Van Nostrand Reinhold Soil Science Series

Editor: Charles W. Finkl, Jnr., Florida Atlantic University

Related Titles of Interest

LAND EVALUATION

Edited by
DONALD A. DAVIDSON
University of Strathclyde, Glasgow, Scotland

A Hutchinson Ross Publication

 VAN NOSTRAND REINHOLD COMPANY
New York

Copyright © 1986 by **Van Nostrand Reinhold Company Inc.**
Van Nostrand Reinhold Soil Science Series
Library of Congress Catalog Card Number: 85-31486
ISBN: 0-442-21807-9

Manufactured in the United States of America.

Published by Van Nostrand Reinhold Company Inc.
115 Fifth Avenue
New York, New York 10003

Van Nostrand Reinhold Company Limited
Molly Millars Lane
Wokingham, Berkshire RG11 2PY, England

Van Nostrand Reinhold
480 Latrobe Street
Melbourne, Victoria 3000, Australia

Macmillan of Canada
Division of Gage Publishing Limited
164 Commander Boulevard
Agincourt, Ontario MIS 3C7, Canada

15   14   13   12   11   10   9   8   7   6   5   4   3   2   1

Library of Congress Cataloging in Publication Data
Main entry under title:
Land evaluation.
   (Van Nostrand Reinhold soil science series)
   "A Hutchinson Ross publication."
   Includes index.
   1. Land use—Planning—Addresses, essays, lectures.   2. Soil geography—
Addresses, essays, lectures.
I. Davidson, Donald A.   II. Series.
HD108.6.L354   1986   333.73   85-31486
ISBN 0-442-21807-9

CONTENTS

Contents

PART IV: LAND CAPABILITY

PART V: SOIL SURVEY INTERPRETATION

PART VI: LAND INFORMATION SYSTEMS

PART VII: RATING INDICES AND YIELDS

SERIES EDITOR'S FOREWORD

The Van Nostrand Reinhold Soil Science Series attempts to provide cogent summaries of the field by reproducing classical and modern papers, ones that provide keys to understanding of critical turning points in the development of the discipline. Scientific literature today is so vast and widely dispersed, especially in a multifaceted discipline like soil science, that much valuable information becomes ignored by default. Many pioneering works are now coveted by libraries, and retrieval from the archives is not easy. In fact, many important papers published in the ephemeral literature are no longer available to serious or committed researchers through interlibrary loan. Other professionals devoted to teaching or burdened with administrative duties must be hard pressed to keep up with comprehensive arrays of technical literature spread through scores of journals. Most of us can, at best, skim only a few select journals to make copies of tables of contents, abstracts and summaries, and reviews in order to remain abreast of specialized and often limited aspects of the robust field of soil science as a whole.

This series in soil science, developed as a practical solution to this problem, reprints key papers and investigative landmarks that relate to a common theme. The papers are reproduced in facsimile, either in their entirety or in significant part, so readers can follow major original events in the field, not peruse paraphrased or abbreviated versions of others. Some foreign works have been especially translated for use in the series. Occasionally short, foreign language articles are reproduced from French or German journals.

Essays by the volume editor provide running commentaries that introduce readers to highlights in the field, provide critical evaluation of the significance of the various papers, and discuss the development of selected topics or subject areas. It is hoped that the volume editor's comments will ease the transition for the seasoned investigator who wishes to step into a new field of research as well as provide students and professors with a compact working library of most important scientific advances in soil science.

Areas of specialization in soil science are divided by the International Society of Soil Science into seven divisions or "commissions." The first six commissions cover soil physics, chemistry, mineralogy, biology, fertility, and technology. Because the scope of the field is so great, we concentrate initially on topics traditionally devoted to the seventh commission: soil morphology, genesis, classification, and geography. The series thus begins with volumes dealing with the major soils of the world: their recognition, characteristics, formation, distribution, and classification. Other volumes concentrate on topics in agronomy, soil-plant relationships, soil engineering topics, or melds of pure science with soil systems. The Van Nostrand Reinhold Soil Science Series plows deeply through the field, picking significant but timely topics on an eclectic basis.

Each volume in the series is edited by a specialist or authority in the area covered by the book. The volume editor's efforts reflect a concerted worldwide search, review, selection, and distillation of the primary literature contained in journals and monographs and in industrial and governmental reports. Individual volumes thus represent an information-selection and repackaging program of value to libraries, students, and professionals.

The books contain a preface, introduction, and highlight commentaries by the volume editor. Many volumes contain rare papers that are hard to locate and obtain, as well as landmark papers published in English for the first time. All volumes contain author citation and subject indexes of the contained papers, usually twenty to fifty key papers in a given subject area.

This volume deals with the applied science of land evaluation. Also sometimes referred to as 'terrain evaluation,' land evaluation is generally considered to encompass all aspects involved in the assessment of the suitability of land for man's use. Typical uses include, for example, agriculture, forestry, engineering, hydrology, regional planning, recreation, military and others. Concepts of land evaluation in these fields have largely proceeded independently but there is sufficient common ground in their principles and problems to warrant recognition of a discrete discipline. Land evaluation, then, is a comprehensive integrating science that incorporates a wide array of natural resource attributes including climate, land form, geology, soil, vegetation, fauna, and water. Because these features are time-variable in a manner that is not readily predictable, they are not spatially fixed, land evaluation is not something that can be done once and for all. It must be repeated when significant changes take place, particularly in the human resource base.

Land classification lies at the heart of land evaluation schemes. Various approaches are used to synthesize landscapes, depending on the nature of special purpose surveys. Attempts to derive distinctive land units by repeated subdivision on the basis of causal environmental factors are often grouped together under the genetic, ecological, landscape, and parametric approaches. Each approach defines land characteristics along orderly principles that permit the categorization and comparison of land types. These different approaches are often combined to reinforce each other, particularly at the planning stage when regions are selected for development or redevelopment.

It is important to note, as brought out in this volume, that land evaluation as an advanced science still faces certain basic problems that are inherent in the nature of land itself. There are, for example, problems of complexity that arise from the multitude of land attributes, their variations, and inter-relationships. Other problems are associated with differing spatial expressions of land attributes, which are often further complicated by concepts of land that are bound by cartographic or parametric limits. Still other problems to overcome are those of association. Because land can not be fully understood in terms of local controls acting in isolation, methods of land evaluation must determine relationships in terms of interacting units at various scales.

This volume traces the evolution of important concepts of land development. The role and scope of principles and techniques, particularly those associated with soil survey interpretation and soil information systems, are reviewed for benchmark papers that are reproduced here in facsimile form. Editorial commentaries highlight significant advances in the field and provide insight into the impact of these important contributions to the development of land evaluation.

CHARLES W. FINKL, JNR.

PREFACE

Land evaluation is an applied science and has as its objective the assessment of land in terms of suitability or yield for particular uses. Any land evaluation project is thus oriented toward eventual decisions on land use and management policy. In no way can land evaluation be claimed to be a new subject. Archaeological evidence suggests that the earliest neolithic farmers exercised judgment on their land in terms of their selection of areas for cultivation, and ever since then, farm management strategies are influenced to varying extents by the nature of land. Engineers obviously find that assessment of land conditions is vital to the choice of locations and the design of structures. Although land evaluation has been practiced for millennia, it is only in the last 30 years that it has begun to appear as a distinct subject. Forces behind this emergence include the increasing availability of soil, geological, and climatic maps and the need to present this information in a more comprehensible form; the adoption of land planning policies in most countries; the ever-increasing concern about population growth and global land resources; and technological developments in computing, which permit the much easier handling and processing of vast quantities of data.

Land evaluation spans a wide diversity of disciplines ranging from the environmental, agricultural, and biological sciences to economics and sociology. Such diversity poses major problems to any compiler of benchmark papers since the ultimate selection is bound to reflect the outlook of the editor. Nevertheless an attempt has been made to reproduce papers that demonstrate both the diversity and the integrity of the subject. An explanation of the book's structure is given in the Introduction. Each of the eight parts is introduced by a review which attempts to place the reproduced papers in a broader context. The hope is that these sectional reviews fuse the papers into an integrated text.

Brief comment is necessary on specific themes that are not included in the book. Land evaluation is taken to be concerned with the assessment of *areas* rather than *sites*. Therefore, site evaluation methods as used in engineering geology or soil mechanics are not discussed. The issue of land evaluation for irrigation projects is crucial for the agricultural development of arid and semiarid areas. It was concluded that the inclusion of one or two papers would not do justice to this important topic. Hence this aspect has been largely avoided with the view that it merits a text of its own.

Despite the so-called information boom, there still seems a serious dearth of detailed land resource information for many areas of the world, a topic discussed in Paper 1. Any land evaluation analysis is dependent upon the availability of land resource data and it is a sad fact that many countries devote little priority to basic soil and geological mapping. This must be due to a lack of awareness about the potential application of such information to land use planning. Thus the importance of land evaluation is not appreciated. While this book is directed primarily toward students and practitioners of the subject, it is hoped they will increasingly convince government bodies and planning authorities that more attention should be given to the results of land evaluation research.

I am grateful for the help and cooperation of authors and publishers in the preparation of this set of papers. I acknowledge with pleasure the advice and encouragement given by the series editor, Dr. Charles Finkl. I dedicate this book to my three girls, Caroline, Louise, and Lorna, who provide the reason for all I try to do.

DONALD A. DAVIDSON

CONTENTS BY AUTHOR

LAND EVALUATION

Introduction

In the most general sense the purpose of land evaluation involves the assessment of the suitability, potential, or yield of one or more land uses in relation to the actual nature and properties of the Earth's environment. Thus the key components in the evaluation process are the choice of land uses for the analysis, the determination of the land requirements of these land uses, and the selection of relevant land attributes. The most critical aspect in the procedure is the comparison of land use requirements with the nature of the actual area to provide the overall assessment. Most land evaluation studies are limited to an ecological assessment whereby the ecological suitability of land uses is determined. A further stage leads into economic assessment when the success of potential land uses is expressed in economic terms.

A simple example should help to summarize the essential nature of land evaluation. A country, province, or region might wish to encourage the expansion of a particular crop—say oilseed rape—but such a crop will perform better in certain localities and the question is where? The process of land evaluation in this instance involves the determination of the climatic and soil requirements for this crop and then the comparison of these land use requirements with the actual climatic and soil conditions. At the first stage, land might be graded according to suitability for oilseed rape and this might be all that is required to aid planning policy. On the other hand, a fuller ecological and economic evaluation may be required in order to predict crop yields and economic returns for different areas. This brief example is sufficient to illustrate the breadth of land evaluation since this interdisciplinary subject ranges from the compilation of land resource inventories of many types through to economic and sociological analysis. Land evaluation encompasses a broad range of techniques and approaches. This book presents a selection of papers drawn from the many aspects of land evaluation in the hope of providing a comprehensive range of studies. Some papers with a methodological or philosophical focus are included, but particular emphasis is given to a wide variety of case studies. Much consideration should be given to the conceptual basis of land evaluation, but increasing attention needs to be given to the application rather than to the development of more refined systems.

THEMES IN LAND EVALUATION

Land evaluation is possible only if a resource inventory is available. The foundations of land evaluation can be traced back to the beginnings of geological mapping on a scientific basis. In the United States scientific geological surveys date from the mid-nineteenth century with the first director of the Geological Survey being appointed in 1879. Geological maps have always been regarded as inventories of land resources given their orientation toward practical uses. Climatic attributes are another set of basic land resource characteristics but classification problems loom large with this subject. Early attempts are associated with Köppen who published in 1900 a classification based on vegetation zones. Such a scheme can be viewed as an early land evaluation analysis since climatic characteristics were evaluated with reference to plants. A similar objective was attempted by Thornthwaite who in 1931 produced his first classification based on indices of precipitation effectiveness and temperature efficiency. This scheme in revised form has been widely adopted and, as will be shown in Part IV, is integral to some present-day land use capability schemes. Soil survey, to complete the environmental triumvirate, had its foundations at the turn of the century—the United States Soil Survey, for example, was founded in 1898 by Milton Whitney—but most soil maps have been published since 1945. The usual situation is for Soil Survey Institutes to be funded by ministries of agriculture and this necessarily has given soil surveys a clear applied bias toward agricultural needs. Thus although geological, climatic, and soil surveys may appear to give prime emphasis to the compilation of resource inventories, such research is of particular relevance to land evaluation given the orientation toward land use.

As already indicated the focus of land evaluation is the assessment of suitability or potential of land for one or more land uses. Despite a clear objective, land evaluation encompasses a wide range of approaches and techniques. This book is divided into parts containing related papers on similar methodologies. Each part begins with an introductory review summarizing the broader issues associated with each topic. The final part draws the themes together and summarizes the editor's views on the present and future status of land evaluation. For the remainder of this introduction it is useful to state the section themes with the intention of explaining the overall structure to the book.

Part I describes the scope of land evaluation and illustrates the methodology and philosophy of approaches. The first clear step toward land evaluation can be traced to the rise in interest in land classification—exemplified by the writings of G. V. Jacks and C. E. Kellogg. This move was in part stimulated by land management and planning problems from the 1930s onward. The formation of the U.S. Soil Conservation Service was a response to the soil erosion problem and one result was the land use capability scheme. In wartime Britain, fast appraisal of land took place to aid planning of food production. Concern with land classification raises the question of what is meant by land, a topic discussed in Part I. The evolution from rather static methods of land classification to a more flexible approach is best expressed in the *Framework for Land Evaluation,* published by the Food and Agricultural Organization (FAO) of the United Nations in 1976. This report was the culmination of consultations over a number of years by an international team, the prime aim of which was to formulate a methodology of land evaluation applicable to any scale or in any land use situation. It is thus a set of guiding principles and is not a definitive classification system. Without doubt, the FAO Framework has been a watershed in land evaluation.

The FAO Framework is ecological in emphasis, and this is the theme for

Part II. The central issue of an ecological approach to land evaluation is the degree of interrelation between all the aspects—in essence, a holistic viewpoint. The merits of such an approach to land were identified long before the FAO Framework. Perhaps the best-known studies in this respect are the Australian ones dealing with land systems. During the 1940s, a rapid resource appraisal was required for much of Australia and a fast method had to be devised. This was achieved by extensive use of aerial photographs. Land complexes were delimited largely on the basis of aerial photo pattern and tone, the idea being that such areas would have similar environmental attributes with respect to land use. In recent years increasing attention has been given to landscape ecological analysis at the detailed scale. Land units are defined on ecological criteria, and, as will be demonstrated, statistical analysis can support the integrity of these units. Landscape ecological surveys therefore have application not only to rapid reconnaissance appraisal, but also to detailed local planning issues such as those in urban areas.

In Part III a selection of papers is presented under the heading "Terrain Evaluation." It is impossible to make a clear-cut distinction between the ecological landscape approach and terrain evaluation; in Australia, for example, the land systems approach has been developed into a method of terrain analysis for engineering purposes. But the emphasis with terrain evaluation is on evaluating the geological and geomorphological attributes of land, although vegetation is usually accepted as an integral component. The best way of introducing terrain evaluation is to mention some of the applications. Geological and geomorphological maps can be interpreted to yield distributions of particular resources or hazards. Maps showing sand and gravel deposits, or areas liable to slope failure, are obvious examples. As already indicated, specialist terrain surveys can be executed using a land systems methodology in order to yield geotechnical information of planning value.

Part IV has land capability as its theme. Soil surveys have always been deemed to be of practical value but soil maps have been underused largely because of their complicated and technical nature. A land use planner usually does not want to know the technical details about soils in an area; instead, he requires a statement on the occurrence of different grades of soil for agricultural purposes. A map showing areas categorized as prime agricultural land is of particular planning value since policies can then be devised to retain this land for agriculture. Soil survey data can thus provide the basis for grading land for general agricultural purposes; land can be similarly evaluated in terms of suitability for specific crops if the growing requirements of these crops are known. Land capability maps depend upon the interpretation of soil survey and climatic data, a theme that is pursued in Part V. The papers in this section exemplify the increasing trend of interpreting soil survey data for a broad range of land uses, many of them nonagricultural. Examples are included in Part V, but perhaps the best-known North American application is the assessment of soils in terms of suitability for septic tank operation. A growing area of application is the use of soil and topographic data to aid planning and management of recreational areas.

Part VI is a continuation of the preceding one in terms of topic except that emphasis is given to computer-based techniques of data storage, retrieval, and presentation. This section is called "Land Information Systems." As in the previous section the assumption is made that technical inventories of land (climate, geology, topography, soils) are too complicated for the non-specialist user, and techniques need to be devised to present information in as simple a form as possible relevant to particular needs. The merits of a computer-based approach in terms of efficiency, capacity, and flexibility require no emphasis. Within land evaluation this is the area of greatest scope for research and development. Interpretative maps will increasingly be produced by techniques of computer graphics, but in no way does this downplay the critical role of the initial field survey. Part VII continues with a quantitative approach to land evaluation, but with an emphasis on numerical measures of land quality. Such a quantitative approach leads into techniques for predicting yields. Finally, Part VIII attempts to pull together many land evaluation themes by presenting papers that give particular priority to land use planning issues.

Each part is introduced by an editorial review in order to place each theme in context. Guidance on further reading is also given in these introductory reviews. However, it is useful to indicate here some general sources on land evaluation. The scope and development of the subject are expressed in the edited volumes by Stewart (1968), Simonson (1974), Swindale (1978), and the Soil Conservation Service (1981). Texts on land evaluation are provided by Vink (1975), Beek (1978), Davidson (1980), Dent and Young (1981), Olson (1981), McRae and Burnham (1981), and Vink (1983). Articles on land evaluation appear in a wide variety of journals and reports; especially recommended are the *Journal of Soil and Water Conservation* and the journal *Soil Survey and Land Evaluation*. An effective way of searching for new publications on land evaluation is to consult an abstracting journal such as *Soils and Fertilizers*.

REFERENCES

Beek, K. J., 1978, *Land Evaluation for Agricultural Development,* International Institute for Land Reclamation and Improvement Publication No 23, Wageningen.

Davidson, D. A., 1980, *Soils and Land Use Planning,* Longman, London.

Dent, D., and A. Young, 1981, *Soil Survey and Land Evaluation,* George Allen and Unwin, London.

Köppen, W., 1900, Versuch einer Klassification der Klimate, vorzugsweise nach ihren Beziehungen zur Pflanzenwelt, *Geographischen Zeitschrift,* **6:**593-611, 657-679.

McRae, S. G., and C. P. Burnham, 1981, *Land Evaluation,* Oxford University Press, Oxford.

Olson, G. W., 1981, *Soils and the Environment,* Chapman and Hall, New York.

Simonson, R. W., ed., 1974, *Non-agricultural Applications of Soil Surveys.* Elsevier, Amsterdam.

Soil Conservation Service, 1981, *Soil Resource Inventories and Development,* Tech. Monograph No. 1, U.S. Department of Agriculture, Washington, D.C.

Stewart, G. A., ed., 1968, *Land Evaluation,* Macmillan of Australia, South Melbourne.

Swindale, L. D., ed., 1978, *Soil Resource Data for Agricultural Development,* Hawaii Agricultural Experimental Station, Honolulu.

Thornthwaite, C. W., 1931, The Climates of North America According to a New Classification, *Geographical Review* **21:**633-655.

Vink, A. P. A., 1975, *Land Use in Advancing Agriculture,* Springer Verlag, Berlin.

Vink, A. P. A., 1983, *Landscape Ecology and Land Use,* Longman, London.

Part I

The Scope of
Land Evaluation

Papers 1 and 2: Introductory Review

1 **DUDAL**
   Land Resources for Agricultural Development

2 **DENT**
   Land Suitability Classification

In June of 1978 the International Society of Soil Science held its Eleventh Congress at Edmonton in Canada. The theme for that Congress was "Optimum Soil Utilization Systems under Differing Climatic Constraints." In his presidential address, Professor C. F. Bentley selected agricultural land resources as his main topic, and he demonstrated for Canada—and indeed for the world as a whole—that there is much overestimation of the amount, quality, and productive potential of land (Bentley, 1978). He explained the massive decrease in Canadian farmland in terms of farm abandonment in the more marginal areas along with substantial losses from urban encroachment in southern Ontario and Quebec. This pattern is reflected to varying extents in many developed countries. Concern over loss of land to urban sprawl is frequently expressed in planning legislation designed to preserve good land for agriculture. The maintenance of agriculture in more marginal areas of the western world is dependent upon support schemes. A continuing major issue in the countries belonging to the European Economic Community (EEC) is the massive extent to which agricultural policy is designed to subsidize farming in marginal localities. The development of policy to either protect good quality agricultural land or to support farming in less favored areas is dependent upon some evaluation of land.

Despite such trends in western Europe and North America, agricultural output in these areas has been high. In Europe the overproduction of dairy foods has been particularly outstanding. The situation is in marked contrast in many of the developing countries. The Food and Agricultural Organization (FAO) reported that at the end of 1983, 35 countries were suffering from food shortages, 24 of them in Africa. In the words of the FAO report (1984a, p. 4), there is ". . . a profound mismatching of needs and resources between high and low income countries." Issues of people, food and land resources are highlighted by the continuing state of human misery in the Sahel belt. This zone first became internationally known during the drought that peaked in 1972-1973 and then recurred 1983-1984. Overall the current dry period began in the late 1960s and has been prolonged. The decade of 1910-1920 was also a time of extreme drought while the 1930s and 1950s experienced above-average rainfall. The Sahel belt is accumulating a massive deficit in food production accentuated by high population growth rates (ca. 2.6% per year), by landscape degradation and by decreasing per capita food production (198 kg of cereals per capita in 1969-1971 compared to 172 kg per capita for 1980-1982 for the countries of Cape Verde, Chad, the Gambia, Mali, Mauritania, the Niger, Senegal, and Upper Volta). Despite these considerable problems, another report by FAO (1984*b*) identifies considerable potential for improving agricultural production in the Sahel. Ultimate success will depend upon the solution of a wide range of economic, political, social, and educational issues, but progress can only begin to be made if areas are subject to land evaluation analysis to determine agro-ecological potential.

GLOBAL LAND RESOURCES

It may be surprising to begin a book on land evaluation with an analysis of land resources at the global scale, but this can be justified on the grounds of human importance. Paper 1 is by Professor Dudal who, as Director of the Land and Water Development Division of FAO, reviewed global land resources at the Eleventh Congress of the International Society of Soil Science. His address marked an important advance in global land resource assessment since prior to the publication of the 1:5,000,000 FAO-UNESCO World Soil Map there was no comprehensive soil map cover based on soil survey in every country. Earlier attempts at global land resource appraisal have been distinguished by striking variability in estimates and some of these are summarized by Dudal. A generalization frequently encountered is that 25% of ice-free land in the world is potential farmland and only about half of that is currently being farmed. According to a report by FAO (1981*b*), in the 90 developing countries, 750 million hectares of arable land were being farmed in 1980—just over 40% of their total potential arable area of about 1,843 million hectares. Although extension of arable areas will obviously produce more food, the bulk of required increases will come from higher yields (no less than 60% of total increases) and from higher cropping intensities (especially from a reduction in shifting cultivation). Increases in agricultural output will be achieved in varying proportions—for example, in Latin America FAO anticipates that extension of arable area will be the greatest contributing factor, while in the Far East reliance will be on achieving higher yields and cropping intensities. Another prediction by FAO is that irrigated areas could provide almost 50% of the required 1980-2000 expansion in food production. If the FAO projections on arable land extensions are achieved by 2000, land shortage will then become a critical constraint for about two-thirds of the population in developing countries.

Dudal's description of FAO research on global land resources indicates the vital contribution of the *Framework for Land Evaluation* (FAO, 1976). If space had permitted, the full report would have been reproduced in this book. However, Dudal summarizes and exemplifies the approach. Nevertheless, it is worth quoting the definition of land as eventually agreed for the FAO *Framework*.

> Land comprises the physical environment, including climate, relief, soils, hydrology and vegetation, to the extent that these influence potential for land use. It includes the results of past and present human activity, e.g. reclamation from the sea, vegetation clearance and also adverse results, e.g. soil salinization. (FAO, 1976, p. 9)

Thus land was interpreted in a physical environmental sense but also in relation to actual or potential land use significance. Dudal summarizes the six principles underlying land evaluation and suggests that the first is the most important — that is, land suitability can only be assessed with reference to a specific land use. This immediately indicates the interdependent nature of land evaluation whereby the significance of soil, relief, and climatic conditions vary according to crop or land use. Land evaluation following the FAO *Framework* can be thought of as two parallel sets of operations once the objectives of a project have been set: (1) specification of kinds of land uses (includes details of input levels, farm structure, etc.) and land use requirements, and (2) land resource survey and mapping of land units followed by assemblage of a data bank on land characteristics and qualities of component land units. The crucial aspect is when these two strands are brought together in the process of matching; this involves determining the extent to which land use requirements of individual land uses are met by land units. One major difficulty in the matching process is the lack of availability of quantitative guidance on crop requirements, though Dent and Young (1981, pp. 172-175) provide a useful summary. The Soil Resources Management and Conservation Service (1983) of FAO have published a substantial report designed to give detailed guidance on how to carry out a land evaluation project using the FAO *Framework* for rainfed agriculture. Similar guidelines are planned for irrigated agriculture and forestry. In many ways this more recent report is an easier document to understand than the original one. The results are usually expressed using a land suitability classification: examples are given in the original FAO *Framework* and subsequent *Guidelines,* as well as by Beek (1978); Young and Goldsmith (1977) provide a detailed study for Malawi. Progress in applying the FAO *Framework* within member countries of the EEC is examined in the proceedings of a seminar edited by Haans, Steur, and Heide (1984).

Most of Paper 1 is devoted to presenting initial results from the Agro-Ecological Zones Project. The background to this FAO study stemmed from the variability in estimates of global land resources: the completion of the FAO *Framework* as well as the availability of the FAO-UNESCO World Soil Map provided methodological and data bases for such an evaluation. The first report dealt with Africa (FAO, 1978*a*) and the project at that stage is summarized by Dudal. Combinations of soil and climatic conditions are assessed in terms of suitability for 11 crops at two input levels. Subsequent reports dealt with Southwest Asia (FAO, 1978*b*), Southeast Asia and South and Central America (FAO, 1981*a*). The results from some of these studies are summarized in Table 1.

**Table 1.   Maximum extents of land assessed as very suitable, suitable or marginally suitable to rainfed cultivation of some crop
(Figures in million hectares)**

	South America	Central America	Southwest Asia[1]	Southeast Asia
Low inputs	810.4	73.5	26.4	281.8
High inputs	709.0	66.0	21.6	271.0
Actual cultivated area	95.1	28.5	50.9	262.5

[1]Assessment done for only one crop (wheat) in this area.

At face value the results in this table indicate a lack of opportunity for extending rainfed arable activities in Southeast Asia while the area currently under wheat in Southwest Asia appears to be overextended by a factor of two. Scope for agricultural expansion is indicated for Central America and in particular for South America. A ninefold expansion is proposed for the latter, with the bulk of this taking place in Brazil. Of course many aspects of these results are open to question and no doubt the FAO team is fully aware of all the assumptions and problems with their method. But the results are based on thorough agro-ecological analysis and merit greater attention than they have been given.

The results of the Agro-Ecological Zones Project are being developed in terms of potential population supporting capacity (PPSC) of land (FAO, 1982). For each country the maximum potential calorie production is calculated using the results from the agro-ecological analysis. This figure can then be divided by the individual calorific requirements of the people in each country as well as by the available land area to give the number of people who could be supported per hectare. This figure can then be compared to the actual population density to produce what is called the PPSC ratio. The example of Kenya is quoted by FAO: in 1975 Kenya had a population density of 0.24 per hectare. In contrast its PPSC at a low input level is only 0.065 people per hectare to give a PPSC ratio of 0.065/0.24 or 0.27. Thus Kenya is supporting a population much greater than it can theoretically support. Kenya faces a high rate of population increase and consequently will suffer increasing land resource problems.

LAND SUITABILITY ASSESSMENT

Dudal's analysis of global land resources demonstrates current and critical concerns within land evaluation. As already stated, a major problem in many land evaluation analyses is the specific identification of soil and climatic conditions. Thus there is much merit in selecting a paper that deals in some detail with one crop. Paper 2 has the advantage of not only focusing on rice, the staple food for over half the world's population, but also of reviewing a variety of approaches to the classification of land for rice suitability. Dent's study further demonstrates the scope of land evaluation.

The selection of wetland rice immediately illustrates the importance of identifying the environmental requirements specific to this crop. In marked contrast to most crops, it prefers flooded to well-drained soils. Dent reviews a variety of classification schemes and he demonstrates in his Table 1 the varying ratings of limiting factors as used in studies in the Republic of Korea, Thailand, Malaysia, Indonesia, and the Philippines. Examples of some of the limiting factors are drainage, soil texture, effective soil depth, salinity/alkalinity, soil reaction, permeability, slope, flooding incidence, and ease of mechanical cultivation. The influence of the United States Department of Agriculture (USDA) land capability scheme (see Part IV) can be discerned in the earlier classifications described by Dent while the later ones are influenced by the methodology of the FAO *Framework*. Dent, in his Table 2, lists land qualities and major land characteristics relevant to rainfed and irrigated rice production.

The assignment of land or soil units to land classes is unfortunately some-times described as being qualitative, inferring a lack of measurement of properties.

In contrast the proper application of the FAO *Framework* ought to be viewed as being quantitatively and rigorously based, though a subjective element is necessarily involved in the definition of suitability classes. In fact it is sometimes forgotten that any land evaluation must involve judgment. The inference sometimes is that if an index is based on a number of soil or land properties such as described by Dent, then the resultant index is a nonsubjective indicator if it can be shown to correlate with crop yield. Nevertheless, decisions need to be made in terms of selecting factors and how they are going to be weighted in an index. The merit of this parametric approach is the scope for computerization once the index is defined and tested. Methods of developing rating indices are examined in Part VII.

As discussed by Dent in the final part of Paper 2, quantitative suitability evaluation involves more than the incorporation of measured properties as in the definition of diagnostic criteria. According to the FAO *Framework,* quantitative land suitability requires distinctions to be drawn in common numerical terms, usually economic ones. Thus an economic input-output analysis is necessary. For example, Young and Goldsmith (1977) in their Malawi study calculated net income per hectare and per capita for different land utilization types on the various land units. A useful introduction to the economics of land evaluation and in particular to gross margin analysis and discounted cash-flow analysis is given by Dent and Young (1981). The FAO *Framework* stresses that the ultimate task of land evaluation is the incorporation of economic analysis: Young and Goldsmith (1977) in their Malawi study draw some salutory conclusions from such an exercise. In essence they emphasize that the results from economic analysis can be short-lived through changes in commodity prices and in the assumptions about discount rates. They quote the example of coffee, which changed from being an uneconomic to an economic crop from 1975 to 1977. It is for such reasons that land evaluation projects incorporating an economic assessment are still comparatively rare.

What observations might a newcomer to land evaluation make from this short review outlining the scope of the subject? The reader is probably first impressed by the diversity of the subject in terms of scale and type of analysis. He or she should also be very conscious of the current emphasis on an ecological approach, be this at the global scale as in the Agro-Ecological Zones Project or at the individual field level in terms of assessing its suitability for a crop such as rice. A second observation that the reader should make is that resource inventories in themselves are of no practical value: they become of significance only when land use requirements are matched with land qualities of specific land mapping units. A third impression the reader may gain is the pace of recent developments in the subject; the early, rather static approach to land classification has been replaced by the thinking inherent in the FAO *Framework.* Also the flexibility of approach and data presentation is continually being extended by developments in computing (Parts VI and VII). One potential danger to any new research worker in land evaluation is that he or she will become engrossed in the challenge of continually refining a particular land evaluation technique. This can be a very real danger when computer systems are being developed. It must always be remembered that the subject has as its core a practical objective — the evaluation of land to aid the planning and management of land. Land evaluation scientists must always ensure that their results can be easily understood and incorporated into land use planning procedures.

REFERENCES

Beek, K. J., 1978, *Land Evaluation for Agricultural Development,* International Institute for Land Reclamation and Improvement Publication No. 23, Wageningen.

Bentley, C. F., 1978, Canada's Agricultural Land Resources and the World Food Problem, *Plenary Papers, Internat. Soc. Soil Sci. 11th Congr.* **2:**1-26.

Dent, D., and A. Young, 1981, *Soil Survey and Land Evaluation,* George Allen and Unwin, London.

FAO, 1976, A Framework for Land Evaluation, *FAO Soils Bull. 32.*

FAO, 1978a, Report of the Agro-ecological Zones Project: Volume 1, Methodology and Results for Africa, *World Soils Resources Rept. 48.*

FAO, 1978b, Report of the Agro-ecological Zones Project: Volume 2, Results for Southwest Asia, *World Soils Resources Rept. 48/2.*

FAO, 1980, Report of the Agro-ecological Zones Project: Volume 4, Results for Southeast Asia, *World Soils Resources Rept. 48/4.*

FAO 1981a, Report of the Agro-ecological Zones Project: Volume 3, Methodology and Results for South and Central America, *World Soils Resources Rept. 48/3.*

FAO, 1981b, *Agriculture: Toward 2000,* FAO, Rome.

FAO, 1982, *Potential Population Supporting Capacities of Lands in the Developing World,* FAO, Rome.

FAO 1984a, The State of Food and Agriculture 1983, *FAO Agriculture Series 16,* Rome.

FAO 1984b, *World Food Report 1984.* FAO, Rome.

Haans, J. C. F. M., G. G. L. Steur, and G. Heide, ed., 1984, *Progress in Land Evaluation,* A. A. Balkema, Rotterdam.

Soil Resources Management and Conservation Service, 1983, Guidelines: Land Evaluation for Rainfed Agriculture, *FAO Soils Bull. 52.*

Young, A., and P. F. Goldsmith, 1977, Soil survey and land evaluation in developing countries: a case study in Malawi, *Geog. Jour.* **143:**407-431.

1: LAND RESOURCES FOR AGRICULTURAL DEVELOPMENT

R. Dudal

*Director, Land and Water Development Division, Food and Agriculture Organization of the United Nations, Rome**

Introduction

The determination of the "carrying capacity" of the world's lands has engaged the minds of men for the last two hundred years. The estimates made over this time-span vary considerably: at the end of the nineteenth century, when the world population was 1.5 billion, Ravenstein (1890) estimated that lands of the globe still available for settlement could carry 6 billion people. At the first Congress of the International Society of Soil Science, in Washington, Penck (1928) suggested that the world could produce food for 16 billion people. More recently Revelle (1976) suggested a carrying capacity of up to 40 billion people, while Buringh (1975) estimated that, under optimal conditions, agriculture could produce thirty times the presently available quantity of food.

Appraisals of total areas of arable land vary from 2.8 billion hectares (Ballod 1912), to 3.2 billion hectares (Kellogg and Orvedal 1969) up to 7 billion hectares (Pawley 1971). These great variations show that within a finite total land area the portion that is considered arable, and the possible production therefrom, are highly flexible and depend on the technology which is being envisaged, and on the various social and economic conditions which prevail (FAO 1976; Higgins 1977).

During the last 20 years - from 1957 to 1977 - the area of arable land increased by 135 million hectares, that is about 9 percent of to-day's total 1.50 billion hectares of cultivated land in the world. During the same period, the world's population has increased from 2.8 to 4 billion, that is by 40 percent. In terms of increased production, the increase in arable land at a low level of agricultural inputs would have sufficed only to feed an additional 400 million people. The food supplies for the 800 million additional people have been obtained from an intensification of agriculture on land already cultivated, reflected by a spectacular increase of fertilizer use - from 24 million tons of plant nutrients in 1957 to 88 million tons in 1976/1977 - and a considerable expansion of irrigation. It is significant, however, that of the 110 million hectares added arable land, 70 percent was opened, in developing countries while intensification of production took place in industrialized countries which consumed 85 percent of the world's fertilizer production.

---

*This paper is based on the work carried out by consultants and FAO staff contributing to the FAO Agro-ecological Zones Project. Coordinator, G.M. Higgins; Consultant agro-ecologists: A.H. Kassam, J.M. Kowal, S. Sarraf; bio-meteorology: M. Frère, J.Q. Rijks; land and water development: P. Arens, H. Arnoldus, R. Dudal, F.W. Hauck, A.J. Pécrot, J. Riquier, H. van Velthuizen.

The additional production resulting from extension of cultivated land in developing countries is lagging far behind that required by the increase of population. Although global estimates of land resources indicate the presence of large tracts of potentially arable land, they hardly permit concrete and practical conclusions with regard to prospects for future trends (Dudal 1969). There is an urgent need to qualify the concept of "arable land" in respect to: specific types of land use, production potential, technical and financial inputs which are required, hazards of soil degradation which may occur and the location of the lands still available. Furthermore, global estimates have to be complemented by land evaluation at the country level since different countries vary greatly in their land resources endowment, and limitations of transportation are often obstacles to massive transfers of food products from one area to another. The solution of the world food problem requires that each community uses its land to its best advantage.

In order to obtain a more precise assessment of the production potential of the world's land resources, and so provide the physical data base necessary for planning future agricultural development, FAO has recently initiated a study of potential land use by major agro-ecological zones. The general methodology for this study is presented herewith together with a few preliminary results for Africa.

A Global Land Evaluation

The methodology to assess the agricultural potential of the world's land resources uses six principles which are fundamental to any sound evaluation of land, land being defined as the physical environment including soils, climate, relief, hydrology and vegetation:

i.   land suitability is only meaningful in relation to a specific use, e.g. land suited to the cultivation of cassava is not necessarily suited to the cultivation of pearl millet;

ii.   the evaluation of production potential needs to be made in respect of specified input levels, e.g. whether fertilizers are being applied or not, if pest control is effected, if machinery or hand tools are being used;

iii. suitability must refer to use on a sustained basis, that is the envisaged use of land must not result in its depletion, e.g. through wind erosion, water erosion, salinization or other degradation processes;

iv.   evaluation involves comparison of more than one alternative type of land use, e.g. suitability for millet or sorghum or maize, and not just for a single crop;

v.   different kinds of land use are compared at least on a simple economic basis; that is, suitability for each use is assessed by comparing the value of the produce to the cost of production;

vi. a multidisciplinary approach is adopted, the evaluation being based on inputs from crop ecologists, agronomists, climatologists and economists, in addition to those from pedologists.

These principles are among those formulated in "A Framework for Land Evaluation" (FAO 1976) developed over the past years through international cooperation.

The 1:5 000 000 FAO/Unesco Soil Map of the World, and a generated climatic inventory, form the basis of the study. Main climatic divisions, and isolines delineating various lengths of growing periods, are superimposed on the appropriate Soil Map of the World sheets. This compilation results in the delineation of 'agro-ecological zones' which reflect areas with similar soils and climates. Area measurement of these soil/climatic zones is effected through a 2 mm (100 km^2) grid count and the results corrected for the reported total areas of countries' land masses. The total areas of soil units - whether occurring as dominant soils, associated soil or inclusions - sub-divided by phases, slope classes and texture classes were calculated by major climatic divisions and lengths of growing period, on a country basis. The results are finally interpreted and presented as extents of land variously suited to the production of eleven important main crops, by major climatic zones and lengths of growing periods.

Available quantitative data on surface and groundwater resources was insufficient to include irrigated production in the study. While such water resource data do exist for a number of individual countries, it is not available on a regional basis and the present study is therefore confined to rainfed cultivation only. When the available water resources of regions are quantified with development costs, the study could be extended to include irrigated production potential. Major land improvements such as regional drainage schemes, are also not considered in the study. Although grazing is an important form of land use in drier areas, the assessment of grazing potential could not be included in the present study. It will be given due attention in a second stage.

The crops considered in the study were selected from listings of the twenty most important crops in the world, with regard to area occupied. They comprise wheat, rice, maize, pearl millet, sorghum, white potato, sweet potato, cassava, phaseolus bean, soybean and cotton, i.e. five basic foodgrains, three root crops, two leguminous and one cash crop (cotton).

Two levels of inputs - low and high - are considered. The former approximates to a low technological level involving hand cultivation, no or insufficient fertilizer application, local cultivars, no chemical pest, disease and weed control, fallow periods, small farm holdings and some untimely operations because of labour bottlenecks.

The high input level involves mechanical cultivation, sufficient fertilizer, high yielding cultivars, chemical pest, disease and weed control, timely operations and a generally high standard of management with simple conservation practices.

A total of twenty two alternative land uses are thus considered in the assessment, i.e. two each for eleven crops. The low and high input levels are characterized as follows:

Attribute	Low Inputs	High Inputs
Produce	Sole cropping only, no multiple cropping	
Market orientation	subsistence production, priority to food production	commercial production, priority to optimum economic production
Capital intensity	low	high
Labour intensity	high, including uncosted family labour	low, family labour costed
Power sources	manual labour with hand tools	mechanization including harvesting
Technology	no fertilizer, local cultivars, no chemical pest and disease control, fallow periods	adequate fertilizer application, improved cultivars, pest and disease control, no fallow periods
Infrastructure	market accessibility not essential, inadequate advisory service	communications and market accessibility essential, high level of advisory services
Land holdings	small, sometimes fragmented	large, consolidated
Income levels	low	high

Following the identification of the alternative land uses to be considered in the assessment, it is necessary to define their soil and climatic requirements. Such is difficult because of the lack of detailed information on soil requirements in specific climatic conditions and the lack of precise information on climatic requirements (particularly moisture) under specific soil conditions. A start has been made to define such parameters and this work is to be followed up as part of FAO's programme on land evaluation.

In the present study the soil requirements were formulated by experience and review of literature. The climatic requirements were compiled from similar literature review including information on the photosynthesis pathway of the crops and response to temperature regimes.

Subsequently the climatic and soil requirements of the crops are individually "matched" with the climatic and soil conditions of the agro-ecological zones. Each crop and level of input is considered separately in respect of climatic and soil requirements.

The final evaluation of potential land suitability is obtained by superimposing the soil assessment on the climatic suitability assessment, giving areas of lands:

very suitable, suitable, marginally suitable or not suitable,

for the production of each crop, at each of the two levels of inputs considered. The four classes are related to the anticipated yield as a percentage of the maximum attainable in the optimum climatic and soil conditions. These physical suitability classes are being related to input/output and price/cost relations and provide data on the production potential in any given area. In a second stage the evaluation will be adjusted according to land degradation hazards which may result from certain types of land use.

In summary, the study assesses the potential use of the developing world's land resources for the rainfed production of a limited number of main crops by climatic zones, at two input levels, using existing soil information, generated climatic data and simple production cost factors.

The soil and climatic inventories being used in the study, and the way in which soil and climatic characteristics have been matched with crop requirements, are described in the sections that follow.

The Soils Inventory

From the beginning of this century, a number of world soil maps have been compiled at scales varying from 1:20 000 000 to 1:100 000 000. These maps were based on general information rather than on actual surveys. The distribution of soils shown differed with the various schools of thought on soil genesis and on factors that govern their formation. The correlation and interpretation of different classification systems and source material, of different scales and origins, met with great difficulties and estimation of global land resources was arduous.

From the early fifties onwards, soil survey activities expanded considerably. Soil investigations extended into tropical areas and knowledge of the world's soils increased markedly. The 6th Congress of the International Society of Soil Science (ISSS), held in Paris in 1956, recommended that special attention be given to the classification and correlation of the soils of great regions. As a result, soil maps covering Africa, Australia, Asia, Europe, South America and North America - at scales ranging from 1:5 000 000 to 1:10 000 000 - were presented at the 7th ISSS Congress in Madison, U.S.A. in 1960. While these maps reflected a vast amount of new data on the properties and distribution of soils in different parts of the world, nomenclature, survey methods, legends and systems of classification varied so widely that comparisons between different regions remained difficult.

In 1961 FAO and Unesco, in cooperation with the ISSS, embarked on the preparation of a soil map of the world at scale of 1:5 000 000. The project was carried out under the scientific authority of an international advisory panel.

Intensive soil correlation was an important element of the programme. First drafts of maps and legends were presented at the 8th ISSS Congress, in Bucharest in 1964, and international agreement on the legend was reached at the 9th ISSS Congress, in Adelaide, Australia in 1968. The first published sheets were exhibited at the 10th Congress of the ISSS in Moscow in 1974. The publication was completed in 1978 and the entire coverage of 19 maps (FAO, 1969-1978) was presented at the 11th Congress at Edmonton, Canada. The maps covering a continent or large region are accompanied by an explanatory volume.

The FAO/Unesco Soil Map of the World is characterized by being based on actual survey material, integrating available knowledge into a unified legend and benefitting from wide international cooperation. It is this material that is being used in the potential land use study.

The reliability of the Map differs from one area to another depending on the accuracy and detail of the material used for its compilation. Table 1 shows the sources of information available in the different parts of the world and, at the same time, provides a picture of soil survey coverage at a global scale. Class I areas are systematic soil surveys in which the boundaries are based on physiographic data while the composition of the mapping units is based on field studies; in Class II and Class III areas, boundaries are derived from interpretation of general information on landforms, geology, climate and vegetation, and from scattered soil studies.

It appears that only about a fifth of the world's soils have actually been surveyed. The highest percentage of survey coverage is found in Europe, and the lowest in Africa. When percentages are calculated after deduction of arid regions and permafrost areas, which are surveyed only in few instances, Class I surveys cover respectively 10.8, 23.3, 15.4, 80.2, 46.1, 15.0 percent of the regions listed in Table 1 and 28.2 percent of the world.

Table 1 - Soil Survey Coverage (percent)

	Class I	Class II	Class III
Africa	7.5	38.0	54.5
Asia	19.0	49.0	32.0
Australasia	11.0	61.0	28.0
Europe	76.3	23.7	-
North & Central America	28.0	16.0	56.0
South America	14.6	45.9	39.5
World	21.0	40.0	39.0

A major obstacle to starting the global soil inventory in 1961 was the lack of a generally accepted system of soil classification. In order to obtain international agreement,a common denominator between the different systems in use had to be established.

To secure reliable identification and correlation in areas far apart, the soil units are defined in terms of measurable and observable properties of the soil itself. The key properties have been selected on the basis of generally accepted principles of soil formation and on their relevance to the use of the soil. The definition of diagnostic features and horizons has drawn on the successive approximations of the USDA Soil Classification and are in accord with Soil Taxonomy (Soil Survey Staff, S.C.S., USDA 1975).

With regard to nomenclature, an attempt has been made to use as many "traditional" names as possible, for instance, Chernozems, Podzols, Planosols, Solonchaks, Rendzinas. A number of terms such as Podzolic soils, Prairie soils, Lateritic soils, Brown forest soils, though firmly established in soils literature, could not be retained without perpetuating the confusion which the dissimilar use of these names in different countries had created. For a limited number of soils it has therefore been necessary to coin new names such as Luvisols, Phaeozems, Nitosols, Cambisols.

The legend comprises 106 soil units which, for the sake of presentation, have been clustered into 26 major groupings. When compared to other classification systems these groups correspond either to orders or to suborders. The definitions, correlation and nomenclature of these units are given in Volume 1, Legend, of the Soil Map of the World (FAO 1974).

The map units are associations of soils which occur within the limits of physiographic entities. Each association is composed of a dominant soil and of associated soils, the latter covering at least 20 percent of the area of the mapping unit. Important soils which cover less than 20 percent of the areas are added as inclusions. The textural class of the dominant soil and the general slope class are given for each association. Important land characteristics, not reflected by the soil associations themselves, are shown on the maps as overprints of various phases, such as the occurrence of salinity or of hard layers at shallow depth. Areas of dunes or shifting sands, salt flats and rock debris are also shown separately.

The distribution of major soils as shown on the Soil Map of the World (Table 2) differs in certain respects from earlier estimates. The soils of tropical areas show a greater diversity than is commonly assumed. Ferralsols occupy only 8 percent of the world's land area and this proportion may decrease further with ongoing surveys in the equatorial zone of South America. On the contrary, the areas covered by Acrisols and Nitosols may be underestimated. While soils high in metallic oxides and of low fertility are common in the tropics these regions also comprise large areas of soils with more favourable base status and retention capacity, e.g. Vertisols, Luvisols, Nitosols and Cambisols.

Table 2 - Distribution of the Major Soils of the
Soil Map of the World and Africa

Soil associations dominated by	World		Africa	
	000 ha	percent	000 ha	percent
Fluvisols	316 450*	2.40	101 390	3.35
Gleysols	622 670*	4.73	130 420	4.32
Regosols and Arenosols	1 330 400*	10.10	594 030	19.73
Andosols	100 640	0.76	5 430	0.16
Vertisols	311 460	2.36	104 960	3.49
Solonchaks and Solonetz	268 010	2.03	69 410	2.32
Yermosols	1 175 980	8.93	373 770	12.42
Xerosols and Kastanozems	895 550	6.79	103 710	3.46
Chernozems, Greyzems and Phaeozems	407 760	3.09	340	0.03
Cambisols	924 870*	7.02	111 650	3.72
Luvisols	922 360	7.00	256 990	8.54
Podzoluvisols	264 120	2.00	-	-
Podzols	477 700	3.63	11 340	0.36
Planosols	119 890	0.91	15 880	0.53
Acrisols and Nitosols	1 049 890	7.97	191 110	6.34
Ferralsols	1 068 450	8.11	322 500	10.69
Lithosols, Rendzinas and Rankers	2 263 760*	17.17	401 450	13.33
Histosols	240 200*	1.82	12 270	0.40
Miscellaneous land units (icefields, salt flats, rock debris, shifting sands, etc.)	420 230	3.18	204 760	6.81
	13 180 390	100.00	3 011 330	100.00

*Large parts of these occur in areas with permafrost.

Since Vertisols and Andosols have not been identified in certain classification systems it is likely that their extension may be greater than the figures indicate. The same applies to Planosols, the large extension of which, however, is already indicative of their importance at a global scale (Dudal 1973). Drought prone soils, Yermosols, Xerosols, Kastanozems, Solonetz, Solonchaks, Arenosols and Regosols occupy near to 28 percent of the world's lands. Soils limited by shallowness, Lithosols, Rendzinas and Rankers represent 17 percent of the earth's surface. Podzols occupy a smaller area than could be implied from the importance attributed to them in certain classification systems. A strict application of the definition of this unit might entail a decrease of its extension in northern areas. On the other hand, soil surveys in progress reveal additional extensions of Podzols in the tropics.

The soils pattern of Africa - as shown in Table 2 and Map 1 - is characterized by a high proportion of drought-prone areas, 38 percent as compared to 28 percent for the world's average. Ferralsols occupy near to 11 percent of the continent. Luvisols which occur extensively mostly belong to the ferric groups, often with petro-ferric hard layers at shallow depth. Africa has large tracts of Vertisols and well characterized stretches of Andosols and Nitosols.

Africa offers an illustration of the occurrence of certain soil groups, i.e. Luvisols, Vertisols, Acrisols and Ferralsols over different climatic regions entailing marked diversification of their suitability for different types of land use.

In formulating the soil requirements for the FAO potential land use study, attention was naturally paid to those soil properties used for defining the soil units of the Soil Map of the World. The requirements were collated from available literature and summarized into ranges of properties necessary and most suitable for the yield of the crop, e.g. pearl millet: optimum soil pH is 5.5 - 7.5, necessary range of soil pH is 5.2 - 8.2.

Prevalent amongst the data used were reports and working papers from FAO land evaluation projects, particularly those in Indonesia, Philippines and the Sudan.

Slope, soil depth, soil drainage, soil texture, fertility, salinity, pH, free calcium carbonate and gypsum are the properties, interpretable from the Soil Map of the World, which were used in assessing soils for crop growth. It was not possible to define fertility requirements quantitatively, other than to state that these were low, moderate or high for each individual crop.

The method of matching the soils inventory with the crop soil requirements is described in a subsequent section.

The Climatic Inventory

Any climatic inventory used in assessing land suitability must take into account the crops' climatic requirements. Previous

Map 1

SOIL ASSOCIATIONS - AFRICA

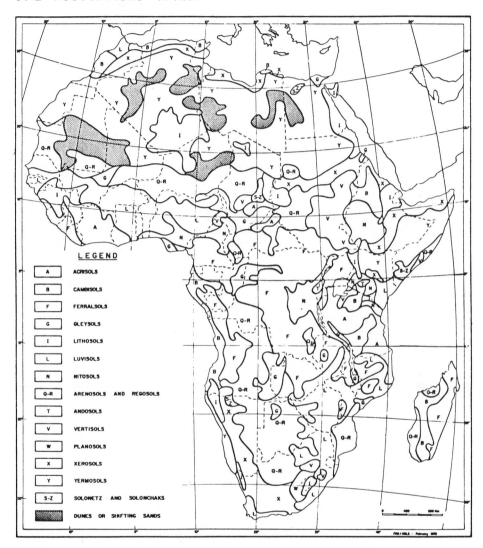

LEGEND

A	ACRISOLS
B	CAMBISOLS
F	FERRALSOLS
G	GLEYSOLS
I	LITHOSOLS
L	LUVISOLS
N	NITOSOLS
Q-R	ARENOSOLS AND REGOSOLS
T	ANDOSOLS
V	VERTISOLS
W	PLANOSOLS
X	XEROSOLS
Y	YERMOSOLS
S-Z	SOLONETZ AND SOLONCHAKS
	DUNES OR SHIFTING SANDS

FAO / AGLS - February 1978

attempts to quantify these requirements have well recognized the importance of rainfall and soil moisture, however, equal emphasis needs to be given to temperature. Similarly important is the nature of the photosynthetic pathway of the crop itself (Kowal and Kassam 1978).

Accordingly, for the global assessment, crops are grouped on the basis of their requirements for photosynthesis, for subsequent matching to existing climatic conditions. Five main groups of crops are recognized.

Two major pathways of CO_2 assimilation are considered in the grouping: one in which the first product of photosynthesis is a 3-carbon organic acid (C3), while in the second one there are 4-carbon organic acids (C4). In general, the C3-species are adapted to lower temperatures (15 - 20° C) than the C4-species (30 - 35° C) and have relatively lower rates of CO_2 exchange and lower growth rates. These C3 and C4-species constitute groups I and III respectively of the crop grouping.

Because breeding and selection have changed the temperature response of photosynthesis in some species, there are some C3 groups (e.g. cotton, groundnut) whose optimum temperature is in a medium to high range (25 - 30° C), and there are some C4-species (e.g. maize, sorghum) where, for temperate and tropical highland cultivars, the optimum temperature is in a low to medium range (20 - 30° C). These C3 and C4-species constitute groups II and IV respectively of the crop grouping effected.

The final group (V) comprises species evolved and adapted to operate under xerophytic conditions. No crops of the assessment are included in this group.

To take account of these attributes and the moisture requirements of the crops, the climatic inventory is made by concomitantly:

a) inventorying the period of days when water availability and temperature regime permit crop growth, that is the growing period, and

b) classifying into major climatic divisions (to cater for the photosynthesis temperature requirements of the four crop groups used in the assessment).

Part a) is achieved by computer calculation of the number of days when available water and temperature regime permit crop growth, i.e. the continuous period during the year, from the time when rainfall exceeds half potential evapotranspiration (calculated by the Penman method) until the time when rainfall falls below full potential evapotranspiration, plus a number of days required to evaporate an assumed 100 mm of soil moisture reserve. Consequently, a normal growing period must exhibit a humid phase, i.e. a period in which rainfall is greater than potential evapotranspiration. Additionally, it excludes any period when crop growth is not possible in the growing period because of low temperatures (e.g. average mean temperature less than 6.5° C for winter wheat).

Length-of-growing-period data are calculated and plotted on
1:5 000 000 scale maps. Zones with similar lengths of growing period
are delineated by constructing isolines at intervals of 30 days (e.g.
90-119 days, 120-149 days, 150-179 days, etc.). Zones with a
humid phase are designated as normal zones (N). Zones without a
humid phase and consequently unable to meet full crop water requirements from rainfall, are designated as intermediate zones (I). An
additional isoline for a growing period of 75 days was also included
to cover possible interpretations for pearl millet in drier areas.

For each zone thus delineated by the length of growing period
isolines, average values of major climatic elements (radiation, day and
night-time temperature, etc.) characterizing the growing period, are
calculated for subsequent potential biomass and yield calculations.
Concomitantly with this activity, part b) of the inventory was made by
classifying the continent into the 8 major climatic divisions shown in
Table 3.

A generalized presentation of the distribution of major climates
and of 60 day interval isolines for Africa (based on data from 700
meteorological stations) is illustrated on Map 2.

Table 4 shows the extension of areas covered by similar growing
periods - at 60 days intervals - by major climatic divisions in Africa.
The table quantifies the different areas generalized on the map.

It should be noted that cartographic presentation at page size
scale has resulted in considerable displacement of the isolines in
areas of rapid change and the map shown herewith is essentially
illustrative of the methodology.

Matching Soil Requirements of Crops with the Soils Inventory

The grading of the soil units of the FAO/Unesco Soil Map of the
World is made by comparing the properties of the soil units with the
crop's soil requirements. If the soil unit largely meets the crop's
requirements, it is adjudged S1, that is the soil conditions do not
affect the climatically-potential yield. If the soil unit only partly meets
the crop's requirements, it is adjudged S2, i.e. the soil does not
allow the full climatic yield potential of the crop to be attained.
Failure to meet the crops' minimum soil requirements - outside the
range of properties necessary for growth - results in a grading of N,
meaning that the soil cannot adequately support production of the crop.
Similar rules are made for the various slope and texture classes and
soil phases and programmed for computer application.

In the matching exercise Fluvisols are treated separately from
other soil units because in areas where these soils occur, crops are
most frequently produced on residual moisture remaining after rainy
season flooding, as well as rice during the flood season. In other
words, the inventoried climatic conditions of the growing period are
not totally applicable to the period when crop growth is possible on
these soils. Additionally, the irregular flooding conditions cause
major difficulties in assessing suitability from a soil point of view only.

Table 3 – Africa – Characteristics of Major Climatic Divisions

	Div. No.	Suitable for consideration for crop group	24 hr. mean temperature regime over the whole growing period	Average altitude	Descriptive name	Total extent (000ha)
Tropical. All monthly average 24hr. mean temperatures (corrected to sea level) above 18°C	I	II and III	>20°C	<1500m	Tropical lowland or warm tropics	2 029 975
	2	I and IV	<20°C	1500–3000m	Tropical highland or cool tropics	96 604
	3	Not suitable	<10.0–12.5°C with severe risk of night frost.	>3000m	Tropical mountains or cold tropics	2 903
Sub-tropical (summer rainfall). Some monthly average 24hr. mean temperatures (corrected to sea level) below 18°C	4	II and III	>20°C	From >1500m at low latitudes to sea level at high altitudes	Warm sub-tropics (summer)	291 894
	5	I and IV	<20°C	From >1500m at low latitudes to sea level at high latitudes	Cool sub-tropics (summer)	39 900
	6	Not suitable	<10.0–12.5°C with severe risk of night frost	>2500–3000m depending on latitude	Cold sub-tropics (summer)	193
Sub-tropical (winter rainfall). Some monthly average 24hr. mean temperatures (corrected to sea level) below 18°C	7	I	>6.5°C	<1500m	Cool sub-tropics (winter)	543 198
	8	Not suitable	<6.5°C	>1500m	Cold sub-tropics (winter)	6 663

Map 2

ISOLINES OF GROWING PERIODS (IN DAYS) –AFRICA

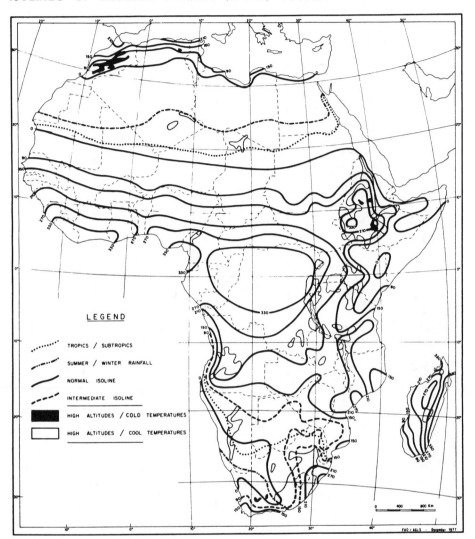

LEGEND

.... TROPICS / SUBTROPICS

—··—··— SUMMER / WINTER RAINFALL

———— NORMAL ISOLINE

– – – – INTERMEDIATE ISOLINE

▬▬▬▬ HIGH ALTITUDES / COLD TEMPERATURES

▭▭▭▭ HIGH ALTITUDES / COOL TEMPERATURES

0   400   800 Km

FAO / AGLS – December 1977

Table 4 — Extension of Areas (000 ha) with Length of Growing
Periods (in days) by Major Climatic Divisions

Length of growing period (days)* \ Major climates	Tropics			Subtropics with summer rainfall			Subtropics with winter rainfall		Total	Percentage
	1 warm	2 cool	3 cold	4 warm	5 cool	6 cold	7 cool	8 cold		
Cold areas	–	–	2 903	–	–	193	–	6 663	9 759	0.32
N. 330 +	222 853	4 638	–	–	–	–	–	–	227 491	7.56
N. 270–329	201 505	14 306	–	549	229	–	–	–	216 589	7.19
N. 210–269	264 557	30 704	–	1 306	1 072	–	9 277	–	306 916	10.19
N. 150–209	401 114	19 927	–	5 549	5 359	–	14 215	–	446 164	14.82
N. 90–149	186 634	12 914	–	–	–	–	14 016	–	213 564	7.09
N. 1– 89	427 705	6 053	–	–	–	–	5 378	–	439 136	14.58
N. 0	183 660	4 078	–	237 744	6 547	–	442 929	–	874 958	29.05
I. 1– 89	91 212	3 887	–	28 530	12 698	–	53 244	–	189 571	6.30
I. 90–149	50 719	97	–	14 108	3 819	–	4 139	–	72 882	2.42
I. 150 +	16	–	–	4 108	10 176	–	–	–	14 300	0.48
Totals	2 029 975	96 604	2 903	291 894	39 900	193	543 198	6 663	3 011 330	100.00
Percentage	67.41	3.20	0.10	9.69	1.33	0.01	18.4	0.22		100.00

* N. Zones with a humid phase
  I. Zones without a humid phase

26

Some basic concepts in the matching exercise are:

a) the gradings are made on the assumption that there have been
no major land improvements. This is necessary because the
location of such improved areas is not known on a global
scale. It is appreciated that in many instances the gradings
will have to be changed if major land improvements have
already been effected in an area;

b) account is taken of the actual quantitative definitions of the
soil units, e.g.

- the Gleyic soil units, defined as having hydromorphic
properties "within 50 cm", have been treated as Gleysols
in the gradings, i.e. are judged N under both low and
high inputs for most crops. Where the definition states
that the hydromorphic properties occur "below 50 cm" the
soil units are adjudged S2 under both inputs for most
crops;

c) Dystric and humic soil units have usually been rated as S2
under low management and S1 under high management,
assuming that appropriate amounts of fertilizers are used
at the high input level.

Modifications are applied to the soil unit gradings, to take into
account limitations imposed by phase conditions, e.g. difficulties with
mechanized cultivation in stony and lithic soils; shallow rooting
volume in soils with hardpans at shallow depth; sensitivity to high
calcium carbonate content of certain crops in petrocalcic soils;
depression of yields as a result of salinity or sodicity.

Modifications to the soil unit gradings are also made for slope
classes. Areas with slopes of 8-30 percent, i.e. "b" slopes, are
modified as follows: for low level inputs, i.e. hand cultivation, one-
third of the area remains unchanged, one-third is decreased by one
class and the remaining one-third is downgraded to N. For high level
inputs one-third of the extent of "b" slope land remains unchanged, but
the remaining two-thirds are downgraded in entirety to N, as mechanized
cultivation is normally not possible on some two-thirds of these slopes.
All extents of "c" slopes, that is steeper than 30 percent, are downgraded
to N for 85 percent of the area, the remaining 15 percent being considered as "b" slopes and the modifications for that slope class apply.

Effected texture modifications are governed by the following
rules: all extents of group 1 textures are decreased by one class,
except for soil units where light texture limitations have already been
applied in the soil unit gradings, e.g. Podzols and Arenosols. All
textures in groups 2 and 3 remain unchanged, no modifications being
necessary as limitations imposed by heavy textures are dealt with in
the soil unit gradings.

Soil/crop gradings have been established for each of the crops
under study at each of the levels of input considered, and for each of the
soil units in the legend of the Soil Map of the World. These gradings

are used as modifiers to the "climatic suitability" assessment described in the following section.

Matching Crop Climatic Requirements and the Climate Inventory

The climate matching exercise is, in essence, undertaken by consecutively:

a) comparing the photosynthesis temperature requirements of each crop group with the main temperature regimes during the growing period in the major climates inventoried and, if the crop's temperature and phenological requirements are met;

b) ascertaining if the prevailing length of growing periods will permit any yield of the crop and, if so,

c) calculating potential net biomass and yield of crops in the various adequate lengths of growing periods inventoried, according to the climatic factors therein.

Mention has already been made, in the climatic inventory section, of the relationship between the main crop groups and major climates, e.g. crops in groups II and III can be considered in major climates 1 (warm tropical lowlands) and 4 (warm subtropical areas with summer rainfall) with mean temperatures of more than 20°C during the growing period. Adequate versus inadequate lengths of growing periods were, for the crops considered, designated as: less than 75 days - inadequate; more than 75 days - adequate, i.e. areas with lengths of growing periods of less than 75 days duration were considered as not suitable for the crops of the assessment.

Calculations of net biomass production and yields of crops use the information on the climatic factors of radiation and temperature within the growing periods, together with the actual photosynthesis capacity of crops and the fraction of the net biomass which crops can convert into economically useful yields. When the climatic pheno- logical requirements are met, the computed values indicate what is possible at the upper limit of crop performance when agro-climatic and soil constraints to growth and yield, including pests, diseases and weeds, are minimal. Such constraints are taken into account in the final land suitability assessment.

Examples of the computed potential net biomass production and yield are given in Table 5.

Crop characteristics considered in the potential net biomass and yield calculations comprise length of normal growth cycle, yield for- mation period, leaf area index at maximum growth rate and harvest index.

Pertinent to the calculation are the facts that: (a) within zone generalized radiation and temperature data are used to arrive at the predicted values (b) climatic requirements for phenological behaviour are taken into account before the calculated values become applicable and (c) climate does affect the fraction of net biomass that can be economically converted into economically useful yield.

The methodology used has the attribute of quantifying all potential yields of the crops of the assessment, in appropriate major climatic divisions and lengths of growing periods. It dispenses with the need, early in the evaluation exercise, to arbitrarily decide on climatic parameters which are hopefully associated with various classes of suitability tied to anticipated yields. In the present study all potential yields are maintained for all "yielding" growing periods and major climates, immaterial of their levels.

T a b l e 5 - Potential net biomass (Bn) and yield (By) in t/ha dry weight of selected crops by various lengths of growing periods in the warm tropics 1/

Growing Period (days)		75-89	120-149	180-209	240-269	300-329
Crop						
Pearl millet	Bn	12.0-16.7	11.6-16.2	10.9-15.3	10.8-15.3	10.4-14.6
	By	3.0- 4.2	2.9- 4.0	2.7- 3.8	2.7- 3.8	2.6- 3.6
Maize	Bn	11.3-14.5	14.3-20-6	13.7-20.1	13.4-19.5	12.7-18.7
	By	1.9- 4.9	5.0- 7.2	4.8- 7.0	4.7- 6.8	4.4- 6.5
Cassava	Bn	3.3- 4.2	7.7-10.9	14.2-17.7	20.7-22.6	23.1-24.8
	By	0.5- 0.8	2.4- 4.7	7.8- 9.7	11.4-12.4	12.7-13.6

1/ Major climate 1.

Soil Degradation Hazards

While the soil and climatic conditions of a tract of land may be suitable for the growth of a specific crop, sustained yields may not be possible because of progressive soil degradation. Certain types of land use may provide short-term returns but may, in the long run, result in the depletion of the soils production potential. Land evaluation must therefore take into account hazards of water erosion, wind blowing, salinization, acidification, compaction or loss of organic matter. Although these processes are well known, with described mechanisms, little precise knowledge is available on area of occurrence and on the relationship to different types of soils. It has been estimated that lands already lost through adverse use are in excess of those presently used (Kovda 1977) and that 5 to 7 million hectares of arable land deteriorate every year. These figures illustrate the gravity of the problem and point to the need to evaluate it more accurately.

In order to obtain a more precise picture of the incidence of soil degradation FAO, in cooperation with Unesco and the support of

UNEP, is currently carrying out an assessment of soil degradation hazards on a world-wide basis. A methodology has been developed to measure the risks of different types of soil degradation quantitatively. The assessment is made first on the basis of the physical factors of the landscape (soil, climate, slope) which reflect the risks of soil degradation without protection of a vegetative cover. Since degradation hazards are closely related to the type of land use, the actual degradation needs to be assessed taking into account the present or envisaged type of soil cover and the management techniques applied. A map output showing the processes and the degrees of degradation risks is being prepared on the basis of the 1:5 000 000 Soil Map of the World. A parametric method is being tested to quantify degradation hazards by multiplying factors related to soil characteristics, climatic aggressivity and slope.

Maps of actual degradation can be prepared subsequently in combination with existing land use data, or on the basis of projected land use plans which involve the human factor in respect of management.

It is obvious that land evaluation has to take into account the hazards of soil depletion. Consequently the prognosis of degradation hazards makes it possible to estimate inputs required for land improvement, erosion control measures or corrective cultural practices, the cost of which will in turn influence the economic parameters of land evaluation.

The assessment of soil degradation was not sufficiently advanced to be included in the present appraisal of land resources. It is planned, however, that elements of both studies will be combined so as to obtain an evaluation which assesses not only present suitability but has a predictive value in respect of maintaining a balance between production and environment.

The Suitability Classification

The previously described matching activities of the potential land use study provide anticipated climatically-potential crop yields by major climatic divisions and lengths of growing period, with identification of the degree and extent of various soil limitations in those areas.

These climatically-potential yields, however, do not take into account yield reductions due to climatic (rainfall) variability, moisture stress, excess moisture, and losses due to pests, diseases and weeds (Kassam 1976). Such calculations have been effected for Africa, the constraints varying according to the zone, e.g. endemic pest, disease and weed losses are relatively higher in longer growing period areas. Climatic variability has been included as a constraint, particularly in short growing period areas. The constraints are rated as nil to slight, moderate or severe and corresponding yield reductions of 0, 25 or 50 percent are applied where such constraints occur, e.g. constraints to cotton in the growing period 270-299 days under low inputs, due to bollworm, sucking bugs and leaf curl attack, result in a yield reduction (of the climatically-potential yield) of 50 percent to arrive at the agronomically attainable yield.

The yields so calculated are for high input/ideal soil conditions. Agronomically attainable low input yields are calculated in a similar manner, the climatically potential yield under low inputs being 25 percent of the climatically potential yield under high input conditions.

The agro-climatic suitability assessment for each crop at both input levels, was achieved by considering the whole agronomically possible yield range and classifying each individual growing period yield into one of four classes, defined in terms of a percentage range of the maximum attainable without constraints. Growing period zones, capable of yielding 80 percent or more of the maximum yield attainable, were classified as very suitable; zones yielding less than 80 percent to 40 percent as suitable; zones yielding less than 40 percent to 20 percent as marginally suitable and zones yielding less than 20 percent as not suitable. This activity results in an agro-climatic crop suitability assessment of each main climatic division and length of growing period. Application of this methodology of assessing agro-climatic suitability, to the rainfed production of pearl millet, maize and cassava in Africa, has given the results shown in Table 6. The distribution of the areas of different agro-climatic suitability are illustrated by Maps 3, 4 and 5 respectively.

For each crop and level of input, appropriate production costs are being calculated. Results to date indicate that, with the exception of millet and low level input cotton, the division between not suitable and marginally suitable relates to the break-even point of the value of the produce in comparison to production costs.

In the final assessment of potential land suitability, the soil assessment is being superimposed on the agro-climatic assessment. In the case of areas of soils adjudged S1 for a particular crop, no change will be made in the agro-climatic suitability assessment. Areas of soils adjudged S2 will have the agro-climatic suitability assessment downgraded by one land suitability class. Areas of soils adjudged as N will result in a final suitability assessment of that land as not suitable, the very severe soil limitations overriding all the climatic attributes.

Preliminary results available at the time of the preparation of this paper, on extents of land suitable for pearl millet, maize and cassava in Africa, show that soil constraints markedly limit the areas of very suitable and suitable land for the growth of these crops. In certain areas differences between the land suitability assessment and the agro-climatic suitability assessment show reductions up to 80 percent for very suitable areas and up to 60 percent for suitable areas due to soil limitations.

The global land suitability assessment will give areas of lands: very suitable; suitable; marginally suitable; not suitable, for the production of each crop, at each of the two levels of inputs considered. The four classes will be related to the anticipated yield as a percentage of the maximum attainable under optimum agro-climatic and soil conditions, and will therefore provide the necessary data for calculation of the production potential of any given area.

Table 6 - Agro-Climatic Suitability Assessment (000 ha) for Pearl Millet, Maize 1/ and Cassava in Africa

| CROP | AREAS OF LAND | | | | | 1975 |
	Very suitable	Suitable	Marginally suitable	Not suitable	Total area	Area cultivated to crop and average yield 3/
MILLET						
Extent 2/	234 001	465 619	160 939	2 150 771	3 011 330	16 415
Percent of total area	7.8	15.5	5.3	71.4	100.0	0.6
Anticipated yields (t/ha)						
Low inputs	1.0-0.8	0.8-0.4	0.4-0.2	<0.2		
High inputs	3.9-3.1	3.1-1.6	1.6-0.8	<0.8		0.6
MAIZE						
Extent 2/	472 352	470 746	187 021	1 881 211	3 011 330	17 401
Percent of total area	15.7	15.6	6.2	62.5	100.0	0.6
Anticipated yields (t/ha)						
Low inputs	1.8-1.4	1.4-0.7	0.7-0.4	<0.4		
High inputs	7.1-5.7	5.7-2.8	2.8-1.4	<1.4		1.4
CASSAVA						
Extent 2/	201 115	719 546	176 774	1 913 895	3 011 330	6 057
Percent of total area	6.7	23.9	5.9	63.5	100.0	0.2
Anticipated yields (t/ha dry weight)						
Low inputs	4/	2.7-1.4	1.4-0.7	<0.7		
High inputs	13.6-10.9	10.9-5.4	5.4-2.7	<2.7		2.4

1/ in warm tropics and warm subtropics with summer rainfall
2/ averaged for both levels of inputs
3/ includes irrigated production; source: FAO Production Yearbook (1975)
4/ only applicable to high level of input conditions; no very suitable areas under low levels of inputs because of virus infected planting material

MILLET

Map 3

GENERALIZED AGRO – CLIMATIC SUITABILITY ASSESSMENT FOR
RAINFED PRODUCTION

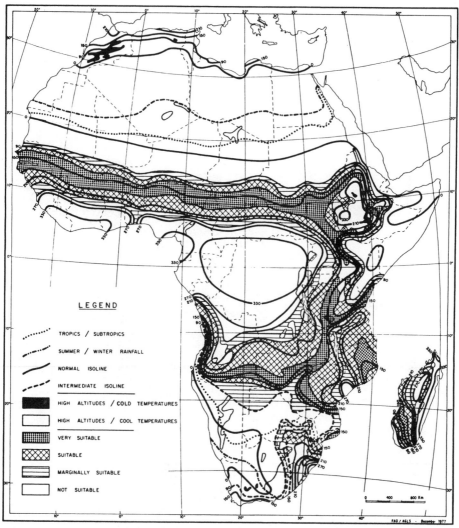

LEGEND

- ········· TROPICS / SUBTROPICS
- –··–··– SUMMER / WINTER RAINFALL
- ——— NORMAL ISOLINE
- – – – INTERMEDIATE ISOLINE
- HIGH ALTITUDES / COLD TEMPERATURES
- HIGH ALTITUDES / COOL TEMPERATURES
- VERY SUITABLE
- SUITABLE
- MARGINALLY SUITABLE
- NOT SUITABLE

FAO / AGLS – December 1977

NOTE: THE ASSESSMENT IS FOR RAINFED PRODUCTION ONLY. A SEPARATE ASSESSMENT IS NECESSARY FOR IRRIGATED PRODUCTION

MAIZE

Map 4

GENERALIZED AGRO – CLIMATIC SUITABILITY ASSESSMENT FOR
RAINFED PRODUCTION

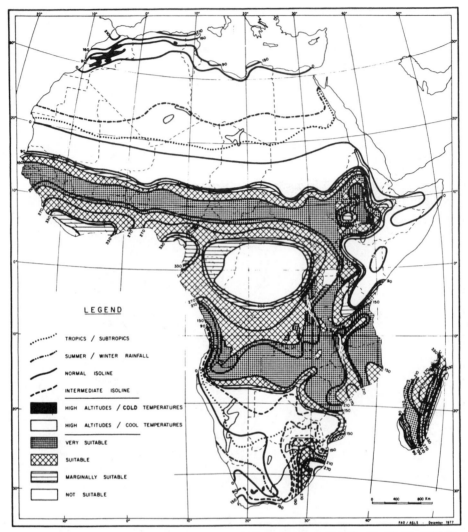

LEGEND

⋯⋯⋯⋯ TROPICS / SUBTROPICS

–⋅–⋅– SUMMER / WINTER RAINFALL

——— NORMAL ISOLINE

– – – INTERMEDIATE ISOLINE

■ HIGH ALTITUDES / **COLD** TEMPERATURES

☐ HIGH ALTITUDES / COOL TEMPERATURES

▦ VERY SUITABLE

▨ SUITABLE

▤ MARGINALLY SUITABLE

☐ NOT SUITABLE

0 400 800 Km

FAO / AGLS · December 1977

NOTE: THE ASSESSMENT IS FOR RAINFED PRODUCTION ONLY. A SEPARATE ASSESSMENT IS NECESSARY FOR IRRIGATED PRODUCTION

CASSAVA

Map 5

GENERALIZED AGRO – CLIMATIC SUITABILITY ASSESSMENT FOR
RAINFED PRODUCTION

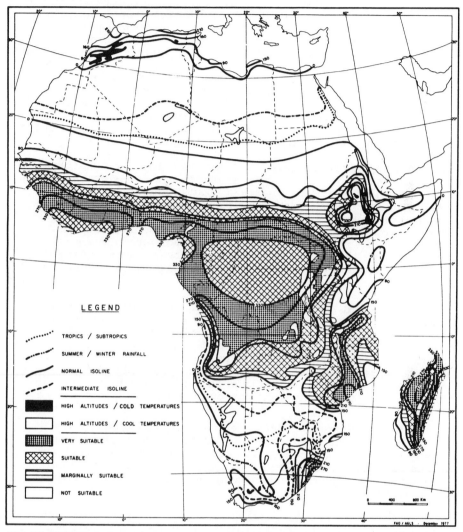

LEGEND

· · · · · · · · · TROPICS / SUBTROPICS

– · – · – · – SUMMER / WINTER RAINFALL

———— NORMAL ISOLINE

– – – – INTERMEDIATE ISOLINE

HIGH ALTITUDES / COLD TEMPERATURES

HIGH ALTITUDES / COOL TEMPERATURES

VERY SUITABLE

SUITABLE

MARGINALLY SUITABLE

NOT SUITABLE

0   400   800 Km

FAO / AGLS - December 1977

NOTE: THE ASSESSMENT IS FOR RAINFED PRODUCTION ONLY. A SEPARATE ASSESSMENT IS NECESSARY FOR IRRIGATED PRODUCTION

Conclusions

From global appraisals it appears that vast tracts of land are still available for cultivation. These estimates however, as reflected by their great variability, do not take into account differences in potential production when it is calculated for different crops, with widely differing requirements and different levels of inputs and technology. Such factors must be taken into account to arrive at realistic estimates of the potential agricultural production of the various lands of the world.

Equally important is the problem that the world's land resources are immobile and unevenly distributed both with regard to extension and quality. Not all crops can be grown in all areas and expansion of production, through increased inputs and investment, will need to be planned and achieved in the context of a sound inventory of land and its production potential for various types of land use.

Although great progress has been made during the last three decades in identifying the world's major soils, a considerable amount of work remains to be done to assess their production potential. At present the interpretation of soil survey results is seriously limited by a lack of information on soil requirements of specific crops. Precise knowledge on climatic requirements of various crops is equally scarce especially in relation to the moisture regimes of different soils. While soil properties have been carefully defined and recorded, their significance for soil management is still insufficiently determined.

Future land resource surveys need to specifically inventory those parameters of importance to crop growth, combining soil and climatic factors. Information now required for agricultural development should reach beyond the assessment of overall areas of "arable land". Land evaluation needs to be made in respect of specific types of land use, taking into account input levels required and degradation hazards to be overcome. Soils must be used according to their suitability in order to conserve and improve the world's land resources.

While evaluations of land are originally based on physical attributes, it should be stressed that economic and social factors need to be taken into account. However, since socio-economic conditions vary considerably from one country to another, it has not been possible to include these elements in detail in the described global study.

Soil science has and is playing an important role in raising agricultural production. Additional tasks lie ahead for characterizing land requirements which can be quantitatively incorporated into economic assessments. To achieve this objective, more intensive cooperation will need to be established with other disciplines which should in turn be cross fertilized with the input from soil scientists. The present study is an attempt in this direction. Because of its global character it is necessarily general in nature. It is hoped, however, that the methodology on which it is based can be used at the country level for practical land use planning.

BALLOD, K. 1912. Wieviel Menschen kann die Erde ernahren? Schmollers Jabrb.f. Gesetzgebung, Verwaltung und Volkswirtschaft, XXXVI, 2:881.

BURINGH, P., VAN HEEMST, H. J. D. and STARING, G. J. 1975. Computation of the absolute maximum food production of the world. Agric. University, Wageningen, The Netherlands.

DUDAL, R. 1969. Arable Land. Pages 13-29 in Annual Report, 1969, Int. Institute for Land Reclamation and Improvement, Wageningen, The Netherlands.

DUDAL, R. 1973. Planosols. Pages 275-285 in E. Schlichting and U. Schwertmann, eds. Pseudogley and gley genesis and use of hydromorphic soils. Comm. V and VI, Int. Soc. Soil Sci. Trans. Verlag Chemie GmgB, Wienheim.

FOOD AND AGRICULTURE ORGANIZATION OF THE UNITED NATIONS. 1971. FAO-UNESCO Map of the World, Vol. IV - South America. Unesco, Paris.

FOOD AND AGRICULTURE ORGANIZATION OF THE UNITED NATIONS. 1974. FAO-UNESCO Map of the World, Vol. I - Legend. Unesco, Paris.

FOOD AND AGRICULTURE ORGANIZATION OF THE UNITED NATIONS. 1975. FAO-UNESCO Map of the World, Vol. II - North America. Unesco, Paris.

FOOD AND AGRICULTURE ORGANIZATION OF THE UNITED NATIONS. 1975. FAO-UNESCO Map of the World, Vol. III - Mexico and Central America. Unesco, Paris.

FOOD AND AGRICULTURE ORGANIZATION OF THE UNITED NATIONS. 1975. Production Yearbook, Vol. 29.

FOOD AND AGRICULTURE ORGANIZATION OF THE UNITED NATIONS. 1976. FAO-UNESCO Map of the World, Vol. VI - Africa. Unesco, Paris.

FOOD AND AGRICULTURE ORGANIZATION OF THE UNITED NATIONS. 1977. A Framework for Land Evaluation. Soils Bull. No. 32. Rome.

FOOD AND AGRICULTURE ORGANIZATION OF THE UNITED NATIONS. 1977. Assessing Soil Degradation. Soils Bull. No. 34, Rome.

FOOD AND AGRICULTURE ORGANIZATION OF THE UNITED NATIONS. 1978. Report on the Agro-ecological Zones Project, Vol. I. Methodology and Results for Africa. World Soil Resources Report No. 48.

HIGGINS, G. M. 1977. Land classification. Pages 59-77 in Soil Conservation and Management in Developing Countries. Soils Bull. No. 33.

KASSAM, A. H. 1976. Crops of the West African Semi-arid Tropics. ICRISAT, Hyderabad, India.

KELLOGG, C. E. and ORVEDAL, A. C. 1969. Potentially arable soils of the world and critical measures for their use. Adv. Agron. 21: 109-170.

KOVDA, V. A. 1977. Soil loss: an overview. Agro-Ecosystems 3: 205-224.

KOWAL, J. M. and KASSAM, A. H. 1978. Page 420 <u>in</u> Agricultural Ecology of Savanna. Oxford University Press.

PAWLEY, W. H. 1971. In the year 2070. Ceres 4(4): 22–27.

PENCK, A. 1928. Das Hauptproblem der Physischen Anthropogeographie. Proc. and Papers, 1st Int. Congr. Soil Sci. Vol. II: 98–116.

RAVENSTEIN, E. G. 1890. Lands of the globe still available for European settlement. Proc. Roy. Geog. Soc. XIII: 27.

REVELLE, R. 1976. The resources available for agriculture. Scientific American 235(3): 164–178.

SOIL SURVEY STAFF, Soil Conservation Service, U.S. Dept. of Agric. 1975. Soil taxonomy, a basic system of soil classification for making and interpreting soil surveys. Agriculture Handbook No. 486, U.S. Government Printing Office, Washington, D.C.

2: LAND SUITABILITY CLASSIFICATION

F. J. Dent

Attempts to develop land suitability classifications for Asian wetland rice since 1913 are reviewed.

Evaluation procedures compare relevant kinds of land use and their environmental requirements with land mapping units and their qualities or attributes. Diagnostic criteria and suitability ratings developed for individual classifications reviewed are intimately related to the physical, economic, and social context of the areas they are to serve.

Early approaches were primarily concerned with effect rather than cause, being largely based on and designed for rice cultivation in areas within a country with a relatively limited range in environmental characteristics. Modern approaches are primarily qualitative — even if parametric methods are utilized — and are empirical assessments based on assumed relationships between crop performance and diagnostic criteria. Parametric methods, however, are at least potentially quantitative if both inputs and products can be related to land qualities in numerical terms. Advances in trial design, site location, and transferability of data are required for more precise information on quantitative environmental land use relationships.

Recent work raises the possibility of formulating a crop-yield prediction equation by means of multiple regression analysis. Such an equation, when linked with soil material classification, offers future potential in suitability classification for wetland rice.

DURING THE PAST 70 YEARS various systems of land evaluation or land classification were developed in many countries. Jacks (1946) viewed land classification as it "relates to the grouping of lands according to their suitability for producing plants of economic importance." Today, land evaluation systems encompass virtually all aspects of land use. Such systems, however, do not evaluate the suitability of special crops or farming systems such as wetland rice cultivation. Nor do they allow for parallel evaluations of alternative uses on the same land except in general terms, i.e. arable or nonarable.

FAO project manager, Land Capability Appraisal Project, Soil Research Institute, Jalan Ir. H. Juanda 98, Bogor, Indonesia.

To meet those needs a framework for land evaluation (FAO, 1976) that provides for parallel land suitability evaluation was developed.

Before the development of the proposed framework, wetland rice was one of the few special crops subjected to separate studies for soil or land suitability evaluations. The principal efforts to develop a soil or land classification system for wetland rice emerged from tropical Asia where more than 25% of the world's population depends on rice for their continued existence from some 82 million ha of wetland rice cultivated annually.

DEVELOPMENT OF SUITABILITY CLASSIFICATION FOR WETLAND RICE

Appraisal of suitability of specific types of land (soil or land mapping units) for a given kind of use (such as wetland rice cultivation) is achieved by *matching* land use with land. In its simplest form matching is the confrontation of the physical requirements of a specific crop to give a prediction of crop performance based on the functional relationships that exist between the land qualities, the possibilities for land improvement, and the requirements of land use.

Unlike most food crops, wetland rice does not require well-aerated soils and thrives under flooding. Certain land attributes that would be considered limiting for most crops are often favorable for wetland rice.

Environmental requirements and limitations for the sustained cultivation of wetland rice

The main soil requirements and limitations of wetland rice follow:
- The optimum texture range is from loams to clays.
- A depth greater than 40 cm is considered advantageous.
- Permeability ranges are from moderate to slow.
- Drainage ranges are from well to very poorly drained. Short periods of deep flooding are tolerated and certain rice varieties will grow where floodwaters rise up to 3 m if the current is not too strong and the water level rise is not greater than 10 cm/day.
- Fertility requirement ranges from low to high.
- Soil reaction ranges are from pH 4.0 to 7.0, the optimum being pH 5.0 to 6.0.
- Organic matter content greater than 65% by weight and more than 60 cm deep are commonly limiting for wetland rice production.
- Excess salt and acid are growth-limiting factors.

Early attempts to classify rice lands in tropical Asia

Barritt (1913) classified some wetland rice areas in Malaysia into two groups according to the labor requirement for cultivation. Jack (1923) proposed a classification of land in Malaysia that grouped soils into three classes in terms of yield, with peaty soils considered separately as uneconomic for rice cultivation.

In Indonesia investigations into the productivity of irrigated paddy fields in East Java (De Vries and Joosten, 1929-30) were primarily concerned with risk of rice yield decrease. From a study of yield figures and soil characteristics from over 10,000 sites in East Central Java during the period 1950-1954, Hauser and Sadikin (1956) concluded that no simple relationship between the soil units and rice yield existed. Two factors, however, appeared to play a major role in determining a soil's productivity level for rice. The dominant factor was the parent material, and the second factor was the state of weathering of that material.

Ng (1968) attempted to classify the *padi* soils of West Malaysia on the basis of drainage limitations, groundwater quality, texture, and humus content. Soils with no limitations were grouped in Class I. Soils with slightly poor drainage and slight salinity effects from groundwater were grouped in Class II. Soils with slightly excessive drainage, sandy plow layer, low humus content, and moderate salinity effects from groundwater were grouped in Class III. Class IV soils included those with poor drainage, extreme acidity, and sulfurous conditions. Class V soils were poorly drained and subject to flooding by sea water, and had extreme salinity.

The foregoing attempts at classification were largely based on, and designed for, rice cultivation in areas within a country with a relatively limited range in environmental characteristics. However, the use of new techniques has led to the development of evaluation or classification systems of wider applicability.

Qualitative suitability classification
Land suitability classification is the process of appraising and grouping specific types of land in terms of their absolute or relative suitability for a specified kind of use (FAO, 1976). Qualitative suitability classification is an empirical assessment based on assumed relationships between crop performance and diagnostic criteria. A diagnostic criterion is defined as a variable, which may be a land quality, a land characteristic, or a function of several land characteristics that has an understood influence on the output from, or the required inputs to, a specific kind of land use (FAO, 1976).

Moormann and Dudal (1965) identified water supply, soil characteristics, soil horizons, and other factors (topography, climate, etc.) as the major criteria for assessing the capability of soil in which rice is grown. (As classification systems developed the term capability was increasingly replaced by the term suitability.)

As with the land capability classification of the U.S. Department of Agriculture, individual soil or land mapping units form the building stones of the systems developed. Individual mapping units with the same relative degree of hazard or limitation for continuous cultivation of rice are placed in the same suitability group or class, with suitability being expressed in qualitative terms. The number of groups or classes utilized varies: the first group or class has no significant limitations, successive groups or classes have progressively greater risks of damage or limitation in use.

The suitability groups or classes group soil or land mapping units according to the degree of hazard or limitation only; they give no indication of the kind of limitation, or of the management practices required. Consequently, they are divided into subgroups or subclasses consisting of individual mapping units with the same kind of dominant limitation. Placement of individual mapping units in their appropriate suitability group or class, and hence subgroup or subclass, is achieved by comparing their characteristics with environmental requirements or limitations for rice. Various guidelines have been developed denoting limiting factors (diagnostic criteria) and the degree of limitation by suitability group or class (Table 1).

In the Republic of Korea (Chun Soo Shin, 1971), soil and land characteristics — slope, natural drainage, texture, erosion, available soil depths, content of gravels or stoniness, conductivity, and the presence of acid sulfatic layers — are the determining factors of a qualitative paddy land suitability classification that does not consider the availability of water and irrigation systems. Four suitability groups are defined with the degree of limitation increasing from P 1(well-suited) to P 4(very poorly suited).

The suitability groups are divided into suitability subgroups on the basis of main limitations, which are designated by letter symbols.

• Subgroup e, where the main limitation is risk of erosion and slippage of paddy berms because of steeper slopes.

•Subgroup w, where the main limitation is excessive wetness because of high groundwater table.

• Subgroup s, where the soil is limited mainly because of coarse texture or rapid permeability.

• Subgroup g, where the soil is limited mainly because of gravels or stoniness.

• Subgroup x, where the soil is limited because of toxic substances.

• Subgroup r, where the soil is well-drained or has low water table.

Rating of diagnostic criteria for placing land or soils in the four suitability groups for paddy are in Table 1. The attributes used in determining suitability are almost entirely physical soil characteristics. Fertility or relative nutrient status appears to have been discounted.

In Thailand the development of a qualitative soils suitability classification for rice was largely based on the factors proposed by Moormann and Dudal (1965). Dent (1969) made a tentative assessment of crops (including rice) suitable for a diversification program in peninsular Thailand. He used a three-point grading (favorable, marginal, and unfavorable) in assessing soil suitability for each crop, depicting increasing demands on capital inputs and managerial skills as soil conditions become more adverse. Major diagnostic

Table 1. Summary of guidelines denoting limiting factors and their degree of limitation by suitability group for six qualitative suitability classifications for wetland rice.

Limiting factors	Ratings for soil/land suitability classifications					
	Chun Soo Shin, 1971 (Republic of Korea)	Dent, 1969 (Peninsular Thailand)	FAO/Land Classifi-cation Division, 1973 (Thailand)	Kanapathy, 1975 (Malaysia)	Harrop, 1974 (Indonesia)	FAO/Bureau of Soils, 1976 (Philippines)
Drainage	P1–somewhat poorly P2–mod. well, poorly P3–well, very poorly P4– —	Favorable–poorly to very poorly Marginal–moderate Unfavorable–well	PI –somewhat poor-to poorly PII – " PIII–somewhat poorly to very poorly PIV–well to very poorly PV –	I –moderately II –poorly III –very poorly IV–very poorly and excessively	PII(I+II)–poor PIII –well (fine textured soils) very poor PIV–well - very poor PV –excessive	
Soil texture [1]surface soil only and thickness of topsoil where indicated	P1–fine clayey, fine loamy fine silty P2– " P3–coarse, loamy coarse silty P4–sandy	Favorable–silty clay loam, clay loam, clay Marginal–sandy clay loam Unfavorable–sandy loam loamy sand, sand	PI –clay, silty clay, clay loam, silty clay loam, sandy clay PII –clay, silty clay, sandy clay, silty clay loam, sandy clay loam, clay loam PIII –sandy loam to clay PIV–loamy sand to clay PV –	I –clay silty clay, silty clay, loam (20–12 cm) II–very heavy clay, sandy clay, silty clay loam (12–8 cm) III–sandy loam, fine sandy loam (<8%) IV–loamy sand, sand	PII –fine — medium PIII –fine — medium PIV–fine — medium PV –coarse	
Effective soil depth [2]irrigated rice [3]rainfed rice	P1–>100 cm P2– 100 — 50 cm P3-50–25 cm[a] P4-50–20 cm to hardpan or rock, 20–10 cm to gravel cobbles or sand	Favorable–>100 cm Marginal–50–100 cm Unfavorable–<50 cm	PI –>50 cm PII –>50 cm PIII –>25 cm PIV–>25 cm PV – —	I ->50 cm II –50-25 cm III –25-15 cm IV–<15 cm	PII –deep — med. PIII –deep — med. PIV–med.- shallow PV – —	S1–>50 cm[2] >100 cm[3] S2–30-50 cm 50-100 cm S3–30-50 cm 50-100 cm N –<30 cm <50 cm

(continued on next page)

Table 1. continued

			Ratings for soil/land suitability classifications			
Limiting factors	Chun Soo Shin, 1971 (Republic of Korea)	Dent, 1969 (Peninsular Thailand)	FAO/Land Classification Division, 1973 (Thailand)	Kanapathy, 1975 (Malaysia)	Harrop, 1974 (Indonesia)	FAO/Bureau of Soils, 1976 (Philippines)
Surface stoniness, boulders, rock outcrops [a]rainfed rice	P1-<3% P2-3-15% P3-15-50% P4->50%		PI -none PII -none to slightly gravelly PIII -none to slightly gravelly and slightly stony PIV-none to gravelly and slightly stony PV			S1-none[a] S2-locally S3-1-10% N ->10%
Salinity/alkalinity	P1-<4 P2-<4-8 P3-8-16 P4->16 (mm hos/cm at 25°C)		PI -<1500 PII -<2500 PIII-<2500 PIV-<4000 PV - (EC 5 × 10⁴)		PII -none PIII -none PIV-mod. — severe PV -severe	
Soil acidity hazard	P1->100 cm P2->100 cm P3- 100-50 cm P4- 50-20 cm (expressed as depth to acid sulphate layer)				PII -none PIII -none PIV-none — mod. PV -none — severe	
Soil reaction (pH) [b]Inherent fertility CEC and pH		Favorable-5.0-6.5 Marginal-4.0-8.4 Unfavorable->4.0 (dry soil pH 1: 1 H$_2$O	PI -5.0-7.5 PII -4.5-8.0 PIII -4.0-8.0 PIV-3.5-8.5 PV - (dry soil pH 1: 1 H$_2$O surface layer)	I->20 meq >4.5 II -20-6 meq 4.0-4.5 III-<2 meq 3.5-4.0 IV-3.5'	PII -slightly acid-neutral PIII -strongly acid to alkaline PIV-extremely acid to alkaline PV -below pH 3.5	
Fertility [c]Content of available nutrients			PI -high-mod. PII -high — mod. low PIII high — low PIV-high— low PV - (rated on CEC, BS%, O.M., avail. P)	I -high-mod, high II -moderate III-low IV-very low	PII -high — med. PIII -high — low PIV-high — very low PV -	S1-high — medium S2-low S3-low N -- (rated on CEC, pH, avail. P and K, free ferric oxide, BS%)

Permeability	Favorable–slow to very slow Marginal–moderate Unfavorable–rapid or very rapid	PI – <0.5 cm/h, slow PII – <1.5 cm/hr, slow to moderately slow PIII – <5 cm/h, slow to moderate PIV – <15 cm/h, slow to mod. rapid (slow to moderate if well drained) (subsoil permeability)		PII – >50% of unit 0–8% slope PIII – 30–50% of unit 0–8% slope PIV – 10–30% of unit 0–8% slope PV – <10% of unit 0–8% slope	S1 – <8 mm/day, low-medium S2 – <8 mm/day high S3 – >8 mm/day, high N — (deep percolation)
Slope %	P1– <2% P2–2–7% P3–7–15% P4–15–30%	Favorable–<2% Marginal–2–8% Unfavorable–>8%	PI <1% PII <2% PIII <3% PIV <5% PV —	I – <1% II –1% III–1–2% IV–>2%	S1–<2% S2–2–8% S3–2–8% N –>8%
Water availability ²irrigated rice		PI –no damage PII –occasional slight damage PIII–mod. damage occasional severe <4 yrs in 10 PIV–mod.to severe damage <6 yrs in 10, occasional complete loss. PV — (risk of damage water shortage)	I –nil, quality good –occasional or slight, quality good III –mod. damage (3 yr in 10), slightly acid or saline IV–mod. to severe damage (6 yr in 10), (risk of damage by water shortage, excess or quality	PII –no restriction* PIII –no restriction PIV–mod. restriction PV –severe restriction * >250 mm/month during preparation and crop growth	S1 –>2 crops² S2 –>1–2 crops S3–1 crop N – 0 (potential cropping intensity)
Flooding ²irrigated rice ³rainfed rice		PI – <1 in 10 yr PII –occasional mod. <3 in 10 yr PIII–mod. occasional severe<4 in 10 yr PIV–severe<6 in 10 yr		PII –slight PIII –mod. — severe PIV–severe — very severe PV —	S1–none to slight S2–slight to mod. S3–severe N –very severe² severe³

(continued on next page)

45

Table 1. *continued*

Limiting factors	Ratings for soil/land suitability classifications					
	Chun Soo Shin, 1971 (Republic of Korea)	Dent, 1969 (Peninsular Thailand)	FAO/Land Classification Division, 1973 (Thailand)	Kanapathy, 1975 (Malaysia)	Harrop, 1974 (Indonesia)	FAO/Bureau of Soils, 1976 (Philippines)
Soil erosion	P1-none — slight P2-none — slight P3-eroded P4-eroded					
Microrelief			PI ->80% land is smooth, little levelling PII -levelling PIII ->50% land is smooth, mod. levelling PIV->40% land is smooth, much levelling PV —			
Presence of laterite		Favorable-nil Marginal-fragmental 15–30 cm thick Unfavorable-fragmental >30 cm thick or massive				
State of redox potential and amount of organic matter				I -O.M. 3–7% II -O.M. 8–15% and 2–3% III -O.M. 15–25% and 1–2% IV-O.M. >25%		
Ease of mechanical cultivation				I -good II -very soft or slightly hard III -very hard IV-very hard		

criteria used in assessing soil suitability for rice were terrain (% slope), effective soil depth in relation to impenetrable subsoil layer or permanent water table, texture, presence of laterite, pH, permeability, and drainage. Ratings for each property, by grade, are summarized in Table 1.

Further developments in soil suitability classification for rice in Thailand were reported by Robinson and Steele (1972) preliminary to the presentation of "Soil Suitability Groups for Paddy (Wetland Rice)" (FAO and the Land Classification Division, 1973). This classification system assumed that the availability of water in a specific area was the most important factor in its suitability for rice. Consequently, soil and water supply were considered together in determining suitability of an area.

In the Thai classification, soil mapping units are placed in groups showing suitability according to soil qualities and the prevailing conditions in which most of the soil occurs. If the water supply is changed by large irrigation projects or stream diversion, the soil is regrouped to show a new suitability. Five paddy suitability groups were defined. Soils placed in groups P I through P IV receive enough water and have characteristics that enable them to hold water on the surface for periods long enough to allow one crop of rice to mature in most years. Soils in group P V are not suited for wetland rice, but may be well suited for other crops.

The suitability groups, except P I which has no significant limitations, are divided into subgroups according to the kind of dominant limitations. The kinds of limitations that mark the subgroups are denoted by a letter symbol and are defined as follows:

• *s – Soil limitation in the root zone.* Soils in subgroup *s* have such features as shallowness, unfavorable texture, rapid permeability, gravel and stones, and low fertility that is difficult to correct.

• *m – Lack of water for plant growth.* Soils in subgroup *m* have limitations that result from insufficient rainfall or stream flow in the normal growing season.

• *f – Flooding.* Soils in subgroup *f* are susceptible to flash floods or excessively prolonged and deep flooding. Frequency, duration, depth of water, speed with which the water moves, rate of rise, and possibility of salt water from the sea must be considered in determining degree of flood hazard.

• *t – Unfavorable topography.* Soils in subgroup *t* have high topographic position or distinct microrelief. It may be difficult or impossible to impound water on these soils, and land leveling may be necessary for paddy.

• *x – Salinity or alkalinity.* Soils in subgroup *x* have too much salt or alkali for crop growth.

• *a – Soil acidity.* Soils in subgroup *a* have high total acidity that is difficult to correct, as in acid sulfate soils.

The Thai classification takes into account rice requirements and limitations other than those that are based purely on soil characteristics. Thus, it offers

wide application in evaluation surveys. Because of its comprehensive
nature, this classification has proved an attractive base for the development
of suitability classifications for rice elsewhere.

In Malaysia, Kanapathy (1975) considered climate, water-related factors,
and soil characteristics as principal factors in classifying land suitability for
rice production. But in recommending land for rice he regarded slope or
terrain as the first factor to consider and availability of good water for
irrigation as of secondary concern. The climatic factor relates to reduction of
rice yields due to poor weather, with specific reference to the requirement of
a relatively dry period during flower emergence and grain formation.
Water-related factors are primarily those of supply, susceptibility to flooding, and susceptibility to drought. The quality of water (acid or saline) is
considered a minor factor, while the topographical factor, which affects the
distribution of water, is important. Soil characteristics considered important
for rice production in Malaysia are

1. Effective soil depth,
2. Texture of surface soil,
3. Thickness of topsoil,
4. Facility for mechanical cultivation,
5. State of redox potential or amount of humus,
6. Inherent fertility or cation exchange capacity and pH, and
7. Contents of available nutrients.

Four suitability classes for *padi* were proposed but not defined. A guideline
was developed, however, for rating soils- and water-related factors by suitability class (Table 1).

In Indonesia (Harrop, 1974), the Philippines (FAO and Bureau of Soils,
1976), and Sudan (FAO and Soil Survey Department, 1975), the new
framework for land evaluation (FAO, 1976) that incorporates land suitability
classification for rice was tested. The framework has the same structure of
suitability-classification categories in all kinds of interpretations. Each
category retains its basic meaning within the context of different classifications and as applied to different kinds of land use. Four categories of
decreasing generalization are recognized.

1. Land suitability orders reflecting kinds of suitability
     Order S: Suitable
     Order N: Not suitable
2. Land suitability classes reflecting degrees of suitability within orders
     Class S1: Highly Suitable
     Class S2: Moderately Suitable
     Class S3: Marginally Suitable
     Class N1: Currently Not Suitable
     Class N2: Permanently Not Suitable
3. Land suitability subclasses reflecting kinds of limitation, or main kinds
     of improvement measures required within classes.

4. Land suitability units reflecting minor differences in required management within subclasses.

In all the three countries the approach to evaluation was basically qualitative. The distinctions between classes of suitability were expressed in qualitative terms, indicating the significance of the degree of limitation to the sustained application of a given use (e.g. wetland rice) with regard to reductions in productivity of benefits, or increase in required inputs. As with previous qualitative evaluations for rice suitability, guidelines were proposed for rating land qualities (complex attributes of land that act in a manner distinct from that of other land qualities in their influence on the suitability of land for a specified kind of use) by suitability class. In the Indonesian example (Harrop, 1974) six land qualities are identified (proposed ratings are in Table 1):

1. Soil — depth, texture, fertility, drainage, and reaction.
2. Flooding damage
3. Topography — a wider slope range (0-8%) was allowed to accommodate areas in which terraced rice cultivation predominates.
4. Salinity or alkalinity
5. Soil acidity
6. Water availability — assumed a basic requirement of more than 250 mm rain/month during land preparation and crop growth period.

The Philippine example of the reconnaisance land resource survey of the Bicol River Basin (FAO and Bureau of Soils, 1976) identified land qualities for two rice-based, land-use alternatives or land utilization types (proposed ratings are in Table 1):

1. Irrigated wetland rice
    a. slope (%)
    b. soil depth,
    c. fertility,
    d. percolation,
    e. flooding, and
    f. potential cropping intensity (based on available surface water resources).
2. Rainfed wetland rice multicropped with upland field crops
    a. slope (%)
    b. boulders, outcrops,
    c. soil depth,
    d. fertility,
    e. percolation, and
    f. flooding.

In the Sudan a manual for land suitability classification for agriculture (FAO and Soil Survey Department, 1975) identified land qualities and their related major individual land characteristics — rated through measurement

Table 2. Major land qualities for rainfed and irrigated rice production, and major individual land characteristics.

Land quality	Major land characteristics
Moisture availability for the plants	Soil depth, available water capacity (texture, structure, O.C.), degree of runoff, climatic moisture regime.
Chemical soil fertility	Content of N, P and K, microelements, CEC, base saturation, and pH.
Conditions for seedling establishment	Texture, structure, aggregate stability, consistence, bulk density, stoniness, surface gravel.
Flooding hazards[a]	Depth and current of floodwater and period and frequency of inundation
Workability[a]	Consistence (stickiness and plasticity), structure, stoniness, presence of hard pans.
Salinity	Electrical conductivity and content and kind of soluble salts.
Sodicity (alkalinity)	Exchangeable sodium percentage, soil reaction.
Erosion hazards	Slope, infiltration rate (texture, structure, bulk density, soil depth, and aggregate stability).
Possibilities for mechanization[b]	Slope, relief, bearing capacity (n-value), consistence (texture, type of clay), stoniness, availability of shallow pans.
Capability of maintaining surface water	Slope, microrelief, drainage, subsoil permeability.
Soil toxicity (other than that caused by salts or sodium)	Surplus of certain elements such as Fe, Al, S, extremely low pH.
Adequacy of topography (for gravity irrigation)[b]	Slope, microrelief, slope complexity, elevation in regard to supply level.
Soil drainability (for irrigated agriculture)[b]	Groundwater level, infiltration rate, permeability.

[a]For rainfed rice production only. [b]For irrigated rice production only.

or estimation — for both rainfed and irrigated wetland rice (Table 2). Parametric approaches to suitability classification.

Parametric approaches to suitability classification

To make land evaluation less subjective, attempts have been made to formulate quantitative productivity indexes utilizing parametric methods. The indexes compare the soils of an area with the best soils known in the region or with a hypothetical, ideal soil. Comparisons are made by judging or rating the limitations of the soils being evaluated with the best or ideal soil.

One of the best known parametric approaches is that of Storie (1937) who evolved an index for rating the agricultural value of soils based on four factors. Each factor was evaluated on the basis of 100%, being the ideal or most favorable condition for each factor. The index rating for any soil was then determined by multiplying the four factors.

Riquier et al. (1970) developed a parametric system of soil appraisal in terms of actual and potential productivity where productivity is the theoretical optimum soil yield when possible damages from pests, unsound husbandry, poor seed, or plant disease are discounted. As with the Storie index, factors are evaluated on the basis of 100%, with the index rating for any soil determined by multiplying the factors. Nine soil properties or factors were chosen: (H) soil moisture content, (D) drainage, (P) effective soil depth, (T) texture and structure of the root zone, (N) average nutrient content, (S) soluble salt content, (O) organic matter in the Al or Ap horizon, (A) mineral exchange capacity and nature of clay in the B or C horizon, and (M) reserves or weatherable minerals in the B or C horizon. Five productivity classes were recognized: excellent (rating 65-100), or good (35-64), average (20-34), poor (8-19), and extremely poor to nil (0-7).

Although the system was not specifically intended for rice suitability classification, Dent (1974) tested the significance of the various soil properties and their tentative ratings, as proposed by Riquier, against actual rice yields on 14 soil series in Thailand. Although the water requirements of rice are unlike those of the majority of field crops, it was felt that a meaningful correlation could be made if the drainage factor (D) was calculated at 100% as waterlogging is not a limiting factor for rice. Findings indicated that the productivity index is a true expression of productive capacity (Table 3; Fig. 1).

Frankart et al. (1972) utilized a similar parametric approach and found good correlation between an actual productivity index and the yields of irrigated rice on seven soils in northeast Thailand. More recently, Tessens et al. (1977) evaluated physical land characteristics for rice cultivation in South Kalimantan. Twelve lowland mapping units were identified and described with regard to their physical land characteristics. Individual physical land characteristics are evaluated according to a qualitative relative limitation scale and a numerical parametric rating, resulting in the grouping of mapping units in orders and classes as defined in the FAO framework (FAO, 1976) and indicating both the qualitative degree of limitation and the numerical index rating. Physical land characteristics considered are topography, characteristics at the origin of wetness limitations (drainage and flooding), characteristics with regard to physical soil conditions (texture and depth to sulfuric horizon), and characteristics with regard to soil fertility that are not readily correctable (exchange capacity, base saturation and organic matter). Findings indicated that the qualitative and parametric approaches produced similar results.

Multivariate statistical approach to suitability classification

Since 1963 Japanese workers have been engaged in a comparative study of paddy soils in tropical Asia. A total of 410 soil samples collected from India

Rice yield (t/ha)

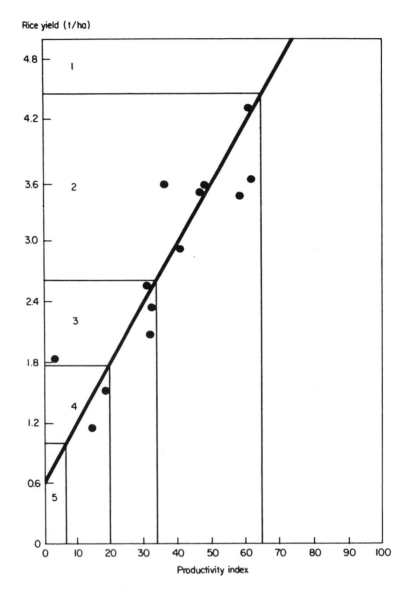

1. Rating of soil productivity for wetland rice as a function of soil characteristics (after Dent, 1974). Equation for straight line = $Y = 1.7X - 10.4 - r = 0.89$. $t = 6.76$ highly significant ($P = 0.01$).

(eastern part), Bangladesh, Sri Lanka, part of Burma, Thailand, Cambodia, Malaysia (West), Indonesia (Java), and the Philippines were utilized. Although the procedure and intensity of sampling were not uniform and the number of samples taken was not in proportion to the extent of rice land in each country, the samples from all countries except Burma were regarded as

Table 3. Comparison between productivity index and actual yield figures for wetland rice-producing soils in Thailand (adapted from Dent, 1974).

Soil series	Soil properties rating[a]								Product-ivity index	Mean rice yield (t/ha)
	H	P	T	N	S	O	A	M		
Bang Khen	100	100	50	100	80	80	100	100	32.0	2.1
Rangsit	100	100	50	50	15	80	100	100	2.3	1.8
Bangkok	100	100	50	100	80	80	100	100	32.0	2.3
Samut Prakan	100	100	80	80	80	80	95	100	36.4	3.5
Deum Bang	100	100	90	80	100	70	90	90	40.8	2.9
Chai Nat	100	100	90	80	100	100	90	95	61.6	4.3
Ban Mi	100	100	80	100	40	100	100	100	32.0	2.6
Nakhon Pathom	100	100	100	80	100	80	90	100	57.6	3.4
Sara Buri	100	100	80	80	100	80	95	100	48.6	3.5
Roi Et	80	100	90	60	100	80	90	90	19.0	1.5
Ubon	80	100	30	100	100	70	90	90	13.6	1.2
Hang Dong	100	100	90	80	100	100	90	95	61.6	3.6
Pran Buri	90	100	100	80	100	80	90	90	46.6	3.4
Bangnara	100	100	80	50	100	100	90	95	34.2	2.8

[a]H = soil moisture content; P = effective soil depth; T = texture and structure; N = average nutrient content; S = soluble salt content; O = organic matter content; A = mineral exchange capacity; M = reserves of weatherable minerals.

representative of the major rice-growing regions of each country.

The comparative study progressed through five stages.

1. The samples were analyzed for pH, total carbon, total nitrogen, ammoniacal nitrogen, total and available phosphorus, cation exchange capacity, exchangeable cations, and available silica (Kawaguchi and Kyuma, 1974a).

2. Characteristics more directly connected with the soil material, i.e. textural composition, clay mineralogical composition, and total chemical composition, were described (Kawaguchi and Kyuma, 1974b).

3. Fertility and material characteristics were subjected to correlation and regression analysis (Kawaguchi and Kyuma, 1975a) as a preliminary step towards material classification and fertility evaluation of the soil samples. Results indicated that

• Characters related to base status, texture, and clay mineralogy are mutually highly correlated;

• Characters related to organic matter status are mutually highly correlated, but only slightly to insignificantly with other characters; and

• Characters related to phosphorus status showed a trend similar to that for characters of organic matter status.

4. A numerical taxonomy of 10 soil material classes was set up (Kawaguchi and Kyuma, 1975b). Each class was characterized in terms of texture, base status, mineral composition, etc., based on data processing of total chemical and mechanical composition (Table 4).

5. Data processing for fertility evaluation used two multivariate statistical methods, i.e. principal component analysis and factor analysis (Kawaguchi and Kyuma, 1975c). It resulted in the extraction of three

Table 4. Soil material classification (after Kawaguchi and Kyuma, 1975b).

Soil material class	Description
Class I	Fine-textured, moderate base status (some are of pyroclastic origin), 14–7 clay with very little 10 Å minerals[a]
Class II	Medium-textured, low base status (typically low humic gley soils on terraces), highly siliceous, 7 Å-clay dominant with moderate 14 and 10 Å minerals.
Class III	Fine-textured, low base status (many derived from deltaic sediments), slightly siliceous, MgO > CaO, 7–14 clay with moderate 10 Å minerals.
Class IV	Medium-textured, high base status (some are of pyroclastic origin), 14–7 clay with little 10 Å minerals.
Class V	Coarse-textured, moderate base status (often occurring on river levees), moderately siliceous, high potash, 14–7 clay with moderate 10 Å minerals.
Class VI	Fine-textured, high base status (typically calcareous alluvial soils and grumusols, many are of pyroclastic origin), 14–7 clay with very little 10 Å minerals.
Class VII	Medium-textured (silty), moderate base status (mostly of Ganges-Brahmaputra sediments origin), very high potash, 7–10–14 clay.
Class VIII	Very coarse-textured, very low base status (strongly weathered sandy terrace or plateau material), very highly siliceous, 7 Å clay dominant with little 14 Å and very little 10 Å minerals.
Class IX	Coarse-textured (low silt), low base status (typically local alluvial sediments in acidic rock area), moderately siliceous, 7 A clay dominant with moderate 14 Å and very little 10 Å minerals.
Class X	Coarse-textured, high base status (almost exclusively of pyroclastic origin), very high alkaline earth bases, 14–7 clay with little 10 Å minerals or amorphous clay (allophane).

[a]7 Å = clay minerals of the kaolin group; 10 A = clay, illite or clay micas; 14 A = montmorillonite, vermiculite, and Al-interlayered vermiculite-chlorite intergrades.

mutually independent and clearly definable fertility component factors — inherent potentiality, organic matter-nitrogen status, and status of available phosphorus.

Kyuma (1973) showed that those three fertility component factors alone accounted for about 60% of variability on rice yield data reported by Malaysian farmers. Inherent potentiality is closely related to the nature and amount of clay and the base status of the soil. In addition, it shows a close relationship with the soil material classification. It follows, therefore, that inherent potentiality should correlate with soil material classes.

Consequently, the 10 soil material classes were arranged according to decreasing mean inherent potentiality scores. Furthermore, a percentage distribution, among five inherent potentiality classes recognized (very high, high, intermediate, low, and very low), of samples belonging to each soil material class indicated that the majority of the samples in each material class fell into a narrow range of inherent potentiality classes (Fig. 2). This supports the view that use of the 10 soil material classes as basis for soil family separation in soil surveys would improve homogeneity of lower taxonomic units — soil series — and make their interpretation easier and more valid in soil suitability assessment for rice.

DISCUSSION

The comparison of land use with land is the focal point in an evaluation procedure leading to suitability classification. Diagnostic procedures utilized in the process include
• Direct measurement from trials on different types of land in the study area;

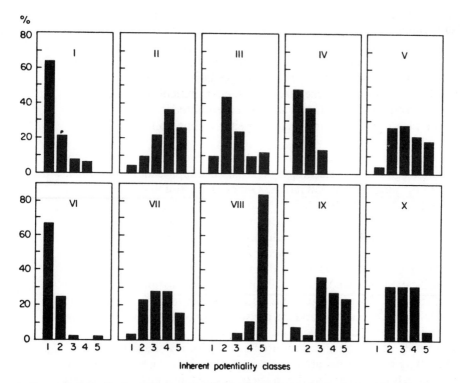

2. Percentage distribution of the samples of each of 10 soil material classes (1 ~ X) among five inherent potentiality classes (after Kawaguchi and Kyuma, 1975c).

- Simulation methods using mathematical models, which establish relationships between crop performance (yield) and diagnostic criteria (land qualities, land characteristics, or functions of several land characteristics); and

- Empirical assessment based on assumed relationships between crop performance and diagnostic criteria.

The advantages of the first procedure are obvious; it also provides standards for the second and third procedures. Advances in trial design, site location, and transferability of data are required for more precise information on quantitative environmental-land use relationships. When that is achieved, simulation methods using mathematical models will have a potential for future suitability assessments.

The majority of the soil or land suitability classifications reviewed utilize assumed relationships between crop performance and diagnostic criteria. In these classifications, the conversion tables show diagnostic criteria that are related to different classes or groups of suitability for rice production. The suitability rating of the land or soil unit depends on the degree to which the land qualities or characteristics satisfy the land use requirements. Herein lies the key to successful suitability classification. Soil requirements for wetland rice cultivation are outlined in the foregoing narrative; but it must be realized that soil forms only one facet of the environment. Climate, relief, elevation, and growing period must also be incorporated if adequate matching between environmental crop requirements and prevailing land conditions is to be achieved.

These classifications are essentially qualitative, even if numerical values are used for diagnostic criteria, although parametric approaches may give an impression of quantitative evaluation. Quantitative suitability evaluation requires the relation of both benefits (yields or product) and inputs (costs) to diagnostic criteria in numerical economic terms. To date, parametric approaches relate benefits — but not inputs — to diagnostic criteria. In this respect, parametric methods are at least potentially quantitative.

The choice of diagnostic criteria differs to a greater or lesser extent for each classification reviewed, as do suitability ratings for similar diagnostic criteria (Table 1). That is largely due to differences in basic assumptions adopted for each classification and the physical, economic, and social setting of the land area the classifications are to serve.

The majority of the classifications are basically for the suitability evaluation of existing rice-growing areas. Consequently, the choice of diagnostic criteria is largely determined by the range of observable land characteristics occurring in areas presently used for rice.

Empirical assessment is then based on assumed relationships between crop performance and these diagnostic criteria, with ratings for each criterion being determined by setting up local standards based, where possible, on direct measurement, or by applying international standards, where they exist. Interrelationships between individual criteria, however, are not well understood and a single criterion is unlikely to influence suitability independently of other criteria unless it represents an extreme condition that overrides other considerations.

In the case of wetland rice, water requirements are of principal concern. If they cannot be met, either naturally or through irrigation, then land is unsuitable for rice production regardless of other favorable qualities. In countries where rice production is restricted to low-lying lands.on which water inundates naturally or can be introduced by gravity, it is argued that the importance of soil physical properties is relatively small (Kyuma and Kawaguchi, 1972) as long as the soils are waterlogged.

In countries where sloping land is terraced for rice cultivation, however, soil physical properties are of greater importance, although use of such land for rice cultivation is a result of socioeconomic pressures rather than the land's natural adaptation to rice.

Consequently, land that is considered unsuitable for rice in one physical, economic, and social context may be judged suitable in a different environmental setting if the cost of achieving the objective is justified. It follows, therefore, that diagnostic criteria and suitability ratings developed for individual classifications are intimately related to the physical, economic, and social context of the areas they are to serve.

Comprehensive studies on paddy soils in tropical Asia (Kawaguchi and Kyuma, 1974a,b, 1975a,b,c) utilizing multivariate statistical methods showed that the soil fertility of tropical Asian paddy soils is made up of at least three major components: organic matter status, available phosphorus status, and inherent potentiality. The latter is independent of the former two. Inherent potentiality is a compound character closely related to soil material characteristics. Correlation between it and the 10 soil material classes identified (Kawaguchi and Kyuma, 1975b) can be expected.

That raises the possibility of formulating a gross-crop yield prediction equation by means of multiple regression analysis in which the three fertility components are used as independent variables together with others, such as climatic and management factors. Such an equation, when linked with soil material classification, which is suggested as a basis for soil family separation in resource surveys, offers future potential in suitability classification for wetland rice, provided that it is understood that such an equation will only be valid within a defined social and economic setting and at a defined (constant) level of inputs. However, comparison between benefits and inputs, both of which generally vary on different kinds of land, is normally required to provide realistic estimates of land suitability.

Finally, there is need to stress that land evaluation comprising suitability assessment for only one kind of land use, such as wetland rice, is inadequate for land-use planning purposes. Modern land evaluation is only reliable if benefits and inputs for any given kind of use can be compared with at least one, and usually several alternatives. If only one use is considered there is the danger that, while the land may indeed be suitable for that use, some other and more benefiicial use may be ignored.

REFERENCES CITED

BARRITT, N.W. 1913. The economics of padi planting. Agric. Bull. Fed. Malayan States 2:443.

CHUN SOO SHIN. 1971. Land suitability classification in Korea. World Soil Res. Rep. 41:215–217. FAO, Rome.

DENT, F.J. 1969. General land suitability for crop diversification in Peninsular Thailand. Soil Survey Division, Dep. Land Dev., Bangkok, Thailand. Soil Surv. Rep. No. 76:26–28.

DENT, F.J. 1974. The agricultural potential of the soils of Peninsular Thailand. M.S. thesis, University of Hull, England.

DE VRIES, E., and J.H.L. JOOSTEN. 1929–30. The productivity of irrigated fields for paddy in three residencies of East-Java [in Dutch, English summary]. Bogor, Indonesia. Landbouw 5(6):405–476.

FAO (FOOD and AGRICULTURE ORGANIZATION). 1976. A framework for land evaluation. Soils Bull. 32. FAO, Rome.

FAO (FOOD and AGRICULTURE ORGANIZATION) and Bureau of Soils. 1976. Bicol River Basin. AGO:PHI/74/003 Field Document 2. Dep. Agric., Philippines: 52–56.

FAO (FOOD and AGRICULTURE ORGANIZATION) and the Land Classification Division. 1973. Soil interpretation handbook for Thailand. Chapter VII. Dep. Land Dev., Bangkok, Thailand:19–30.

FAO (FOOD and AGRICULTURE ORGANIZATION) and the Soil Survey Department. 1975. Manual for land suitability classification for agriculture. Part II. Guidelines for soil survey party chiefs. Wad Medani, Sudan.

FRANKART, R., C. SYS, and W. VERHEYE. 1972. Contributions to the use of the parameter method for the evaluation of the classes in the different categories of the land evaluation proposed by the working group. Wageningen. FAO Consultation on Land Evaluation 1972. (mimeo. rep.)

HARROP, J.F. 1974. Design and evaluation of land development units for Indonesia. ALG/INS/72/011. Soil Research Institute, Bogor, Indonesia. Working Paper No. 9:93–97.

HAUSER, G.F., and R. SADIKIN. 1956. The productivity of the soils of East Central Java based on the yields of sawah rice. Contrib. Gen. Agric. Res. Stn., No. 144 Bogor, Indonesia.

JACK, H.W. 1923. Rice in Malaya. Agric. Bull. Fed. Malayan States 1:103.

JACKS, G.V. 1946. Land classification for land-use planning. Tech. Comm. No. 43. Imperial Bureau of Soil Science, Harpenden, England.

KANAPATHY, K. 1975. Special land characteristics for rice production. Dep. Agric., West Malaysia. (mimeo.)

KAWAGUCHI, K., and K. KYUMA. 1974a. Paddy soils in tropical Asia. Part 1. Description of fertility characteristics. Southeast Asian Stud. 12(1):3–24.

KAWAGUCHI, K., and K. KYUMA. 1974b. Paddy soils in tropical Asia. Part 2. Description of material characteristics. Southeast Asian Stud. 12(2):177–192.

KAWAGUCHI, K., and K. KYUMA. 1975a. Paddy soils in tropical Asia. Part 3. Correlation and regression analyses of the soil data. Southeast Asian Stud. 13(1):45–57.

KAWAGUCHI, K., and K. KYUMA. 1975b. Paddy soils in tropical Asia. Part 4. Soil material classification. Southeast Asian Stud. 13(2):215–227.

KAWAGUCHI, K., and K KYUMA. 1975c. Paddy soils in tropical Asia. Part 5. Soil fertility evaluation. Southeast Asian Stud. 13(3):385–401.

KYUMA, K. 1973. A method of fertility evaluation for paddy soils. III. Third approximation: synthesis of fertility constituents for soil fertility evaluation. Soil Sci. Plant Nutr. 19:19–27.

KYUMA, K., and K. KAWAGUCHI. 1972. An approach to the capability classification of paddy soils in relation to the assessment of their agricultural potential. Proc. Second ASEAN Soil Conference, Jakarta. 1:283–294.

MOORMANN, F.R., and R. DUDAL. 1965. Characteristics of soils in which paddy is grown in relation to their capability classification. Soil Surv. Rep. No. 32, Dep. Land Dev., Bangkok, Thailand.

NG, S.K. 1968. Padi soils of West Malaysia. Soil Sci. Div. Dep. Agric., Malaysia. (mimeo.)

RIQUIER, J., D.L. BRAMAO, and J.P. CORNET. 1970. A new system of soil appraisal in terms of actual and potential productivity (first approximation), AGL:TESR/70/6, FAO, Rome. (mimeo.)

ROBINSON, G.H., and F. STEELE. 1972. Classification and evaluation of soils for wetland rice. FAO. Int. Rice Comm., Bangkok.

STORIE, E.R. 1937. An index for rating the agricultural value of soils. Bull. 556, Berkeley, California.

TESSENS, E., ISMANGUN, and C. SYS. 1977. Evaluation of the physical land charactristics for padi rice cultivation in Riam Kanan (South Kalimantan, Indonesia). CLAMATROPS. Kuala Lumpur, Malaysia.

Part II

Ecological Approaches

Papers 3, 4, and 5: Introductory Review

3 **MOSS**
Landscape Synthesis, Landscape Processes and Land Classification, Some Theoretical and Methodological Issues

4 **LAWRANCE et al.**
The Use of Air Photo Interpretation for Land Evaluation in the Western Highlands of Scotland

5 **SONDHEIM and KLINKA**
The Relationship of Soil and Physiographic Attributes to an Ecological Classification System

The centrality of ecological thinking and analysis to land evaluation has been introduced in Part I. It thus seems important to examine the various ecological approaches to land evaluation. Paper 3 by Moss is a comprehensive review of approaches to landscape synthesis. Paper 4 by Lawrance et al. is a case study designed to test the application of a land systems approach, while Paper 5 by Sondheim and Klinka presents a contrasting investigation, with the emphasis on determining if an ecological classification system can yield land units that are homogeneous in terms of soil and physiographic properties.

A long-standing core concept has been the notion of approaching land as a functional entity. Thus emphasis has been given to devising methods that permit the delimitation of land units deemed to express a degree of ecological unity. Vink (1983) describes various approaches: for example, he summarizes the phytocentric method whereby landscape-vegetation relationships are the basis to landscape analysis. The identification of patterns on aerial photographs has played a crucial role in aiding the delimitation of landscape ecological units at a broad range of scales.

Moss argues in Paper 3 that there is much need for developing a more process-oriented approach to landscape ecological analysis. In this way a dynamic or functional element can be incorporated into the analysis of landscape ecological units. The key inputs are energy and moisture; data on these inputs along with a knowledge of control processes should then be the basis for defining functional land entities. The benefits of such a process-oriented approach are not only to aid land classification, but, more importantly, to permit modeling of primary productivity, nutrient and soil moisture movement, and overall water budgets. Reference will be made later to current concerns regarding the sensitivity of ecosystems to acid deposition; again, process data are essential to predicting outcomes.

To exemplify the approach, Moss demonstrates how it is possible to map ecodistricts according to potential primary productivity rates. Indeed, it is very interesting to observe the long-standing tradition in Canada of an ecological approach (Davidson, 1984). The distinguished contributions of such landscape ecologists as G. A. Hills (see Hills, 1976, for a detailed paper on his approach) and P. Dansereau (see Dansereau and Pare, 1977) in part explain this tradition. The sheer size and ecological diversity of Canada has very much encouraged the development of efficient land survey based on ecological principles. The focus for this research is the Canada Committee for Ecological Land Classification, and a substantial number of reports have now been produced in the *Ecological Land Classification Series* of the Lands Directorate, Environment Canada. Much effort was devoted to developing a classification, summarized by Moss (Fig. 5). Such methods are particularly suited to land survey in northern areas such as the Northern Yukon (Wiken et al., 1981) and the Lockhart River area, Northwest Territories (Bradley, Rowe, and Tarnocai, 1982). Results from land ecological surveys are being applied to a wide range of land management and planning issues including, for example, national parks (Parks Canada, 1980). As already mentioned, a topic of much current concern is the effect of acid precipitation. One avenue for research in the Lands Directorate has been toward assessing ecological sensitivity to this input using 1:1,000,000 ecodistrict data base (Cowell, Lucas, and Rubec, 1981). Such assessments can be made only if information is available on the effects of throughfall, foliar deposition, filtering and leaching—the essential point of Moss's argument.

It should not be concluded that an ecological approach is suited only to dealing with large areas. In fact, the approach seems particularly relevant at two very contrasting scales: the regional or national as already described for Canada, and at the local, very detailed level such as within cities or urban fringe localities where there is extreme pressure on land. One of the early reports by the Lands Directorate focuses attention on ecological land classification in urban areas (Wiken and Ironside, 1977). Vink (1983) presents examples of detailed landscape ecological maps in the Netherlands and in Italy. Planners encounter many difficulties in devising land use planning strategies for urban fringe areas. There seems to be a great need to develop techniques of landscape ecological analysis particularly suited to these objectives.

No book on land evaluation would be complete without discussion of the *integrated* or *land systems* approach. It is interesting to observe the similarity between Canada and Australia—large countries that required efficient methods of yielding land resource inventories. In Australia the result was integrated surveys, with 39 published by CSIRO over the period 1952 to 1977. The technique is largely associated with Christian and Stewart (1968); recurring patterns called land systems are identified on aerial photographs and these patterns are taken to express the distinctive integration of relief, climate, vegetation, hydrology, and soils. The whole approach is ecological, given this integration emphasis. Its merit is that it is an efficient reconnaissance method. Substantial areas of northern, central, and southeast Australia as well as Papua New Guinea have been surveyed in this way. The United Kingdom Land Resources Development Centre (LRDC) has until recently used the land systems approach for land resource inventory research; for example, between 1968 and 1978 a team from LRDC surveyed 230,000 km^2 in central Nigeria with the data being interpreted to show land suitability for crops, livestock, and forests.

In recent years LRDC has swung away from basic inventory-type projects to much more specific and issue-oriented development planning. If requested today, broad reconnaissance-type surveys are likely to be based on interpretations of satellite-derived imagery. Nevertheless, there is still a need to develop the land systems approach at a more detailed scale. A related requirement is for studies to be made on the statistical purity of land properties within mapping units. Land facets as subdivisions of land systems are appropriate units for mapping at scales of between 1:20,000 and 1:50,000. Webster and Beckett (1970), in a trial project in Oxfordshire, carried out statistical tests to determine if mapped facets were internally homogeneous in terms of specific variables: overall their results supported the validity of the approach.

Paper 4 by Lawrance et al. follows a similar vein and it is included in this book because it discusses three important questions: (1) Can land facets be applied to a very different type of environment—the Scottish Highlands? (2) What degree of concordance is there between identification of facets by different researchers with varying degrees of knowledge of the study locality? (3) To what extent is there a relationship between facets and soil properties? The paper compares and contrasts the results from the photo-interpretation team based in Oxford with those of soil surveyors with local knowledge. Despite many points of difference, the overall impression is of broad agreement. This should be no surprise because a land facet interpretation is an ecological analysis based on aerial photo patterns. The whole approach of the free method of soil survey is also based on an appreciation of landscape ecology but primarily from a field stance.

As already stressed, the land systems or land facet approach is based on the distinctive landscape expression of land properties ranging from geology through to vegetation. A more specific approach is to define landscape ecological units on the basis of particular properties. For example, Kwakernaak (1982) selected altitude, slope type, slope value, and slope aspect as four independent variables, with the following variables as dependent ones: soil properties, slope processes, hydrology, vegetation, and land management. He was thus able to define landscape ecological units for his study area in Switzerland. Relationships between the dependent and independent variables were determined using cluster analysis. As a result Kwakernaak was able to predict information values for these variables.

An analogous landscape ecological analysis is presented by Sondheim and Klinka in Paper 5, but the distinctive feature of their project is the use of a phytosociological classification. The aim of their study in British Columbia was to determine the extent to which variation in soil and physiographic properties can be related to their ecological units, defined primarily on the identification of climax plant communities. They follow Braun-Blanquet's taxonomy of plant communities to group associations into alliances, orders, and classes. From 60 sample plots, a data bank of 40 soil and physiographic properties was obtained. Much of their paper is devoted to the statistical analysis of these data, in particular, analysis of variance. In their discussion Sondheim and Klinka question the value of the hierarchical ecological classification given the limited partitioning of soil and physiographic values. In contrast they obtain quite the opposite results when the classification levels are analyzed on an independent basis. In particular they find the best relationships are achieved at the association level, especially for physiographic variables.

Sondheim and Klinka conclude that it is unrealistic to expect one taxonomic system to account for variability in such a broad range of variables. One important general implication for landscape ecological analysis is that it is undesirable to define taxonomic and thus mapping units on too narrow an ecological basis, say, limited to plant communities. Instead the merit of an ecological approach seems to depend upon a classification based on a broad range of ecological attributes.

REFERENCES

Bradley, S., J. S. Rowe, and C. Tarnocai, 1982, *An Ecological Land Survey of the Lockhart River Map Area, Northwest Territories,* Ecological Land Classification Series No. 16, Lands Directorate, Environment Canada, Ottawa.

Christian, C. S., and G. A. Stewart, 1968, Methodology of Integrated Surveys, in *Aerial Surveys and Integrated Studies,* UNESCO, Paris, pp. 233–280.

Cowell, D. W., A. E. Lucas, and C. D. A. Rubec, 1981, *The Development of an Ecological Sensitivity Rating for Acid Precipitation Impact Assessment,* Working Paper No. 10, Lands Directorate, Environment Canada, Ottawa.

Dansereau, P., and G. Pare, 1977, *Ecological Grading and Classification of Land-occupation and Land-use Mosaics,* Geographical Paper No. 58, Lands Directorate, Environment Canada, Ottawa.

Davidson, D. A., 1984, Recent Canadian advances in land evaluation, *Soil Survey and Land Evaluation* **4:**71-76.

Hills, G. A., 1976, An Integrated Iterative Holistic Approach to Ecosystem Classification, in *Ecological (Biophysical) Land Classification In Canada,* Ecological Land Classification Series No. 1, Lands Directorate, Environment Canada, Ottawa, pp. 73-97.

Kwakernaak, C., 1982, Landscape Ecology of a Prealpine Area, *Publication of the Physical Geography Department, Amsterdam University No. 33.*

Parks Canada, 1980, *Ecological Inventories in National Parks,* Natural Resources Division, National Parks Branch, Parks Canada.

Vink, A. P. A., 1983, *Landscape Ecology and Land Use,* Longman, London.

Webster, R., and P. H. T. Beckett, 1970, Terrain Classification and Evaluation Using Air Photography: A Review of Recent Work at Oxford, *Photogrammetria* **26:**51-75.

Wiken, E. B., and G. R. Ironside, 1977, *Ecological (Biophysical) Land Classification in Urban Areas,* Ecological Land Classification Series No. 3, Lands Directorate, Environment Canada, Ottawa.

Wiken, E. B., D. M. Welch, G. R. Ironside, and D. G. Taylor, 1981, *The Northern Yukon: An Ecological Land Survey,* Ecological Land Classification Series No. 6, Lands Directorate, Environment Canada, Ottawa.

3: LANDSCAPE SYNTHESIS, LANDSCAPE PROCESSES AND LAND CLASSIFICATION, SOME THEORETICAL AND METHODOLOGICAL ISSUES

Michael R. Moss

Department of Geography, University of Guelph, Ontario

Abstract: Systems of land classification are discussed as important procedures in landscape synthesis. Existing systems are examined and found to have limited application because of their lack of functional integration of landscape/environmental components, their lack of focus upon the active components of the landscape and their limited ability to predict land capability and the consequences of environmental impact. An alternative procedure is suggested whereby process data can be used. The basics of the method are described and the system illustrated by reference to different environments. By adopting this approach the links between classification, capability assessment and impact assessment are more clearly understood.

Introduction

The concept of landscape synthesis is broad (Mazúr and Drdos 1981). The term is used here in a somewhat specific sense by acknowledging the fact that the "land" or the "landscape" can be viewed as a composite of a range of physico-geographic components which, when linked together, have an inherent functional value and as such provide an important input to systems and methods of land and environmental management. Such functionally interrelated components can be viewed at different scales and for different purposes. At the small scale regional synthesis traditionally deals with the interaction between human and physical components of the environment in producing distinct landscapes. At the intermediate scale physico-geographic regionalization has frequently become the focus for interpreting the general interrelationships between components of the physical environment. At the larger scale detailed analysis of component data has been used as an important adjunct to urban, regional and local planning (for example, Bartkowski, 1981, Richling, 1976).

The two latter fields mentioned above provide the scale and the focus for this paper. In focussing upon the implications of a synthetic approach to the landscape a basic requirement must be an understanding of the systems of synthesis and of the classification of these synthesized areas into land units in a form, and by a method, which yields appropriate data for land and environmental management. At the same time it may be argued that a successful classification scheme must not only satisfy the objectives of the user but must also reflect an awareness of the more significant aspects of what exactly produces the land units identified. If there is no understanding or appreciation of how the landscape components work then the prescriptive value of the classification system is limited to assumptions only. And how a land unit is ultimately used will affect to a great deal the working of the processes in that land unit.

A fundamental problem for landscape synthesis, therefore, is the procedure used to classify the relevant land-based information. There exist many classification systems, which are variously referred to as, for example, land evaluation procedures, systems of geocomplexes, biophysical and/or ecological land classification procedures and land systems classifications. It is the objective and the relevance of these approaches that will be examined here in the context of the requirements stated above.

Theoretical Basis and Theories of Land Classification

To develop the theme it is essential initially to consider what is meant by the "land" and what the problems are in providing a basis for land classification[1]. "Land" is generally understood to be the equivalent of what is traditionally seen in physical geography to be the physical components of geographic environment, that is, the bedrock, soils, vegetation, wildlife with various hydrological and atmospheric components added. This combination of environmental components is recognized as forming the critical zone of integration in the earth/atmosphere system relevant to man. Mabbut (1968) defines the land as "a complex of surface and near surface attributes significant to man" and Gardiner (1976) quotes the statement that "land refers to all those physical and biological characteristics of the land surface which affect the possibility of land use." However, most land classification systems take a somewhat broader view and attempt to encompass all environmental components, whether or not they are relevant directly, or indirectly, to man's use of the land. And perhaps herein lies a basic problem for land classification systems in that they take too broad a view of what is necessarily required for decision making and often therefore confuse or mislead by providing excess or extraneous material.

It is possible to subdivide the land into those components of the environment which are active and those which are relatively inactive. The former components are those which respond quickly to environmental change, either natural or more specifically man-induced changes. They are the components which change and in which process changes take place which can be measured on a time scale of human activities and which reflect the thermodynamic aspects of environmental interaction, again measured in the time frame of current human activity. Such land-based impacts almost always, inevitably, focus initially upon the vegetation and biotic component of the environment. This includes the organic fraction of the soil and has direct and immediate consequences for the more dynamic aspects of the soil, for example, soil chemical balance, moisture retention etc. It is probably a truism to state, with some significant degree of accuracy, that virtually all human impact upon the "land", both past and present, has been initially upon, and as a result of, vegetation change by whatever cause. Examination of some of the major volumes on man/environment interaction are, in fact, studies of man's impact upon the vegetation component and the resulting consequences, for example, upon the soil, microclimate, hydrological balance, river runoff etc. (Thomas 1956, and Goudie 1982). This focus clearly distinguishes such impacts from the inactive component of the environment. For instance, forest removal may alter the local microclimate but not the regional climatic patterns and may alter soil moisture and chemical balances but not, on a reasonable time scale, the overall inorganic mineral and textural make-up of the soil, and certainly not the underlying bedrock to any significant degree. Consequently, when man's past, present, and immediate future impacts upon the land are examined the environmental or land components which respond on a time scale where impacts may be measured are restricted to those dynamic or active components in the landscape which are functionally separable in time and in space from those which respond only on a longer, or geological time scale.

What then are the problems of developing land classification schemes to reflect such situations? Within most existing schemes the fundamental unity of the physical environment is recognised as are the functional interrelationships between all components. But an understanding of why this is so is less clear. There are many reasons for this but perhaps the most important is the fact that with the exception of a few Soviet geographers attempts to understand functional interrelationships within the environment as a whole have, to a large extent, been neglected as being too complex to understand given the present state of knowledge. Consequently, other approaches from other disciplines, more concerned with one particular environmental component, have tended to assume a greater value and to attach a greater significance to one subsection of the field than is warranted. Also these approaches have tended to suggest that one component is more significant than the others and is therefore seen to have greater causal value than any other component. Furthermore, where attempts have been made to use all environmental component data little or no distinction has been made between the active and the more passive components. And the significance of functions and dynamics has been underrated at the expense of assumptions based on answers assumed to be found by the superimposition of component data.

The majority of systems of land classification are structured in a hierachical manner encompassing, in the same scheme, units of land from the subcontinental scale down to units relevant for individual land use functions. The commoner, more-universally accepted schemes have been reviewed elsewhere (Moss 1975). However, in almost every case the criteria used to determine the differences between units at the different levels in the hierarchy differ. For instance, at the higher levels distinctions are often made on the basis of regional climate, geological structure or major vegetation forms, whereas at the lower levels attributes such as plant community composition and soil profile description are examples of descriptors used. One of the more basic requirements of a hierarchical structure is, however, to show the significance of a small areal unit within a broader spatial framework and to enable the user to bring out the significance of the juxtaposition of units. But if different criteria are used can the significance of a particular event on one unit at a lower level be seen to have any significance within a broader spatial framework where different criteria may have been used? For example, can information on species composition, which may have been used to distinguish a low level unit, be seen to have any significance to a higher level where units may be determined for example, by ground surface morphology? The recently developed scheme of the Canada Committee on Ecological Land Classification in part overcomes this problem in that all levels in the hierarchy assess attributes of the same components (Wiken 1980), that is, geomorphology, soils, vegetation, climate, water and fauna. However, the attributes of these components at the various levels in the hierarchy are descriptive rather than functional.

Other classification schemes are based upon the assumed dominance or greater relevance of one environmental component. Damman (1979), for example, recognizes the major importance of vegetation in both detailed and reconnaisance work. This system also recognizes the fact that different factors control vegetation units at different scales but the main focus is basically upon appreciating the significance of patterns of vegetation; vegetation being described by species composition and related to soil profile and hydrologic sequence. Likewise, soil mapping units may be considered the most valuable indicators of land and land potential. In many cases soil units are considered the same as land units. Since most systems of soil classification are themselves hierarchical there are logically distinct parallels drawn between both procedures. But soil classification procedures and the taxa defined are often based upon soil profile description and related horizon properties. In some instances, however, as in the vast tropical rain forests soil profile description may be of little or no value in determining land potential. The reason for this being that only the top 0.5 m can be considered the active part of the soil and that the important inherent fertility of this thin horizon is often of quite different character from the chemical composition of the thick weathered regolith.

Terrain classification (surface morphology) has been extensively used as a basis for land classifications. Ollier (1977, p. 300) states that terrain classification is a good basis for soil mapping and that two factors of soil formation (parent material and topography) are built into the system. The other factors of soil formation (climate, organisms and time) lead to greater variation, but with the exception of the time factor it is the two other functions, climate and organisms, which separate out the more dynamic factors from the inactive factors in the landscape, thus inevitably leading the user back once again to an emphasis on description rather than dynamics. Gardiner (1976) states quite categorically that land evaluation must be based upon an initial classification of terrain and documents the long and established tradition of this approach underpinning, in particularly, British (see, for example, Beckett and Webster 1965, Mitchell 1973) and Australian work (for example, Christian and Stewart 1968) in the field. It has often been stated that the form of the land must necessarily control, or be controlled by, all other factors in the physical environment (Gardiner 1976, p. 13) although this assumption often remains unacceptable or irrelevant in a land classification context since many aspects of surface

morphology are related to past events, such as glaciations, and not to present day processes.

Other classification procedures are developed upon the notions of superimposition of inventory data on environmental components. The underlying logical value of this approach, in the context of the physical environment, is, however, outweighed by the problems already raised in using quite different criteria and methods for each unit derived at each level. For example, there are some fundamental problems in defining vegetation units for land mapping purposes. These problems revolve around the issue of whether it is possible to recognize discrete bounded vegetation units on the ground or whether vegetation cover should be approached by viewing it as a spectrum of continually changing species interrelationships in both space and time. Similarly quite radical changes in systems of soil classification have been developed in the last two decades to overcome, in part, the difficulties in recognizing the transitional nature of the intergradation between typical soil profiles which have been traditionally used as the basis for soil mapping units (Hole 1978).

Local and regional systems of climatic classification, which could be useful as data bases for land classifications, are almost non-existant whereas global systems of climatic classifications are common. Mapping of small climatic regions is extremely difficult due to the more gradual nature of spatial change in climatic elements. However, these are often based on simple temperature and precipitation values although some, such as the Thornthwaite system (Thornthwaite and Mather 1957) reinterpret these parameters as energy and moisture indices and the *Klimadiagramm-Weltatlas* (Walter and Lieth 1960) provides a useful basis for interpreting climatic data in a more practical sense (Mueller-Dombois 1981). But in using basic climatic data can the functional interrelationships between climate and vegetation, possibly measured as species composition, be related further to a soil profile description using a limited range of pedological descriptors?

Consequently, although there is a strong intuitive and logical basis for the existing systems of land classifications the underlying problems are such that they do not satisfy the demands of a classification which seeks to identify the key dynamics of the landscape as a prerequisite.

Towards a Method of Process Data Incorporation

What emerges from the foregoing discussion is a need to develop land classification procedures in which land units are determined by focussing upon those components of the land where current processes and process dynamics can be recognized and made distinct from conditions within the less active components of the environment. These should be derived by using common criteria, or functionally-related criteria. The object must be to produce land-based data which has direct application and value rather than indirect value through assumption and inference. The only possible approach to satisfying these objectives is either to build into, or to develop upon, existing systems a procedure based upon an awareness of existing environmental scientific knowledge. A structure must be based upon processes operating *within* the land rather than a system based upon inventory of certain characteristics of the land components themselves.

An awareness of the need for process studies as an integrative funtion in the land has strong roots in geographic tradition and methodology, but only modest advances have been made in developing ideas on the subject. Without the work of predominantly Soviet geographers (for example, Isachenko 1973) the development of this apporach would have been restricted to only a few very recent publications of the last 10 to 15 years. The most serious attempt to overcome the effects of the splintering of modern physical geography, wherein perhaps lies the root of the problem, was the viewpoint outlined in 1972 by Carter et al. This publication appeared at about the same time that greater emphasis was beginning to emerge toward fulfilling the need for a more integrated approach to environmental problems in instruct-ional and educational materials. However, the approach still has not developed far as a research focus. Similarly the acceptance of General System Theory as a paradigm in physical geography and the popular attractiveness of ecosystem theory clearly provided a methodological basis for outlining a structure, a recognition of the significance of process, and of component interaction within environmental systems.

Advances in this and related fields may be seen in attempts to understand more fully the nature of environ-mental interrelationships (for example, Phipps 1982). Richling's work on geocomplexes in parts of Poland is another illustration of this type of work (Richling 1976). However, whereas such approaches may take us further in answering the question of *which* components are interrelated and to some extent *why* this is so, it still does not answer *how* the components are functionally linked.

The process problem has, in part, been overcome by Prokayev, 1962 and Bazelevich et al., 1971, and others, but much of the work is restricted to the large scale units (facets/sites/facies etc.) of land and tends to neglect the significance of this site specific work within the broader small scale land units.

If the problem is approached in a systems sense it can readily be recognized that any unit of land is not only a functional part of a greater whole but that it is functionally linked within this structure by particular pathways followd by the flows of energy and moisture. This environmental systems approach means that different processes operating within the environment have certain controls which determine the efficiency of these processes and which are determined, to a large degree, by energy/moisture interaction. Consequently, since energy/moisture interaction will vary spatially the efficiency of the different component processes must also vary spatially and so limits can be set as boundaries of land units within which certain processes will take place, will interact with other processes, and will produce an environmental response of characteristics giving the land unit a degree of uniqueness. Such process-response characteristics (for example, nutrient levels and cycling efficiency, biomass accumulation, occurrence of land slips) must been seen in this context. This can then be combined with the traditional inventory approach to incorporate evidence, useful in its own right, but which is not necessarily functionally related. Species composition, for example, may be much more significant for synecological relevance (i.e. plant-plant relationships) rather than autecological functions (plan-environment relationships). Similarly particular landforms may be the result of, for example, former glaciations. Here the emphasis should be upon the processes now operating upon these landforms for which the glacial characteristics may or may not be relevant. Likewise, where soil profile descriptions are used the significant point is that only certain profile-related properties reflect processes. But it is often not the processes-response aspects that are measured (for example, organic decay-decomposition rates, nutrient storage capacity, moisture retention) but non-process or indirect evidence (for example, parent material, stoniness etc.).

Ecosystem studies have been identified as a solution to the problem. However, it is suggested that the ecosystem model is largely inappropriate as a model in land system analysis except where ecosystems are seen to be objects at a particular scale as systems in a hierarchy of environmental systems. Unfortunately by taking an ecosystematic approach to land systems analysis the original, and really workable meaning of the term "ecosystem" has achieved only generalized statements about component interaction at the simplest level. Serious ecosystem analysis, which could provide a model for land system analysis, and therefore ultimately classification, at a scale low in the hierarchy (e.g. ecosite and ecosection level[2])) is both time consuming and expensive (Van Dyne et al. 1978) in land system analysis where objectives are primarily of a reconnaissance nature. Ecosystem work generally produces data on species interaction and species interaction with other biotic and abiotic variables. The focus is generally upon the vertical integration of objects within the system and models provide little relevant information on spatial interaction, for example, between adjacent land units. Ecosystem work tends to be site-specific and though essential at one level of knowledge provides little in advancing the type of land system work discussed here. Generally it does not consider environmental process as a dominant focus, stressing attributes rather than processes and process responses. The term biophysical is preferable to ecosystematic for these reasons.

A suggestion has been made previously as to how a more process oriented approach may be developed (Moss 1979, 1981, 1982). Fig 1 provides a model for this method. The

Fig 1 A model to illustrate a methodology for the incorporation of process data into land classification (based on Moss, 1979, 1981, 1982).

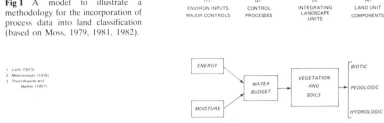

1 Lieth (1973)
2 Meetemeyer (1978)
3 Thornthwaite and
   Mather (1957)

basis for this approach is the recognition that it is the integration of energy and moisture as active inputs (column 1) that provides the driving mechanism for predicting the nature, the seasonality and the efficiency of the biophysical processes operating at any point on the earth's surface. The nature of this energy/moisture interaction can be determined by the standard approaches to water budgeting (column 2). The Thornthwaite method of water budget analysis (Thornthwaite and Mather 1957) is perhaps the most widely accepted procedure and has the advantage of using basic temperature and precipitation data recorded at any standard meteorological station. With respect to the biophysical environment, in the strict sense, it is the occurrence of these processes in the soil/vegetation systems that is important (column 3). By concentrating upon these integrating units this approach allows us to focus upon the significance of the primary inputs into the environment at any scale or at any level in the hierarchy. At the same time these soil types and vegetation communities are readily observable and mappable as environmental components whose boundaries are often (but not always) determined by these same energy and moisture inputs. From these units one may proceed to a study of the significant processes that occur within these areal units thereby giving a spatial framework in which certain key biotic, pedologic and hydrologic processes operate (column 4).

What then are these processes in the biophysical environment that are controlled and which can be determined in this way? Column 5 lists some of these and column 6 summarizes the 'state of the art' in terms of obtaining quantifiable data. The determination of potential net primary productivity is of fundamental importance to this issue. Not only is this process perhaps the key process in the functioning of any environment, it is of special relevance as an indicator of land potential for development, in the cycling of nutrients and hence in relation to inherent fertility levels, in the efficiency and maintenence of the stability of the system itself, and also in hydrologic control. Values can be determined for major regions by equations based upon the relationship between actual evapotranspiration and net primary productivity. Such data can indicate, not only the ecological potential of a region in terms of its potential productivity

(Moss 1978), but when used in conjunction with similarly based organic decay and decomposition models (Meetemeyer and Elton 1977) give a significant picture of the natural organic turnover at a site.

Other biophysical processes are, for example, leaching of nutrients by moisture which moves downwards in the soil after the primary evapotranspiration demands on that soil moisture have been satisfied. By the same water budgeting techcniques moisture movement through the soil, moisture retained in the soil, or runoff over the ground surface can be determined. The seasonality and relative efficiency of each of these processes can also be determined by the use of these same water budget techniques in allocating excess moisture to the various components in the biophysical environment.

Classification and mapping of this process data into land units (in the general sense) should, therefore, provide an addition to existing approaches to land classification. Functionally singnificant units of land can be indentified, not only from the point of view of their potential but also from the stand-point of how other processes are functionally related within a designated area. This, when used in conjunction with the data inventory on vegetation characteristics, soils, surface morphology etc. should yield a much improved data base for land capability and environmental impact assessment.

Illustrations of the Approach

Fig 2 is an attempt to illustrate the basis of the theory outlined above. The dominant biophysical processes at the smaller scales are those which reflect energy and moisture interaction as reflected in primary productivity, organic decay and decomposition rates, and nutrient cycling in different environments. Compare, for example, the effects on all processes of high energy and moisture interaction in the tropical rain forest with the divergent effect on values in desert environments (high energy/low moisture), and in tundra environments (low energy/low moisture).

The use of a part of this approach is shown in Fig 3 where the existing ecodistrict mapping units have been assigned a value for perhaps the most important land process,

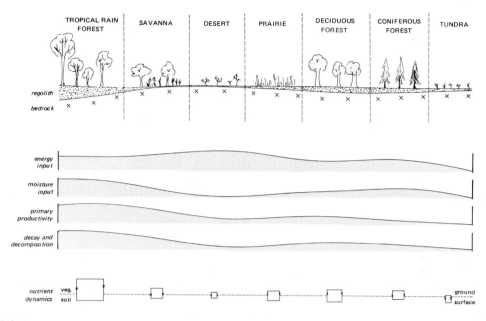

Fig 2 Relevant process interaction within the major biomes (scales and values approximate only). Primary productivity and decay and decomposition are process responses to energy and moisture inputs. Nutrients dynamics are shown by both the volume and the location of major storage reservoirs (vegetation in the tropics, soil in the tundra).

primary productivity. The values (in g/m²/yr) have been added to each ecodistrict which has been previously identified by remote sensing and aerial photography and described by field description of soil, vegetation and geomorphic properties. In this case the potential primary productivity

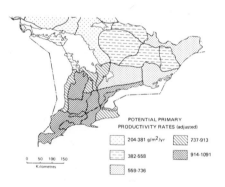

Fig 3 Part of southern Ontario, Canada, where values for one process-response, primary productivity, adjusted by soil performance, have been assigned to ecodistricts already determined by traditional methods.

values determined by existing equations have been modified from the ecoregion level to the finer ecodistrict level by building in the constraints imposed by soil properties on basic organic activities. So that whereas values for potential primary productivity range from 1250 g/m²/yr for the area when unadjusted, when subjected to a soil productivity factor (Moss and Davis 1982) are reduced from a high of 986 g/m²/yr to as low as 44 g/m²/yr on unfavourable sites within ecodistricts on the Canadian Shield areas in the north of the map.

Fig 4 illustrates the basis of this approach for larger scale units, in this case a river valley section where land units would be mapped at the ecoelement level (scale 1:10,000 to 1:2,500). Work is currently in progress in Peninsular Malaysia to incorporate relevant processes data within the land classification procedures. Within broader regions where the dominant biological processes have been evaluated further subdivision can be based upon the most important variable that changes within the environment as a result of forest clearance. This is rainfall impact. In Peninsular Malaysia lowland rain forest sites attain primary productivity values as high as 2400 g/m²/yr and lows of 1600 g/m²/yr in highland areas (Moss 1978). Decay and decomposition rates are annually greater than 200 % in lowland forests and slightly less than 100 % in uplands. Forest clearance, as a result of

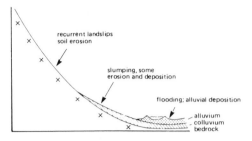

Fig 4 Several process-responses, in this case illustrated by reference to current geomorphic activities, identified at the ecoelement scale. Three ecoelements could be recognized on the valley section (upper slope, lower slope, flood-plain) in which the different processes would affect land use development.

different larger land units. The consequences for land unit recognition in high energy geomorphic environments has also been applied to areas in the Rocky Mountain foothills of Alberta, Canada by Sauchyn (1982). Fig 5 summarises much of the foregoing discussion.

Conclusions

The key to the further development of this process approach lies in the value of overcoming many of the problems inherent in traditional systems of landscape synthesis and regionalization for derivation of land units. It tends to avoid the problem of causal factors, which will differ for different levels in a hierarchical system by concentrating on functional

LEVEL IN HIERARCHY		PROCESS DATA	ENVIRONMENTAL VALUE OF DATA	USE OF DATA
1:1,000,000+ (e.g. Ecoregion)	expression of energy/moisture interaction in active components	• Potential primary productivity • Decay and decomposition	• Land surface dynamics (fundamental land/biotic function controls)	• Major regional decisions concerning land capability
1:125,000+ (e.g. Ecodistrict)		• Modification of above values by soil properties	• Modification of basic functions by local controls (soil capability)	• Ranking of potential value for regional decisions, carrying capacity etc.
1:50,000+ (e.g. Ecosection)		e.g. 1. geomorphic/ hydrologic process data 2. changes in precip. impact on soil surface (e.g. due to deforestation)	• Local expression of changes in controls by various processes	• Wildland planning • Soil erosion potential
1:10,000+ (e.g. Ecosite)		3. slope processes		• Specific site use determination geomorphic hazards

mp

Fig 5 Summary table of processes, measurement and use at different scales in a land systems hierarchy (CCELC terminology used).

extensive land development means a significant alteration to one major input, that is precipitation and its impact upon the soil. The consequences of this action within regions of different rainfall regimes and on different slope sections must have quite considerable consequences not only for soil erosion on the slopes but also for river regimes, flooding potential etc. In other words, in dealing here with different processes at this finer scale the efficiency of these different geomorphic processes can be assumed to vary within the

links and the nature of interrelationships within environmental systems at all scales. And whereas the applications of the method are restricted to areas with an accumulation of basic data or where this may be readily obtained it should provide an important adjunct to existing schemes.

Furthermore, the properties measured are those which are important in understanding man/environment interaction which at the same time can be directly applied to such

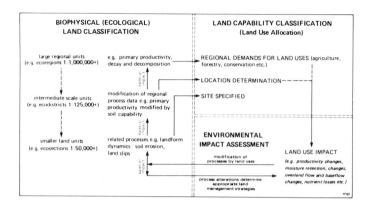

Fig 6 Diagram to show the interrelationships between biophysical land classification, land capability classification and environment impact assessment. The value of a process approach to linking these three procedures is identified.

requirements as land capability assessment and environmental impact analysis and many other aspects of regional land development which are related to the 'land'. These links are outlined further in Fig 6.

Finally, landscape synthesis, as expressed here through systems of land classification cannot be divorced from other landscape processes. And although such a scheme may develop further as a scientific understanding of these processes improves' emphasis on spatial patterns and spatial links between land units and the importance of impact measured in terms of the stability, resistance and resilience of land units' will more effectively encompass the rapidly developing field of landscape ecology, for which land classification can again provide the basic component information.

Footnotes

1) In this paper "land" and "landscape" are used interchangeably. It is recognized that "land" is more commonly used in the English language whereas "landscape" (≡ landschaft) has more familiar useage in continental Europe.

2) Throughout this paper, unless stated otherwise, the land unit terminology follows that of the Canada Committee for Ecological Land Classification (Wilken 1980).

References

Bartkowski, T.: Town eco-geosystems versus rural geocomplex: casestudy of the Poznan agglomeration. In: Perspectives in landscape ecology, pp. 185−194, Tjallingii, S.P. and de Veer, A.A., eds., Wageningen, Pudoc 1982.
Bazilevich, N.I., Rodin, L. Ye and Rozov, N.N.: Geographical aspects of biological productivity. Soviet Geography, Review and Translation 12, 293−317 (1971)
Beckett, P.H.T. and Webster, R.: A classification system for terrain. M.E.X.E. Report 872, M.E.X.E., Christchurch, Hampshire 1965.
Carter, D.B., Schmudde, T.H. and Sharpe, D.M.: The interface as a working environment: a purpose for physical geography. Association of American Geographers, Technical Paper 7. Washington 1972.
Christian, C.S. and Stewart, G.A.: Methodology of integrated surveys. In: Aerial surveys and integrated studies, pp. 233−280, Paris, UNESCO 1968.
Damman, A.W.H.: The role of vegetation analysis in land classification. The Forestry Chronicle 55(5), 175−182

Gardiner, V.: Land evaluation and the numerical delimitation of natural regions. Geographia Polonica 34, 11−30 (1976)
Goudie, A.: The human impact. Man's role in environmental change. Cambridge, Mass. M.I.T. Press 1982.
Hole, F.A.: An approach to landscape analysis with emphasis on soils. Geoderma 21, 1−23 (1978)
Isachenko, A.G.: Principles of landscape science and physical-geographic regionalization. Melbourne, Melbourne University Press 1973.
Lieth, H.: Primary production: terrestrial ecosystems. Human Ecology 1, 303−332 (1973)
Marbutt, J.A.: Review of concepts of land classification. In: Land evaluation, pp. 11−28, Stewart, G.A., ed., Australia, Macmillan 1968.
Mazur, E. and Drdos, J.: IGU Working Group on "Landscape Synthesis." GeoJournal 5(2), 192−196 (1981)
Meentemeyer, V. and Elton, W.: The potential implementation of biogeochemical cycles in biogeography. Professional Geographer 29(3), 266−271 (1977)

Mitchell, C.W.: Terrain analysis. London, Longman 1973.

Moss, M.R.: Biophysical land classification schemes: a review of their relevance and applicability to agricultural development in the humid tropics. Journal of Environmental Management 3(4), 287–307 (1975)

Moss, M.R.: The potential primary productivity of Peninsular Malaysia. Journal of Environmental Management 6, 171–183 (1978)

Moss, M.R.: Climate and related process data in ecological land classification. Newsletter, Canada Committee on Ecological (Biophysical) Land Classification, Lands Directorate, Environment Canada, 8, 4–6 (1979)

Moss, M.R.: A process approach to biophysical land classification: some applications to Peninsular Malaysia. In: Assessing Tropical Forest Lands, pp.2 202–207, Carpenter, R.A., ed., Dublin, Tycooly International 1981.

Moss, M.R.: Process and related data inputs to systems of land classification. Symposium on Landscape Synthesis. IGU Working Garoup on Landscape Synthesis: Bratislava, Czechoslovakia 1981.

Moss, M.R. and Davis, L.S.: The potential and actual primary productivity of Southern Ontario's agro-ecosystem. Applied Geography 2(1), 17–37 (1982)

Mueller-Dombois, D.: The ecological series approach to forest land classification. In: Assessing Tropical Forest Lands, pp. 105–140, Carpenter, R.A. ed., Dublin, Tycooly International 1981.

Ollier, C.D.: Terrain classification: methods, applications and principles. In: Applied Geomorphology, pp. 217–316, Hails, J.R., ed., Amsterdam, Elsevier 1977.

Phipps, M.: Information theory and landscape analysis. In: Perspectives in landscape ecology, pp. 57–64, Tjallingii, S.P. and de Veer, A.A., eds., Wageningen, Pudoc 1982.

Prokayev, V.I.: The facies as the smallest unit in landscape science. Soviet Geography, Review and Translation 3(6), 21–29 (1962)

Richling, A.: Frequency and force of interdependences between components of the geographical environment. Geographia Polonica 33, 55–66 (1976)

Sauchyn, D.: Geomorphic/hydrologic systems versus land ecosystems: implications for ecological land survey. Annual Meeting, Canadian Association of Geographers, (Abstracts p. 114), Ottawa, Canada 1982

Thomas, W.L.: Mans role in changing the face of the earth. Chicago, Chicago University Press 1956.

Thornthwaite, C.W. and Mather, J.W.: Instructions and tables for computing potential evapotranspiration and the water balance. Centerton, New Jersey, Laboratory of Climatology, Publications in Climatology 1957.

Van Dyne, G.M., Joyce, L.A. and Williams, B.K.: Models and the formulation and testing of hypotheses in grazing land ecosystem management. In: The breakdown and restoration of ecosystems, pp. 41–84, Holdgate, M.W. and Woodman, M.J., eds., New York, Plenum 1978.

Walter, H. and Lieth, H.: Klimadiagramm-weltatlas. Jena, VEB Fischer Verlag 1960.

Wiken, E.: Rationale and methods of ecological land surveys: an overview of Canadian approaches. In: Land/wildlife integration, pp. 11–19, Taylor, D.G., ed., Ecological Land Classification Series No. 11; Ottawa, Lands Directorate, Environment Canada 1980.

4: THE USE OF AIR PHOTO INTERPRETATION FOR LAND EVALUATION IN THE WESTERN HIGHLANDS OF SCOTLAND

C. J. Lawrance[1], R. Webster[2], P. H. T. Beckett

Soil Science Laboratory, University of Oxford

J. S. Bibby and G. Hudson

Macaulay Institute for Soil Research, Craigiebuckler, Aberdeen

SUMMARY

Classifications of terrain, into land systems and land facets, relying largely on air photo interpretation are justified in two ways:

(i) that recognition of the pattern of variation within a *land system*, and its description by means of diagrams and annotated air photos, facilitates the identification of distinct sub-areas within it (*facets* or *elements*), particularly by staff with limited local experience.

(ii) that the classes are useful for indexing existing information on natural resources, including soil, and as strata for economic sampling when obtaining new data.

Such schemes have been widely used, for one or both reasons, but not so far in the intricately varying landscapes shaped by glacial and periglacial processes on hard rock. This paper reports a study in which attempt was made to classify such terrain in the Western Highlands of Scotland using the same philosophy and procedures, and the result checked.

It proved reasonably easy to classify a trial area into distinct land systems, which are mapped. Division of the land systems was more problematic since each subdivision was itself a complex, termed a "patterned facet", consisting of several elements of more or less contrasting land with different potentials for use. Elements were not consistently recognized correctly by air photo interpretation, though elements of the more specifically soil complexes could be recognized by surveyors with considerable local experience.

ZUSAMMENFASSUNG

Überwiegend auf Luftbildauswertungen beruhende Landschaftsklassifikationen in "land systems" and "land facets" sind wie folgt gerechtfertigt:

I Die Kenntnis der Varianz innerhalb von "land systems" and ihre Beschreibung mit Hilfe von Diagrammen and Luftbildkommentaren erleichtert die Identifizierung "facets" oder "elements" besonders für Luftbildbearbeiter mit beschränkten Ortskenntnissen.

---

1) now Transport & Road Research Laboratory, Crowthorne, Berks.
2) now Soil Survey of England & Wales, Rothamsted Experimental Station, Harpenden, Herts.

II Die Klassifikation ist sinnvoll für die örtliche Fixierung vorhandener Informationen über Naturressourcen einschließlich Böden und als Hilfsmittel erneuter Datenerhebung im Bedarfsfall.

Solche Schemata werden entweder für einen oder beide aufgeführten Gründe häufig genutzt, allerdings nicht für komplizierte, durch Glazial- und Periglazialprozesse geformte Gebiete in Festgesteinen. Diese Veröffentlichung informiert über eine Arbeit, in der versucht wurde, Gebiete im westlichen Hochland Schottlands nach den angezeigten Verfahren zu klassifizieren und die Ergebnisse zu überprüfen. Es erweist sich als relativ einfach, ein Versuchsgebiet in "land systems" zu klassifizieren. Die Untergliederung der "land systems" ist problematischer, da jede Untereinheit für sich selbst wieder einen Komplex bildet, den wir als "patterned facet" bezeichnen, und der aus mehreren "elements" besteht, die hinsichtlich des Nutzungspotentials mehr oder weniger unterschiedlich sind. Diese "elements" konnten nicht genau genug kartiert werden, obwohl einige "elements" mit spezifischen Bodengesellschaften durch Kartierer mit guten Ortskenntnissen ausgeschieden werden konnten.

1. INTRODUCTION

Air photography made rapid surveys of land resources, including soil, feasible. By the mid 1960s much reconnaissance soil survey and land evaluation, especially in Australia and Africa, was being carried out remotely and cheaply, based on a two-tier classification of land into *land systems* and *land facets*. Land facets were the basic reasonably homogeneous classes that could be treated as uniform for practical purposes. Land systems were patterns consisting of a few land facets that recur in characteristic fashion (BRINK et al. 1966). BECKETT & WEBSTER (1965), who were developing methods for survey of remote areas, showed that it was entirely practicable to classify land in southern England quickly in this way, and that the result was useful (eg WEBSTER & BECKETT 1968). However, a brief experience in Canada suggested that the remote surveyor would find it more difficult to classify recently glaciated terrain on hard rock in this simple way. (This has since been confirmed privately by J.T. PARRY for the Canadian Shield and by A. WELLVING in northern Sweden.) The problem obviously needed to be explored.

The Soil Survey was also interested in a cheap means of surveying the Western Highlands. In this area of intricate land form and complex soil pattern maps showing conventional soil series would be very time-consuming to make. Further, the economic potential of the land there is considerably less than elsewhere in the country, and the cost of mapping conventional soil series would be quite unjustifiable. The Survey would almost certainly have to recognize complex soil mapping units of some kind, even though it was locally based for field work.

The two groups of workers, C.J.L., R.W. and P.H.T.B. at Oxford, and J.S.B. and later G.H. of the Soil Survey based in Oban, thus had a common interest. The former wished to explore the practicability of the two-tier scheme of land classification in an area of intricate terrain, the latter to evaluate this essentially physiographic approach to mapping soil in the Western Highlands. Nevertheless, the two groups we are operating under different constraints. The Oxford workers were remote from the area. They were intentionally exploring the problem of the remote surveyor. One member if the Soil Survey (J.S.B.) had experience of West Highland conditions, gained largely outside the study area, and this influenced his approach. In the following account we make clear where this difference affected the conduct of the study and its outcome.

The study was planned primarily:
a) to ascertain whether land system - land facet classifications could be devised for areas in the Western Highlands, and, if so,
b) whether the result could provide a basis for the acquisition of information on soil and on land capability.

Land use in that area is most affected by climate, land form and soil. To be useful any survey procedure must be able to provide information at least on land form
and on significant soil characteristics, of which stoniness, rockiness, wetness,
and the presence of a thick organic horizon, are probably the most important.

1.1. Land system - land facet classification

The main.aim of these classifications is to define mapping units that are as easily recognizable on air photographs, and yet have as consistent properties for a
particular land use, as possible. Accordingly their definitions give considerable
weight to land form and those aspects of materials and hydrology that have external expression, and less weight to the soil profile as such.

The *land facet* is the basic unit of the classification:
(i)   It is a distinguishable part of the landscape, with simple and characteris-
       tic form, rock, soil, and water regime;
(ii)   it is recognizable on air photographs, and
(iii) it can be managed uniformly under at least moderately intensive forms of
       land use.

Ideally individual occurrences of land facets are of an extent that can be mapped
conveniently at scales of about 1 : 50 000, though the mapping scale may be as
large as 1 : 20 000 in areas of intricate terrain and could be as small as
1 : 80 000 in areas where changes are less frequent. Particular parts of a land
facet, with significantly different effects on land use, may be distinguished and
called *land elements*.

Land systems are composite landscape units, patterns of land, distinguishable on
air photographs, and each consisting of a few facets that are linked together over
a wide area in the same recurrent and consistent relationship to one another. Land
systems are normally mapped at scales between 1 : 250 000 and 1 : 1 million, depending on the intricacy of the terrain.

Commonly, the customer or user is presented with a map of land systems, with instructions and visual aids (mainly block drawings and annotated air photographs)
to enable him to distinguish and delineate the unmapped land facets within each
land system.

The land system map is intended to serve regional or national planners, for whom
the minimum area of interest is likely to be about 1000 ha, which covers about
2 cm^2 on a 1 : 250 000 map. The land facet classification is provided as a vehicle
for the more detailed information required by the local planner, agricultural ad-
viser or road engineer, for whom the smallest planning unit is perhaps 1 - 5 ha.
It is assumed that if they want local facet maps at 1 : 20 000 - 50 000 such
users will employ the identification aids to locate the facet boundaries by air
photo interpretation.

Such classifications have proved useful in many situations. But their use pre-
supposes that most of the landscape is occupied by bodies of fairly uniform soil,
of reasonable size, which are recognizable on air photographs from their close
association with vegetation and land form and their occurrence in a recognizable
recurrent pattern. Indeed, for staff with limited local experience, the recognition of the pattern of occurrence of the different facets is a significant stage
in the recognition of individual land facets. Conversely a land system classification is unlikely to be helpful where soil bodies, different enough to need different management, are small or occur in no recognizable or definable pattern, or
lack consistent external expression.

1.2. Requirements

So this study would need to ascertain, for a typical area of the Western Highlands,
either i) is it possible to define land facets that are both recognizable, and

relatively uniform in features that affect land use?

and if so, do these occur in recognizable patterns, whose limits can be
mapped as land system boundaries?

or ii) are there distinguishable blocks of land of size comparable to land
systems?

and if so, can they be subdivided into smaller recognizable units, in recurrent pattern, comparable to land facets?

2. PROCEDURE

2.1. Trial area

An area of Argyll was chosen for examination (Fig. 1), extending from Loch Creran, north of Oban, to the Mull of Kintyre. It included the mountainous Ben Cruachan, composed of granites, and the andesites of the Lorne volcanic plateau in the north; the quartzites, epidiorites, phyllites and slates of central Argyll; the mica schists of Kintyre; and the hilly landscapes underlain by Old Red Sandstone and Carboniferous porphyrites South of Campbeltown.

A major glaciation (maximum 17 000 – 18 000 years B.P.) had strongly eroded the landscape in north and central Argyll, and on its retreat (complete by 13 000 B.P.) had deposited till widely in Kintyre. The Loch Lomond readvance (10 800 – 10 000 B.P.) was confined to the valleys of Loch Etive and parts of Loch Awe and Loch Fyne. Low areas of gravel, sand and silt are extensively developed near Campbeltown, Lochgilphead and at the mouth of Loch Etive and much of them are overlain

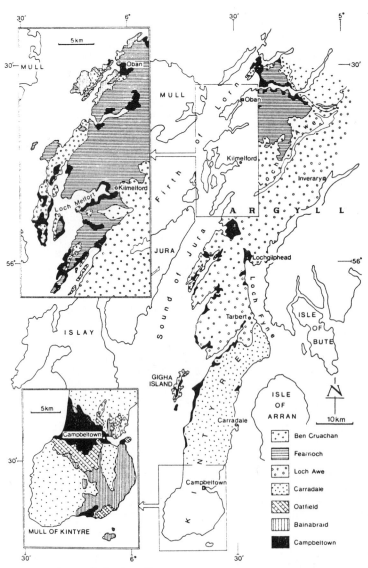

Fig. 1: Land System Map

by peat. The climate now is mild and wet. Mean annual rainfall ranges from 1250 mm near the south coast to over 2500 mm in the hills. Land use is dominated by rough grazing and grassland, with arable production of animal feed mainly in the south.

2.2. Trials

Evaluation of a mapping procedure necessarily involves making a map of all or parts of an area, and then examining the truth of the map in an unbiased way. In this study the trial fell into four stages:
1) to make a land system classification and map for the area;
2) to produce a detailed land façet classification for a representative part;
3) to select randomly a set of test sites and, using only the aids provided, to identify the land facet at each and predict conditions there;
4) to visit the sites to assess the truth of these predictions.
The procedure and results are presented for each stage in turn.

2.3. Stage one - land systems

C.J.L. and R.W. spent three weeks in the area, in the field with J.S.B., to gain local experience and to relate soils and physiography to features perceptible on air photographs, and to the visual patterns to which these gave rise. With this experience and general background information, and with a cover of air photographs at 1 : 10 000 and maps of solid geology at 1 : 63 360, they distinguished several landscapes on their characteristic air photo patterns. These appeared to exhibit reasonably distinctive ranges of terrain conditions so they were mapped as tentative land systems (Fig. 1). Since many of the land system boundaries observed on the air photographs corresponded quite closely to boundaries on the geological maps, the boundaries of some of their smaller occurrences were taken from these.

Field examination and air photo analysis both showed that the land systems consisted of many small areas, different enough to require different management, too small to be mapped as land facets, and some of them not consistently distinguishable on air photographs. They are therefore *land elements*.

2.3.1. "Patterned facets"

Many of the elements appeared to occur in characteristic groups; that is the landscapes could be divided into sub-areas, each of which contained several but not all of its elements in a reasonably simple and recurrent pattern. These sub-areas were of comparable extent to the simple land facets mapped elsewhere at scales of 1 : 20 000 - 80 000, so we have tentatively called them "patterned facets".

The pattern of elements was especially intricate in the andesite landscape in the northern part of the area, where several of the sub-divisions at this level contained most of the elements in the landscape, though in different proportions. Since it is possible to describe these patterned facets more precisely than the land systems in which they occur, they convey more precise information than the land systems. Having established that it was possible to define and map land systems, the study moved to stage 2 concentrating on Carradale land system. Although extensive in Kintyre, no soil survey had so far been conducted on it. It will be convenient to describe it before continuing.

2.3.2. Carradale land system

The Kintyre peninsula is asymmetric, with an eastern zone of rounded hills, up to 460 m high, penetrated by valleys, which are narrow except where close to the sea. The valleys are short and steep on the eastern flanks, but somewhat longer on the west. Between Tarbert and Campbeltown the peninsula is dominated by mica-schists, crossed by a belt of Green Beds (epidiorite, chlorite and hornblende schists) from the north east to the south west, with small Tertiary dykes, and some outcrops of schistose marble north of Campbeltown. Ground moraine or till from the last glaciation, sandy loam to fine sandy loam in texture, covers most of the low ground and contains a mixture of local schistose rocks with material of Old Red Sandstone age from the Clyde basin. It thins out on the upper slopes of the hills and exhibits well marked "crag-and-tail" features in central Kintyre, being deeper (up to 15 m) on the west or downflow side of the hills. Frost shattering above ice-level had produced rocky debris on the hill crests and many such areas now display crenellated bedrock, often boulder strewn, and the shallow till on the upper slopes is sandier and grittier than that below. Outwash and alluvial deposits covered the valley floors locally, but widespread solifluction during the ice-retreat mantled many lower slopes and valley floors. Indurated and stony horizons were formed locally, and deflation and wind deposition produced complicated patterns of stony and sandy material. Some of the till, particularly that near drainage channels, has been water-modified, and patchy removal of clay has produced mosaics of loam, sandy loam and fine sandy loam.

Following post-glacial uplift the drainage cut numerous gullies into slope-till and bedrock, and incised the valleys. Peat is now widespread. Its depth tends to increase with altitude, particularly within the range from 150 m to 450 m. In places it is subject to local erosion, or "hagging", which leaves tabular relics on gentle slopes and slip features on steeper slopes. Subsurface water flow, has produced a mosaic of seepage points or "flushes" on the slopes often at the lower limits of peat patches or near the upper limits of continuous till.

Fig. 2 of the upper and lower extremes of the Carradale land system, and Fig. 5 a-c illustrate the degree of complexity that has resulted.

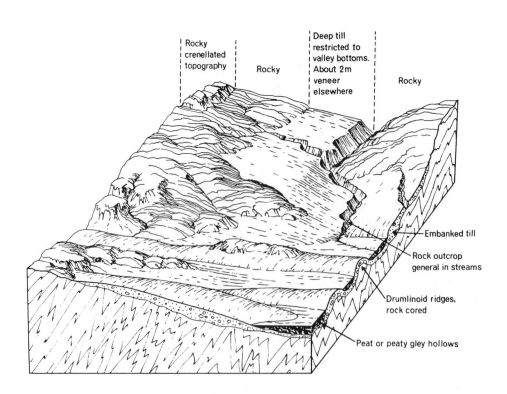

Fig. 2: Compound landscape to illustrate the extremes of Carradale land system.

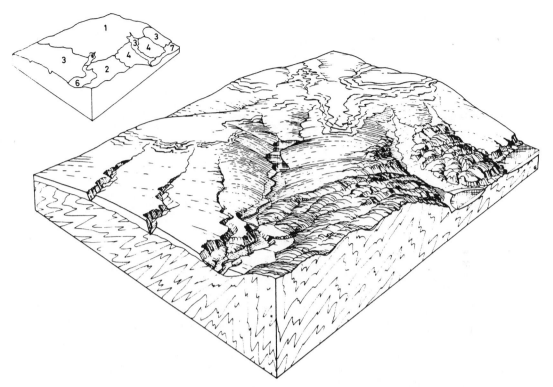

Fig. 3: Definitive block diagram of Carradale land system: facets numbered as in Table 1 (a).

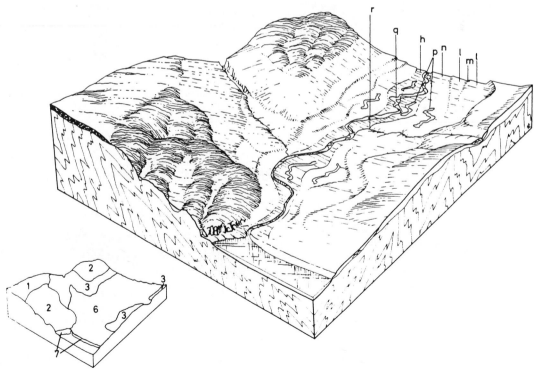

Fig. 4: Definitive block diagram of Oxford facet No. 6.: elements numbered as in Table 3 (a).

INTERPRETATIVE DIAGRAM OF SAMPLE AREA 4

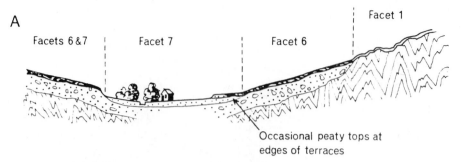

A

Facet 1

Facets 6 & 7   Facet 7   Facet 6

Occasional peaty tops at
edges of terraces

INTERPRETATIVE DIAGRAM OF SAMPLE AREA 15

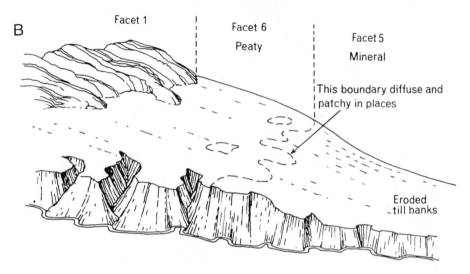

B

Facet 1   Facet 6
Peaty

Facet 5
Mineral

This boundary diffuse and
patchy in places

Eroded
till banks

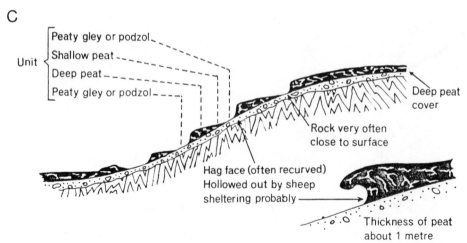

C

Peaty gley or podzol
Shallow peat
Deep peat
Peaty gley or podzol

Unit

Deep peat
cover

Rock very often
close to surface

Hag face (often recurved)
Hollowed out by sheep
sheltering probably

Thickness of peat
about 1 metre

Fig. 5: a, b: Interpretative diagrams of sample areas 4 and 15 to illustrate some
Oban facets (Table 1 (b)). c: Peat hagging.

Table 1: PATTERNED FACETS WITHIN CARRADALE LAND SYSTEM

(a) Recognized remotely (Oxford)	(b) Recognized locally (Oban)
1) Hill tops. Gently convex, undulating or occasionally hummocky crests. Dominated by blanket bog and gentle peaty slopes, not more than 10°. Rare rock outcrops. Rarely extends far down slope, though can occur as isolated patches anywhere on slope.	1) Rocky hills with peaty topsoils. Very extensive, occupying up to 60 % of hill ground; mainly below 250 m: dominated by rocks but with only limited rock outcrop (Fig. 5a, 5b, 5c).
2) Areas of thin soil over rock. Smooth and gentle slopes of thin soils with mineral or peaty topsoil dominate but are obviously underlain by bedrock at no great depth, of which the structure is often evident. Rock outcrops are frequent, but small.	2) Rocky hills with mineral topsoils. Limited area, mainly on steep slopes and low coastal hills, below 200 m rock more prevalent than (1); mainly steep to moderate slopes.
3) Long smooth slopes developed on deeper solifluction or drift deposits, with mineral or peaty topsoils: smooth with no rock outcrops nor evidence of rock structure beneath.	3) Crenellated, very rocky hills with peaty topsoils. Mainly on mountain tops, and above 250 m; dominated by steep and moderate slopes; conspicuous rock outcrops with peaty hollows between, often "hagged".
4) Crenellated rocky slopes many of them steep, with more than 50 % rock outcrop separating extents of mainly mineral soils of variable depth; strong evidence of geological structure.	4) Crenellated, very rocky hills with mineral deposits; restricted to steep slopes on the flanks of major valleys.
5) Floors of small valleys.[+]	5) Rolling topography on tills with mineral topsoils, usually below 150 m; comprises most of the agricultural land in the area (Fig. 5b).
6) Floors of major valleys.[+]	6) Rolling topography on till, with peaty topsoils; mainly on valley hills, or on the drumlinoid ridge hills of the lower ground (Fig. 2); reclamation for agriculture may be attempted (Fig. 5a, 5b).
7) Coastline features.[+]	7) Valley bottoms.[+]
	8) Peat basins.[+]
	9) Coastline features.[+]

[+] not further defined, except by the lists of elements (Table 3)

2.4. Stage two - land facets in Carradale land system

When the land system map had been agreed, C.J.L. and R.W. in Oxford produced a list of tentative land facets for Carradale land system. While doing so, further examination of the air photographs revealed uncertainties that their field work had not resolved. So they drew up a list of questions to clarify doubtful points. J.S.B. from Oban visited the sites they had chosen to illustrate these, and answered their questions in detail, and they produced a revised facet classification.

Table 2: EXAMPLE OF DESCRIPTION OF A PATTERNED FACET MADE BY THE REMOTE GROUP
          (OXFORD). PATTERNED FACET No. 2. THIN SOILS OVER ROCK

Rock outcrops are frequent but small; smooth and gentle slopes of shallow soils
with mineral or peaty topsoil dominate, but are obviously underlain by bedrock at
no great depth, of which the structure is often evident.

Elements

a) Gentle slopes
   Smooth, gentle slopes, usually extensive; the dominant element of the facet
   and occupies most of the area between rock outcrops.
   i) with mineral topsoil - probably not much more than 1,5 m of till over
                             bedrock.
   ii) with peaty topsoil   - at least 1 m peat over till as (i); often "hagged",
                             and difficult to distinguish on air photographs if
                             not.

b) Rock outcrops
   Sometimes bare rock, but often with thin soil cover up to 0,5 m over rock.
   Gentle and steep slopes, up to 20 m high and 500 m long, but commonly a few
   metres high and a few tens of metres long: forms the main part of facet 2 in
   alternation with (a).

c) Flushes
   Usually triangular in plan, widening downhill from a narrow source; permanently
   wet with water at or near surface; may be a few tens of metres long; several
   flushes may link up round the hill to form a springline; rushy.

d) Peat basins
   Deep peat; up to 100 m across; wet and poorly drained; infrequent and mostly
   small.

e) Minor valley floors
   Up to 100 m wide, including the stream itself; soils as in element (a), but
   often wetter; water table probably within 1 - 1,5 m; discontinuous.

f) Lochans
   Permanent open water; up to 200 m wide; infrequent.

The two groups agreed on the limits of the land system, and largely agreed on its
major elements (once "steep slopes" proved to be rare). But not only were the land
facets patterned, with 2 or 3 contrasting major elements and from 3 to 6 minor
elements in each, but the elements of the land system could be grouped in different ways and there could be no unique facet classification for Carradale land
system. Patterned facets defined by the two groups (Table 1) contained different
combinations of elements (Table 3).

C.J.L. and R.W. followed techniques they had used already in mainly erosional and
unglaciated landscapes, and depended heavily on the general appearance of the terrain on air photographs: for lack of local knowledge they probably failed to
identify or draw sufficient inferences from some of the features that contributed
to this general appearance. Thus their facet 1 was distinguished largely on its
topographic position, and facets 2, 3 and 4 on their rockiness or on evidence of
the underlying rock structure, and the smoothness or otherwise of their slopes,
as indications of the thickness of their drift cover. They supposed facet 1 was
dominated by peaty topsoils, and facet 4 by mineral topsoils, but their facets 2
and 3 comprised both peaty of mineral topsoils. Following standard practice the
land system as a whole was represented by a block diagram (Fig. 3) of a composite
landscape showing the facets in their correct inter-relationships, and by a list
of patterned facets (Table 1 (a)). Two examples are included in this paper to

Table 3: ELEMENTS IN CARRADALE LAND SYSTEM

a) Remote classification

Elements	Patterned facets							
	1	2	3	4	5	6	7	8
a) Moderate to gentle slopes and blanket bog								
i) less than 1,5 m till	+p.m(25)	+p,m(3)		+m,?p				
ii) more than 1,5 m till			+p,m(22)					
b) Rocky slopes and rock outcrop	+(2)	+	+	+				
c) Flushes	+(1)	+	+(9)	+	?	+		
d) Peat basins	+	+		+				
e) Small streams and gully sides	+	?	+(2)	?				
f) Minor valley floor and bottomlands	+	+	+(1)	+	+(2)			
g) Lochan	+	↲	+		+			
h) Floodplain					+	+		
j) Peat flat					+			
k) Small mounds					+			
l) High terraces						+(5)		
m) Terrace bluffs						+		
n) Lower terraces						+(1)		
p) Abandoned channels						+(2)		
q) River						+		
r) Small fans						+		

b) Local classification

Elements	1	2	3	4	5	6	7	8
a) Steep slopes	+p	+m	+p	+m	+m	+p		
b) Moderate slopes	+p(1)	+m	+p	+m	+m(2)	+p(3)		
c) Gentle slopes	+p(23)	+m(2)	+p(4)	+m	+m(4)	+p(15)		
d) Peat basins	+	+	+			(1)		+
Small peat basins					+	+		
e) Rock outcrops	+	+	+	+	+	+	+	+
Boulder accumulations					+	+		
f) Flushes	+(1)	+	+	+	+(4)	+(5)	+	+
g) Small water courses	+	+	+	+	+	+		
h) Lochans	+	+	+		+	+		+
i) Screes		+	+	+				
j) Banks					+	+	+	
k) Stream							+	
l) River							+	
m) Floodplain or alluvial strata							+(4)	
n) Terrace							+(6)	
p) Abandoned channels							+	
q) Peat flat							+	

p = peaty topsoil; m = mineral topsoil; + = part of facet definition.
Numbers in parentheses are the numbers of test sites encountered in the sample.

show how the patterned facets were defined. Table 2 describes the elements of facet 2 in detail, while Fig. 4 shows the elements of facet 6 and their relationships to one another.

On the other hand J.S.B. at Oban, with more knowledge of the West Highlands, was confident that he could distinguish peaty from mineral topsoils, till from non-till soils, and three classes of slope, on air photographs. So his patterned facets were defined on particular combinations of topsoil, slope and parent material (Table 1 (b)). Fig. 5 illustrates some of their interrelations. The Soil Survey has used similar criteria to define and describe soil complexes in several areas of Scotland (MUIR 1956, BOWN 1973, BIBBY 1973). Soil complexes are grouped into larger units, soil associations which differ from land systems mainly in the emphasis placed on their soil parent material. In the lowlands one land system may comprise several soil associations, but in the uplands, where changes in physiography are often closely allied to underlying rock type, the boundaries of soil associations and land systems are often the same.

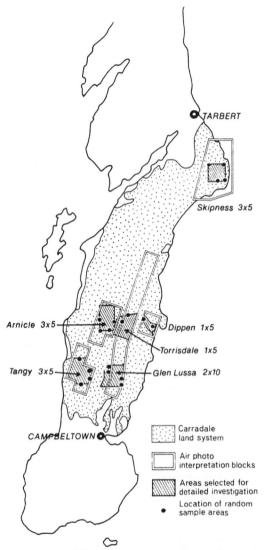

Fig. 6: Areas selected for field check, and random sample areas within them. 2 x 5 indicates that 5 sites were successfully visited in each of 2 samples areas.

The contrast between the two approaches is significant. The Soil Survey approach distinguishes the elements on particular features, recognizable on air photographs, and then defines landscape units, each to be dominated by a combination of these features. The remote classification divides the land system into areas in which distinctive air-photo appearances occur in characteristic pattern, which can then be described in terms of the elements they contain. To some extent the former could be said to recognize landscape units directly from their features, and the latter to depend more on the recognition of their patterns and interrelations.

2.5. Stage three - selection of check sites

The field check was designed to compare the two classifications. Check sites were chosen as follows:
a) Six blocks were chosen which had good cover of air photographs (Fig. 6), and which had not been the subject of any of the preliminary investigations.
b) Within each block two or four intersections on the 1 km national grid (marked on Fig. 6) were selected randomly.
c) An area of 50 ha was established round each intersection and five sites within it were selected randomly.

The sites were marked on the 1 : 10000 air photographs. Then without further ground check C.J.L. and J.S.B. separately identified the facet and element present at each site. Their lists of identifications were then put away ("office" lists).

2.6. Stage four - field check

The field check was carried out by another soil surveyor (G.H.) unfamiliar with this area and with no previous connections with the study. He was equipped with the alternative lists of facets for Carradale land system, and their definitions, and the air photographs on which the test sites were marked. He found that he could locate the sites to within 5 m, but some of the sites under a dense cover of young trees planted since the air photographs were taken were omitted. Fig. 6 indicates the 75 sites that were visited. He identified the element and facet on both classifications represented at each site ("field" lists). He examined the soil profile by spade, and peat deeper than 50 m by probe. Where possible he re-corded all the features in Table 4, using the classes given there. Some records were incomplete; for example it proved impracticable to examine the mineral soil beneath deep peat.

Table 4:

Drainage class of whole profile.	P Free; P - PH Imperfect; PH Poor; HP Very Poor.
Texture of mineral soil	(s, ls, sl, fsl, l, gravel) in Topsoil (0-20 cm); and Subsurface (20-40 cm)
Depth of peat or of peat domi-nated horizons.	H1 0-5 cm; H2 5+-15 cm; H3 15+-50 cm; H4 50+-100 cm; H5 >100 cm; Soils with 5-50 cm peat are 'peaty', with 50-100 cm 'shallow peat', more than 100 cm 'deep peat'.
Depth of mineral soil including unconsolidated till or alluvium.	MO 0-5 cm; M1 >5 cm; M2 >15 cm; M3 >45 cm; M4 >1 m; M5 > 2 m; M6 > 3 m; Each site is allocated to the deepest class to which the (sometimes incomplete) records allow it to be allocated
Slope at the site	GO 0-1°; G1 2-5; G2 6-9; G3 10-20; G4 >20°. 'Gentle' slopes are 0-9°, 'Moderate' 10-20°, 'Steep' are greater than 20°.
Parent Material	Bedrock, Till, Head and Colluvium, Alluvium.
Major Soil Subgroup	Organic or Peat, Peaty Podzol, Peaty Gley, Peaty Lithosol, Peaty Flush/Flush Gley, Podzol, Brown Podzolic, Non-Calcareous Gley, Flush Gley, Alluvium.

3. RESULTS

Table 3 records the number of times each land element was encountered in this sample. The high proportion of sites of "poor" drainage (78 - 85 %), and the num-ber of flushes encountered, confirm the prevailing wetness of the region. While facet 1 in both classifications is dominated (25/28 or 23/25) by broadly the same element and might have been presented as a simple facet, facet 3 of the remote group (Oxford) and the corresponding facets 5 and 6 of the local surveyor (Oban) are clearly patterned.

Table 5 compares the success of the authors of the two classifications at identi-fying the elements of their land systems. The more conspicuous features of the major valley floors were easily distinguished, but minor elements of the upland facets (such as flushes, minor streams and peat basins) less so. The local surveyor

Table 5: RECOGNITION OF ELEMENTS: NO. OF SITES RECOGNIZED IN "OFFICE" AND "FIELD"

a) Oxford

"Office" predictions

		Facets 1 - 4						Facet 6			
		a		b	c	e	f	l	n	p	
		i	ii								
a	i	25	3								28
	ii	10	11			1					22
b		2		O							2
c		4	4		1		1				10
e			2			O					2
f						1	2				3
l								4	1		5
n									1		1
p										2	2
		41	20	O	1	2	3	4	2	2	75

("Field" observations — row labels at left)

b) Oban

"Office" predictions

		Facets 1 - 6									Facet 7			
		a		b		c		d	e	f	g	m	n	
		p	m	p	m	p	m							
a	p	O												O
	m		O											O
b	p			2		2								4
	m		2		O									2
c	p			4	1	26	3	5		1	1			42
	m				1		4			1				6
d								O			1			1
e									O					–
f				3		2	1	1		O	3			10
g											O			–
m												2	2	4
n													6	6
		O	2	9	3	30	8	6		2	5	2	8	75

("Field" observations — row labels at left)

had considerable success in distinguishing sites with and without peaty topsoils, whereas the remote photo-interpreter had felt too uncertain to make a facet separation. The local surveyor, however, had over-estimated gradients.

Table 6:

"Field" observations		"Office" predictions			
		OXFORD		OBAN	
		No. of sites on		No. pf sites on	
		Shallow till (facets 1,2,6)	Till (facets 3)	Shallow till (facets 1-4)	Till (facets 5-6)
	Shallow till	25	3	20	2
	Till	10	11	2	20
		For element a		For elements a, b, c	

Table 7: PARENT MATERIAL OBSERVED

"Office" predictions		Facet and Element	Bedrock	Till	Alluvium
	Oxford	1a	9	14	1
		3a,c	1	18	
		3f		1	2
	Oban	1b,c	8	2	
		5c		8	
		6b,c,f		19	1

Table 8: DEPTH OF MINERAL SOIL OBSERVED

"Office" predictions		Facet and Element	MO	M1	M2	M3	M4	M5	M6
	Oxford	1a	3	1	2	1	2	6	1
		3a	1		1	6		7	1
	Oban	1b,c	4			1	2		
		5c,6b,c,f		1	3	6		13	2

Table 9: DEPTH OF ORGANIC SURFACE OBSERVED

"Office" predictions		Facet and Elelemt	H1	H2	H3	H4	H5
	Oxford	1a	1	6	7	8	18
		3a	7	3	8	1	1
	Oban	1b,c		2	4	5	11
		5c	4	1	3		
		6b,c		6	8	2	3

Table 6 compares their success in distinguishing those elements on slopes which lay over more than 1 - 2 m till. Again, J.S.B. had proved more successful at recognizing a particular feature on the air photographs.

The remaining comparisons are limited to elements represented by more than one site. Tables 7 - 11 group the sites according to their "office" identification. Both classifications are reasonably successful at identifying elements on deep till within the facets dominated by till (Table 7) but in facet 1 higher up the slopes the elements identified by the local surveyor (1b, c) were slightly more uniform in parent material and depth (Table 8) than those identified remotely (1a).

The elements identified locally were more uniform in their presence or absence of peaty surface horizons (Table 10), and in the depth of their humose or peaty surfaces (Table 9) than those

Table 10: SOIL SUB-GROUP OBSERVED

Facet and Element		Peat	Peaty topsoil				Mineral topsoil		
			Gley	Podzol	Lithosol		Gley	Well-drained	
Oxford	1a	24	9		5	14	1		1
	3a	2	8	1	1	10	4	2	6
Oban	1b,c	14	2		6	8			
	5c		3	1	-	4	3	1	4
	6b,c	5	13	1		14		-	1

("office" predictions — shown at left)

Table 11: SOIL TEXTURE OBSERVED

Facet and Element		Topsoil					Subsoil				
		S	LS	SL	FSL	L	S	LS	SL	FSL	L
Oxford	1a	1	2	8					6	2	
	3a,c,f		4	12	2	2		5	7	3	
Oban	1b,c			3					1		
	5c			4	1	1		1	4	1	
	6b,c,f		5	11		1		4	6	4	

("Office" predictions — shown at left)

interpreted remotely. C.J.L. had defined facet 1 as a hill crest feature and thereby picked out the sites of more sandy topsoil (Table 11) in contrast to J.S.B. whose facet definitions make no reference to their position in the landscape. None of the elements of either group are very uniform in soil texture.

4. CONCLUSIONS

Land systems can be defined for the Highlands of Scotland to serve as aids to regional planning. Also, it is not difficult to define *land elements*, each to comprise a kind of terrain that presents particular and fairly uniform problems of management or conservation, but most of these are too small in extent to be mapped at a reasonable scale or used as a basis for local planning. Over much of this area it was not possible to define simple facets, larger than elements, uniform enough to be managed as single units even if only for moderately intensive land use. While it was possible to define *"patterned facets"*, that could be distinguished on air photographs and mapped at scales of 1 : 20 000 - 1 : 50 000, many of these consisted of 2 or 3 major elements in recognizable pattern and several minor elements, so they are not uniform enough to be treated as single management units under moderately intensive land use.

As stated earlier, land facets had to be created as units for the detailed mapping of simple landscapes in any one of which a few simple facets recurred to form a characteristic pattern. The recognition of the pattern and of the position of any site within it is then a significant stage in the identification of the facet at any particular site, and staff with little local experience need not distinguish land facets on subtle or unfamiliar diagnostic features.

Clearly these conditions do not apply to Central Argyll, where the landscape patterns are complex and not always clear, and several of the larger facets could not be associated with particular positions in the landscape. In such cases it will be better to distinguish areas on any particular soil characteristics, such as peaty topsoil or shallowness, that are associated with specific features on air photographs. The mapping units that result will be similar to soil complexes, already mapped in some areas, that contain two or more different kinds of soil. They can be grouped within soil associations, according to parent material, to fit the classification structure already used in Scotland, and they can be mapped quickly by locally based surveyors with good experience. Staff with little local experience and those who must work remotely will find it difficult to map specifically soil complexes from their air photo appearance. They can map patterned facets, and though such units may be less useful than classes defined strictly on soil characters, they may be adequate for some forms of land evaluation.

BIBLIOGRAPHY

BECKETT, P.H.T. & WEBSTER, R. (1965): A classification system for terrain. Report No. 872, Military Engineering and Experimental Establishment, Christchurch.
BIBBY, J.S. (1973): In: Island of Mull - Survey and proposals for development. Special Report No. 10. Highlands and Islands Development Board, Inverness.
BOWN, C.J. (1973): The soils of Carrick and the country round Girvan (Sheets 7 and 8) Mem. Soil Surv. Scotland. H.M. Stationery Office, Edinburgh.
BRINK, A.B.A., MABBUTT, J.A. WEBSTER, R. & BECKETT, P.H.T. (1966): Report of the working group on land classification and data storage. Report No. 940, Military Engineering Experimental Establishment, Christchurch.
MUIR, J.W. (1956): The soils of the country around Jedburgh and Morebattle (Sheets 17 and 18). Mem. Soil Surv. Scotland. H.M. Stationery Office, Edinburgh.
WEBSTER, R. & BECKETT, P.H.T. (1968): Quality and usefulness of soil maps. Nature, London, 219, 680 - 682.

5: THE RELATIONSHIP OF SOIL AND PHYSIOGRAPHIC ATTRIBUTES TO AN ECOLOGICAL CLASSIFICATION SYSTEM

M. W. Sondheim[1] and K. Klinka[2]

[1]*Surveys and Resource Mapping Branch, British Columbia, Ministry of Environment, 777 Broughton Street, Victoria, B.C., V8V 1X5; and*
[2]*Research Branch, B.C.*
Ministry of Forests, 4595 Canada Way, Burnaby, B.C., V5G 4L9

The ability of a phytosociologically based, ecological classification system to explain the variability of soil and physiographic properties is tested. Sixty stands from a research forest in southwestern British Columbia are defined in terms of three categorical levels of the ecosystem taxonomy of V. J. Krajina. The stands belong to 14 associations, eight alliances, and three orders. Using these taxa, nested and one-way analyses of variance are performed on 40 soil and physiographic properties of the included ecosystems. Because the hierarchy tested is unbalanced and the samples are of unequal size, the estimates and significance of the variance components for both analyses are determined by approximation techniques. The results from the one-way analyses show that for mineral soil pH and for most physiographic factors between one-half and two-thirds of the variability can be explained by the classification of the ecosystems into associations. For the other properties and for the alliances and orders, this proportion is typically much lower. The study suggests that for general pedologic and environmental characterization there may be little justification for using the alliance and order categories.

Key words: Soil-plant relationships, taxonomy, biogeocoenose, integrated classification

L'aptitude d'un système de classification phytosociologique à expliquer la variabilité des propriétés du sol et du modèle est mise à l'essai. Soixante peuplements forestiers du sud-ouest de la Colombie-Britannique sont caractérisés selon trois niveaux de la taxinomie écosociologique de Krajina. Les peuplements appartiennent à 14 associations, 8 alliances et 3 ordres. Utilisant ces taxons, on a effectué des analyses de la variance groupées et à une variable sur les propriétés pédologiques et physiographiques des divers écosystèmes. Etant donné que le système hiérarchique est en déséquilibre et que les échantillons sont de taille inégale, les estimées et le degré de signification des composantes de la variance sont déterminées par approximation. Les résultats des analyses à une variable montrent que pour le pH du sol minéral et pour la plupart des facteurs physiographiques, de la moitié aux deux tiers de la variabilité observée peuvent être expliqués par la classification des écosystèmes en associations. Pour les autres propriétés, et pour les alliances et les ordres, la proportion est beaucoup plus basse. Cette étude porte à conclure que pour la caractérisation générale des terres selon les facteurs pédologiques et écologiques, il y a peu d'avantage à utiliser le classement par alliances et par ordres.

Mots clés: Relations sol-plante, taxinomie, biogéocoénose, classification intégrée

During the past decade there has been increased interest in North America in an ecosystem approach to forest resource management (Kimmins 1977). In western Canada this has led to the development and utilization of several types of ecosystem classification schemes. Among those successfully applied in British Columbia is the system developed by Krajina (1960, 1965, 1969, 1972, 1977) and his colleagues (Wali and Krajina 1973; Kojima and Krajina 1975; Klinka 1976; Klinka and Skoda 1977; Annas and Coupe 1979; Klinka et al. 1979, 1980). Discussions of Krajina's system may also be found in some standard textbooks (Mueller-Dombois and Ellenberg 1974; Daniel et al. 1979; Spurr and Barnes 1980).

Krajina's classification is considered to be ecological in scope; however, it is based primarily on the identification of climax plant communities. Use of the system is of particular interest to soil scientists in British Columbia because of the following assumption inherent in the system: an ecological classification, essentially phytosociological in nature, can be employed profitably to explain the variability of those soil and physiographic properties thought to interact strongly with the vegetation. An in-depth analysis of this assumption is the object of this paper. The manner of investigation is discussed after a brief description of the classification system.

Krajina's approach to classification involves several "levels of integration" (Krajina 1977), two of which are relevant here. The first concerns the definition of a biogeocoenosis. Similar to the term ecosystem (Tansley 1935), a biogeocoenosis refers to a concrete entity on the ground with finite boundaries, containing both uniform vegetation and site characteristics (Sukachev and Dylis 1964). Thus, it contains vegetational, faunal, microbiological, climatic, and soil elements which are conceptualized as being in dynamic equilibrium. The vegetation within a biogeocoenosis composes a phytocoenosis, the plant community. Taxonomically, climax plant communities are classified into plant associations. Where different biogeocoenoses are characterized by the same association, their overall climatic, moisture, and chemical regimes are presumed to be approximately equivalent (Klinka 1976; Klinka and Skoda 1977).

A second level of integration of Krajina's system involves the construction of a phytosociological classification (Krajina 1977). The classification follows Braun-Blanquet's taxonomy of plant communities (Braun-Blanquet 1964), whereby associations are grouped hierarchically into alliances, orders and classes. The groupings are based mainly on the floristic properties of the ecosystems. Krajina (1969) presumes that the higher the taxonomic category, the broader is the spectrum of some of the associated pedologic and physiographic attributes. Biogeocoenoses are classified on the basis of their phytocoenoses, and it is assumed that this classification reflects a meaningful classification of other biogeocoenotic elements, including climate and soils.

The present study analyzes the relationship of 40 pedologic and physiographic properties to the association, alliance, and order catgories of the system. The class category is not considered because of data base limitations and because of its very limited usage in the literature. Two major issues are addressed. (1) To what extent does the variability of each of the properties increase as the degree of generalization increases through the categories? (2) Ignoring the categorical rank, how much does the organization of the biogeocoenoses into associations, alliances, and orders help explain the variability of each of the properties?

The two questions can be examined appropriately in a univariate context with the use of nested and one-way analyses of variance, respectively. Because univariate analyses are used exclusively, the study does not examine the ecological principle of compensating factors. Note as well that the legitimacy of the taxonomy as a phytosociological classification is not questioned. Rather, the study simply attempts to ascertain the extent to which the three selected categories of Krajina's taxonomic system explain the variability of a number of soil and physiographic properties.

DATA BASE

The data come from an ecological study by Klinka (1976) (The numbers of the plots in Klinka (1976) from which the data were taken are as follows: 2, 3, 4, 5, 6, 7, 8, 12, 13, 14, 16, 19, 20, 22, 23, 24, 25, 26, 27, 28, 29, 30, 31, 32, 33, 36, 37, 39, 41, 42, 44, 46, 52, 53, 54, 55, 56, 60, 62, 63, 74, 75, 79, 82, 87, 89, 90, 97, 99, 100, 104, 111, 114, 116, 119, 148, 150, 153, 155, 158.) at the University of British Columbia Research Forest in southwestern British Columbia. The environmental characteristics of the location are also described by Sondheim and Lavkulich (1982). Klinka mapped the biogeocoenoses of the forest and subsequently classified them according to the system of Krajina. In support of the mapping and classification, soils and vegetation data were collected from 158 plots, each modally located in the middle of a biogeocoenosis. The soil horizon samples collected from 60 of the plots underwent comprehensive physical and chemical laboratory analysis. Covering the majority of the forest's ecological diversity, the 60 corresponding biogeocoenoses were hierarchically grouped into 14 associations, eight alliances, and three orders. Figure 1 displays the synopsis, the name of taxa, and the number of biogeocoenoses which each contains. The stands, all naturally established, range in age from approximately 100 yr to greater than 250 yr; they represent mature to old growth stages of succession. Although the time factor has not been held constant, the earlier, most dynamic periods of ecosystem development have been excluded by the sampling scheme.

The properties under investigation include eight physiographic factors, four mineral soil textural characteristics, 15 mineral soil chemical attributes and 13 forest floor (LFH) chemical attributes. Because mineral soil data were collected on a horizon basis, it was necessary to take weighted averages for each of the 19 mineral soils properties. Both arithmetic and exponential weighting procedures were used, bringing the total number of parameters up to 59. The properties with their abbreviations are listed in Table 1.

NUMERICAL METHODS

For each of the mineral soil textural and chemical properties, data for the horizons within the rooting zone of each pedon are reduced to a single value. This was accomplished using both arithmetic and exponential weighting procedures. With the arithmetic method, the single pedon value is defined as follows (Kloosterman and Lavkulich 1973):

$$V_a = \sum_{i=1}^{n} V_i t_i \Big/ \sum_{i=1}^{n} t_i \qquad (1)$$

where, V_a is the new, arithmetically weighted value; n is the number of horizons; V_i is the value of the ith horizon; t_i is the thickness of the ith horizon.

With the exponential technique the weight of a horizon diminishes with depth. The single pedon value is thus determined by the following equation:

$$V_e = \frac{\sum_{i=1}^{n} V_i(\exp(-0.02u_i) - \exp(-0.02l_i))}{\sum_{i=1}^{n} (\exp(-0.02u_i) - \exp(-0.02l_i))} \qquad (2)$$

where, V_e is the new, exponentially weighted value; u_i is the depth of the upper boundary of the ith horizon, l_i is the depth of the lower boundary of the ith horizon.

Work by Russel and Moore (1968) and by Sondheim et al. (1981) shows that for many soils the intensity of pedogenic development and of organic matter accumulation is approximately proportional to the exponential term, $\exp(-0.02d)$, where d is depth in cm. This term may also serve as a rough approximation of the availability of nutrients within the mineral soil. Using Eqs. 1 and 2 two separate data sets for the mineral soil textural and chemical data were created. An alternative to the inte-

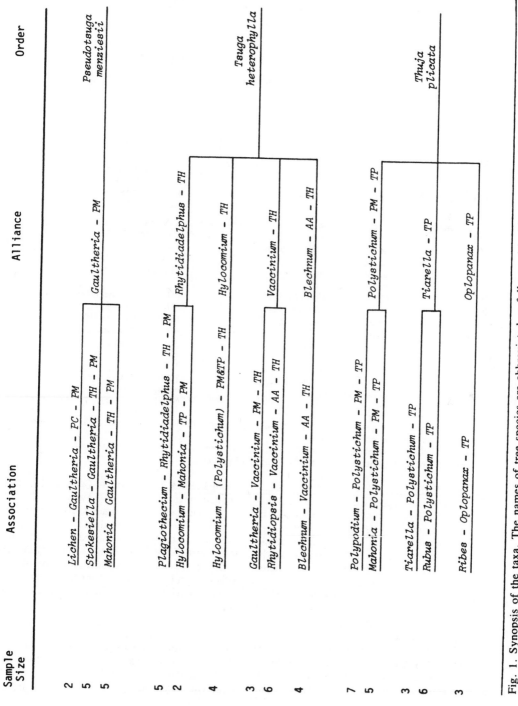

Fig. 1. Synopsis of the taxa. The names of tree species are abbreviated as follows: AA, *Abies anabilis*; PC, *Pinus contorta*; PM, *Pseudotsuga mensiesii*; TH, *Tsuga heterophylla*; TP, *Thuja plicata*.

Table 1. Description of properties

Property	Description	Laboratory reference
General physiographic factors		
EL	Elevation	
SI.	Slope in percent	
RA	Incoming solar radiation (month of May)	Buffo et al. (1972)
COSAS	Cosine of aspect	
PRS	% of ground surface as rock or stone	
PCF	Field estimate of % of soil as coarse fragments (>2 mm)	
DPO	Depth of LFH layer	
DPM	Depth of rooting zone	
Soil textural characteristics†		
COFR	% coarse fragments (>2 mm)	Sieve
SAND	% sand (<2 mm, >50 μm)	Sieve and pipette Jackson (1958)
SILT	% silt (<50 μm, > 2 μm)	Jackson (1958)
CLAY	% clay (<2 μm)	Jackson (1958)
Mineral soil‡ and forest floor§ chemical attributes		
PHH	pH-measured in water	1:1, Peech (1965)
PHC	pH-measured in CaCl₂ solution	1:2, Peech (1965)
C	% carbon content	Leco
N	% nitrogen content	Semimicro–Kjeldahl, Bremner (1965)
CNR	Carbon-nitrogen ratio	
CA	Exchangeable calcium (meq/100 g)	pH 7.0; Chapman (1965)
MG	Exchangeable magnesium (meq/100 g)	pH 7.0; Chapman (1965)
NA	Exchangeable sodium (meq/100 g)	pH 7.0; Chapman (1965)
K	Exchangeable potassium (meq/100 g)	pH 7.0; Chapman (1965)
CEC	Cation exchange capacity (meq/100 g)	pH 7.0; Chapman (1965)
BS	% base saturation	
FEP	Iron by pyrophosphate (ppm)	Bascomb (1968)
ALP	Aluminum by pyrophosphate (ppm)	Bascomb (1968)
FEO	Iron by oxalate (ppm)	McKeague and Day (1966)
ALO	Aluminum by oxalate (ppm)	McKeague and Day (1966)

†For the mineral soil properties both arithmetically and exponentially weighted values for each site were derived from the original horizon data.
‡Mineral soil chemical attributes include all 15 properties listed.
§Forest floor chemical attributes include only the first 13 properties listed.

gration techniques of these equations involves taking data from specified horizons. For example, the pH of the first Bf horizon could be used as a variable. However, since a given type of horizon will vary in its occurrence, thickness, and depth, and in its relationship to the rooting zone, this approach was not considered to be satisfactory.

For the nested analysis of variance, a random effects model is used in which components of variance are assigned to each category of the hierarchy. Because the classification as tested is unbalanced, it is necessary to resort to the approximation procedure developed by Gower (1962). The results for the calculated sums of squares and the estimated sums of squares and

mean squares are shown in Table 2. The calculated mean squares, not shown, are equal to the calculated sums of squares divided by the respective degrees of freedom. Thus, each of the variance components may be evaluated. The total variance, σ_T^2, is equal to the sum of the variance components attributable to the order, alliance, and association categories, and random error within the association categories, respectively

$$\sigma_T^2 = \sigma_{Or}^2 + \sigma_{Al}^2 + \sigma_{As}^2 + \sigma_E^2 \qquad (3)$$

The proportion of the total variance attributable to each of the categories of the hierarchy is readily obtained and graphed from this equation. The statistical significance of the compo-

Table 2. Nested analysis of variance design

Source	Degrees of freedom	Calculated sum of squares	Expectations of	
			Sum of squares	Mean squares
Order	2	$\sum_{i=1}^{3} n_i(x^*_i - x^*)^2$	$2\sigma_E^2 + 9.4\sigma_{As}^2 + 19.5\sigma_{Al}^2 + 38.4\sigma_{Or}^2$	$\sigma_E^2 + 4.7\sigma_{As}^2 + 9.8\sigma_{Al}^2 + 19.2\sigma_{Or}^2$
Alliance	5	$\sum_{i=1}^{3}\sum_{j=1}^{m_i} n_{ij}(x^*_{ij} - x^*_i)^2$	$5\sigma_E^2 + 21.4\sigma_{As}^2 + 31.5\sigma_{Al}^2$	$\sigma_E^2 + 4.3\sigma_{As}^2 + 6.3\sigma_{Al}^2$
Association	6	$\sum_{i=1}^{3}\sum_{j=1}^{m_i}\sum_{k=1}^{m_{ij}} n_{ijk}(x^*_{ijk} - x^*_{ij})^2$	$6\sigma_E^2 + 24.5\sigma_{As}^2$	$\sigma_E^2 + 4.1\sigma_{As}^2$
Error	46	$\sum_{i=1}^{3}\sum_{j=1}^{m_i}\sum_{k=1}^{m_{ij}}\sum_{l=1}^{n_{ijk}} (x_{ijkl} - x^*_{ijk})^2$	$46\sigma_E^2$	σ_E^2

n_i is the number of observations in the ith order; m_i is the number of alliances of the ith order. n_{ij}, n_{ijk}, and m_{ij} are similarly defined for the lower levels of the hierarchy. x^* is the calculated grand mean. x^*_i is the calculated mean of the ith order; x^*_{ij} and x^*_{ijk} are similarly defined for the lower levels of the hierarchy. x_{ijkl} is the lth observation of the kth association of the jth alliance of the ith order. σ_{Or}^2, σ_{Al}^2, σ_{As}^2 and σ_E^2 are the variance components attributable to the orders, alliances, associations, and the variability within the associations (the error), respectively.

nents can be determined approximately by a technique developed by Satterthwaite (1946). With this procedure quasi-F ratios and associated degrees of freedom are calculated using the mean square values. Table 3 shows the results for the association, alliance, and order categories. The calculated mean squares of Table 3 represent the expected mean squares of Table 2. The α, β and γ coefficients in Table 3 are designated such that the expected mean square terms in the numerator and denominator of the quasi-F ratio are identical with the exception of one term in the numerator specific to the level being tested.

The one-way analyses were conducted using the one-factor analysis of variance, random effects model, with unequal numbers of observations (Snedecor and Cochran 1967). This is displayed for each of the categories of the hierarchy in Table 4. As before the total variance can be broken into components. These components can be identified as the among-group variance, σ_A^2, and within-group variance, σ_W^2. As with the nested analyses, the proportion of the total variance attributable to the components σ_A^2 and σ_W^2 is of interest. The ratio of σ_A^2 to $\sigma_A^2 + \sigma_W^2$ is referred to as the intraclass correlation coefficient, ρ_I:

$$\rho_I = \sigma_A^2/(\sigma_A^2 + \sigma_W^2) \qquad (4)$$

RESULTS

Tables 5–8 display the significance results for both types of analyses. For the one-way analyses the estimated intraclass correlations are given only for those variables found statistically significant; for the remaining variables the estimated correlations are less than approximately 0.18, 0.14, and 0.11 for the association, alliance, and order levels, respectively; such levels are too low to be of any interest. Figure 2 shows graphs of percent cumulative variance versus categorical level. The percentages of the total variance of σ_E^2, $\sigma_{As}^2 + \sigma_E^2$, $\sigma_{Al}^2 + \sigma_{As}^2 + \sigma_E^2$, and $\sigma_{Or}^2 + \sigma_{Al}^2 + \sigma_{As}^2 + \sigma_E^2$ are plotted against the error, association, alliance, and order categories, respectively. As an example of the interpretation of these tables and figures, elevation will be discussed in detail.

Looking at the nested analyses of vari-

Table 3. Significance tests for the nested ANOVA

Null hypothesis	Quasi-F ratio	Numerator (nearest integral value)	Denominator	Coefficients
$\sigma_{As}^2 = 0$	$\dfrac{MS_{As}}{MS_E}$	6	46	
$\sigma_{Al}^2 = 0$	$\dfrac{\alpha_{Al}MS_{Al} + \beta_{Al}MS_E}{MS_{As}}$	$\dfrac{(\alpha_{Al}MS_{Al} + \beta_{Al}MS_E)^2}{\dfrac{\alpha_{Al}^2 MS_{Al}^2}{5} + \dfrac{\beta_{Al}^2 MS_E^2}{46}}$	6	$\alpha_{Al} = 4.1/4.3$ $\beta_{Al} = 1 - \alpha_{Al}$
$\sigma_{Or}^2 = 0$	$\dfrac{\alpha_{Or}MS_{Or} + \beta_{Or}MS_{As} + \gamma_{Or}MS_E}{MS_{Al}}$	$\dfrac{(\alpha_{Or}MS_{Or} + \beta_{Or}MS_{As} + \gamma_{Or}MS_E)^2}{\dfrac{\alpha_{Or}^2 MS_{Or}^2}{2} + \dfrac{\beta_{Or}^2 MS_{As}^2}{6} + \dfrac{\gamma_{Or}^2 MS_E^2}{46}}$	5	$\alpha_{Or} = 6.3/9.8$ $\beta_{Or} = (4.3 - 4.7\alpha_{Or})/4.1$ $\gamma_{Or} = 1 - \alpha_{Or} - \beta_{Or}$

MS_{Or}, MS_{Al}, MS_{As}, and MS_E are the calculated mean squares at the order, alliance, association, and error levels, respectively.

Table 4. Design and significance tests for the one-way ANOVAs

	Order	Alliance	Association
Null hypothesis	$\sigma^2_{\mu_i \cdot \mu} = 0$	$\sigma^2_{\mu_i \cdot \mu} = 0$	$\sigma^2_{\mu_i \cdot \mu} = 0$
Degrees of freedom	2, 57	7, 52	13, 46
Calculated sums of squares among groups, SS_a	$\sum_{i=1}^{3} n_i (x^*_i - x^*)^2$	$\sum_{i=1}^{8} n_i (x^*_i - x^*)^2$	$\sum_{i=1}^{14} n_i (x^*_i - x^*)^2$
Calculated sums of squares within groups, SS_w	$\sum_{i=1}^{3} \sum_{j=1}^{n_i} (x_{ij} - x^*_i)^2$	$\sum_{i=1}^{8} \sum_{j=1}^{n_i} (x_{ij} - x^*_i)^2$	$\sum_{i=1}^{14} \sum_{j=1}^{n_i} (x_{ij} - x^*_i)^2$
Calculated mean squares among groups, MS_a	$SS_a/2$	$SS_a/7$	$SS_a/13$
Calculated mean squares within groups, MS_w	$SS_w/57$	$SS_w/52$	$SS_w/46$
Estimated mean squares among groups where n_0 equals†	$\sigma_W^2 + n_0\sigma_A^2$ 19.2	$\sigma_W^2 + n_0\sigma_A^2$ 7.3	$\sigma_W^2 + n_0\sigma_A^2$ 4.2
Estimated mean squares within groups	σ_W^2	σ_W^2	σ_W^2
F, Ratio	MS_a/MS_w	MS_a/MS_w	MS_a/MS_w

$†n_0 = \dfrac{1}{g\text{-}1} \left(\Sigma n_i - \dfrac{\Sigma n_i^2}{\Sigma n_i} \right)$,where g is the number of groups.

For each of the three independent tests: μ is the grand mean and μ_i is the mean of the ith class; x^* is the calculated grand mean and x^*_i is the calculated mean of the ith class; n_i is the number of observations in the ith class; x_{ij} is the jth observation of the ith class; σ_A^2 and σ_W^2 are the among-group and within-group variance components, respectively.

ance results on Table 5 first, it can be seen that for elevation the association component of variance is statistically significant at the 99% level of confidence. At the 95% level, neither the alliance nor the order component differs significantly from zero. In Fig. 2 it is clear from the slope of the line segments that the estimate of σ_{Al}^2 is

Table 5. Significance results, general physiographic factors

Property†	Nested ANOVA			One-way ANOVA‡		
	Assoc.	Alliance	Order	Assoc.	Alliance	Order
EL	**			0.64**	0.53**	0.19**
SL	**			0.66**	0.35**	
RA				0.35**	0.32**	0.17*
COSAS						
PRS	**			0.64**	0.36**	0.15**
PCF	**			0.54**	0.21**	
DPO						
DPM				0.56**	0.51**	0.38**

†EL, elevation; SL, slope in percent; RA, incoming solar radiation (month of May); COSAS, cosine of aspect; PRS, percent of ground surface as rock or stone; PCF, field estimate of percent of soil as coarse fragments; DPO, depth of LFH layer; DPM, depth of rooting zone.

‡For one-way ANOVA results, the intraclass correlation coefficients are given where the among-group variance component is judged significantly different from zero at the 95% or 99% level of confidence.

*,**significant at the 95% and 99%, levels of confidence, respectively.

100 / M. W. Sondheim and K. Klinka

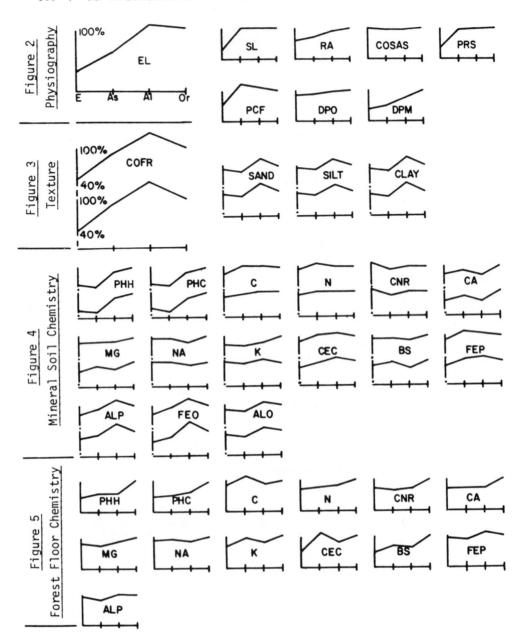

Figs. 2–5. Graphs of percent cumulative variance versus category of the hierarchy from the nested ANOVA. E is error; As is association; Al is alliance; Or is order. Where two graphs occur on the same set of axes, the upper refers to the arithmetic results and the lower refers to the exponential results.

larger than that for σ_{As}^2. The former is not statistically significant because of the fewer degrees of freedom associated with its assessment. The plot shows further that the estimate of σ_{Or}^2 is negative, a result which for practical purposes can be equated with zero.

When the association category is considered as a separate, independent classification, the intraclass correlation coefficient for elevation is estimated to be 0.64, as given on Table 5. This proportion, equal to approximately two-thirds, is significant at the 99% level of confidence; it also implies that among-group variance, σ_A^2, is approximately twice as great as the within-group variance σ_W^2. This suggests that, in terms of understanding the variability of elevation in the data set, knowledge of the association taxa is quite helpful. The alliance and order categories are also tested as independent classifications. Their σ_A^2 estimates are judged significantly different from zero at the 99% level and their intraclass correlations are 0.53 and 0.19, respectively. Though of statistical significance, the latter value is too small to be of much interpretive use.

From this discussion the following points emerge concerning elevation. As independent taxa, both associations and alliances are valuable in that they each account for over half of the total variability. The hierarchical arrangement of ecosystems into associations also appears useful; from the graph and the significance results, it is clear that the percentage of variability explained by the association category is comparatively large and statistically significant. The grouping of associations into alliances seems worthwhile in spite of its apparent lack of statistical significance. The order category appears to be of no value as a level of the hierarchy and of only marginal value as an independent classification.

An examination of the other physiographic factors in Table 5 and Fig. 2 shows that percent slope, percent of soil as coarse fragments (field estimate), and percent of

surface as rock or stone all behave quite similarly. In all three cases σ_{As}^2 appears highly significant and explains well over 50% of the total variance. Their association intraclass correlations are all above 0.5. The alliances and orders, as hierarchical constituents, are of no value; as independent classes the alliances account for only a limited amount of the overall variance, whereas the orders are of even less utility. For incoming solar radiation the nested and the one-way results are of no significance and of minor value, respectively. Cosine of the aspect and depth of the LFH layer do not appear related to the taxa of the system in any way. From its cumulative component graph, depth of the rooting zone can be partially explained by each of the categories, although none are statistically significant. ρ_I for both the associations and the alliance is estimated as greater than 0.5, and for the orders it is nearly 0.4.

Analyses of the textural data are provided on Table 6 and Fig. 3. The upper and lower curves on each of the graphs represent the results from the arithmetic and the exponential weighting procedures, respectively. The marked similarity between the two curves for each variable is noteworthy. For percent of soil as coarse fragments (laboratory determination) both the associations and the alliances appear as valid hierarchical categories; however, only the association level is statistically significant. The intraclass correlation coefficient is over 0.5 for the associations and close to 0.4 for the alliances. Percent sand and percent clay are significant at the 95% level of confidence for the alliance category only on the nested results. From the graphs on Fig. 3, percent silt behaves virtually identically to percent sand and percent clay. For all sand, silt and clay one-way analyses, the estimated ρ_I values are very low to nonsignificant for the association and alliance categories. None of the textural variables show any relationship to the order category.

Table 7 and Figure 4 display the results

for the mineral soil chemistry. Here as well the similarity between the results for the arithmetic and exponential weighting procedures is striking. For both measures of pH the component of variance attributable to the alliance category is highly significant, accounting for approximately 50% of the total variance. As independent classifications all three categories are statistically significant; however, only for the associations and the alliances is the estimate of ρ_I at or above 0.5. Other significant results from the nested analyses include: calcium significant for the order category, sodium for the order category for the arithmetic data only, and base saturation for the order category for the exponential data only. From the graphs on Fig. 4, aluminum by pyrophosphate and iron and aluminum by oxalate appear to have major variance components for the alliance category. Results from the one-way analyses indicate that for the following variables one or more of the ρ_I estimates was found to be significant: carbon, calcium, magnesium, cation exchange capacity, base saturation, iron and aluminum by both pyrophosphate and oxalate. Nevertheless the highest estimate of ρ_I is only 0.33 and in most of these cases it is 0.20 or less. For nitrogen, carbon-nitrogen ratio, and potassium, none of the variance components in any of the analyses are judged significantly different from zero.

Results from the analyses of the forest floor chemical properties are contained in Table 8 and Fig. 5. On the nested analyses, the order estimates of variance for both pH measures are significant at the 99% level of confidence. For the association category the estimate of the nested variance component for cation exchange capacity is highly significant and accounts for over half of the total variance. Other significant results on the nested analyses include the estimates of variance for potassium for the association category, for base saturation for the association and the order category, and for aluminum by pyrophosphate for the

Table 6. Significance results, soil textural characteristics

Property†	Nested ANOVA						One-way ANOVA‡					
	Arithmetic			Exponential			Arithmetic			Exponential		
	Assoc.	Alliance	Order	Assoc.	Alliance	Order	Assoc.	Alliance	Order	Assoc.	Alliance	Order
COFR	**			**			0.53**	0.36**		0.54**	0.36**	
SAND		*						0.20*		0.20*		
SILT		*			*			0.14*				
CLAY							0.18*	0.21*		0.19*	0.22*	

†COFR, percent coarse fragments; SAND, percent sand; SILT, percent silt; CLAY, percent clay.
‡For one-way ANOVA results, the intraclass correlation coefficients are given where the among-group variance component is judged significantly different from zero at the 95% or 99% level of confidence.
*, **significant at the 95% and 99% levels of confidence, respectively.

Table 7. Significance results, mineral soil chemical attributes

Property†	Nested ANOVA						One-way ANOVA‡					
	Arithmetic			Exponential			Arithmetic			Exponential		
	Assoc.	Alliance	Order	Assoc.	Alliance	Order	Assoc.	Alliance	Order	Assoc.	Alliance	Order
PHH		**			**		0.51**	0.36**	0.34**	0.50**	0.56**	0.38**
PHC		**			**		0.50**	0.54**	0.29**	0.49**	0.54***	0.31**
C							0.25**	0.15*			0.14*	
N												
CNR												
CA			*			*		0.15*	0.25**	0.26*	0.20*	0.23**
MG									0.16*	0.20*	0.15*	0.20**
NA			*									
K												
CEC							0.20*			0.22*		
BS						**			0.13*		0.15*	0.15*
FEP	*						0.21*			0.22*		
ALP							0.26*	0.19*		0.23*	0.22*	
FEO							0.28*	0.19*		0.33**	0.30**	
ALO								0.19*			0.20*	

†PHH, pH in water; PHC, pH in CaCl₂ solution; C, percent carbon, N, percent nitrogen, CNR, carbon-nitrogen ratio; CA, exchangeable calcium; MG, exchangeable magnesium; NA, exchangeable sodium; K, exchangeable potassium; CEC, cation exchange capacity; BS, percent base saturation; FEP, pyrophosphate-extractable iron; ALP, pyrophosphate-extractable aluminum; FEO, oxalate-extractable iron; ALO, oxalate-extractable aluminum.

‡For one-way ANOVA results, the intraclass correlation coefficients are given where the among-group variance component is judged significantly different from zero at the 95% or 99% level of confidence.

*, **significant at the 95% and 99% levels of confidence, respectively.

Table 8. Significance results, forest floor chemical properties

Property[†]	Nested ANOVA			One-way ANOVA[‡]		
	Assoc.	Alliance	Order	Assoc.	Alliance	Order
PHH			**	0.41**	0.38**	0.41**
PHC			**	0.39**	0.41**	0.42**
C						
N				0.22*	0.21*	0.20**
CNR				0.25*	0.28**	0.20**
CA				0.23*	0.25**	0.28**
MG					0.18*	0.18*
NA						0.11*
K	*			0.23*		0.14*
CEC	**			0.47**	0.17*	0.17*
BS	*		*	0.42**	0.34**	0.39**
FEP						
ALP		*				

[†]PHH, pH in water; PHC, pH in CaCl$_2$ solution; C, percent carbon; N, percent nitrogen; CNR, carbon-nitrogen ratio; CA, exchangeable calcium; MG, exchangeable magnesium, NA, exchangeable sodium; K, exchangeable potassium; CEC, cation exchange capacity; BS, base saturation; FEP, pyrophosphate-extractable iron; ALP, pyrophosphate-extractable aluminum.
[‡]For one-way ANOVA results, the intraclass correlation coefficients are given where the among-group variance component is judged significantly different from zero at the 95% or 99% level of confidence.
*,**significant at the 95% and 99% levels of confidence, respectively.

alliance category. From the graphs in Fig. 5 calcium and carbon-nitrogen ratio both appear to have major variance components for the order category, though neither were found to be significant. Examining the results from the one-way anlyses it can be seen that all of the variables except carbon, iron, and aluminum have significant variance estimates for at least one of the categories. None of the corresponding intraclass correlation coefficients are above 0.5 and only for the two pH measures, cation exchange capacity, and base saturation are any of the estimated ρ_I values above 0.4.

DISCUSSION

When the classification is viewed as hierarchical, it appears to be of limited value as a means of partitioning the variability of the physiographic factors or the soil attributes. The nested variance components were not judged significant at all three levels of the hierarchy for any of the variables examined. In one case, base saturation of the LFH layer, two of the components were found to be statistically significant. For 14 of the properties only one of the components was found significant. All of the components on the remaining 25 variables were deemed not significantly different from zero. For some variables, such as depth of the rooting zone, the components suggest a desirable trend, in spite of their lack of statistical significance.

Provided that a least some of the variables are significant at each of the three categories of the hierarchy, the classification system could be considered as a legitimate and valuable tool. This contention has been suggested in regard to natural versus artificial soil classification systems (Kubiena 1958). For the system under study, however, there appears to be no inherent logic as to why certain variables are significant for some categories but not for others. Consequently, the worthiness of the classification as an ecologically valid, hierarchical system must be called into question insofar as the pedologic and physiographic properties tested here are concerned.

When the different levels of the system

are considered as independent classifications, a complementary but very different picture emerges. With the one-way analyses only nine (10 with the exponential weighting) of the variables are not statistically significant at any of the three levels. The three levels though must be evaluated separately. At the association level variables found significant and with an estimated intraclass correlation coefficient (ρ_1) of 0.50 or greater include: elevation, slope, percent of surface as rock or stone, depth of the rooting zone, percent coarse fragments (field and laboratory estimates), and the two pH measures for the mineral soil. At the alliance level, four variables have estimated ρ_1 value of 0.50 or greater: elevation, depth of the rooting zone, and the two soil mineral pH measures. At the order level none of the estimated ρ_1 values were equal to or greater than 0.50.

Two further points emerge from an examination of the one-way results. Firstly, of the three categories, the association classification appears to be the most viable in terms of how it relates to the 40 variables included in the study. Secondly, with the association category in particular, those variables best explained by the system are primarily physiographic in nature. The only exceptions to this are the soil pH measures.

There are two explanations for the apparent significance of many of the physiographic variables. The first relates to mapping procedures. A physiographic bias may result during mapping, when an attempt is made for mapping convenience to link landform boundaries to ecosystem delineations; since the vegetation of these delineations is directly involved in the recognition and definition of taxa, a relationship between physiography and taxonomy can be expected. The second explanation, which also serves as justification for the first, is that physiography undoubtedly does exert a strong influence on ecosystems and thus in turn on associations. The nature of this influence would seem to involve the moisture (Soil Survey Staff 1975)

and temperature regimes of the soil. Elevation, slope, percent of surface as rock or stone, rooting depth, and percent coarse fragments are all clearly related to the hydrologic dynamics within the rooting zone. To varying degrees these factors influence the soil's thermal characteristics within the rooting zone as well. The finding that physiographic attributes are the major differentiating criteria in the research forest is corroborated by the work of Eis (1962). The importance of physiography on climax communities is also discussed by Daubenmire (1952).

Most of the nonphysiographic properties do not appear to show a strong relationship to the categories of the hierarchy examined. Data from a study conducted in the interior of British Columbia (Wali and Krajina 1973) indicate that the environmental tolerances of most species are sufficiently wide that associations of these species may not fall within unique physical or chemical ranges. Other factors, such as fire history, past management practices, and seed dispersal patterns may also influence species location. In theory these factors are irrelevant to the definition of a taxon defined on the basis of climax characteristics; in practice it may be difficult to discount them completely. The existence of genetic variability within individual species also complicates the picture. Yet another taxonomic difficulty involves compensating factors. In biogeocoenoses where higher values of an attribute may partially offset lower values of another, the variability of these attributes within the associated taxa is increased. Such increases lower the likelihood that the classification will prove meaningful for the attributes. The possibility that a single taxonomic sytem can explain a major proportion of the variability of floristic, physiographic, and pedologic characteristics may simply be asking too much. This would seem to be particularly true, as in the case here, where that classification is based on only the floristic attributes of the ecosystems.

CONCLUSIONS

The study indicates that a statistically significant relationship exists between the ecosystem groupings, as defined by the plant associations, and many physiographic and soil variables. For elevation, slope, percent of surface as rock or stone, depth of the rooting zone, and percent coarse fragments, the association classification explains one-half to two-thirds of the variability. It is suggested that the significant physiographic properties manifest their ecological importance primarily through their effects on the soil moisture and temperature regimes within the rooting zone. Of the mineral soil chemical properties, one-half of the variability for pH is explained by the association classification. Of the forest floor properties, 40–50% of the variance estimates for pH, cation exchange capacity, and base saturation are also explained by the association classification. Results for other properties are considerably lower. Whether viewed as categories of a hierarchy or as independent classifications, the alliances and orders appear to bear little or no relationship to most of the attributes included in the study. A possibility for improving the results for the alliances and orders might be to redefine the classes and structure of the system such that environmental characteristics are taken directly into account. However, such a redefinition would result in an increase of the variation within the vegetation parameters.

ACKNOWLEDGMENTS

Special thanks are extended to Dr. Malcolm Greig of the University of British Columbia Computing Centre for his constructive critique of the statistical techniques employed in the paper. Mr. Jace Standish, R.P.F., of Talisman Projects Inc., Vancouver, and Drs. L. M. Lavkulich and T. Ballard of the University of British Columbia Department of Soil Science, all provided worthwhile commentary at various stages of the research.

ANNAS, R. M. and COUPE, R. 1979. Biogeoclimatic zones and subzones of the Cariboo Forest Region. British Columbia Ministry of Forests, Victoria, B.C. 103 pp.

BASCOMB, C. L. 1968. Distribution of pyrophosphate-extractable iron and organic carbon in soils of various groups. J. Soil Sci. **19**: 251–267.

BRAUN-BLANQUET, J. 1964. Pflanzensoziologie, 3rd ed., Springer-Verlag, Vienna.

BREMNER, J. 1965. Total nitrogen. Pages 1171–1175 *in* C. A. Black, ed. Methods of soil analysis. Part 2. Am. Soc. of Agronomy, Madison, Wis.

BUFFO, J., FRITSCHEN, L. J. and MURRAY, J. L. 1972. Direct solar radiation on various slopes from 0 to 60 degrees north latitude. U.S. Dep. Agric. For. Serv. Res. Pap. PNW-42, Portland, Oreg.

CHAPMAN, H. D. 1965. Cation exchange capacity. Pages 891–902. *in* C. A. Black, ed. Methods of soil analysis. Part 2. Am. Soc. of Agronomy, Madison, Wis.

DANIEL, T. W., HELMS, J. A. and BAKER, F. S. 1979. Principles of silviculture. 2nd ed. McGraw-Hill, New York.

DAUBENMIRE, R. F. 1952. Forest vegetation of northern Idaho and adjacent Washington, and its bearing on concepts of vegetation classification. Ecol. Monogr. **22**: 301–330.

EIS, S. 1962. Statistical analysis of several methods for estimation of forest habitats and tree growth near Vancouver, B.C. Faculty of Forestry Bull. 4, Univ. British Columbia, Vancouver, B.C. 76 pp.

GOWER, J. C. 1962. Variance component estimation for unbalanced hierarchical classifications. Biometrics **18**: 537–542.

JACKSON, M. L 1958. Soil chemical analysis. Prentice-Hall, Englewood Cliffs, N.J.

KIMMINS, J. P. 1977. On the need for ecological classification of forests. Pages i–vi. *in* J. P. Kimmins, ed. Proceedings — Ecological classification of forest land in Canada and northwestern U.S.A. Sponsored by Forest Ecology Working Group of the Canadian Institute of Forestry and Centre for Continuing Education, Univ. British Columbia, Vancouver, B.C.

KLINKA, K. 1976. Ecosystem units, their classification, interpretation and mapping in the University of British Columbia Research Forest. Ph.D. Thesis, Microfiche edition, National Library of Canada, Ottawa, Ont.

KLINKA, K., NUSZDORFER, F. and SKODA, L. 1979. Biogeoclimatic units of central and southern Vancouver Island. British Columbia Ministry of Forests, Victoria, B.C. 120 pp.

KLINKA, K. and SKODA, L. 1977. Synecological map of the University of British Columbia Research For. Chron. **53**: 348–352.

KLINKA, K., VAN DER HORST, W. NUSZDORFER, F. and HARDING, R. 1980. An ecosystematic approach to a subunit plan — Koprino River watershed study. British Columbia Ministry of Forests, Victoria,B.C. 118 pp.

KLOOSTERMAN, B. and LAVKULICH, L. M. 1973. Grouping of Lower Fraser Valley soils of British Columbia by numerical methods. Can. J. Soil Sci. **53**: 435–443.

KOJIMA, S. and KRAJINA, V. J. 1975. Vegetation and environment of the coastal western hemlock zone in Strathcona Provincial Park, British Columbia, Canada. Syesis **8** (Suppl. 1): 1–123.

KRAJINA, V. J. 1960. Ecosystem classification. Silva Fennica **105**: 107–110.

KRAJINA, V. J. 1965. Biogeoclimatic zones and classification of British Columbia. Ecol. Western No. Am. **1**: 1–17.

KRAJINA, V. J. 1969. Ecology of forest trees in British Columbia. Ecol. Western No. Am. **2**: 1–147.

KRAJINA, V. J. 1972. Ecosystem perspectives in forestry. The H. R. MacMillan Lectureship in Forestry. Univ. British Columbia, Vancouver, B.C. 31 pp.

KRAJINA, V. J. 1977. On the need for an ecosystem approach to forest land management. Pages 1–11. *in* J. P. Kimmins, ed. Proceedings — Ecological classification of forest land in Canada and northwestern U.S.A. Sponsored by Forest Ecology Working Group of the Canadian Institute of Forestry and Centre for Continuing Education, Univ. British Columbia, Vancouver, B.C.

KUBIENA, W. L. 1958. THE CLASSIFICATION OF SOILS. J. Soil. Sci. **9**: 9–19.

McKEAGUE, J. A. and DAY, J. H. 1966. Dithionite and citrate extractable iron and aluminum as aids in differentiating various classes of soils. Can. J. Soil Sci. **46**: 13–22.

MUELLER-DOMBOIS, D. and ELLENBERG, H. 1974. Aims and methods in vegetation ecology. John Wiley and Sons, Toronto.

PEECH, M. 1965. Hydrogen-ion activity. Pages 914–926. *in* C. A. Black, ed. Methods of soil analysis. Part 2. Am. Soc. of Agronomy, Madison, Wis.

RUSSEL, J. S. and MOORE, A. W. 1968. Comparison of different depth weightings in the numerical analysis of anisotropic soil profile data. Trans. 9th Int Cong. Soil Sci. **4**: 205–213.

SATTERTHWAITE, F. E. 1946. An approximate distribution of estimates of variance components. Biometrics **2**: 110–114.

SNEDECOR, G. W. and COCHRAN, W. G. 1967. Statistical methods. 6th ed. Iowa State Univ. Press, Ames, Iowa.

SOIL SURVEY STAFF. 1975. Soil taxonomy. Agricultural Handbook No. 436. U.S. Dep. Agric. Washington, D.C.

SONDHEIM, M. W. and LAVKULICH, L. M. 1982. Comparison of some podzolic horizons using chemical criteria and the multivariate density equation. Can. J. Soil Sci. **62**: 91–96.

SONDHEIM, M. W., SINGLETON, G. A. and LAVKULICH, L. M. 1981. Numerical analysis of a chronosequence, including the development of a chronofunction. Soil Sci. Soc. Am. J. **45**: 558–563.

SPURR, J. E. and BARNES, B. V. 1980. Forest ecology, 3rd ed. John Wiley, New York. 687 pp.

SUKACHEV, V. A. and DYLIS, N. 1964. Fundamentals of forest biogeocoenology (Translation of Osnovy lesnoi biogeotsenologii by J. M. MacLennan). Oliver and Boyd, Edinburgh and London.

TANSLEY, A. G. 1935. The use and abuse of vegetation concepts and terms. Ecology **16**: 284–307.

WALI, M. K. and KRAJINA, V. J. 1973. Vegetation-environment relationships of some subboreal spruce zone ecosystems in British Columbia. Vegetatio **26**: 237–381.

Part III

Terrain Evaluation

Papers 6 and 7: Introductory Review

6 GRANT
The PUCE Programme for Terrain Evaluation for Engineering Purposes. I. Principles

7 WERMUND et al.
Test of Environmental Geologic Mapping, Southern Edwards Plateau, Southwest Texas

An immediate question arising from this topic is the difference between *land* and *terrain*. As already discussed, land is taken to refer to all the components of the physical environment (climate, relief, soils, hydrology, and vegetation) to the extent to which these may influence human activities on the earth's surface. One interpretation of terrain would be to view it in the same way. However, terrain evaluation is usually taken to have a narrower focus than land evaluation since the emphasis is given to terrain in terms of engineering properties or trafficability. As Benn and Grabau (1968, p. 64) express it: "The function of terrain evaluation is to provide military planners, civil engineers, foresters, and other users with a reliable estimate of the effect of the terrain on their activities or machines." Much of the early research on terrain analysis was directed toward military users; for example, Strahler and Koons (1960) undertook an analysis with the aim of assessing the restrictive forces imposed by terrain in relation to military movement. The methods of terrain analysis as developed at Oxford in the 1960s also had a military objective (Webster and Beckett, 1970). Since then, the scope of terrain analysis has broadened, but overall an engineering or geotechnical focus remains. Thus terrain evaluation should be viewed as a limited part of land evaluation. The tradition that seems to have evolved is that any assessment of land in terms of plant or crop growth is a project in land evaluation and not one in terrain analysis.

The concerns of civil or soils engineers are usually site specific. In other words they have to investigate a small area in order to aid the design of a structure planned for the site. Although they will obviously use experience gained from working on similar sites, their ultimate recommendations will be based on field and laboratory data as derived from the actual site. The objective of terrain analysis is to determine spatial patterns of terrain units that possess similar engineering properties so that predictions can be made over likely engineering hazards. This is not to negate the importance of site investigations, which will always be necessary prior to major engineering projects, but the merit of a preceding terrain analysis is that likely problems can be anticipated at an earlier stage.

These principles are described by Grant in Paper 6. He has done much research in Australia concerned with terrain evaluation for engineering purposes— his Pattern-Unit-Component-Evaluation (PUCE) system. In essence his system can classify and map terrain at four scales according to topography, lithology and tectonic attributes, soils, and vegetation. The details are given in his paper; the other critical set of operations is the mapping of terrain units. Aerial photo-interpretation in combination with field checks is the basis of the method. Emphasis is given to the delimitation of photo-patterns, very similar to the land systems technique but at a more refined level. His four scales are called *province, pattern, terrain unit,* and *terrain component* (see his Table 7). In Table 9 he relates different engineering activities to these terrain classes. This is only possible through the compilation of a data bank on the geotechnical properties of terrain at these different scales. Reference needs to be made to Part II of his report (Grant, 1975) which is a manual of instruction in terrain classification.

An example of the technique is provided by Grant et al. (1981) for the Albury-Wodonga area of New South Wales and Victoria. A great deal of geotechnical data is given on the terrain classes, but of greatest relevance to planners must be the assessments made of each terrain pattern for the following uses:

1. Urban
   a. Residential and associated uses
   b. General commerce, industry, and associated uses
   c. Large-scale and extensive industries
2. Open Urban
   a. Open space uses requiring large, flat surfaces
   b. Major transport corridors
3. Nonurban Open Lands
   a. General rural
   b. Special agriculture
   c. Sylviculture
4. Nature Conservation, Geological Features, Flora, Fauna
5. Aesthetic Evaluation, Unique Scenery, Evocative Qualities

Central to terrain analysis, as in all land evaluation projects, is the need to identify terrain or land mapping units. In Grant's PUCE system, the identification of patterns on aerial photographs is crucial, but there are other possible approaches. One is to use geomorphological mapping whereby data on surface form, superficial deposits, landforms, active geomorphological processes, and hydrological regime are collected by field survey and aerial photo analysis. Systems of geomorphological mapping have been developed by Tricart (1965), Verstappen and Zuidam (1968), and Demek (1972). These systems give details on use of symbols and shading grades for geomorphological features and superficial deposits. The resultant maps are extremely complex and difficult to use by the nonspecialist. Thus priority is given to producing interpretative maps designed to illustrate geomorphological attributes for specific land use issues. In review of geomorphological mapping, Cooke and Doornkamp (1974, p. 353) summarize applications (based on Demek, 1972) as shown in Figure 1. A more

I. *Land Use:*

Territorial planning
Regional area planning
Conservation of the natural and cultural landscape

II. *Agriculture and Forestry*

Potential utilization
Soil conservation
Soil erosion control
Reclamation of destroyed or new areas
Soil reclamation
Drainage and irrigation

III. *Underground and Surface Civil Engineering*

Reconstruction and replanning of settlements, especially of towns
Designing of industrial buildings
Communications (roads, railways, canals, harbours)
Hydro-engineering:
    reservoirs and dams
    regulation of rivers
    natural and artificial waterways
    irrigation canals
    harbour construction
    shore protection
    fishing projects

IV. *Prospecting and Exploitation of Mineral Resources*

Prospecting
Geological survey
Exploitation
Mining
Potential and actual damage done by mining
Reclamation of abandoned open-cast mines
Landslip areas and regions of subsidence due to mining
Reclamation of areas destroyed by mining and waste dumps

Figure 1. Applications of geomorphological mapping in planning and economic development. *(From Cooke and Doornkamp, 1974, p. 353)*

recent review of geomorphological mapping techniques is given by Crofts (1981). One of his examples illustrates how a slope map is helpful to the search for industrial sites connected with the oil industry in northeast Scotland.

There was much enthusiasm for geomorphological mapping in the 1960s and early 1970s. The essential view was that a comprehensive geomorphological inventory could provide the basis for a wide variety of evaluations. Two difficulties can be stressed. First the approach is very much oriented toward features rather than to their intrinsic properties. Thus if a landscape was dominated by long smooth rectilinear slopes, little would be mapped while it would be difficult to include all the symbols in valley floor situations where there was an intricate pattern of landforms. Related to this emphasis on landforms and their genesis is the lack of emphasis on geotechnical properties—the very strength of the Australian PUCE system. The second problem is that the significance of geomorphological features varies according to land use activity. The obvious example to quote is slope value: different slope thresholds must be defined according to land use operation. Thus a geomorphological survey could select slope categories not suited to particular activities. The solution is for specific techniques of geomorphological mapping to be shaped to particular requirements. For example, Brunsden et al. (1975) demonstrate how geomorphological mapping can assist with highway design.

Greater emphasis is given to the geotechnical properties of superficial deposits in systems of engineering geological mapping. In a review of this subject, Strachan and Dearman (1983) distinguish between engineering geological maps used for planning on a regional scale and engineering geological plans produced for individual engineering projects. They demonstrate how the nature and thickness of glaciogenic deposits can be mapped. Of course a geomorphological appreciation of landforms is essential to such mapping. Particular emphasis is given to issues of slope stability caused by geotechnical properties of glacial deposits. The International Association of Engineering Geologists (1982) has produced a system for mapping engineering geology.

The mapping of engineering geology is primarily directed toward the assessment of hazards. This is the subject of the text by Griggs and Gilchrist (1977) who give consideration to such issues as earthquakes, volcanic activity, landslides and mass movement, subsidence, coastal erosion, flooding, groundwater contamination, and waste disposal. The importance of identifying environmental risk is therefore emphasized. Mathewson and Piper (1975) take this a stage further when they translate geological risk into economic terms for a small tract of land in the Padre Island National Seashore, in south Texas. For different coastal landform units (e.g., lagoon, washover zone, wind tidal flats, etc.), they assessed geological-economic values through a combination of cost and risk evaluations. The resultant map displays in a simple way geological hazards to land investors and property developers. In Texas there appears to be a tradition of research in environmental geology geared to resource management and development (Wermund, 1982).

Paper 7 deals with similar issues, also in Texas. The study by Wermund et al. describes in detail a method of environmental geological mapping developed for the southern Edwards Plateau. As the authors state, this area was becoming subject to a range of land use pressures—residential development, recreation, and water supply. The need was to provide planners with data on the environmental geology, the prime aim being to conserve groundwater resources. Environmental units were defined primarily on the basis of geomorphology with extensive use being made of aerial photographs. The resultant units are distinct not only in terms of topography and solid geology, but also with respect to processes and superficial deposits. The section of the paper dealing with geology and land use planning is an excellent demonstration of how an analysis of environmental geology can offer guidance on such important issues as septic tank operation, groundwater pollution, protection of recharge zones, and soil erosion. Such a terrain analysis ought to be of particular value to land use planners.

REFERENCES

Benn, B. O., and W. E. Grabau, 1968, Terrain Evaluation as a Function of User Requirements, in *Land Evaluation,* G. A. Stewart, ed., Macmillan of Australia, South Melbourne, pp. 64-76.

Brunsden, D., J. C. Doornkamp, P. G. Fookes, D. K. C. Jones, and J. M. H. Kelly, 1975, Large Scale Geomorphological Mapping and Highway Engineering Design, *Quart. Jour. of Engineering Geology* **8:**227-253.

Cooke, R. U., and J. C. Doornkamp, 1974, *Geomorphology in Environmental Management,* Oxford University Press, Oxford.

Crofts, R. S., 1981, Mapping Techniques in Geomorphology, in *Geomorphological Techniques,* A. Goudie, ed., George Allen and Unwin, London, pp. 66-75.

Demek, J., ed., 1972, *Manual of Detailed Geomorphological Mapping,* Academia, Prague.

Grant, K., 1975, *The PUCE Programme for Terrain Evaluation for Engineering Purposes. II. Procedures for terrain classification,* Division of Applied Geomechanics Technical Paper No. 19, CSIRO.

Grant, K., T. G. Ferguson, A. A. Finlayson, and B. G. Richards, 1981, *Terrain Analysis, Classification, Assessment and Evaluation for Urban and Regional and Developmental Purposes of the Albury-Wodonga Area, New South Wales and Victoria,* Vol. 1 and 2, Division of Applied Geomechanics Technical Paper No. 30, CSIRO.

Griggs, G. B., and J. A. Gilchrist, 1977, *The Earth and Land Use Planning,* Duxbury Press, North Scituate, Mass.

International Association of Engineering Geologists, 1982, Recommended Symbols for Engineering Geological Maps, Report on the IAEG Commission on Engineering Geological Maps, *Bull. of the International Assoc. of Engineering Geologists* **24.**

Mathewson, C. C., and D. P. Piper, 1975, Mapping the Physical Environment in Economic Terms, *Geology* **3:**627-629.

Strachan, A., and W. R. Dearman, 1983, Engineering Geological Mapping in Glaciated Terrain, in *Glacial Geology,* N. Eyles, ed., Pergamon Press, Oxford, 229-246.

Strahler, A. N., and D. Koons, 1960, *Objective and Quantitative Field Methods of Terrain Analysis,* Final Report of Project NR 387-021, Contract No. 266-50 O.N.R., Department of Geology, Columbia University, New York.

Tricart, J., 1965, *Principles et Methodes de la Geomorphologie,* Masson, Paris.

Verstappen, H. Th., and R. A. van Zuidam, 1968, I.T. C. System of Geomorphological Survey, *I. T.C. Textbook of Photo-Interpretation,* Ch. VII.2, Delft.

Webster, R., and P. H. T. Beckett, 1970, Terrain Classification and Evaluation Using Air Photography: A Review of Recent Work at Oxford, *Photogrammetria* **26:**51-75.

Wermund, E. G., 1982, Texas Geology Translated to Land and Water Resources Mapping for Planning Development of Mineral and Energy Resources, *Proceedings of the First Internat. Symposium on Soil, Geology and Landforms,* Bangkok, G4, pp.1-45.

6: THE PUCE PROGRAMME FOR TERRAIN EVALUATION FOR ENGINEERING PURPOSES. I. PRINCIPLES

K. Grant*

I. Introduction

The PUCE (Pattern–Unit–Component–Evaluation) Programme of terrain evaluation for engineering purposes has been developed in Australia in an attempt to rationalize certain procedures for the gathering and processing of engineering information for the pre-planning, planning, and project stages of civil engineering works. It also provides a method for storing engineering information for retrieval for future use.

Terrain evaluation does not aim to answer specific questions at specific sites; rather it gives a probability of the occurrence of particular sets of conditions at particular sites. Terrain evaluation does not supersede normal site investigation; rather it provides site investigation with a rational basis upon which to proceed.

Terrain evaluation in one form or another has been in use for many years, but no standard system has hitherto evolved. The history of the subject was reviewed by Aitchison and Grant (1968*a*).

In an endeavour to standardize procedures, a Terrain Evaluation System for Engineering (Grant 1968) was prepared as a guide for engineers contemplating adopting terrain evaluation procedures. The concepts and definitions set out in that publication have now been refined and extended. Detailed procedures for conducting various aspects of terrain evaluation have been standardized.

The procedures of terrain evaluation are now being used by many engineers in Australia. This treatise, which supersedes the earlier publication, has been prepared firstly to guide engineers in the use of terrain evaluation procedures and secondly to coordinate and standardize procedures in use in the interests of effective communication of information between engineers and between generations of engineers.

The concept of this treatise is of a series of parts each dealing with some aspect of terrain evaluation. Part I will deal with the principles of terrain evaluation. Part II will deal with procedures to be followed for terrain classification necessary as a preliminary to engineering evaluation.

Parts that may be published later would deal with procedures for the engineering evaluation of the classified terrain and for the processing, including collating, storing, and retrieving, of engineering information collected in earlier stages of the evaluation process.

II. The Analysis of Terrain

Evaluation of terrain for any given purpose depends upon the ability to analyse terrain and, as a result of the analyses, to subdivide it into classes in which the members

* Division of Applied Geomechanics, CSIRO, P.O. Box 54, Mount Waverley, Vic. 3149.

of each class are essentially homogeneous with respect to the properties of the critical natural terrain attributes that require evaluation for the purpose in hand. Prominent among these attributes are the natural materials, such as soil and rock that form the surface and subsurface layers, and the three-dimensional profile, i.e. the shape of the surface, the vegetation that grows in the surface soil, and the use to which the particular land is presently put.

Whilst some of these attributes can be considered to be independent variables, others cannot. For instance, underlying lithology and rock structure are basic and independent of all other attributes, but soil developed upon the rock and derived from this rock parent material by weathering, i.e. by climatic interactions, cannot be considered to be an independent variable. Nor can topography be considered as an independent variable, for it is formed by interaction between geologic and climatic factors. Similarly vegetation and land use, both of which depend, at least to some extent, upon the nature of the soil and on climatic influences, are not completely independent variables.

The overall nature of each terrain attribute can be considered as the resultant of the summation of all its properties. (Of course, in any process of terrain evaluation, not all the properties of all terrain attributes need be evaluated; indeed, only those properties pertinent to the purpose in hand require evaluation.) Again, as for terrain as a whole, whilst some of these properties of each terrain attribute are independent variables, others are not. For example, whilst the size of the particles that comprise the soil can be regarded as independent, the amount of water in the soil is not only dependent upon ambient climatic influences and the capacity of the soil to absorb and hold water, i.e. the porosity and capillarity of the soil, but also upon the capacity of plants growing in the soil to remove water (evapotranspiration). The final amount of water in the soil is the resultant of the interaction of all these variables.

Similarly, some properties both of terrain and of its attributes may vary continuously, but others vary discontinuously. Again, some may vary continuously in one circumstance but discontinuously in another. For instance, continuous variation in topography is exemplified by a surface undulating in such a manner that the undulations gradually increase in wavelength and/or amplitude, and in a soil by a gradational soil profile in which the clay content increases gradually with depth. Obvious types of discontinuous variation occur in topography where a plateau surface which in itself may show continuous variation gives way abruptly to an escarpment and in stratified soils where a layer of sand may be overlain abruptly by a layer of clay; both layers of this soil may contain elements that vary continuously.

Also, whilst many of the properties of both terrain and its attributes can be measured quantitatively, others can be conveyed only in descriptive terms, i.e. qualitatively. For instance, it is a relatively simple task to measure the configuration of the ground surface or the strength of materials occurring at or near the surface, but it is a much more difficult task to express quantitatively the composition of a complete soil profile or the vegetation association or formation that grows in surface soil. Indeed, as Aitchison (1968) has pointed out, some terrain properties may be incapable of quantitative expression.

Thus, terrain can be considered as the complex variable that may vary in both a continuous and a discontinuous manner on both the macro- and micro-scales, formed as the resultant of the summation of terms that represent all the properties and inter-actions between properties of all terrain attributes. Some of the terms representing these properties can be expressed quantitatively, but some are difficult, if not impossible, to quantify. These can be expressed in a qualitative manner only. Whilst each of the terms representing attribute properties may be separately evaluated, either quantitatively or qualitatively, the expression representing the attributes and the more complex expression representing terrain must also be evaluated with points of discon-tinuity marked and the pattern of continuous variation resolved.

The terrain analysis may be made by the solution of a mathematical model formulated as above, but there are obvious inherent difficulties firstly in formulating some of the terms and secondly in solving the model to produce the required analysis. More conventionally, the analysis may be made in a less rigorous manner by defining naturalistic terrain classes using criteria based upon recognizable changes in properties of the terrain attributes. A terrain classification can then be made in a semi-quantitative manner with a map produced to relate class descriptions to the ground.

Terrain can be considered to be the product of the interaction of geology and climate with time as the operator. A logical extension of this proposition is "products such as terrain with all its attributes that have evolved from similar starting materials through a similar geologic process possess similar properties". This principle forms the basis of a practical system of terrain classification upon which can be erected a scheme for evaluating the engineering properties of any given area of terrain at any desired level for any particular engineering purpose.

III. TERRAIN CLASSIFICATION IN THE PUCE PROGRAMME FOR TERRAIN EVALUATION

The PUCE (Pattern–Unit–Component–Evaluation) Programme for terrain evaluation was proposed by Aitchison and Grant (1967) and subsequently elaborated in detail by Grant (1968). The Programme requires that the terrain of an area in which civil engineering work is projected should be classified in accordance with a system defined upon naturalistic principles as enunciated previously. The terrain classification system adopted for the Programme uses as criteria only easily recognizable features of the landscape. No special skills are required for its implementation.

The basis of the terrain classification system is that any area of land can be defined in terms of its topography, i.e. slope characteristics, underlying lithologic and structural (tectonic) characteristics, and soil and vegetation characteristics; by defining allowable limits of variation in these terrain characteristics at suitable significant levels, valid naturalistic terrain classes may be erected.

The system operates at four levels of generalization, viz. terrain component, terrain unit, terrain pattern, and province. The terrain component can be defined uniquely. The terrain unit can then be defined as the limited association of terrain components that form recognizable, distinctive terrain features and the terrain pattern can be defined as the limited association of terrain units that form recognizable, dis-tinctive landscapes. The province can be defined as the limited association of terrain patterns that are underlain by a constant suite of rocks of a defined kind.

In this hierarchical system of terrain classification, each member of each class is composed of a limited number of repetitive members of the preceding class in a constant form of association, i.e. a province consists of a constant repetitive association of terrain patterns, a terrain pattern consists of a constant repetitive association of terrain units, and a terrain unit consists of a constant repetitive association of terrain components. However, the limited number of members of one class associated to form a member of the next highest class in the hierarchy may be as low as one, i.e. for some areas, two adjacent members of the hierarchy may be coincident.

```
Province - Constant  │ geology at group level
                     │ association of terrain patterns

■  Terrain Pattern - Landscape within province
                     Constant association of terrain units
                     (background, foreground)

●  Terrain Unit - Physiographic feature of landscape
                  Constant association of terrain components

▼  Terrain Component - Constant │ slope type
                               │ lithology
                               │ soil (USC and PPF)
                               │ vegetation formation
```

Fig. 1.—Terrain classification.

In the definition of the terrain classes present, climate has not been included among the criteria for the recognition of members of each class, because changes in climate will be reflected in changes in topography, soil, and vegetation characteristics. The inclusion of these soil and vegetation characteristics among the criteria for recognition of the members of the classes ensures that the effects of different climates cannot be ignored when the terrain classification is established.

The relationship between the members of this hierarchical classification is depicted in Figure 1.

(a) Definition of the Terrain Classes

The definition of the terrain component which is basic to the definition of all other terrain classes depends upon the definition of critical slope, rock, soil, and vegetation characteristics.

The definition of slopes can be regarded as a problem in three-dimensional geometry. As such, any slope can be referred to a set of three axes in space. Because terrain is, in general, of low symmetry, these axes may not be orthogonal. They can be defined in such a way that two axes are at right angles, but the third axis may be oblique, i.e. terrain may possess symmetry as low as monoclinic, although in some instances higher symmetry is possible./ One axis can be regarded as horizontal. The other two axes may be defined as follows:

"The major axis of a slope can be regarded as the line on the surface, ignoring minor irregularities, that forms the intersection of the surface and a plane normal to the surface passing through the highest and lowest points of the particular slope."

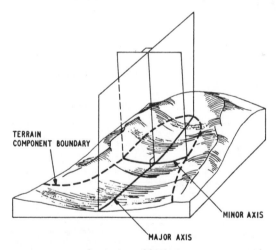

Fig. 2.–Diagrammatic representation of major and minor axes of a slope.

"The minor axis of a slope may be regarded as the line of maximum extent on the surface, ignoring minor irregularities, that forms the intersection of the surface and a plane cutting both the surface and the major axis of the slope at right angles at the point of intersection. It should be noted that the plane of the minor axis is at right angles to the surface and is not necessarily vertical." The major and minor axes of a slope are depicted diagrammatically in Figure 2.

With reference to the major and the minor axes, three types of slopes can be recognized, viz. concave, convex, and planar. Concave and convex slopes are of curved section.

TABLE 1 UNIFIED SOIL CLASSIFICATION,

Field identification procedures (Excluding particles larger than 3 inches and basing fractions on estimated weights)					Group symbols [1]
Coarse grained soils — More than half of material is *larger* than No. 200 sieve size [2] (The No. 200 sieve size is about the smallest particle visible to the naked eye)	Gravels — More than half of coarse fraction is larger than No. 4 sieve size (For visual classifications, the ¼″ size may be used as equivalent to the No. 4 sieve size)	Clean gravels (Little or no fines)	Wide range in grain size and substantial amounts of all intermediate particle sizes		GW
			Predominantly one size or a range of sizes with some intermediate sizes missing		GP
		Gravels with fines (Appreciable amount of fines)	Non-plastic fines (for identification procedures see ML below)		GM
			Plastic fines (for identification procedures see CL below)		GC
	Sands — More than half of coarse fraction is smaller than No. 4 sieve size	Clean sands (Little or no fines)	Wide range in grain sizes and substantial amounts of all intermediate particle sizes		SW
			Predominantly one size or a range of sizes with some intermediate sizes missing		SP
		Sands with fines (Appreciable amount of fines)	Non-plastic fines (for identification procedures see ML below)		SM
			Plastic fines (for identification procedures see CL below)		SC
Fine grained soils — More than half of material is *smaller* than No. 200 sieve size		Identification procedures on fraction smaller than No. 40 sieve size			
	Silts and clays Liquid limit less than 50	Dry strength (crushing characteristics)	Dilatancy (reaction to shaking)	Toughness (consistency near plastic limit)	
		None to slight	Quick to slow	None	ML
		Medium to high	None to very slow	Medium	CL
		Slight to medium	Slow	Slight	OL
	Silts and clays Liquid limit greater than 50	Slight to medium	Slow to none	Slight to medium	MH
		High to very high	None	High	CH
		Medium to high	None to very slow	Slight to medium	OH
Highly organic soils		Readily identified by color, odor, spongy feel and frequently by fibrous texture			Pt

[1] *Boundary classifications:*– Soils possessing characteristics of two groups are designated by
[2] All sieve sizes on this chart are U.S. standard.

INCLUDING IDENTIFICATION AND DESCRIPTION

Typical names	Laboratory classification criteria
Well graded gravels, gravel-sand mixtures; little or no fines	$C_u = \dfrac{D_{60}}{D_{10}}$ Greater than 4 $\quad$ $C_c = \dfrac{(D_{30})^2}{D_{10} \times D_{60}}$ Between one and 3
Poorly graded gravels, gravel-sand mixtures; little or no fines	Not meeting all gradation requirements for GW
Silty gravels, poorly graded gravel-sand-silt mixtures	Atterberg limits below "A" line, or PI less than 4 / Above "A" line with PI between 4 and 7 are *borderline* cases requiring use of dual symbols
Clayey gravels, poorly graded gravel-sand-clay mixtures	Atterberg limits above "A" line with PI greater than 7
Well graded sands, gravelly sands; little or no fines	$C_u = \dfrac{D_{60}}{D_{10}}$ Greater than 6 $\quad$ $C_c = \dfrac{(D_{30})^2}{D_{10} \times D_{60}}$ Between one and 3
Poorly graded sands, gravelly sands; little or no fines	Not meeting all gradation requirements for SW
Silty sands, poorly graded sand-silt mixtures	Atterberg limits below "A" line, or PI less than 4 / Above "A" line with PI between 4 and 7 are *borderline* cases requiring use of dual symbols
Clayey sands, poorly graded sand-clay mixtures	Atterberg limits above "A" line with PI greater than 7

The following legends run vertically in the central column of the table:

- Use grain size curve in identifying the fractions as given under field identification
- Determine percentages of gravel and sand from grain size curve. Depending on percentage of fines (fraction smaller than No. 200 sieve size) coarse grained soils are classified as follows:—
  - Less than 5% — GW, GP, SW, SP,
  - More than 12% — GM, GC, SM, SC,
  - 5% to 12% — *Borderline* cases requiring use of dual symbols

Typical names (fine grained soils)
Inorganic silts and very fine sands, rock flour, silty or clayey fine sands with slight plasticity
Inorganic clays of low to medium plasticity, gravelly clays, sandy clays, silty clays, lean clays
Organic silts and organic silt-clays of low plasticity
Inorganic silts, micaceous or diatomaceous fine sandy or silty soils, elastic silts
Inorganic clays of high plasticity, fat clays
Organic clays of medium to high plasticity
Peat and other highly organic soils

Plasticity chart

For laboratory classifications of fine grained soils

combinations of group symbols. For example GW-GC, well graded gravel-sand mixture with clay binder.

Any area of land can be regarded as being homogeneous with respect to slope when the slopes in section, measured along both the major and minor axes, each independently retain constant rates of change of curvature; rates of change of curvature of planar slopes and slopes of circular section are, of course, zero.

Lithology requires little definition. In hard rock areas, it will suffice for terrain evaluation for engineering purposes to consider sedimentary rocks as conglomerate, sandstone, shale, or limestone, metamorphic rocks as phyllite, schist, gneiss, hornfels, quartzite, or serpentine, granitic rocks as granite, granodiorite, diorite, or gabbro, and volcanic and hypabyssal rocks as rhyolite, dacite, andesite, or basalt (dolerite). In areas where these underlying rocks are massive, no problem in defining homogeneity arises; in other areas, where sedimentary rocks are thinly bedded, the overall combined lithology can be taken as the basis of the definition of homogeneity, e.g. for sandstone and shale interbeds, the combined lithology is sandstone, shale. In many areas, terrain is developed on soft deposits such as alluvium, colluvium, or aeolian material; homogeneous lithology can then be considered as sand, silt, clay, or gravel, or as a combination of these materials; if they are mixed, then such terms as sandy clay are appropriate or if they are stratified, terms such as sand and clay (stratified) can be used.

Soil is a material variable with respect to both areal and vertical components. For the purposes of terrain definition, limits must be placed upon the amount of variability in texture allowed in the areal sense and upon the amount and manner of textural variability in the vertical sense. The Unified Soil Classification system as in Table 1 (U.S. Department of the Interior 1963) defines such textural limits for each layer in a soil profile whilst Northcote (1971) has devised a system of soil classification (for all soils other than those alluvially stratified) that includes a definition of intervals for the manner of textural variation vertically in a soil profile. Therefore, for terrain evaluation for engineering purposes, provided that the soil is not alluvially stratified, a soil may be regarded as sensibly homogeneous if the textural properties of each layer in the soil profile fall within one class in the Unified Soil Classification system and the manner of textural change in the profile falls within one subdivision of the primary profile form (Northcote 1971). For alluvial or aeolian stratified soils a sufficient criterion is that each layer in the soil must fall within one class of the Unified Soil Classification system and that it is stated that the soil is alluvially or aeolianly stratified.

Vegetation also presents a problem in defining limits of allowable variation. Rarely does any area carry a vegetation community that is unispecific. Usually there is present a number of genera and species including trees, shrubs, grasses, and forbs. In the botanical sense, a vegetation association (Anon. 1968) refers to a restricted vegetation structural unit that may contain a diversity of genera and species, but such genera and species occur in a community that has a distinct relationship within itself and also a relationship to its immediate surroundings.

A vegetation association can therefore be regarded as sensibly homogeneous and an area containing such an association as being homogeneous with respect to vegetation.

(i) Terrain Component

A terrain component, apart from microtopography and certain other features defined below, has along each of a pair of lines parallel to the major and minor axes of the slope a constant rate of change of curvature always in the same sense, i.e. either convex or concave but not concavo-convex.

It has a constant underlying lithology in a constant structural environment.

It has a consistent association of soils such that each layer of the soil can be expressed within one class in the Unified Soil Classification (USC) system (Table 1) and the whole soil profile within one class of a subdivision of the primary profile form (Northcote 1971) (except alluvially or aeolianly stratified soils which are expressed in terms of the Unified Soil Classification only).

It has a constant vegetation association, i.e. while more than one species or genus may be present, the species or genera always occur in the same spatial relationship to each other and there is no discontinuity in their occurrence.

Features not to be considered when rate of change of slope is determined are as follows:

(1) Microtopography which consists of small-scale natural topographic features, i.e. an inherent part of the particular piece of landscape and not of foreign material introduced accidentally into that particular piece of landscape. It is considered arbitrarily that any such topographic feature with a relief amplitude of not more than 1 metre and an areal extent of not more than 100 square metres falls into this category.

(2) Rounded, angular, or irregular rock outcrop. Such outcrop may be of any size, but mostly will not be of large dimensions.

(3) Elements such as rocks, boulders, cobbles, etc., derived from another part of the general landscape and introduced accidentally into the particular piece of landscape. Such elements may be of any size, but mostly they will not be of large dimensions.

While elements of microtopography, rock outcrop, or accidental introduction, as defined above, are specifically excluded from slope considerations in the recognition of terrain components, they must enter into the descriptive phase of terrain component recognition as surface features. In these circumstances, a terrain component with any of these features will be essentially different from one similar in all other respects but containing either no, or different, surface features.

The exclusion of these features from slope considerations is based upon the principle that in any form of terrain classification that is to be workable, arbitrary lower limits must be placed upon the amount of variation allowed in any of the recognition criteria for each class. If all possible variations on a continuously varying medium are considered separately, an infinite number of varieties is possible; any system so based must be unworkable.

(ii) *Terrain Unit*

A terrain unit can be defined as the area covered by a single land form feature which has a characteristic soil association and a characteristic natural vegetation formation.

The terrain unit so defined can be regarded as being composed of a limited number of terrain components which always recur in the same spatial relationships within the terrain unit. The slopes and soil and vegetation characteristics of the terrain unit will be those produced by a synthesis of those of the terrain components associated to form the terrain unit.

Topographically, the terrain unit will fall into classes and, within each class, will have a characteristic association of slopes and a consistent local relief amplitude. The classes so far recognized are listed as follows, but the list is not exhaustive.

(1) Surfaces, flat or with varying degrees of undulation, i.e. undissected, dissected, and/or eroded. These surfaces are not necessarily tied to specific erosional or depositional surfaces, i.e. the same terrain unit may occur on more than one erosional or depositional surface; such occurrences will be separated by a terrain unit classified under (2).

(2) Slopes between surfaces as in (1); gentle, steep, or escarpment-like.

(3) Isolated hills, ridges, etc. except those with flat tops; in the latter case the flat tops and surrounding slopes have been given independent terrain unit status in accordance with (1) and (2) respectively.

(4) Drainage lines, lakes, etc.

The characteristic soil association of the terrain unit will be dominated by one of the following textural types:

Rock outcrop, pockets of shallow soil or gravel	Sand over clay soils (G)
Clay soils (Ug)*	Sand over clay soils (D)
Clay soils (U or G)	Sandy soils (U or G)
Clay soils (D)	Stratified soils
Silty soils	Organic soils

The characteristic vegetation formation will be dominated by one of the following vegetation classes:

Bare, sparse grass, occasional tree or shrub	Woodland
Grassland	Forest
Shrubland	Rain forest
Open woodland	Fresh-water swamp forest
Savannah woodland	Salt-water swamp forest

(iii) *Terrain Pattern*

A terrain pattern can be defined as an area containing a recurring topography, soil associations and natural vegetation formations. A terrain pattern has a constant local relief amplitude, a constant drainage pattern and a constant drainage density. The terrain pattern can be regarded as being composed of a limited number of recurring terrain units always associated in the same spatial relationship, and should be coincident with the area represented by a distinctive pattern or an aerial photograph of suitable scale.

Criteria for the delineation and recognition of terrain pattern boundaries are:

(1) The continuous terrain unit or group of terrain units changes.

(2) Terrain units included within the continuous terrain unit or group of terrain units change.

(3) The continuous terrain unit or group of units and included terrain units do not change, but relative dominance of continuous and included terrain units changes.

(4) Type or density of the drainage net changes significantly.

(5) Local relief amplitude changes significantly.

(iv) *Province*

A province can be defined as an area of *constant geology* at the group level (Anon. 1973), and is composed of a limited number of recurring terrain patterns always associated in the same spatial relationship.

* The symbols refer to the classification system used in the 'Atlas of Australian Soils' (Northcote, 1971).

(b) *Systematic Nomenclature of Terrain Classes*

To be effective, any system of classification must incorporate a scheme of nomenclature whereby each member of each class can be uniquely differentiated from all other members of the same or other classes. The PUCE Programme uses a scheme of decimal numerical nomenclature to achieve this purpose. The use of such a scheme has the advantage that it is simple to operate, does not depend upon a knowledge of local names, and is completely compatible with a digital computer as a storage and retrieval medium.

Whilst in Section III(*a*) the definition of the terrain component was basic for the definition of the other classes, it is usually convenient to refer to a piece of terrain firstly as a member of a province, secondly as a member of a terrain pattern class within that province, thirdly as a member of a terrain unit class within that terrain pattern, and fourthly as a member of a terrain component class within that terrain unit. Therefore the decimal numerical nomenclature will be given in that order, i.e. province, terrain pattern, terrain unit, terrain component, rather than in the order of definitions.

(i) *Provinces*

Provinces are enumerated firstly on a rock age basis (2 digits) and secondly serially in order of recognition (3 digits) as shown in Table 2.

TABLE 2

NUMERICAL SYSTEM OF NOMENCLATURE – PROVINCES

Archaean	1	General	10
Proterozoic	2	General	20
		Lower	21
		Middle	22
		Upper	23
Palaeozoic	3	General	30
		Cambrian	31
		Ordovician	32
		Silurian	33
		Devonian	34
		Carboniferous	35
		Permian	36
Mesozoic	4	General	40
		Triassic	41
		Jurassic	42
		Cretaceous	43
Cainozoic	5	General	50
		Tertiary	51
		Quaternary	52

Provinces within each age class above are then numbered serially in numerical order as encountered, using a three-digit system which allows 999 provinces per system; e.g. the Brighton Group, which occupies an area near Melbourne, Victoria, is Tertiary in age and is the ninth Tertiary province recognized in Australia; therefore it is numbered as Province 51.009.

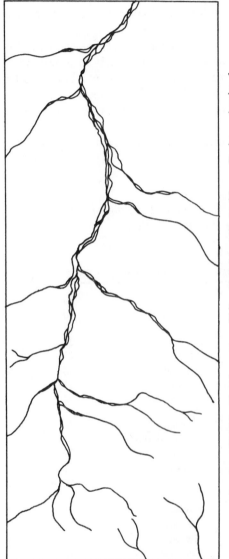

Province 43.001.   Terrain pattern 01/3.   Relief amplitude 15 m.   Drainage density 1.

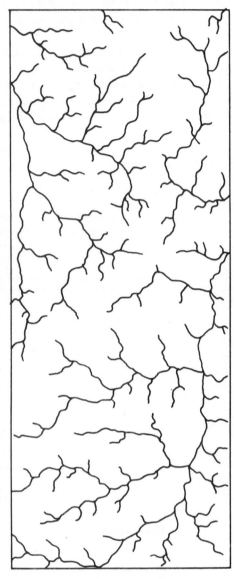

Province 42.002.   Terrain pattern 34.   Relief amplitude 150 m.   Drainage density 4.

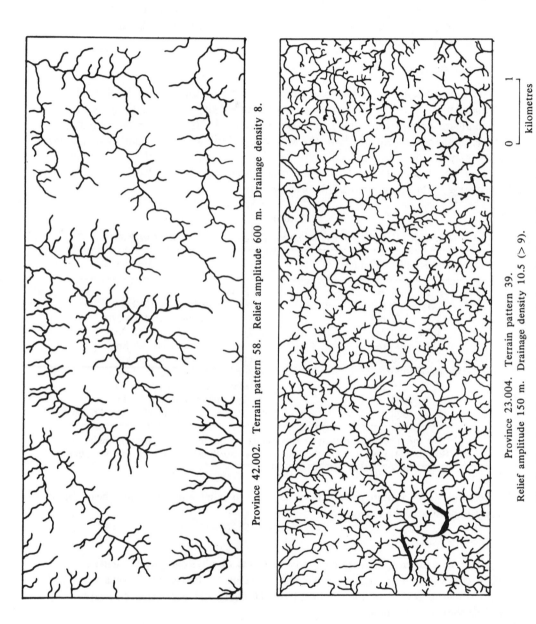

Province 42.002. Terrain pattern 58. Relief amplitude 600 m. Drainage density 8.

Province 23.004. Terrain pattern 39.
Relief amplitude 150 m. Drainage density 10.5 (> 9).

Fig. 3.—Terrain pattern numbering – relief amplitude – drainage density.

0   1
kilometres

It is recognized that a geological group is defined as a stratigraphic, not time, unit (Anon, 1973). However, most geological groups fall predominantly into one geological system, although a system, of course, may consist of more than one geological group. For convenience in the PUCE Programme the numerical nomenclature of groups is in accordance with the age of the predominant system in which they fall. Two or more groups falling into the one system are differentiated by the use of the three-digit serial numbers.

(ii) *Terrain Patterns*

Terrain patterns are enumerated firstly in terms of the greatest local relief amplitude that occurs with the terrain pattern (one digit) and secondly in terms of its mean drainage density (one digit) as shown in Table 3. If two or more terrain patterns in the same province have the same local relief amplitude and mean drainage density they are differentiated serially in order of recognition by the use of a third digit separated from the first two digits by a stroke, e.g. Terrain Pattern 01; Terrain Pattern 01/2; Terrain Pattern 01/3; etc.

TABLE 3

NUMERICAL SYSTEM OF NOMENCLATURE – TERRAIN PATTERNS

Greatest local relief amplitude	Mean drainage density*
0 To 15 m	0 No surface drainage
1 To 30 m	1 One stream-line per 1.6 km
2 To 75 m	2 Two stream-lines per 1.6 km
3 To 150 m	3 Three stream-lines per 1.6 km
4 To 300 m	4 Four stream-lines per 1.6 km
5 To 600 m	5 Five stream-lines per 1.6 km
6 To 1200 m	6 Six stream-lines per 1.6 km
7 To 2400 m	7 Seven stream-lines per 1.6 km
8 To 3600 m	8 Eight stream-lines per 1.6 km
9 > 3600 m	9 Nine or more stream-lines per 1.6 km

*The mean drainage density is the average of the number of stream-lines of any order (Horton 1945) per 1.6 km that intersect (*a*) north–south, and (*b*) east–west lines of an appropriately oriented orthogonal grid.

The relationship of terrain pattern nomenclature to relief amplitude and mean drainage density is illustrated in Figure 3.

(iii) *Terrain Units*

Terrain units are enumerated firstly in terms of physiography (1 digit) and surface configuration (1 digit) and secondly in terms of texture and primary profile form (Northcote 1971) of the dominant soil (1 digit), and vegetation association (1 digit) as shown in Table 4.

(iv) *Terrain Components*

Terrain components are enumerated in terms of slopes (3 digits), soil profile (2 digits), land use or surface cover (whichever is applicable) (1 digit), and vegetation association (2 digits), as shown in Table 5.

TABLE 4

NUMERICAL SYSTEM OF NOMENCLATURE – TERRAIN UNITS

Topography	Soils dominantly	Vegetation dominantly
1. Flat to undulating or sloping smooth surfaces usually with relatively deep soil	0. Rock outcrop, pockets shallow soil and gravel	0. Bare, sparse grass, occasional tree or shrub
1.1 Flat surface	1. Clay soils (Ug)	1. Grassland
1.2 Gently undulating surface (to 2°)	2. Clay soils (U or G)	2. Shrubland
1.3 Undulating surface (to 5°)	3. Clay soils (D)	3. Open woodland
1.4 Strongly undulating surface (to 10°)	4. Silty soils	4. Savannah woodland
1.5 Sloping surface (to 2°)	5. Sand over clay soils (G)	5. Woodland
1.6 Sloping surface (to >2°)	6. Sand over clay soils (D)	6. Forest
1.7 Undulating sloping surface	7. Sandy soils (U or G)	7. Rain forest
1.8 Strongly undulating surface (to >10°)	8. Stratified soils	8. Fresh-water swamp forest
	9. Organic soils	9. Salt-water swamp forest
2. Irregular subhorizontal to undulating eroded surfaces, usually with rock outcrop or shallow soil		
2.1 Flat surface		
2.2 Eroded surface		
2.3 Benched surface		
2.4 Undulating eroded surface		
2.5 Strongly undulating eroded surface		
2.6 Moderately dissected surface		
2.7 Moderately dissected eroded surface		
2.8 Strongly dissected surface		
2.9 Strongly dissected strongly eroded surface		
3. Slopes, including escarpments, between surfaces		
3.1 Smooth steep slope		
3.2 Rough rocky steep slope		
3.3 Gentle slope		
3.4 Dissected slope (to 5°)		
3.5 Dissected slope (to 10°)		
3.6 Benched slope		
3.7 Dissected slope (to >10°)		
4. Isolated hills		
4.1 Conical hill including pap and butte		
4.2 Rounded hill		
4.3 Complex hill		
4.4 Razor-backed hill		
4.6 Steep knoll, mamelon, volcanic plug		
4.7 Small volcanic vent		
4.8 Elongated rounded hill		
4.9 Dissected hill		

TABLE 4 (*Continued*)

Topography

5. Isolated ridges, etc.
5.1 Low ridge (to 5° slope)
5.2 Dissected ridge
5.3 Strongly dissected ridge
5.4 Rough irregular ridge
5.5 Linear strike ridge
5.6 Razor-back ridge
5.7 Linear ridge (other than strike ridge)
5.9 Sand ridge

6. Irregular eroded sloping surfaces, usually
   with rock outcrop or shallow soil
6.2 Eroded sloping surface
6.3 Undulating eroded sloping surface
6.5 Undulating dissected eroded sloping surface

7. Mountains
7.3 Moderately dissected mountain
7.8 Heavily dissected mountain

8. Not allocated

9. Drainage systems
9.1 Major stream channel
9.2 Minor stream channel
9.3 Braided stream channel system
9.4 Incised gully, ravine, etc.
9.5 Lake, lagoon, billabong
9.6 Reticulated stream channel system (flood-out)
9.7 Tidal channel
9.8 Swamp or marsh
9.9 Sink hole

Example.—An area of gently undulating surface to 2° slope with clay soils (Ug) and grassland is terrain unit 1.2.11

NOTE

Land use is used as a criterion for terrain component definition in developed areas; surface cover is similarly used in underdeveloped areas that are either essentially unused or used for pastoral purposes only.

(v) *Example of Numerical Terrain Classification*

Province	Terrain pattern	Terrain unit	Terrain component
52.009	22/2	1.7.11	431 032 01

means

Province	52	Quaternary
	.009	Ninth recognized province of Quaternary age
Terrain pattern	2	Relief amplitude to 75 m
	2	Drainage density 2 stream-lines per 1.6 km
	/2	Second recognized terrain pattern with the above parameters

TABLE 5

NUMERICAL SYSTEM OF NOMENCLATURE – TERRAIN COMPONENTS

	A	B	C	D	E	F	G	H
Slope profile								
Maximum magnitude parallel to major axis								
Maximum magnitude parallel to minor axis								
Soil profile								
Land use or surface cover								
Vegetation association								

A Slope profile

	Parallel to	
	major axis	minor axis
1	Planar	Planar
2	Planar	Concave
3	Planar	Convex
4	Concave	Planar
5	Concave	Concave
6	Concave	Convex
7	Convex	Planar
8	Convex	Concave
9	Convex	Convex

B C Slope – Maximum magnitude parallel to major axis or minor axis

0	Flat
1	1°
2	2°
3	5°
4	10°
5	20°
6	40°
7	60°
8	$> 60°$
9	Vertical

D E Soil profile – Consistent within one class of the Unified Soil Classification and one sub-division of the primary profile form (Northcote 1971) – Numbered serially within each province

F Land use or surface cover where applicable

Land use		Surface cover	
0	Unused	0	Not present
1	Forestry	1	Silcrete, rounded
2	Pasture	2	Silcrete, angular
3	Agriculture	3	Ironstone, rounded
4	Recreation	4	Ironstone, platy
5	Urban development	5	Porcellanite
6		6	Quartzite
7		7	Calcrete
8		8	Salt
9		9	Rock outcrop and rubble of appropriate lithology

G H Vegetation association – Numbered serially within each province

Terrain unit	1.7	Undulating sloping surface
	.1	Clay soils (Ug)
	.1	Grassland
Terrain component	4	Slopes — major axis concave, minor axis planar
	3	— major axis to 5°
	1	— minor axis to 1°
	03	Soil profile (serial within province)
	2	Land use — pasture
	01	Vegetation (serial within province)

An example of the classification into terrain patterns, terrain units, and terrain components of terrain consisting of a single province is illustrated in Appendix VII of Part II of this treatise.

(c) Measurement of Terrain Parameters Relevant to the Terrain Classes

In order to ensure that members of the terrain classes are essentially homogeneous with respect to the physical feature of the terrain it is necessary to measure a number of terrain parameters. These parameters include dimensions of areas represented by members of the terrain classes, the relief amplitude and slopes, and stream and vegetation densities. Because terrain varies continuously a large array of values for these parameters is possible. To avoid such an array, the admissible values of these parameters in the PUCE Programme have been classified using what are considered to be significant intervals, as shown in Table 6.

IV. THE IMPLEMENTATION OF THE PUCE PROGRAMME

The PUCE Programme is implemented first by classification of the relevant terrain, followed by the evaluation for the required purpose of each member of each known class recognized. Lastly all information obtained during the classification and evaluation stages may be processed and stored for future use.

(a) Classifying the Terrain

In the terrain classification stage, the PUCE Programme is implemented by a process of aerial photograph interpretation (Grant 1971) followed by a period of field checking with consequent amendment of the interpretation to ensure that the terrain concerned has been analysed and interpreted truly and accurately.

When the terrain classes as defined in Section III(a) above are derived by the interpretation of aerial photographs alone without ground checking, a different nomenclature is used because the classes are those of pattern images on aerial photographs. These classes are not necessarily the same as classes of terrain as seen on the ground.

A land form component is the photo-interpretive equivalent of a terrain component. A land form unit is the photo-interpretive equivalent of a terrain unit. A photo-pattern is the photo-interpretive equivalent of a terrain pattern.

For land form unit and photo-pattern identification in the photograph interpretation stage, relatively small-scale aerial photographs are examined minutely in order to recognize the land form units, i.e. the photographic equivalents of terrain units. The land form units are described as far as possible by the interpretive process in terms of

TABLE 6

TERRAIN PARAMETERS – CLASS INTERVALS

Classes of length and width of terrain units	
1 To 10 m	6 2000 m
2 To 50 m	7 4000 m
3 To 100 m	8 8000 m
4 To 500 m	9 Extensive
5 To 1000 m	

Classes of length and width of terrain components	
1 To 2 m	6 To 100 m
2 To 5 m	7 To 500 m
3 To 10 m	8 To 1000 m
4 To 20 m	9 Extensive
5 To 50 m	

Classes of relief	
1 To 1 m (microtopography)	6 To 75 m
2 To 3 m	7 To 150 m
3 To 6 m	8 To 300 m
4 To 15 m	9 To >300 m
5 To 30 m	

Classes of tree spacings, heights, and girth diameter		
1 To 2 m	1 To 2 m	1 To 0.05 m
2 To 3 m	2 To 3 m	2 To 0.1 m
3 To 6 m	3 To 6 m	3 To 0.2 m
4 To 30 m	4 To 12 m	4 To 0.3 m
5 Scattered	5 To 18 m	5 To 0.5 m
6 Occasional	6 To >18 m	6 To 0.6 m
		7 To >0.6 m

Classes of stream densities
1 <0.5 total streams/1.6 km
2 0.5 total streams/1.6 km
3 1.0 total streams/1.6 km
4 1.5 total streams/1.6 km
5 2.0 total streams/1.6 km
6–9 Increasing at 0.5 intervals

Classes of slope	
0 Level	5 To 20°
1 To 1°	6 To 40°
2 To 2°	7 To 60°
3 To 5°	8 > 60°
4 To 10°	9 To vertical

Classes of rubble sizes	
1 To 0.025 m	5 To 0.3 m
2 To 0.05 m	6 To 0.6 m
3 To 0.1 m	7 To 2 m
4 To 0.2 m	8 To >2 m

their occurrence, topography, soil, land use or surface cover (whichever is applicable), and vegetation characteristics. Aerial photograph patterns representing constant repetitive associations of land form units are recognized and delineated as the basis for later terrain pattern delineation. This delineation may require some amendment when the interpretation has been amended as found necessary by ground checking. Any points of uncertainty in the interpretation are noted. Sampling sites are then chosen in such a way that

(1) sites are apparently representative of the terrain represented photographically by each interpretive land form unit;

(2) the terrain represented by each land form unit is examined adequately in relation to its properties and the properties of its attributes;

(3) all points of uncertainty are physically examined;

(4) the sites are, if possible, reasonably accessible.

In the ensuing period of field work, all points of uncertainty are resolved and sampling and examination of the terrain conducted at the chosen and other (as found necessary) sites. The interpretive descriptions of land form units and patterns and the delineated pattern boundaries are amended in accordance with the information obtained so that the terrain is classified and described accurately. The land form units and photo patterns are now tied to the terrain rather than to photographic representations of it and become terrain units and terrain patterns respectively. The smaller terrain parameters that are more easily estimated in the field are determined during this stage.

Following the ground survey, a re-examination is made of the aerial photographs in order to extrapolate the results of the field work over the whole area. Macro-terrain parameters necessary are estimated from the aerial photographs using photogrammetric techniques.

Terrain patterns are then mapped at 1 : 250,000 or larger scale and final terrain descriptions in terms of terrain patterns and terrain units are prepared. An example of a terrain pattern map is included as Appendix VII(*d*) of Part II of this treatise.

Detailed instructions for the classification of terrain in accordance with the above procedure are given in Part II.

For terrain-unit terrain-component identification, a similar process can be followed if aerial photographs of a suitably large scale are available. In this case, terrain pattern boundaries are transferred from the smaller-scale aerial photographs used previously for terrain-pattern terrain-unit identification to the larger-scale photographs. Terrain units are then delineated on these larger-scale photographs. Land form components (the photographic equivalents of terrain components when ground checked) are then recognized on the photographs and described by interpretation in terms of occurrence, slopes, soil, land use or surface cover (whichever is applicable), and vegetation. The interpretive land form components are then checked in the field using a similar procedure to that used for checking at terrain-unit terrain-pattern levels. In this stage, soil and vegetation are identified at the required level and all necessary terrain parameters are estimated. After amendment as found necessary in the field, terrain units and terrain components can be mapped (scales 1 : 50,000 and 1 : 5,000 or larger respectively) and appropriate descriptions prepared.

TABLE 7

ESTABLISHMENT AND EXPRESSION OF THE TERRAIN CLASSIFICATION

Initial stage in classification			Final stage in terrain classification			
Source of non-contact information (1)	Relevant factor in classification (2)	Title (3)	Supplementary source of information (4)	Relevant factor in classification (5)	Title (6)	Mode of expression (7)
Geological maps or aerial photographs* on scale of the order of 1 : 10⁶	—	—	—	Areas of constant geology at the group level Areas of similar air-photo pattern†	Province	Map 1 : 250,000 or larger
Aerial photographs* on scale of the order of 1 : 10⁴	Areas of similar air-photo pattern as defined by a constant association of land form units	Air-photo pattern	Ground study of physiography and association of terrain units	Areas of similar air-photo pattern† Areas with constant local relief amplitude, constant drainage pattern and density	Terrain pattern	Map 1 : 250,000 or larger Statement (and block diagram) of association of terrain units
Photogrammetric studies of air-photos at scale of the order of 1 : 10⁴	Single land form	Land form unit	Ground study for recognition and assessment of dimensions of land forms (where not obtained from air-photo studies) Ground study of association of earthen materials associated and vegetative cover Studies of association of terrain components	Areas occupied by single land form with characteristic earthen materials association and vegetation formation Areas with similar associations of terrain components	Terrain unit	Map 1 : 50,000 or larger Statement of characteristic land form and earthen material association and vegetation formation, percentage of terrain pattern, and association of terrain components
Photogrammetric studies of air-photos at scale of the order of 1 : 10⁴ Maps contoured at suitable intervals	Land form component	Land form component	Ground studies for recognition of specific slopes, soil, surface cover, and vegetation associations	Areas with constant rate of change of slope Consistent soil at U.S.C. and subdivided primary profile form level Consistent vegetation association	Terrain component	Map 1 : 1000 to 1 : 10,000 Statement of characteristic combination of slopes, vegetation and soil and of relative dominance within terrain unit

* Or equivalent presentations of data from remote sensors.   † Or similar patterns defined by other sensing devices on an appropriate scale.

TABLE 8

DESCRIPTION AND QUANTIFICATION ASSOCIATED WITH TERRAIN CLASSIFICATION

Level in terrain classification (1)	Terrain factors suitable for descriptive expression (2)	Terrain factors suitable for quantitative expression (3)	Methodology of quantification (4)
Terrain pattern	Physiography Basic characteristics of soil, rock, vegetation common among constituent terrain units Drainage pattern	Relief amplitudes Stream frequencies	Air-photo or ground study Air-photo study
Terrain unit	Physiography Principal characteristics of soil, rock, vegetation	Dimensions of terrain unit (relief amplitude, length, width)	Air-photo or ground study
Terrain component	Slope type Lithology Soil type Vegetation association	Dimensions of terrain component (relief amplitude, length, width, slopes)	Measured *in situ*
		Dimensions of vegetation (height, diameter, spacing)	Measured *in situ*
		Dimensions of surface obstacles including rock outcrops and termitaria	Measured *in situ*
		Properties of earthen materials throughout profile (depth, particle size gradation, consistence, strength, permeability, suction, mineralogy)	Measured in field where practicable, otherwise by standard laboratory procedures
		Quantities of earthen materials	Measured or estimated *in situ*

136

If aerial photographs of suitable scale are not available for this level of working, the classification must be done by field study alone. A terrain component map can then be prepared only if a base map of the area at a suitable scale and contoured at suitable intervals is available. Such a contoured base map also materially assists in the field work, whether aerial photographs are available or not. An example of a terrain component map is included as Appendix VII(*e*) of Part II of this treatise.

Detailed instructions for the classification of terrain in accordance with the above procedure are given in Part II.

The complete process of terrain classification is summarized in Table 7 and description and quantification of parameters associated with terrain classification are summarized in Table 8.

(b) *Engineering Evaluation of Terrain*

The classification of terrain is the necessary preliminary process to evaluation. The evaluation stage consists of specifying

(1) the properties of the terrain and its attributes that are critical for the desired purpose;

(2) for those properties, the level of detail required to be estimated for each phase in the planning and construction processes;

(3) estimating the recording values of these necessary parameters in terms of the level in the terrain classification appropriate to them. Those parameters significant at province level can be gathered and recorded against the appropriate province, those at terrain pattern level against the appropriate terrain pattern, those at terrain unit level against the appropriate terrain unit, and those at terrain component level against the appropriate terrain component.

The technique of terrain evaluation is equally applicable to the planning of new developments in the open countryside or of redevelopment of city areas that are no longer viable in their present context within the city scene; each type of development, of course, imposes its own constraints on the purposes of and methods used for evaluation. In areas of new development, the number of degrees of freedom for location is generally large; in areas of redevelopment the number of degrees of freedom is mostly small.

A flow chart depicting the relationships of the stages of terrain evaluation and its application is illustrated in Figure 4.

Whilst engineering evaluation of terrain may or may not be conducted concurrently with the terrain classification stage, it is essentially a separate procedure. Terrain classification is the necessary tool used as the basis for evaluation, but it is engineering evaluation that supplies the data necessary for engineering planning and construction. Again, whilst terrain classification may be done in an ordered form by relatively unskilled personnel simply following a standard formalized set of instructions, evaluation is always tied to a particular stage in a particular project, whether large or small, and is always done at the behest of and under the control and supervision of the engineer in charge.

The type of information specified to be collected will, of course, depend upon the project and the requirements of the particular engineer. This information may also

contain some items that are essentially intangible in nature (Aitchison 1968). These
items are usually determined from the experience of particular engineers and require
judgment rather than measurement for their collection. Also, Aitchison and Grant
(1968b) have pointed out that whilst geotechnical parameters immediately pertinent
to the terrain classification can be expressed in quantitative form using simple procedures, the complete methodology of expressing quantitatively geotechnical terrain
parameters is in general incapable of finalization, because varying requirements of
various engineering purposes lead to an indefinite, but large, number of parameters;
many of these parameters have been defined, but many more require definition. When
all parameters have been defined it will be possible to erect mathematical analytical
models for each engineering task. The application of such models will allow all
critical terrain parameters for any one purpose to be specified uniquely and it will be
possible to lay down strict standard procedures for the collection of these parameters.

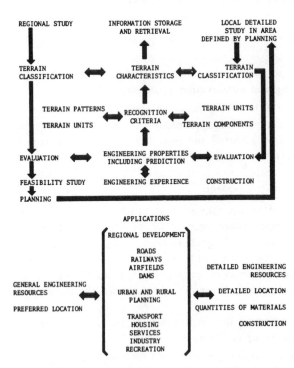

Fig. 4.–Terrain evaluation flow chart.

In using the PUCE Programme, geotechnical information should be collected as
required in terms of significant differences in terrain as determined by the terrain
classification stage of the process rather than in terms of fixed arbitrary distances from
some reference point. That is, information that is appropriate at terrain pattern level
is collected on a terrain pattern basis, that appropriate on a terrain unit level is
collected on a terrain unit basis, and that appropriate at terrain component level is
collected on a terrain component basis. The use of this method can achieve considerable
savings in effort and cost of sampling and testing by eliminating unnecessary sampling

where no significant changes occur in the terrain. The relationship between some stages in engineering construction and the appropriate terrain classes is shown in Table 9, but the items shown in that table are not exhaustive.

TABLE 9

STAGES OF ENGINEERING CONSTRUCTION IN RELATION TO THE TERRAIN CLASSES

Terrain class	Appropriate stage of engineering construction
Province	Deep underground rock examinations General statement only for factors specific at lower levels in the classification

Terrain pattern	Formation for road or railway construction
	    Earthworks – quantity
	              – equipment
	    Bridging frequency
	    Culverting frequency
	Airstrip construction – topographic suitability
	Dam sites – topographic suitability
	Underground excavations affected by surface features
	General statement for factors specific at terrain unit or terrain component level of classification

Terrain unit	Formation for road or railway construction
	    Location
	    Preferred location of grade line
	    Suitability of natural material as base course
	    Source of borrow for embankment
	    Proportion of rock excavation
	Airstrip construction
	    Location
	    Suitability of natural material as a base course
	    Proportion of rock excavation
	Dam sites
	    Location
	    Source of borrow for embankment
	Building construction
	    Location
	General statement for factors specific at terrain component level of the classification

Terrain component	Trafficability of natural surface
	Liability to flood
	Road and airfield pavements
	    Suitability of natural material as subgrade
	    Source of borrow for pavement materials (gravel, crushed rock, screenings, etc.) and estimates of quantities
	    Source of borrow for concreting materials (sand, aggregate, etc.) and estimates of quantities
	Building foundations
	    Susceptibility to volume change with moisture change
	    Susceptibility to settlement under load
	Earth tanks
	    Topographic suitability
	    Material suitability

When it can be shown that any member of any class of terrain is sensibly homogeneous, irrespective of its occurrence, geotechnical information gathered from any one occurrence of the particular class member can be extrapolated to all other occurrences of the same member. Again, by means of this extrapolation procedure, considerable savings in both effort and cost may be made when collecting information.

Each engineering objective requires the collection of sets of information that are essentially different from the sets required for any other objective, although some sets of information may contain some items in common. For any one engineering objective, the required information can be considered as existing in three sets. One set of information is required for feasibility studies, another for planning purposes, whilst another set is required for construction purposes. These sets of information may, of course, overlap and contain some items in common. In general, information required for planning purposes tends to be more broadly based, whilst that required for construction purposes must be detailed. Again, sets of information acquired for planning a number of objectives are likely to contain more common items than do the sets of information necessary for the construction of these objects.

Therefore the PUCE Programme has been designed to operate as a two- or three-stage process although it can just as easily be operated in one stage. Regional evaluation of terrain at province and terrain pattern levels normally produces sufficient information for feasibility studies. More detailed evaluation at terrain unit level over the limited area defined by the feasibility study provides information for planning. More detailed evaluation at all relevant levels including terrain component level can be done later in the more limited area of interest defined by the planning process. In each case the set of information collected will be only that relevant to the purpose in hand. However, when the terrain has been classified, that classification will remain valid for all future purposes in the same area so that additional sets of information may continue to be collected as the necessary occasion arises.

The use of such a system allows consideration of regional as well as local factors in the planning stage. For instance, in planning the route of a new road in the open countryside there is initially a large number of possible locations or, alternatively, for urban planning there is a large number of possible sites for each particular sphere of activity. The best location will depend upon the relative economics, including socio-economic factors, of building in particular areas with different types of topography, or different soils, or from different natural constructional materials, etc. The use of regional terrain evaluation at a relatively coarse level supplies sufficient data for the assessment of all these factors in an integrated form. Such an assessment provides sufficient data for the most economical general location to be determined on a rational basis. When this general location has been determined, the detailed evaluation of the limited area that influences the exact location provides the data for the final design and construction of the project.

An example of broad-scale terrain evaluation for location of materials and route for railway construction purposes and for regional water resources is given in Grant (1970*a*).

However, evaluation of small areas in which the possible freedom of choice is small can be conducted as a one-stage process, with the classification and evaluation conducted simultaneously at terrain pattern, terrain unit, and terrain component levels. Examples of such areas are those defined for redevelopment within an already established community or for projects constrained in their location by already existing development.

The terrain classification stage of terrain evaluation in accordance with the PUCE Programme is so designed that the classification of the terrain of any area is equally valid for all engineering purposes, i.e. once the terrain in any area has been classified as the basis for evaluation for any one engineering purpose, that classification can be validly used as the basis for evaluation for all future engineering purposes. In this regard, it is most important that regional terrain classification at terrain pattern and terrain unit level (for feasibility studies and for planning purposes) should be conducted in such a way that it is consistent and compatible over areas of continental dimensions, because if done properly it need only be done once.

The same arguments, of course, apply equally to the detailed classification of terrain at terrain unit and terrain component levels conducted as the basis of evaluation for design and construction purposes, but because the amount of effort necessary to classify terrain satisfactorily at this detailed level is quite large, it would indeed be uneconomic to conduct this work in any area in which it was unlikely to be of use. Hence this type of terrain classification, for the time being at least, should be conducted only in the area that influences the construction of particular projects. That is, of course, not to say that it should not be conducted over areas that are likely to be subjected to integrated engineering involving a large number of engineering projects that interact with each other even though such projects may be constructed over quite a long period of time. To quote an example: whilst in open countryside engineering projects tend to be widely spaced, although some, e.g. roads, may at times intersect each other, within an expanding city and its environs engineering projects tend to be close together and interact with each other. In both cases regional terrain evaluation at terrain pattern and terrain unit level will supply the data necessary for feasibility studies and for planning engineering projects. In the latter case it will also supply the data necessary for basic town planning, which, of course, includes many aspects of integrated engineering. Also, in both cases detailed terrain evaluation at terrain unit and terrain component level will supply the data necessary for detailed design and construction, but can only be justified economically in areas that influence design and construction. In the former case (open countryside) such areas, whilst they may intersect, occupy only a small part of the region. In the latter case (city and environs) these areas occupy the whole area covered by the city and its environs; in the city itself there is always redevelopment and the provision of new services, and in the environs there is always the new development associated with an expanding city. In this case the detailed classification of the whole area is justified.

Also, if the terrain is evaluated on the basis of the PUCE Programme, once a required set of information has been specified for a particular purpose, a search of the information store (see section (c) below) will reveal whether the specified set of information has been collected previously or, if that set has not been collected previously, whether specified items in the specified set have been collected as components of other sets of information. In either case, the relevant set of items may be retrieved from the information store rather than having to be re-collected. As the storage system is incremental (see section (c) below), a considerable saving in cost and effort can eventually be achieved through the process of information storage and retrieval.

Thus the terrain evaluation procedure may achieve considerable savings in both effort and cost by elimination of unnecessary information collection by

(1) sampling only when significant changes occur in the terrain;

(2) use of the prediction facility inherent in the terrain evaluation process;

(3) use of the storage and retrieval system that is part of the terrain evaluation process.

Terrain evaluation as the basis for urban and rural planning has been discussed by Grant and Aitchison (1970) and for highway engineering by Grant (1970*b*). Examples of terrain classification for urban and rural planning are given by Grant (1972) and as a basis for highway planning by Grant (1970*c*).

(c) Information Processing

An information collating, storage, and retrieval system is an essential and integral part of the PUCE Programme. Indeed, the conception and operation of such a system are the prime purposes for which the PUCE Programme was devised.

In its operation the PUCE Programme requires that:

(1) The terrain be classified into classes, each member of which is essentially homogeneous in accordance with the criteria for class definition, irrespective of its occurrence, as in Section IV(*b*).

(2) Engineering information be gathered for each member of each class as appropriate as in Section IV(*b*).

(3) The collected information be collated and stored using the appropriate member of the terrain classes as the basis for information processing.

The actual system used for information processing must necessarily be of an incremental type in which it is possible to add information continually as it is collected and to retrieve data as required.

Terrain evaluation as formulated in the PUCE Programme allows and, what is more, is designed for the processing of all information relative to the engineering significance of terrain, but it does not require the collection of all that information at any one time. Clearly it would be uneconomic and certainly futile to collect any information other than that which was required specifically for the purpose in hand. Indeed, who can specify what is all information of engineering significance?

Each engineering objective requires the collection of a set of information that is essentially different from the set required for any other objective, although some information may be common to two or more sets. For each objective, the information in the set relevant to it must be specified, then collected.

In any area, once the basic terrain classification has been done to the required level, the set of information collected for any one purpose can be stored as an increment in the system, as can each succeeding set of information. Equally a set of information once placed in the system can be retrieved as a dividend at any time. Also, if a set of required information contains some items that have already been collected in any other set, that information can be retrieved from the system and does not need to be collected again.

Whilst such a system should be capable of handling all data of engineering significance, it can only contain all such data when all engineering works possible have been constructed. As engineering is a continuing process, it is likely that the information in the system can never be complete at any one time.

A key to a successful system for information processing is a method for encoding the information presented to the system. Encoding ensures that information is always presented to the system in a uniform manner that is compatible with the system. Because the same information is always presented in the same way, it avoids duplication. Also, because terminology is standardized, no difficulties can be experienced in interpreting the precise meaning of every item placed in the system, i.e. difficulties in translating from the language used by the collector of the information to that of the information user do not arise. Encoding is independent of the actual information processing system used. Coded information is applicable just as easily to a computer-based information processing system, a file system for use in the office, or a note-book system for use in the field.

Use of the PUCE Programme requires that all information collected should be tied to the appropriate members of the terrain classes and processed in terms of these terrain class members. Therefore criteria for the recognition of the terrain class members must also be stored in the system in an encoded form. A glossary embodying the encoding necessary for the inclusion into the information processing system of information gathered about and recognition criteria for all members of all terrain classes so far recognized in Australia is included as Appendix VI of Part II of this treatise. The glossary should not be regarded as exhaustive.

The actual information processing system used for processing engineering information pertinent to terrain is entirely dependent upon the size of the operation. Probably the ideal type of system is one centralized data bank with continuous access for the addition and retrieval of information. Such a centralized system would certainly be based upon a computer as the medium for information processing. However, the operation of such a system would require the agreement of all engineers and engineering authorities operating in a country, firstly to collect all engineering information in a standard manner, secondly to incorporate all information collected into the data bank, and thirdly to make that information freely available without let or hindrance. Such an agreement is unlikely to be attained. Even if such a system were implemented, unless every engineer and engineering authority possessed a direct linkage to the central computer, it might still be found necessary to have a detailed system for rapid office referral and an abbreviated system based upon the detailed system for field use.

If a centralized system cannot be adopted or if rapid referral is required, it is suggested that:

(1) Large organizations handling large amounts of data and requiring fast access and retrieval of information should use an automatic system based upon computer operation. Direct access lines to the computer would be required. Grant and Lodwick (1968) have discussed certain aspects related to automatic information storage and retrieval of terrain data using a computer medium. They proposed the use of a standard set of data collection sheets compatible with computer processing and gave an example of a computer printout of information pertinent to terrain classification. Such a system can easily be extended to include automatic processing of geotechnical data collected in accordance with the PUCE Programme.

(2) On the smaller scale, when information to be processed is not excessively large, an office filing system can be readily adapted for such a use; Brink *et al.* (1968) describe a system using envelopes within an office filing system for this type of use.

(3) For field use, a note-book system can be devised that records the significant information in abbreviated form. Aitchison and Grant (1968b) have discussed an information recording system for field use and illustrated possible abbreviated methods for handling field data. It should be noted that in these suggested methods, even the code numbers for terrain patterns, terrain units, and terrain components have been abbreviated for ease of working.

V. REFERENCES

Aitchison, G. D. (1968).–Engineering expectations from terrain evaluation. Proc. 4th Conf. Aust. Rd Res. Bd, Vol. 4, Pt 2, p. 1661.

Aitchison, G. D., and Grant, K. (1967).–The P.U.C.E. Programme of terrain description, evaluation and interpretation for engineering purposes. Proc. 4th Reg. Conf. Africa Soil Mech. Fdn Engng, Vol. 1, pp. 1–8.

Aitchison, G. D., and Grant, K. (1968a).–Terrain evaluation for engineering. In "Land Evaluation", ed. G. A. Stewart. (Macmillan: Melbourne.)

Aitchison, G. D., and Grant, K. (1968b).–Proposals for the application of the P.U.C.E. Programme of terrain classification and evaluation to some engineering problems. Proc. 4th Conf. Aust. Rd Res. Bd, Vol. 4, Pt 2, p. 1648.

Anon. (1973).–Australian code of stratigraphic nomenclature. 4th Ed. *J. Geol. Soc. Aust.* **20**, 105–112.

Anon. (1968).–"Van Nostrands Scientific Encyclopaedia." 4th Ed. p. 130. (Van Nostrand: Princeton.)

Brink, A. B. A., Partridge, T. C., Webster, R., and Williams, A. A. B. (1968).–Land classification and data storage for the engineering usage of natural materials. Proc. 4th Conf. Aust. Rd Res. Bd, Vol. 4, Pt 2, p. 1624.

Grant, K. (1968).–A terrain evaluation system for engineering. CSIRO Aust. Div. Soil Mechanics tech. Pap. No. 1.

Grant, K. (1970a).–Terrain evaluation. A logical extension of engineering geology. Premier Congrès International de l'Association Internationale de Géologie de l'Ingénieur, Paris, Vol. 2, pp. 971–80.

Grant, K. (1970b).–Terrain evaluation for engineering purposes. Proc. Symp. on Terrain Evaluation for Highway Engineering, Sp. Rep. 6, p. 81. (Aust. Rd Res. Bd: Melbourne.)

Grant, K. (1970c).–Terrain classification for engineering purposes of the Marree area, South Australia. CSIRO Aust. Div. Soil Mechanics tech. Pap. No. 4.

Grant, K. (1971).–The use of aerial photograph interpretation in terrain evaluation for engineering purposes. Proc. 3rd Int. Symp. for Photo-interpretation, Int. Archives of Photogrammetry, Dresden, pp. 949–74.

Grant, K. (1972).–Terrain classification for engineering purposes of the Melbourne area, Victoria. CSIRO Aust. Div. Appl. Geomechs tech. Pap. No. 11.

Grant, K., and Aitchison, G. D. (1970).–Terrain studies for urban development. Unibeam Building and Estate Management A. Magazine, p. 60. (University of Singapore.)

Grant, K., and Lodwick, G. D. (1968).–Storage and retrieval of information in a terrain classification system. Proc. 4th Conf. Aust. Rd Res. Bd, Vol. 4, Pt 2, p. 1667.

Horton, R. E. (1945).–Erosional development of streams and their drainage basins. Bull. Geol. Soc. Am. No. 56, 275–370.

Northcote, K. H. (1971).–"A Factual Key for the Recognition of Australian Soils." 3rd Ed. (Rellim: Adelaide.)

United States Department of the Interior, Bureau of Reclamation (1963).–"Earth Manual." 1st Ed.

7: TEST OF ENVIRONMENTAL GEOLOGIC MAPPING, SOUTHERN EDWARDS PLATEAU, SOUTHWEST TEXAS

E. G. Wermund, R. A. Morton, P. J. Cannon, C. M. Woodruff, Jr.,

Bureau of Economic Geology, University of Texas at Austin, Austin, Texas

D. E. Deal

Department of Geology, Sul Ross State University, Alpine, Texas

ABSTRACT

The southern Edwards Plateau, southwest Texas, is the recharge area for a thick limestone aquifer that supplies potable water to more than 850,000 people and irrigation water for more than 2,500 sq mi (6,500 sq km) of cropland. Because the increasing population effects a booming residential and recreational development in this region, information on the geological environment of the plateau must be made available to planners so that the aquifer can be safeguarded. A reconnaissance environmental mapping technique has been developed in a pilot study that is to precede a major regional mapping program. Constraints in developing the technique were plateau geology, land use, factors controlling recharge, and available materials, including aerial photography and maps. The basis for defining the environmental mapping units is dominantly geomorphic; lithologic differences are indicated where necessary. The units are: karstic tableland, karstic lowland, deeply dissected carbonate, moderately dissected carbonate, carbonate, shale, alluvial fan, terrace, flood plain, fan plain, and alluvial-colluvial material. Results of this mapping are directly applicable in land use planning.

INTRODUCTION

One of the interesting problems in modern land management involves safeguarding the quality of recharge waters for an aquifer while the recharge area is being developed for food production, recreation, and multiple dwellings. If environmental geology is defined as ". . . a branch of ecology in that it deals with relationships between man and his geological habitat" (Flawn, 1970), then the relevant data needed to plan land use in a recharge zone must be derived from environmental geology. The intent of this paper is to illustrate the formulation of environmental geologic units for mapping a recharge area of a major limestone aquifer in southwest Texas.

The above definition results in two pragmatic approaches to describe environ-mental geologic units. One is to emphasize man and his habitat and relate his cultural environment to the natural habitat and geology; the other is to emphasize the geology and recognize man's cultural overprint. Both approaches have been used by previous authors in environmental geologic studies. Not surprisingly, early environmental geologic papers were concerned principally with urban problems. Toward their solution, Johnson and Smith (1965) and Danehy and Harding (1969) emphasized urban problems and related geology to the urban habitat. Later, Hayes and Vineyard (1969) and LaMoreaux and others (1971) described urban, suburban, and rural areas, to which they related geological properties in their environmental studies.

Brown and others (1971) and Fisher and others (1972) approach the problem of relating man and his habitat by first defining a natural habitat — in their cases, the coastal zone. They have delineated many environmental units of the coastal zone by mapping surficial sedimentary facies and noting the physical properties of these facies. For further understanding of the natural habitat, these workers added data on the effects and interplay of biological activities and physical processes on the facies. On this basis, the coastal zone environment was defined as a geological province, and man's activities were related to this natural habitat. In looking at the full spectrum of environmental geological issues, the approach of studying each unique geological province appears valuable. One such environmental geologic province is a recharge area for a limestone aquifer, the subject of this paper.

We are presently mapping environmental units over a 33,000-sq-mi (86,000-sq-km) area of southwest Texas, which includes the drainage basins of the Nueces, San Antonio, Guadalupe, and Lavaca Rivers. Output from this project includes eight maps depicting: (1) environmental geology, (2) physical properties, (3) physical processes, (4) slopes, (5) biologic assemblages, (6) land use, (7) man-made features, and (8) resources. The project region is being mapped in stages; each stage deals with a natural unit in a geologic province to which man's activities will be related. These provinces are the southern Edwards Plateau, the interior Cretaceous coastal plain, the Tertiary coastal plain, and the coastal zone (Pleistocene-Holocene). The first and second stages of mapping include the southern Edwards Plateau and the interior Cretaceous coastal plain; they are scheduled to be completely mapped within an eight-month period.

The southern Edwards Plateau and the interior coastal plain of this study (Fig. 1) are bounded on the north by the divide between the Colorado River drainage and the drainage of the Nueces and Guadalupe Rivers. They are bounded on the west by the divide between the Rio Grande and Nueces drainages. The eastern boundary is the divide between the Blanco River, a tributary of the Guadalupe River, and the Colorado River. An arbitrary southern limit is drawn south of U.S. Highway 90 and east of U.S. Highway 81, where Quaternary fan plains terminate south and east of the Balcones fault zone and where the base of the Tertiary sequence is exposed.

Because of the requirements of mapping a large area in a short time (3 yr), we are restricted to interpretation of topographic

Figure 1. Location of the southern Edwards Plateau region in Texas relative to some major cities. This region includes areas of both recharge and ground-water withdrawal for a major limestone aquifer that is the water supply of San Antonio.

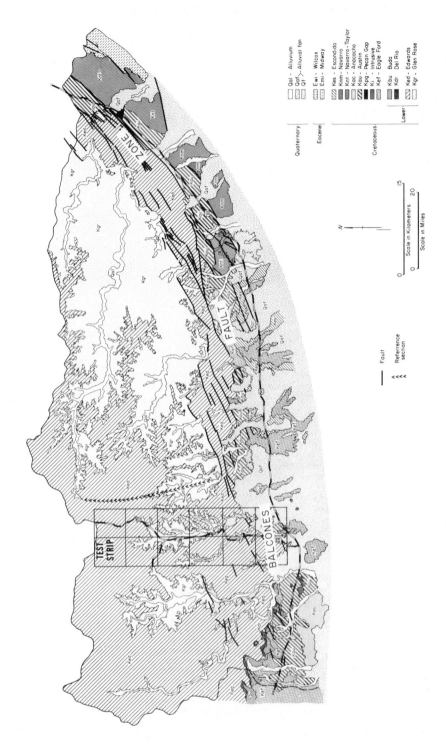

Quaternary
Qal – Alluvium
Qaf – Alluvial fan
Qt

Eocene
Ewi – Wilcox
Emi – Midway

Cretaceous
Kes – Escondido
Knm – Navarro
Knt – Navarro - Taylor
Kac – Anacacho
Kau – Austin
Kpg – Pecan Gap
Ki – Intrusive
Kef – Eagle Ford

Lower
Kbu – Buda
Kdr – Del Rio

Ked – Edwards
Kgr – Glen Rose

—— Fault

<<< Reference
section

N

0   Scale in Kilometers   15
0   Scale in Miles   20

Figure 2. Geologic map of the southern Edwards Plateau region (after V.E. Barnes, in prep.) locating the test strip described in this paper. The Balcones fault zone is a principal area of recharge into the Edwards aquifer.

maps and aerial photographs supplemented by limited field reconnaissance. Topographic maps on a scale of 1:24,000 are available for 80 percent of the region. Available aerial photography is black and white, in the form of controlled mosaics and stereo pairs. From study of topographic maps and aerial photographs, we are reporting the results of compiling an environmental geologic map for a test strip of 12 quadrangles (1:24,000). The test strip is representative of the southern Edwards Plateau (Fig. 1), a recharge region for a major carbonate aquifer supplying potable water to more than 850,000 people and irrigation water for more than 2,500 sq mi (6,500 sq km) of rich agricultural land.

SOUTHERN EDWARDS PLATEAU REGION

General Geology

The Edwards Plateau, according to Fenneman (1931), is a plateau held up by limestone lacking any fluviatile mantle. The maximum elevation of the plateau in the study region is about 2,400 ft (730 m), and the surface slopes gently both southward and eastward. The relatively level surface, which reflects nearly flat-lying rocks, is deeply incised by southward-flowing streams in the Nueces River basin and eastward-flowing streams in the San Antonio and Guadalupe River basins. Elevations are about 750 ft (230 m) where streams discharge from southern limits of the plateau escarpment onto coastal plain rocks.

Most of the streams that erode headward into the plateau form narrow valleys with steep walls of Cretaceous carbonate strata. These valley walls reach heights of nearly 400 ft in one-half mile (150 m in 1 km) transverse to the streams. Only the major streams develop valleys ~3.5 to 5 mi (as much as 8 km) wide. The wider valleys may have formed by both karst development and lateral cutting processes when there was greater rainfall than at present (Pleistocene pluvials?). These modern wider valleys contain underfit streams which catch a present mean annual rainfall of 30 in. (75 cm) in the east and 22 in. (55 cm) in the west of the plateau. More significant is the distribution of the rainfall through the year; 2 to 3 in. (5 to 8 cm) of rain in 1 hr is common.

In the southern Edwards Plateau, only the Glen Rose and Edwards Formations crop out extensively (Fig. 2). The Glen Rose is more than 480 ft (145 m) thick (Stricklin and others, 1971) and the Edwards Formation is about 360 ft (110 m) thick (Rose, 1972) 8 mi (13 km) east of the test strip. The upper Glen Rose Formation comprises alternating beds of limestone, dolomite, and marly limestone; about 60 percent of the section consists of marly limestones. Conversely, the Edwards Formation is composed of limestone and dolomite with only 8 percent marly limestone in which clay beds rarely occur. The marly limestone of both the Edwards and Glen Rose Formations is rapidly weathered and eroded and contains only minor amounts of clay minerals.

With rare exceptions, our reconnaissance of the region substantiates the lateral lithologic continuity of the upper Glen Rose and Edwards rocks described above. In the lower Glen Rose, thick limestones occur in many places. Throughout the region, vertical and horizontal permeability paths have developed in the thicker sections of limestone and dolomite, as evidenced by joints and bedding planes that contain modern solution cavities, older travertine-filled routes, and even caves. Such solution features are abundant in the Edwards aquifer rocks, which have a well-developed open system of fluid communication in outcrop and subcrop of the plateau.

The geologic map (Fig. 2; after V. E. Barnes and others, in prep.) illustrates a number of important regional features. The southern limit of both the Edwards and Glen Rose outcrops is along the Balcones fault zone which strikes east-west in the western part of the map area and nearly northeast-southwest in the eastern part. North of the major faults, broad valleys expose wide outcrops of the Glen Rose Formation; valleys of alluvial deposits narrow just south of the faults as streams incise the down-dropped Edwards Formation. This can be seen on a succession of streams from west to east. Maximum displacement along the Balcones fault zone is about 1,700 ft (520 m) in the eastern part of the map area (DeCook, 1963) and about 700 ft (215 m) in the southwestern part (Welder and Reeves, 1962). Maximum displacement along any one fault is about 500 ft (150 m) in the eastern part of the area; however, displacement decreases to about 200 ft (60 m) toward the southwest.

South of the major Balcones faults and south of the Edwards outcrop area, there is a marked change in the terrain. Maximum relief is about 100 ft (30 m) in low rolling hills. The two units that crop out there are (1) the normal succession of Upper Cretaceous chalks and terrigenous mud rocks, including the Austin, Taylor, and Navarro Groups; and (2) broad, extensive gravel and sand fan plains that appear just south of the Balcones faults. These fans form broad and elongate plains at the base of the escarpment of the Edwards Plateau.

Land Use

Six present land use units are recognized in the southern Edwards Plateau (Fig. 3) from reconnaissance study: (1) hill country, (2) grazing land, (3) mixed grazing and cultivated land, (4) cultivated land, (5) recreational areas, and (6) urban and small communities. The hill country and grazing lands represent about 70 percent of the region. A land use unit, such as the above, is comparable to the resource-capability unit defined by Brown and others (1971, p. 1) as an "... environmental entity — land, water, area of active process or biota — defined in terms of the nature, degree of activity or use it can sustain without losing an acceptable level of environmental quality." It stands then that the present use is a critical feature of resource-capability units. Each of the land use units previously mentioned has clear, identifiable properties. The units best equate to the recent land-classification units of Anderson and others (1972) thus: our urban and small communities unit is their urban and built-up land (level 1); cultivated land is a level 3 category of their cropland and pasture (level 2); mixed grazing and cultivated land is essentially their cropland and pasture (level 2); grazing land is a level 3 unit related to their level 2 chaparral; the hill country is a level 3 unit of their mixed forest land; and they do not account for recreational lands.

Hill country is the local term for rugged scenic upland, the least accessible and most rugged unit in the southern Edwards Plateau. Note on Figure 3 that the hill country occupies nearly all the divides between the major streams. The relief within this unit at many locations approaches 500 ft (150 m) in cliffs. In its natural state, very thin soil and thick brush overlie carbonate bedrock; soil is absent in many places on the steeper slopes. The brush is generally juniper and scrub live oak. Even where the brush is cleared, most domesticated animals find this environment too harsh for survival; only goats graze with limited success on this land. However, deer and wild turkey do well, and important uses of this land unit are hunting, hiking, and observing scenic vistas.

Grazing land is generally level or gently sloping in areas of limestone outcrop. The soil is thin, and the vegetation is prairie-like; juniper and live oak are uncommon, because they are removed from large areas by chaining, root plowing, or chemical spraying. Maximum relief approaches 200 ft (60 m) but is generally much less than that. Grazing of both cattle and sheep is also common in the wider valleys of major streams, where marly limestone is the dominant rock type, and relatively thick alluvium covers much of the area.

Grazed and cultivated land is encountered in the lowland south of the thick limestone of the Edwards Plateau. The outcrops are of shale or marl in many areas, chalk in some, and thin limestones on which prairie grasses and sparse mesquite predominate in a few places. Relief is low — 20

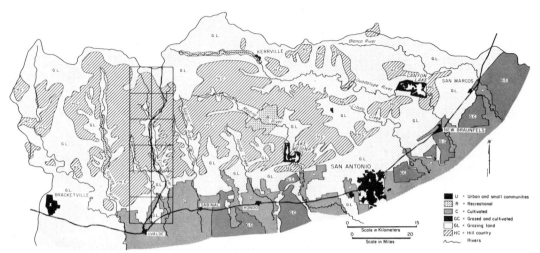

Figure 3. Land use in the southern Edwards Plateau region; location of the test strip is shown. Major impact areas of community growth in the recharge zone are north of San Antonio and around Medina Lake and Canyon Lake.

to 50 ft per mi (4 to 10 m per km). Whether the land is used for grazing or cultivation depends upon the steepness of the slopes in outcrop areas and on how easily the related soil can be plowed.

Cultivated land invariably lies on the extensive fan-plain deposits that begin south of the plateau escarpment, where major streams discharge from the faulted Edwards escarpment. These cultivated fans are composed of a wide range of particle sizes up to and including gravels. The gravels contain both limestone and chert fragments, generally well rounded. At one time, sand-sized limestone fragments were undoubtedly a large proportion of the fan material, but a long period of weathering has changed it all to fines in the soil fraction. The cultivated lands are level surfaces that slope gently southeastward at a rate of less than 40 ft per mi (7.5 m per km).

Recreational land is an overprint on the other categories of land use previously mentioned. In summer, major areas of recreation occur along the main streams in the heart of the plateau. Springs feed the cool, clear streams which flow on carbonate bedrock, and tall mature cypress trees grow on the banks in the headwaters and in lower interrupted courses of the streams. Fishing, boating, swimming, and especially horse-back riding are popular — the scenery is beautiful. The study region (Fig. 3) is a major dude-ranching region in Texas. In the fall and winter, the entire region is one of the major deer- and bird-hunting preserves of Texas. Medina and Canyon Lakes are also important recreational areas, but they are becoming more significant as suburban developments of a major population center,

San Antonio. Therefore, these lakes are classified as urban and more properly belong to the following land use category.

Urban and small communities include, in decreasing order of population, San Antonio, San Marcos, New Braunfels, Kerrville, Uvalde, and Hondo. San Antonio, with a 1970 population of 654,000, is the most important community both as a user of the subsurface limestone aquifer and as a major impact on the natural environment. All the other communities are on the plains south and east of the Balcones fault zone and the Edwards Plateau escarpment. The exception is Kerrville which is in the alluvial valley of the Guadalupe River.

Test Strip

Before mapping the entire region, a pilot study was made of the plateau region. Twelve 7½' topographic quadrangles were selected for a test strip (located on Figs. 2 and 3). The western tier of quadrangles, north to south, are named Bull Head Creek NE, Bull Head Creek SE, York Hollow NE, York Hollow SE, Uvalde 2 NE, and Uvalde 2 SE. The eastern tier, north to south, are Hillcrest Ranch, Circle Bluff, Rio Frio, Magers Crossing, Concan, and Uvalde 1 SW. Most quadrangles are temporary and will have new names. The test strip was selected so that it begins in the north on the drainage divide between southward-flowing Nueces tributaries and northwestward-flowing Pedernales (Colorado) tributaries. This divide is the northern boundary of the southern Edwards Plateau of this paper. The test strip, which extends south of the Balcones fault zone and the last physiographic expression of the plateau into coastal plain

strata, contains all the stratigraphic units described for the plateau region, Balcones normal faulting, and maximum relief of 1,500 ft (460 m). The test strip also includes each of the land use units noted for the region. There is no major urban area included, but the test strip touches the limits of Uvalde with a population of 17,500 — a large community in southwest Texas. The following descriptions of developing units, mapping, and results pertain solely to the test strip.

MAPPING CRITERIA AND METHODS

Bases for Defining Environmental Units

Most previous workers base their derivations of environmental map units on lithologic variations. Exceptions are the hurricane process and biologic units of Brown and others (1971) and Fisher and others (1972). All have considered topography or terrain as a separate problem, often presented on a thematic map. Although their map units also reflect the mapping method, this is not always stated. The map units of this study do reflect the mapping method, indicating that we rely strongly on both aerial photographs and topographic maps. The environmental units also reflect our observations of materials, processes, and terrain which were evaluated in view of current and projected land use, that is, resource capability in a sense.

Pessl and others (1972, p. 3) question that one should map "land-use suitability" or resource capability, because future technological progress alters land use. They are overly negative. We believe that if basic natural capabilities are used to formulate map units, then environmental or resource capability units remain useful to planners.

In the Edwards Plateau headwaters of the Nueces, San Antonio, and Guadalupe Rivers, the recharge process is the dominant environmental factor regulating plans for land use, both current and projected. It is to be expected that recharge will always be the most important environmental factor. Therefore, the geological properties regulating the recharge process become major considerations in building environmental map units. Properties affecting recharge and infiltration rates comprise: (1) rock composition; (2) passageways for fluids, including porosity, permeability, and transmissivity; (3) soil and vegetative cover; (4) slope; and (5) the attitude of the bedrock. From an evaluation of these recharge properties, as related to the geology, we have developed the environmental map units. In part, decisions about units also reflect mapping procedure on topographic bases, where available, and the scales and kinds of available aerial photographs.

Where the rocks are limestone and dolomite, slope is probably the dominant property affecting recharge in the region. Thickness of soil and density of vegetation depend primarily upon the slope and remain constant over different calcareous rocks. Limestone and dolomite behave similarly as soluble, dense fractured rocks yielding similar soils. Their facies can be separated only by means of detailed ground mapping. Attitude is constant — a gentle monoclinal dip of less than 1°.

Steep slopes with convex hilltops are common in the many valley headwaters of streams dissecting the plateau. The steep slopes have rapid runoff nearly unimpeded by sparse, brushy vegetation, and there is little infiltration into a rare, thin, and immature soil. On the divides with flattened slopes and in less dissected carbonate rocks with concave slopes, denser vegetation retards runoff, and thicker mature soil increases infiltration. Fracturing or jointing is also more important in the lesser slopes, but fracturing is consistently evident in the carbonates throughout the region. Where dense limestone and dolomite crop out on low slopes, sinkholes are common, reflecting recharge and infiltration. Some carbonate terrane has very gentle slopes reflecting the occurrence of marly limestone.

Based on recognition of varied carbonate terranes, four carbonate environmental units are named: deeply dissected carbonate, moderately dissected carbonate, karstic tableland, and karstic lowland. Geomorphological criteria, related to processes, are the dominant factors for defining the four units.

Alluvial terranes compose an important area of the test strip, where they are significant in both recharge and flooding processes. Three alluvial units are readily identified as flood plain, terrace, and alluvial fan. They originate as porous and permeable deposits, open to infiltration downward to carbonate bedrock, but are now locally sealed by thick caliche. The alluvial units have distinctive properties that will be described in the following section.

At the heads of the steep-walled valleys, gravity fall, creep, and colluviation commonly occur. It is frequently impossible to separate products of these mass-wasting processes from those of alluvial processes on aerial photographs. Therefore, a mixed alluvial-colluvial environmental unit is defined that includes both mixed colluvial and alluvial materials and even "pure" alluvial units where they are not distinctive at this mapping scale.

South of the southern Edwards Plateau, three units are designated for the physiographic Upper Cretaceous coastal plain. They can be separated lithologically into: calichified shale, thin carbonates, and muddy conglomerates of fan plains. They can also be distinguished topographically as hill-capping, gently rolling carbonates; low-relief shale; and level, broad fan plains. The properties of these environmental units are described in the next section.

Mapping Environmental Units

These descriptions of environmental units reflect the effects of the mapping methods employed, the philosophy of defining environmental units, and the time restrictions imposed by the contract.

Karstic tableland includes thick, fractured, carbonate rocks consisting almost entirely of limestone. The maximum relief is approximately 40 ft (12 m). Sinkholes are relatively common and usually no deeper than 3 ft. Soils are dark, very thin, mildly alkaline clays about 6 in. (15 cm) thick. Soil is locally thicker, over dissolved fractures as well as over local depressions. The vegetation is mainly a prairie-type grass, but locally there are mottes of mature live oak trees.

Karstic lowland includes thick limestone and thin dolomite. The maximum relief is on the order of 100 ft (30 m). In many outcrops, sinkholes, fractures, open fissures, and faults are in evidence. Compared to those in the karstic highlands, these sinkholes are more abundant and deeper, more than 5 ft (1.5 m) deep. The soil is similar to that in the highlands with some local thicker deposits in undrained depressions. Vegetation is predominantly live oak thickets among prairie-type grasses. This land has generally been cleared to increase grass production.

Deeply dissected carbonate terrane includes mostly limestone and dolomite in high-relief areas and sometimes includes interbedded marly limestones along with dolomite and limestone on lower valley slopes. Maximum relief is as much as 800 ft (245 m). Most slopes are convex and represent high runoff areas. Because of the steep slopes, bare rock ledges are common; the sparse soil is generally restricted to dark grayish-brown to black clay in pockets along joints. Vegetation, where present, is mainly stunted junipers and scrubby live oaks.

Moderately dissected carbonate terrane is dominantly limestone and dolomite. The maximum relief is about 100 ft (30 m). Local concentrations of caliche can occur in the stable soil, depending on the slope. Soils developed on resistant carbonate units are similar to those on karstic units, whereas marly limestones yield thicker, lighter colored, more friable soils. The vegetation is generally live oak and juniper. The trees are densely packed along intermittent streams. The divides are grass covered and have fewer trees.

Thin carbonate terrane includes limestone units as much as 20 ft (6 m) thick, which are commonly underlain by shale or marl. The maximum relief is on the order of 40 ft (12 m); the steepest slopes occur at contacts with underlying softer rocks. The limestone is strongly jointed, and many blocks have moved downslope over underlying shale. The soil is fairly well developed, as is that on the karstic tableland, and it does not creep downslope. The vegetation is predominantly juniper with fewer live oaks, and gently sloping areas are cleared in order to increase the grass for grazing. In the test strip, this unit occurs only south of the Edwards escarpment.

Shale, and almost no other rock type, occurs just south of the Edwards Plateau area. In regions of shale, the maximum relief is on the order of 15 ft (5 m). Outcrops are rare, because there is a thick caliche zone at the ground surface. The predominant tree in pastures is mesquite. This environmental unit is commonly cultivated where the slopes are minimal.

Flood plains are constructed of gravel- to mud-sized clasts (Folk, 1954) and are confined to incised, meandering, linear tracts bordered by either steep faces of cutbanks or the first minor escarpments of point bars or terraces of the reaches. Holocene deposits are not very thick or widespread, as the streams are underfit. The stream flows directly on limestone or dolomite bedrock in many places, because the alluvium of a slightly older flood plain has been eroded away. Large cypress trees are ubiquitous on the hill-country flood plains.

Terraces contain gravel- to mud-sized materials, generally rounded; deep caliche cover is common. Borrow pits for road-building material have been dug into the thick caliche cover of stream terraces throughout the area. The surface is nearly flat, frequently with a gravel veneer. On aerial photographs, the terrace morphology is distinctive. A good soil develops on the stream terrace deposits; consequently, these surfaces are usually plowed and cultivated. The soil is a gravelly, calcareous, grayish-brown friable loam over caliche. The natural vegetation is mainly prairie-like grasses. Pecan and walnut trees are indicative of terrace materials throughout the area.

Alluvial fans contain gravel- to mud-sized debris of limestone, dolomite, and chert; they are fan shaped in aerial view. Hand-lens observation suggests that the sand fraction weathers out early during formation of the soil on most fans. Some weathering is contemporaneous with the formation of thick caliche. At the surface of a fan, there is commonly a caliche mat that may be as much as 8 ft (2.5 m) thick. Because of this impermeable caliche, water runs off the slope rather than into the ground, often stripping off any soil that may have developed. The slopes are generally low except at the head of a fan. The soil is similar to that on the terrace deposits in the lower part, grading into soils such as those on the carbonate units near the fan heads. Prairie vegetation is usually found on alluvial fans, although some live oak and cedar occur, giving fan surfaces the appearance one expects in a predominantly carbonate terrane.

Fan plains include widespread areas of gravel and very fine material; it appears that sand has been removed by early weathering and is therefore no longer present in the topsoil. Both the coarse and fine material are composed predominantly of calcareous clasts with a lesser amount of chert. This material weathers to a deep, well-developed soil, enabling extensive fan plains to be generally cultivated. The soil is light reddish-brown, friable, calcareous, gravelly loam or clayey loam. Before extensive cultivation, the natural vegetation was probably dominantly prairie-type grasses, with a few mesquite trees.

Alluvial-colluvial material (undifferentiated) includes all the above alluvial deposits as well as colluviated slopes. This unit is used where one cannot clearly differentiate (on photographs) between colluvial slopes, alluvial fans, terraces, and flood plains. This is especially true of the upper slopes in the higher areas where there has been extreme dissection. A thick caliche horizon has developed in the upper part of this unit. The soil is the dark, alkaline clay soil of the carbonaceous units in the upper part and lighter colored calcareous loam soil near the boundary of the undifferentiated alluvium-colluvium and flood plain. The vegetation is generally the same as that described for the above units; that is, the

vegetation takes on the character of that on the fans or the stream terraces, depending upon location.

Supplementary Mapping

In order to better understand the mapping of environmental units and as part of the project to map properties and processes, slopes were mapped directly on topographic sheets.

Supplementing the environmental-unit mapping, slope mapping further contributed to the over-all understanding of the area. Based on work of the Kansas Geological Survey Study Committee (1968, p. 11, Fig. 1), it was initially thought that the mapping of 0 to 2 percent, 2 to 5 percent, 5 to 15 percent, 15 to 25 percent, and >25 percent slopes would be essential to an over-all understanding of this problem. All of these slopes were mapped experimentally on two topographic sheets. Mapping five

A

B

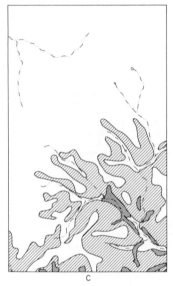

C

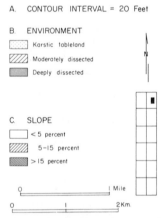

A. CONTOUR INTERVAL = 20 Feet

B. ENVIRONMENT
   Karstic tableland
   Moderately dissected
   Deeply dissected

C. SLOPE
   < 5 percent
   5–15 percent
   > 15 percent

0   1 Mile

0   1   2 Km.

Figure 4. Typical topographic expression (A) of environmental units (B), karstic tableland, deeply dissected thick carbonate, and moderately dissected thick carbonate, related to slope units (C). Box diagram shows location of topographic examples within the test strip indicated on Figures 2 and 3.

slope units produced too little information for the required mapping time. Therefore, the final choice was to map 0 to 5 percent, 5 to 15 percent, and >15 percent slope units; slope maps were hand drawn as described in the Kansas study. This choice seems reasonable, as 0 to 5 percent slopes involve minimal engineering costs in the construction of either highways or buildings; 5 to 15 percent slopes require moderate expenditure and increasingly sophisticated engineering; and 15 percent slopes are near the limit for normal engineering practice, as in the construction of homes or roads. The normally accepted slope limit for the fields of septic tanks is about 10 percent; under extraordinary circumstances, septic tanks may be built on slopes as high as 15 percent.

RESULTS

The results of this study are best shown as a series of maps of the thick carbonate terrane, the alluvial-colluvial landscape, the fault zone, and the coastal plain. The variation in surface features for different terrain environmental units is shown as a series of topographic, environmental, and slope maps of identical areas (Figs. 4 through 7). Contour values vary from map to map to avoid the blocking of small contour intervals on steep slopes.

Thick Carbonate Terrane

Four environmental units are important within the thick carbonate terrane: karstic tableland, karstic lowland, deeply dissected carbonate, and moderately dissected carbonate. The karstic lowland will be left for a later illustration, as this unit is an essential element within the Balcones fault zone. The other three units are distinctive in topography, soils, and vegetation. They differ in morphology and in the kind of active processes determining their characteristics. The topography and the slope, in percent, are varied for each unit.

The karstic tableland is composed predominantly of limestone with rare dolomite. This unit has very low topographic relief, and no slopes were measured greater than 5 percent (Fig. 4). Not only can standing water accumulate in scattered local sinkholes, but there are also local sags, not easily explained by solution, which may contain standing water. However, because of the soil development, water generally infiltrates. There is minor runoff along the dissected edge of the karstic tableland.

The slopes off the dissected margin of the karstic tableland vary in steepness and form (Fig. 4). From the nearly flat karstic tableland, the slope steepens gently and is nearly planar or concave in the moderately dissected unit in which all slopes are less than 15 percent, frequently less than 5 percent. Where there is rapid transition from the level karstic tableland into the deeply

dissected unit, slopes steepen abruptly, and most are convex. Within the deeply dissected unit, all slopes are greater than 5 percent; valley walls of headward-eroding streams generally exceed 15 percent. Some small areas of less than 5 percent slope are too small to map at the final scale and are therefore considered as part of the deeply dissected unit.

Figure 5 shows a clear separation of deeply dissected and moderately dissected units. The moderately dissected unit includes large areas of less than 5 percent slope, whereas the deeply dissected unit has only minor less than 5 percent slopes occurring as narrow floors of steep-walled valleys. The moderately dissected unit contains no slopes greater than 15 percent,

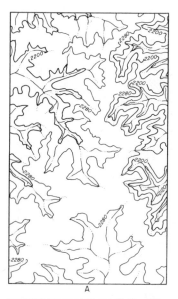

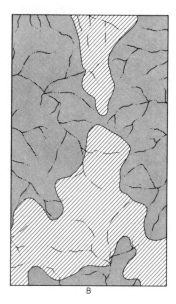

A.   CONTOUR INTERVAL=80 FEET

B   ENVIRONMENT

▨ Moderately dissected

▩ Deeply dissected

C. SLOPE

☐ < 5 percent

▨ 5-15 percent

▩ > 15 percent

0   1 Mile
0   1   2 Km

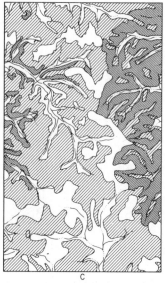

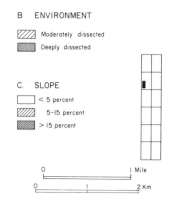

Figure 5. Topographic expression (A) of the deeply dissected and moderately dissected thick carbonate environmental units (B) and the corresponding slope units (C) in the southern Edwards Plateau.

whereas much of the deeply dissected unit has slopes greater than 15 percent. Both units have slopes between 5 and 15 percent. No quantitative expression of percent slope separates moderately from deeply dissected carbonate terrane.

Surfaces of moderately dissected units are commonly root-plowed to remove the trees (Fig. 5). Infiltration and recharge are more important than runoff here. The dominant process in the deeply dissected unit is runoff.

In the fault zone, the downfaulted limestone shows fracturing and solution (Fig. 6) and therefore has been noted as a separate environmental unit — the karstic lowland. The karstic lowland has slopes of less than 15 percent. In areal extent, the classes of slopes of less than 5 percent and from 5 to 15 percent are about equally represented. The sinkholes which occur in slopes of less than 5 percent may be young or old land forms and are frequently filled with clay. A reversal of topography can occur in clay-filled sinkholes; the topographic rever-

sal is generally less than three feet. Aerial photographs of the karstic lowland reveal closely spaced fractures (lineations). This unit appears locally capable of rapid infiltration of precipitation into its moderate soil and, over-all, has greater recharge than runoff.

To approximate the relative areal distribution of each environmental unit, the test strip was placed over a grid and points of intersection of environmental units and grid counted. For the entire test strip, the karstic tableland makes up 2.7 percent of the area, the deeply dissected thick carbonate constitutes 53.5 percent, the moderately dissected carbonate is 3 percent, and the karstic lowland is 5 percent.

Alluvial-Colluvial Landscapes

For the test strip, Figure 7 illustrates a representative distribution of the alluvial-colluvial environmental units: flood plain, terrace, alluvial fan, and the undifferentiated unit. The flood plain is a narrow, linear, slightly sloping area bordering underfit incised streams; it is subject to flooding every one or two years. The perennial stream shown in the flood plain is fed by springs. Most of the wider parts of the stream are generally results of low man-made dams and concrete low-water crossings. Locally resistant limestone or dolomite beds form temporary low dams and may pond water several feet deep far upstream. There is active recharge of the Edwards Limestone throughout the flood plain, both directly from the stream and indirectly through flood-plain alluvium.

Stream terraces occur as at least two consistent mappable levels, possibly three levels, in the test-strip area. Only the terraces are mapped, and levels are not distinguished, because they relate to the same alluvial process and are formed of the same materials. Physical processes, physical properties, slopes, resources, and land use are identical for each terrace level. The terraces, as well as the flood plain, everywhere include slopes of less than 5 percent.

On stereo aerial photographs, the terraces are observed to clearly slope downstream. The terraces are never so level as to naturally pond water; generally they are also so permeable that water will not pond. There are unusual terraces that have caliche on the surface, where standing water may collect. Water is more likely to accumulate on older higher level terraces, as they are more heavily calichified; borrow pits are evident on the photographs of high terrace levels. Where caliche is widespread in the terrace, runoff may exceed recharge; however, the normal process on terraces is for recharge to exceed runoff.

The alluvial fans are clearly distinguished by their shape. The head of the fan usually slopes more than 5 percent (Fig. 7), but the predominant slope is less than 5 percent. Many alluvial fans are cut by relatively deep

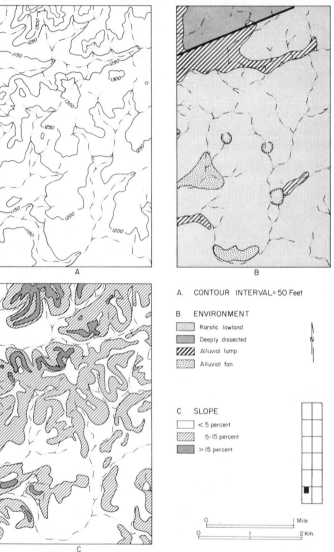

A. CONTOUR INTERVAL = 50 Feet

B. ENVIRONMENT

Karstic lowland
Deeply dissected
Alluvial lump
Alluvial fan

C. SLOPE

< 5 percent
5-15 percent
> 15 percent

0   1 Mile
0   1   2 Km.

Figure 6. Topographic expression (A) of the deeply dissected thick carbonate, karstic lowland, alluvial-fan, and undifferentiated alluvial-colluvial environmental units (B) and the equivalent slope units (C) in the Balcones fault zone, a major recharge area of the Edwards Limestone aquifer.

stream valleys, suggesting that the fans are older features than the modern drainage. In the field, local sliding of new soil on top of caliche is observed. Caliche borrow pits are common in fans, and soil movement is indicated on photographs by an irregularly rippled surface near the toe of fans. In addition to soil movement, there is local colluvial contribution to the fans not readily apparent on photographs. The ratio of recharge to runoff depends on the extent and degree of calichification in each fan.

As noted in the description of the environmental units, the undifferentiated unit generally includes alluvial and colluvial landscapes where it is not possible to accurately map flood plain, terrace, alluvial fans, and colluviation on aerial photographs. As might be expected, the shapes of mapped undifferentiated units are highly irregular. Slopes exceeding 5 percent are not uncommon on the undifferentiated units. Generalizations regarding recharge and runoff would be inaccurate.

The areal distribution of the alluvial and colluvial landscapes in the test strip is 5 percent flood plain, 4 percent terraces, 9 percent alluvial fans, and 9 percent undifferentiated units.

Coastal Plain

The coastal plain is south of most recharge into the Edwards Limestone aquifer; it also lies south of the Balcones fault zone and escarpment. Coastal plain slopes are less than 5 percent except for peripheries of the few relatively resistant limestones over which 5 to 15 percent slopes are mapped. The single dominant environmental unit of the coastal plain is the fan plain, which accounts for 5.3 percent of the test-strip area.

A fan plain is a widespread clastic wedge as much as 30 ft (10 m) thick in local sand and gravel pits, base not exposed, and probably thicker than observed. The fan plain itself is an aquifer. Numerous wells providing water for stock and for dwellings are evidence of the recharge and water-bearing potential of the fan plain. Wherever the fan plain overlies a permeable rock, such as a fractured limestone or chalk, there is possible recharge to the deeper Edwards aquifer so long as the entire lithologic system is open.

Other environmental units mapped in the coastal plain include thin carbonate rock, shale, and flood plain. The thin carbonate terrane of the coastal plain has a subdued topography. In some places, the carbonate rock, where heavily jointed, has slid downslope on the underlying shale.

Two distinctive shale units occur. One type is a homogeneous, dense, slightly calichified clay that when wet is very plastic with high shrink-swell ratio. On aerial photographs, it appears as a homogeneous white tone and underlies the jointed limestone. A second type is a silty shale with discontinuous flaggy sands that are lenticular and thin. On aerial photographs, it appears dark toned and commonly displays a chaotic texture. This shale is heavily calichified at the surface.

GEOLOGY AND LAND USE PLANNING

Until recent years, the southern Edwards Plateau and its major recharge zone were nearly pristine. Land use was dominantly agricultural. Now this land is in great demand locally for urbanization and everywhere for recreation. Most of the urban pressure is on that area within an hour by automobile from San Antonio. Included in that area are two lakes — Canyon Lake and Medina Lake (Fig. 3).

What is going to be the effect of lakeside developments, as at Canyon Lake and

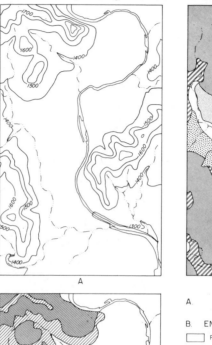
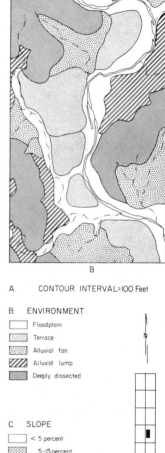

A   CONTOUR INTERVAL=100 Feet

B.   ENVIRONMENT

☐ Floodplain
▨ Terrace
▨ Alluvial fan
▨ Alluvial lump
▨ Deeply dissected

C.   SLOPE

☐ < 5 percent
▨ 5-15 percent
▨ > 15 percent

Figure 7. Topographic expression (A) of a wide valley illustrating the deeply dissected thick carbonate, flood-plain, terrace, alluvial-fan, and undifferentiated alluvial-colluvial environmental units (B) and appropriate slope units (C), indicating gently sloping terrain.

Medina Lake, where fairly large communities are being built, if geologic features are ignored? Along both lakes, some roads and streets are developed on the hills in a rectangular plan, ignoring the topography; moreover, almost all the homes use septic tanks for waste disposal. In steep limestone terrane, rectangular street and lot development may result in heavy erosion, and septic tanks do not have the necessary drainage field to filter wastes. Property owners unaware of the geologic constraints may suffer economic losses, and a loss of quality in aquifers downdip may also result. Fortunately at this time, water quality losses are minimal, but quality could deteriorate in the future. This potential pollution problem needs management. Larger cities with well-developed sewage systems may do less damage to a karst environment than man's unorganized use of previously undeveloped land.

Results of our mapping are directly applicable to the planning of specific suburban projects in the carbonate recharge zone. In the vicinity of the lakes, the suburban planner can use maps of both the environmental units and slopes to identify those steep areas where heavy surficial runoff and inadequate subsurface drainage of septic tanks will cause problems in housing developments. Recharge zones that need protection can be identified; the government planner or private real estate developer may choose either to restrict these zones as greenbelts or to engineer special construction which passes all fluids over and beyond critical zones.

In addition, these results of environmental mapping will be valuable for planning and regulating future recreational use of the hill country. The higher carbonate terrane, including the karstic tableland, the deeply dissected, and the moderately dissected units, will have minor use — mostly hunting and hiking; indeed, the major income in many localities having only these units is from leasing land for hunting. The lowlands, however, will be crowded with temporary and permanent housing, as well as with people fishing, floating, and swimming in spring-fed streams. Along with previously identified problems of construction, flooding will be an important concern. The flood-plain unit of the environmental map floods every one or two years, and certain terrace units are also flooded on rare occasions.

Even in the lowland, the concern remains for maintaining good quality for that water which will recharge the aquifer. It has been generally accepted by Texas hydrologists that major recharge occurs where streams flow over the Balcones faults. In the lowlands, both slope and geologic foundation material are important considerations in most construction projects. For example, construction on highly jointed carbonate rock overlying plastic shale should be avoided.

SUMMARY AND CONCLUSIONS

A technique developed for rapid reconnaissance mapping of environmental geologic units for the southern Edwards Plateau is applicable in any predominantly carbonate region and of particular value where major carbonate rock bodies persist into the subsurface and become important aquifers. The technique includes the study of black-and-white aerial photographs — both mosaics and stereo pairs, along with periodic field reconnaissance.

The selection of environmental geologic units depends upon qualitative assessment of both geologic processes and present and projected land use. The environmental units take into consideration recharge hydrology, urbanization, industrialization, recreation, engineering, ranching, and farming; equally important are variations in rock composition, fracturing and faulting, slopes, pedology, and vegetation.

Compared to earlier environmental mapping by geologists, especially those workers cited on preceding pages, the technique presented herein is significantly different. Prior workers have emphasized rock properties or engineering properties of materials. Our technique emphasizes geomorphic units and their hydrologic characteristics to a greater degree, because ground water (and its recharge) is the most valuable natural resource in this region. For example, it is not so important to separate limestone from dolomite from marl where a thick section of one or more of these rock types occurs on a steep slope. It is more important to recognize that little recharge can occur because of rapid runoff on the steep slope. Furthermore, on a steep slope, there will be little soil and no grass. Therefore, few kinds of domesticated animals can survive, and man will rarely build on this kind of land.

We will be compiling a regional environmental geologic map based on our initial work in this test strip. Such a regional environmental geologic map can be a valuable guide to government and other planners and regulators of land use. It must be recognized, however, that the technique described herein yields a regional map that, as such, is a qualitative guide to the user. For detailed planning, as in construction or sanitary engineering, additional quantitative geologic data must be collected.

ACKNOWLEDGMENTS

For permission to publish this paper, we thank the Bureau of Economic Geology. The work was supported by a Bureau contract with the Texas Water Development Board.

This paper was presented in part before the Annual Meetings of the Geological Society of America in Minneapolis, 1972.

REFERENCES CITED

Anderson, J. R., Hardy, E. E., and Roach, J. T., 1972, A land-use classification system for use with remote-sensor data: U.S. Geol. Survey Circ. 671, 16 p.
Brown, L. F., Jr., Fisher, W. L., Erxleben, A. W., and McGowen, J. H., 1971, Resource capability units, their utility in land- and water-use management with examples from the Texas coastal zone: Texas Univ. Bur. Econ. Geology Geol. Circ. 71-1, 22p.
Danehy, E. A., and Harding, R. C., eds., 1969, Urban environmental geology in the San Francisco Bay region: San Francisco, Assoc. Econ. Geologists Spec. Pub., 162 p.
DeCook, K. J., 1963, Geology and ground-water resources of Hays County, Texas: U.S. Geol. Survey Water-Supply Paper 1612, 72 p.
Fenneman, N. M., 1931, Physiography of western United States: New York, McGraw-Hill, Inc., 534 p.
Fisher, W. L., McGowen, J. H., Brown, L. F., Jr., and Groat, C. G., 1972, Environmental geologic atlas of the Texas Coastal Zone — Galveston-Houston area: Texas Univ. Bur. Econ. Geology, 91 p.
Flawn, P. T., 1970, Environmental geology: New York, Harper & Row, 313 p.
Folk, R. L., 1954, The distinction between grain size and mineralogical composition in sedimentary rock nomenclature: Jour. Geology, v. 52, p. 345–351.
Hayes, W. S., and Vineyard, J. D., 1969, Environmental geology in town and country: Missouri Geol. Survey and Water Resources Educ. Ser. 2, 42 p.
Johnson, S. L., and Smith, R. E., 1965, Urban hydrology of the Houston, Texas, metropolitan area: U.S. Geol. Survey open-file rept., 214 p.
Kansas Geological Survey Study Committee, 1968, A pilot study of land-use planning and environmental geology: Kansas Geol. Survey, Planning for Development "701" Project no. Kans. P-43, Rept. no. 15D, 52 p.
LaMoreaux, P. E., and others, 1971, Environmental geology and hydrology, Madison County, Alabama, Meridianville quadrangle: Alabama Geol. Survey, Atlas Ser. no. 1, 72 p.
Pessl, Fred, Jr., Langer, W. H., and Ryder, R. B., 1972, Geologic and hydrologic maps for land use planning in the Connecticut Valley with examples from the Hartford North quadrangle, Connecticut: U.S. Geol. Survey Circ. 674, 12 p.
Rose, P. R., 1972, Edwards Group, surface and subsurface, central Texas: Texas Univ. Bur. Econ. Geology Rept. Inv. 74, 198 p.
Stricklin, F. L., Jr., Smith, C. I., and Lozo, F. E., 1971, Stratigraphy of Lower Cretaceous Trinity deposits of central Texas: Texas Univ. Bur. Econ. Geology Rept. Inv. 71, 63 p.
Welder, F. A., and Reeves, R. D., 1962, Geology and ground-water resources of Uvalde County: Texas Water Comm. Bull. 6212, 252 p.

MANUSCRIPT RECEIVED BY THE SOCIETY APRIL 9, 1973
REVISED MANUSCRIPT RECEIVED SEPTEMBER 27, 1973
PUBLICATION AUTHORIZED BY THE DIRECTOR, BUREAU OF ECONOMIC GEOLOGY, UNIVERSITY OF TEXAS AT AUSTIN

Part IV

Land Capability

Papers 8 and 9: Introductory Review

8 KLINGEBIEL and MONTGOMERY
Land Capability Classification

9 VAN VLIET, MACKINTOSH, and HOFFMAN
Effects of Land Capability on Apple Production in Southern Ontario

Land capability analysis is probably the best-known topic in land evaluation. This is due to several factors: it has been widely adopted for over 25 years, the resultant maps are easy to understand, and land use planning policies in several countries now depend upon an assessment of land capability. The origins of land capability evaluation can be traced to the reasons for the formation of the United States Soil Conservation Service. The impetus was massive soil erosion, especially in the American Midwest, and the acute need was to identify types of land use that would not lead to environmental degradation. General reviews of land capability are given by Davidson (1980), McRae and Burnham (1981), and Davidson (1982).

This section begins with a reprint of the United States Department of Agriculture (USDA) handbook on land capability classification (Paper 8) written by Klingebiel and Montgomery. In many regards this publication, closely followed by the Food and Agriculture Organization (FAO) *Framework for Land Evaluation* (discussed in Part I), can be proposed as the most significant contribution to land evaluation. The USDA scheme has as its focus the interpretation of soil mapping units according to degree of constraint posed to land use. Three levels of classification are defined: capability class, capability subclass, and capability unit (in increasing order of detail). Eight classes are described, with class I posing little or no limitation to land use while class VIII is only capable of supporting wildlife. Classes I to IV offer varying degrees of possibility for arable cultivation; arable farming is not deemed suitable for lower classes.

The assignment of soil mapping units to classes, subclasses, or units is dependent upon a set of assumptions and these are clearly stated by Klingebiel and Montgomery. For example, in assumption 1, priority is given to assessing permanent soil characteristics in terms of degree of constraint posed to land use. Consideration is also given to the interaction of soil and climatic conditions. Different types of soil can exist within the same capability class but they present similar degrees of constraint. Assumptions are also made about level of management, effects of changes in soil conditions (for example, drainage), and the location and layout of farms. The most critical part of the report is the description of capability classes, subclasses, and units, followed by guidelines in allocating soil mapping units to classes.

Perhaps the outstanding advantage of the land capability classification is its flexibility—it can be interpreted and applied in a form relevant to local conditions. Consequently, the lack of quantitative details on classes, subclasses, and units has distinct merit. The disadvantage of the qualitative approach is the high degree of subjectivity: surveyors could come to different conclusions about the same area. McRae and Burnham (1981) list 12 advantages and 9 disadvantages of the system. Nevertheless, the use that has been made of land capability maps in the U.S. is extensive. There is continuing concern about soil loss—for example, between 1977 and 1982, the area of cropland in the highly erodible classes of IVe, VIe, VII, and VIII increased by 9.2% (Lee, 1984). One major objective of the Soil Conservation Act of 1984 is to prevent farmers who cultivate such land from receiving federal program benefits unless there is approval of a conservation plan. At the other end of the scale, land capability assessment has been crucial to the identification and delimitation of prime agricultural land (see Paper 15).

The U.S. land capability scheme is essentially negative in approach whereby the degree of limitation to land use is assessed. This is in marked contrast to the central concept of the FAO *Framework for Land Evaluation* in which land units are assessed with reference to the requirements of specific land uses. One route for modifying the U.S. system has been to design land classifications geared to particular land uses. Canadian research has very much been in this direction. The Canada Land Inventory—as the body charged with surveying, classifying, and mapping land capability—has developed separate classifications for agriculture, forestry, recreation, and wildlife (Environment Canada, 1970). The approach was based on the U.S. scheme, though the number of classes was reduced from eight to seven. Another strength of the Canadian program has been that, within a few years, land capability maps were available for the whole of the settled area of Canada. Paper 19 demonstrates the application of a capability analysis to planning of the Ottawa urban fringe. The merits of classification schemes remain academic unless planners obtain comprehensive map cover showing the land capability.

The British experience in modifying the U.S. scheme is also of interest. The Soil Surveys of England and Wales and Scotland evolved a *Land Use Capability Classification,* very similar to the American scheme but with seven classes and many more quantitative guidelines (Bibby and Mackney, 1969). Since 1969 the Surveys have been publishing land use capability maps at scales of 1:63,360 (now 1:50,000) and a few at 1:25,000. It is unfortunate that these maps never became integral on a national basis to planning procedures—in part, because of the patchy nature of the map cover, but also because of weaknesses in the original classification. The result has been the much more refined and detailed *Land Capability Classification for Agriculture* (Bibby et al., 1982). Key advances in this new scheme are the greater level of detail given to guidelines, importance given to soil workability and droughtiness, and the subdivision of classes III and IV into two divisions and classes V and VI into three divisions. Classes III and IV in the older scheme were criticized for being too broad, and the introduction of subdivisions solves that problem. Particular importance is attached to the grazing values of upland areas for the subdivision of classes V and VI. In Scotland this land classification has been officially accepted for grading of agricultural land, a decision also made possible by the availability of full map cover.

Much emphasis is given in the American and subsequent land capability classifications to the point that land within the same class is similar in terms of degree of limitation to use. Predictions of yield are not included in the method though some relationship might be expected between degree of limitation and crop response. Yield characteristics are taken into account at the unit level: according to Table 1 in Paper 8, capability units have comparable potential productivity. This scale of capability analysis is relevant to individual farms when the objective might be to introduce a new land conservation scheme. Another objective might be to carry out a cost-benefit analysis of possible farming strategies and this would clearly require estimates of crop yields.

Paper 9 examines the relationships between yields of one crop (apples) and land capability classes as defined in a system for tree fruits. At 171 sampling sites, data were collected on yield, soil, climatic, and management variables. Much of the paper is devoted to statistical analysis, and of particular interest is the section on land capability-yield relationships. After a modification was made to the classification, statistically significant relationships were obtained between average apple yield and capability class though differences were not established between all classes. On the basis of these relationships the authors propose that land capability provides an important framework if planning priority is given to protecting areas very suited to apple production.

The success of this study can largely be explained by the fact that use was made of a land capability classification specific to the crop. In another Canadian study, Peters (1977) examined the relationships between yields of cereals (wheat, oats, and barley), agroclimatic conditions, soil capability, and soil type. What emerged was that climate had the major influence on yields, though certain soils were distinguished by having higher yields. A closer correlation might have been established if climatic and soil conditions had been fused into one capability classification. In the Canadian soil capability classification for agriculture, climatic characteristics are only considered at subclass level. There is much merit, as demonstrated by the British scheme, in combining soil and climatic assessments within one classification.

This introductory discussion of relationships between yield and land capability may well cloud the distinction between land capability and land quality. It is best to consider the former as referring to permanent or semipermanent attributes of land and the extent to which these pose limitations to land use. Land quality, as will be discussed in Part VII, is much more focused on prediction of crop performance; as such, changeable properties such as nutrient status and pH can assume importance. Therefore close relationships should not be expected between crop yield and general land capability classes. It is only when specific classifications are evolved—such as for apple production—that statistical relationships emerge.

REFERENCES

Bibby, J. S., and D. Mackney, 1969, Land Use Capability Classification, Tech. Monograph No. 1, Soil Survey, U. K.

Bibby, J. S., H. A. Douglas, A. J. Thomasson, and J. S. Robertson, 1982, Land Capability Classification for Agriculture, *Soil Survey of Scotland Monograph,* Macaulay Institute for Soil Research, Aberdeen.

Davidson, D. A., 1980, *Soils and Land Use Planning,* Longman, London.

Davidson, D. A., 1982, *The Assessment of Land Use Capability,* Proceedings of the First Internat. Symposium on Soil, Geology and Landforms, Bangkok, G2, pp.1-57.

Environment Canada, 1970, *The Canada Land Inventory: Objectives, Scope and Organisation,* Report No. 1, Lands Directorate, Ottawa.

Lee, L.K., 1984, Land Use and Soil Loss: A 1982 Update, *Jour. Soil and Water Conserv.* **39:**226-228.

McRae, S.G., and C. P. Burnham, 1981, *Land Evaluation,* Oxford University Press, Oxford.

Peters, T. W., 1977, Relationships of Yield Data to Agroclimates, Soil Capability Classification and Soils of Alberta, *Canadian Jour. Soil Sci.* **57:**341-347.

8: LAND CAPABILITY CLASSIFICATION

A. A. Klingebiel and P. H. Montgomery

Soil Scientists, Soil Conservation Service

The standard soil-survey map shows the different kinds of soil that are significant and their location in relation to other features of the landscape. These maps are intended to meet the needs of users with widely different problems and, therefore, contain considerable detail to show important basic soil differences.

The information on the soil map must be explained in a way that has meaning to the user. These explanations are called interpretations. Soil maps can be interpreted by (1) the individual kinds of soil on the map, and (2) the grouping of soils that behave similarly in responses to management and treatment. Because there are many kinds of soil, there are many individual soil interpretations. Such interpretations, however, provide the user with all the information that can be obtained from a soil map. Many users of soil maps want more general information than that of the individual soil-mapping unit. Soils are grouped in different ways according to the specific needs of the map user. The kinds of soil grouped and the variation permitted within each group differ according to the use to be made of the grouping.

The capability classification is one of a number of interpretive groupings made primarily for agricultural purposes. As with all interpretive groupings the capability classification begins with the individual soil-mapping units, which are building stones of the system (table 1). In this classification the arable soils are grouped according to their potentialities and limitations for sustained production of the common cultivated crops that do not require specialized site conditioning or site treatment. Nonarable soils (soils unsuitable for longtime sustained use for cultivated crops) are grouped according to their potentialities and limitations for the production of permanent vegetation and according to their risks of soil damage if mismanaged.

The individual mapping units on soil maps show the location and extent of the different kinds of soil. One can make the greatest number of precise statements and predictions about the use and management of the individual mapping units shown on the soil map. The capability grouping of soils is designed (1) to help landowners and others use and interpret the soil maps, (2) to introduce users to the detail of the soil map itself, and (3) to make possible broad generalizations based on soil potentialities, limitations in use, and management problems.

The capability classification provides three major categories of soil groupings: (1) Capability unit, (2) capability subclass, and (3) capability class.

Reprinted from *USDA Handbook 210*, U.S. Department of Agriculture, Washington, D.C., 1961, pp. 1-21

TABLE 1.—Relationship of soil-mapping unit to capability classification

Soil-mapping unit	Capability unit	Capability subclass	Capability class
A soil mapping unit is a portion of the landscape that has similar characteristics and qualities and whose limits are fixed by precise definitions. Within the cartographic limitations and considering the purpose for which the map is made, the soil mapping unit is the unit about which the greatest number of precise statements and predictions can be made.	A capability unit is a grouping of one or more individual soil mapping units having similar potentials and continuing limitations or hazards. The soils in a capability unit are sufficiently uniform to (a) produce similar kinds of cultivated crops and pasture plants with similar management practices, (b) require similar conservation treatment and management under the same kind and condition of vegetative cover, (c) have comparable potential productivity.	Subclasses are groups of capability units which have the same major conservation problem, such as— e—Erosion and runoff. w—Excess water. s—Root-zone limitations. c—Climatic limitations.	Capability classes are groups of capability subclasses or capability units that have the same relative degree of hazard or limitation. The risks of soil damage or limitation in use become progressively greater from class I to class VIII.
The soil mapping units provide the most detailed soils information. The basic mapping units are the basis for all interpretive groupings of soils. They furnish the information needed for developing capability units, forest site groupings, crop suitability groupings, range site groupings, engineering groupings, and other interpretive groupings. The most specific management practices and estimated yields are related to the individual mapping unit.	The capability unit condenses and simplifies soils information for planning individual tracts of land, field by field. Capability units with the class and subclass furnish information about the degree of limitation, kind of conservation problems and the management practices needed.	The capability subclass provides information as to the kind of conservation problem or limitations involved. The class and subclass together provide the map user information about both the degree of limitation and kind of problem involved for broad program planning, conservation need studies, and similar purposes.	The capability classes are useful as a means of introducing the map user to the more detailed information on the soil map. The classes show the location, amount, and general suitability of the soils for agricultural use. Only information concerning general agricultural limitations in soil use are obtained at the capability class level.

The first category, capability unit, is a grouping of soils that have about the same responses to systems of management of common cultivated crops and pasture plants. Soils in any one capability unit are adapted to the same kinds of common cultivated and pasture plants and require similar alternative systems of management for these crops. Longtime estimated yields of adapted crops for individual soils within the unit under comparable management do not vary more than about 25 percent.[1]

The second category, the subclass, is a grouping of capability units having similar kinds of limitations and hazards. Four general kinds of limitations or hazards are recognized: (1) Erosion hazard, (2) wetness, (3) rooting-zone limitations, and (4) climate.

The third and broadest category in the capability classification places all the soils in eight capability classes. The risks of soil damage or limitations in use become progressively greater from class I to class VIII. Soils in the first four classes under good management are capable of producing adapted plants, such as forest trees or range plants, and the common cultivated field crops [2] and pasture plants. Soils in classes V, VI, and VII are suited to the use of adapted native plants. Some soils in classes V and VI are also capable of producing specialized crops, such as certain fruits and ornamentals, and even field and vegetable crops under highly intensive management involving elaborate practices for soil and water conservation.[3] Soils in class VIII do not return on-site benefits for inputs of management for crops, grasses, or trees without major reclamation.

The grouping of soils into capability units, subclasses, and classes is done primarily on the basis of their capability to produce common cultivated crops and pasture plants without deterioration over a long period of time. To express suitability of the soils for range and woodland use, the soil-mapping units are grouped into range sites and woodland-suitability groups.

ASSUMPTIONS

In assigning soils to the various capability groupings a number of assumptions are made. Some understanding of these assumptions is necessary if

---

[1] Yields are significant at the capability-unit level and are one of the criteria used in establishing capability units within a capability class. Normally, yields are estimated under the common management that maintains the soil resource. The main periods for such yield estimates are 10 or more years in humid areas or under irrigation and 20 or more years in subhumid or semiarid areas. The 25 percent allowable range is for economically feasible yields of adapted cultivated and pasture crops.

[2] As used here the common crops include: Corn, cotton, tobacco, wheat, tame hay and pasture, oats, barley, grain sorghum, sugarcane, sugar beets, peanuts, soybeans, field-grown vegetables, potatoes, sweet potatoes, field peas and beans, flax, and most clean-cultivated fruit, nut, and ornamental plants. They do not include: Rice, cranberries, blueberries, and those fruit, nut, and ornamental plants that require little or no cultivation.

[3] Soil and water conservation practices is a general expression for all practices including but not limited to those for erosion control.

the soils are to be grouped consistently in the capability classification and if the groupings are to be used properly. They are:

1. A taxonomic (or natural) soil classification is based directly on soil characteristics. The capability classification (unit, subclass, and class) is an interpretive classification based on the effects of combinations of climate and permanent soil characteristics on risks of soil damage, limitations in use, productive capacity, and soil management requirements. Slope, soil texture, soil depth, effects of past erosion, permeability, water-holding capacity, type of clay minerals, and the many other similar features are considered permanent soil qualities and characteristics. Shrubs, trees, or stumps are not considered permanent characteristics.

2. The soils within a capability class are similar only with respect to degree of limitations in soil use for agricultural purposes or hazard to the soil when it is so used. Each class includes many different kinds of soil, and many of the soils within any one class require unlike management and treatment. Valid generalizations about suitable kinds of crops or other management needs cannot be made at the class level.

3. A favorable ratio of output to input [4] is one of several criteria used for placing any soil in a class suitable for cultivated crop, grazing, or woodland use, but no further relation is assumed or implied between classes and output-input ratios. The capability classification is not a productivity rating for specific crops.. Yield estimates are developed for specific kinds of soils and are included in soil handbooks and soil-survey reports.

4. A moderately high level of management is assumed—one that is practical and within the ability of a majority of the farmers and ranchers. The level of management is that commonly used by the "reasonable" men of the community. The capability classification is not, however, a grouping of soils according to the most profitable use to be made of the land. For example, many soils in class III or IV, defined as suitable for several uses including cultivation, may be more profitably used for grasses or trees than for cultivated crops.

5. Capability classes I through IV are distinguished from each other by a summation of the degree of limitations or risks of soil damage that affect their management requirements for longtime sustained use for cultivated crops. Nevertheless, differences in kinds of management or yields of perennial vegetation may be greater between some pairs of soils within one class than between some pairs of soils from different classes. The capability class is not determined by the kind of practices recommended. For example, class II, III, or IV may or may not require the same kind of practices when used for cultivated crops, and classes I through VII may or may not require the same kind of pasture, range, or woodland practices.

---

[4] Based on longtime economic trends for average farms and farmers using moderately high level management. May not apply to specific farms and farmers but will apply to broad areas.

6. Presence of water on the surface or excess water in the soil; lack of water for adequate crop production; presence of stones; presence of soluble salts or exchangeable sodium, or both; or hazard of overflow are not considered permanent limitations to use where the removal of these limitations is feasible.[5]

7. Soils considered feasible for improvement by draining, by irrigating, by removing stones, by removing salts or exchangeable sodium, or by protecting from overflow are classified according to their continuing limitations in use, or the risks of soil damage, or both, after the improvements have been installed. Differences in initial costs of the systems installed on individual tracts of land do not influence the classification. The fact that certain wet soils are in classes II, III, and IV does not imply that they should be drained. But it does indicate the degree of their continuing limitation in use or risk of soil damage, or both, if adequately drained. Where it is considered not feasible to improve soils by drainage, irrigation, stone removal, removal of excess salts or exchangeable sodium, or both, or to protect them from overflow, they are classified according to present limitations in use.

8. Soils already drained or irrigated are grouped according to the continuing soil and climatic limitations and risks that affect their use under the present systems or feasible improvements in them.

9. The capability classification of the soils in an area may be changed when major reclamation projects are installed that permanently change the limitations in use or reduce the hazards or risks of soil or crop damage for long periods of time. Examples include establishing major drainage facilities, building levees or flood-retarding structures, providing water for irrigation, removing stones, or large-scale grading of gullied land. (Minor dams, terraces, or field conservation measures subject to change in their effectiveness in a short time are not included.)

10. Capability groupings are subject to change as new information about the behavior and responses of the soils becomes available.

11. Distance to market, kinds of roads, size and shape of the soil areas, locations within fields, skill or resources of individual operators, and other characteristics of land-ownership patterns are not criteria for capability groupings.

12. Soils with such physical limitations that common field crops can be cultivated and harvested only by hand are not placed in classes I, II, III, and IV. Some of these soils need drainage or stone removal, or both, before some kinds of machinery can be used. This does not imply that mechanical equipment cannot be used on some soils in capability classes V, VI, and VII.

13. Soils suited to cultivation are also suited to other uses such as pasture, range, forest, and wildlife. Some not suited to cultivation are suited to pasture, range, forest, or wildlife; others are suited only to pasture or

---

[5] Feasible as used in this context means (1) that the characteristics and qualities of the soil are such that it is possible to remove the limitation, and (2) that over broad areas it is within the realm of present-day economic possibility to remove the limitation.

range and wildlife; others only to forest and wildlife; and a few suited only to wildlife, recreation, and water-yielding uses. Groupings of soils for pasture, range, wildlife, or woodland may include soils from more than one capability class. Thus, to interpret soils for these uses, a grouping different from the capability classification is often necessary.

14. Research data, recorded observations, and experience are used as the bases for placing soils in capability units, subclasses, and classes. In areas where data on response of soils to management are lacking, soils are placed in capability groups by interpretation of soil characteristics and qualities in accord with the general principles about use and management developed for similar soils elsewhere.

CAPABILITY CLASSES

Land Suited to Cultivation and Other Uses

Class I—Soils in class I have few limitations that restrict their use.

Soils in this class are suited to a wide range of plants and may be used safely for cultivated crops, pasture, range, woodland, and wildlife. The soils are nearly level [6] and erosion hazard (wind or water) is low. They are deep, generally well drained, and easily worked. They hold water well and are either fairly well supplied with plant nutrients or highly responsive to inputs of fertilizer.

The soils in class I are not subject to damaging overflow. They are productive and suited to intensive cropping. The local climate must be favorable for growing many of the common field crops.

In irrigated areas, soils may be placed in class I if the limitation of the arid climate has been removed by relatively permanent irrigation works. Such irrigated soils (or soils potentially useful under irrigation) are nearly level, have deep rooting zones, have favorable permeability and water-holding capacity, and are easily maintained in good tilth. Some of the soils may require initial conditioning including leveling to the desired grade, leaching of a slight accumulation of soluble salts, or lowering of the seasonal water table. Where limitations due to salts, water table, overflow, or erosion are likely to recur, the soils are regarded as subject to permanent natural limitations and are not included in class I.

Soils that are wet and have slowly permeable subsoils are not placed in class I. Some kinds of soil in class I may be drained as an improvement measure for increased production and ease of operation.

Soils in class I that are used for crops need ordinary management practices to maintain productivity—both soil fertility and soil structure. Such practices may include the use of one or more of the following: Fertilizers and lime, cover and green-manure crops, conservation of crop residues and animal manures, and sequences of adapted crops,

---

[6] Some rapidly permeable soils in class I may have gentle slopes.

Class II—Soils in class II have some limitations that reduce the choice of plants or require moderate conservation practices.

Soils in class II require careful soil management, including conservation practices, to prevent deterioration or to improve air and water relations when the soils are cultivated. The limitations are few and the practices are easy to apply. The soils may be used for cultivated crops, pasture, range, woodland, or wildlife food and cover.

Limitations of soils in class II may include singly or in combination the effects of (1) gentle slopes, (2) moderate susceptibility to wind or water erosion or moderate adverse effects of past erosion, (3) less than ideal soil depth, (4) somewhat unfavorable soil structure and workability, (5) slight to moderate salinity or sodium easily corrected but likely to recur, (6) occasional damaging overflow, (7) wetness correctable by drainage but existing permanently as a moderate limitation, and (8) slight climatic limitations on soil use and management.

The soils in this class provide the farm operator less latitude in the choice of either crops or management practices than soils in class I. They may also require special soil-conserving cropping systems, soil conservation practices, water-control devices, or tillage methods when used for cultivated crops. For example, deep soils of this class with gentle slopes subject to moderate erosion when cultivated may need one of the following practices or some combination of two or more: Terracing, stripcropping, contour tillage, crop rotations that include grasses and legumes, vegetated water-disposal areas, cover or green-manure crops, stubble mulching, fertilizers, manure, and lime. The exact combinations of practices vary from place to place, depending on the characteristics of the soil, the local climate, and the farming system.

Class III—Soils in class III have severe limitations that reduce the choice of plants or require special conservation practices, or both.

Soils in class III have more restrictions than those in class II and when used for cultivated crops the conservation practices are usually more difficult to apply and to maintain. They may be used for cultivated crops, pasture, woodland, range, or wildlife food and cover.

Limitations of soils in class III restrict the amount of clean cultivation; timing of planting, tillage, and harvesting; choice of crops; or some combination of these limitations. The limitations may result from the effects of one or more of the following: (1) Moderately steep slopes; (2) high susceptibility to water or wind erosion or severe adverse effects of past erosion; (3) frequent overflow accompanied by some crop damage; (4) very slow permeability of the subsoil; (5) wetness or some continuing waterlogging after drainage; (6) shallow depths to bedrock, hardpan, fragipan, or claypan that limit the rooting zone and the water storage; (7) low moisture-holding capacity; (8) low fertility not easily corrected; (9) moderate salinity or sodium; or (10) moderate climatic limitations.

When cultivated, many of the wet, slowly permeable but nearly level soils in class III require drainage and a cropping system that maintains or improves the structure and tilth of the soil. To prevent puddling and to improve permeability it is commonly necessary to supply organic material to such soils and to avoid working them when they are wet. In some irrigated areas, part of the soils in class III have limited use because of high water table, slow permeability, and the hazard of salt or sodic accumulation. Each distinctive kind of soil in class III has one or more alternative combinations of use and practices required for safe use, but the number of practical alternatives for average farmers is less than that for soils in class II.

Class IV—Soils in class IV have very severe limitations that restrict the choice of plants, require very careful management, or both.

The restrictions in use for soils in class IV are greater than those in class III and the choice of plants is more limited. When these soils are cultivated, more careful management is required and conservation practices are more difficult to apply and maintain. Soils in class IV may be used for crops, pasture, woodland, range, or wildlife food and cover.

Soils in class IV may be well suited to only two or three of the common crops or the harvest produced may be low in relation to inputs over a long period of time. Use for cultivated crops is limited as a result of the effects of one or more permanent features such as (1) steep slopes, (2) severe susceptibility to water or wind erosion, (3) severe effects of past erosion, (4) shallow soils, (5) low moisture-holding capacity, (6) frequent overflows accompanied by severe crop damage, (7) excessive wetness with continuing hazard of waterlogging after drainage, (8) severe salinity or sodium, or (9) moderately adverse climate.

Many sloping soils in class IV in humid areas are suited to occasional but not regular cultivation. Some of the poorly drained, nearly level soils placed in class IV are not subject to erosion but are poorly suited to intertilled crops because of the time required for the soil to dry out in the spring and because of low productivity for cultivated crops. Some soils in class IV are well suited to one or more of the special crops, such as fruits and ornamental trees and shrubs, but this suitability itself is not sufficient to place a soil in class IV.

In subhumid and semiarid areas, soils in class IV may produce good yields of adapted cultivated crops during years of above average rainfall; low yields during years of average rainfall; and failures during years of below average rainfall. During the low rainfall years the soil must be protected even though there can be little or no expectancy of a marketable crop. Special treatments and practices to prevent soil blowing, conserve moisture, and maintain soil productivity are required. Sometimes crops must be planted or emergency tillage used for the primary purpose of maintaining the soil during years of low rainfall. These treatments must be applied more frequently or more intensively than on soils in class III.

Land Limited in Use—Generally Not Suited to Cultivation [7]

Class V—Soils in class V have little or no erosion hazard but have other limitations impractical to remove that limit their use largely to pasture, range, woodland, or wildlife food and cover.

Soils in class V have limitations that restrict the kind of plants that can be grown and that prevent normal tillage of cultivated crops. They are nearly level but some are wet, are frequently overflowed by streams, are stony, have climatic limitations, or have some combination of these limitations. Examples of class V are (1) soils of the bottom lands subject to frequent overflow that prevents the normal production of cultivated crops, (2) nearly level soils with a growing season that prevents the normal production of cultivated crops, (3) level or nearly level stony or rocky soils, and (4) ponded areas where drainage for cultivated crops is not feasible but where soils are suitable for grasses or trees. Because of these limitations cultivation of the common crops is not feasible but pastures can be improved and benefits from proper management can be expected.

Class VI—Soils in class VI have severe limitations that make them generally unsuited to cultivation and limit their use largely to pasture or range, woodland, or wildlife food and cover.

Physical conditions of soils placed in class VI are such that it is practical to apply range or pasture improvements, if needed, such as seeding, liming, fertilizing, and water control with contour furrows, drainage ditches, diversions, or water spreaders. Soils in class VI have continuing limitations that cannot be corrected, such as (1) steep slope, (2) severe erosion hazard, (3) effects of past erosion, (4) stoniness, (5) shallow rooting zone, (6) excessive wetness or overflow, (7) low-moisture capacity, (8) salinity or sodium, or (9) severe climate. Because of one or more of these limitations these soils are not generally suited to cultivated crops. But they may be used for pasture, range, woodland, or wildlife cover or for some combination of these.

Some soils in class VI can be safely used for the common crops provided unusually intensive management is used. Some of the soils in this class are also adapted to special crops such as sodded orchards, blueberries, or the like, requiring soil conditions unlike those demanded by the common crops. Depending upon soil features and local climate the soils may be well or poorly suited to woodlands.

---

[7] Certain soils grouped into classes V, VI, VII, and VIII may be made fit for use for crops with major earthmoving or other costly reclamation.

Class VII—Soils in class VII have very severe limitations that make them unsuited to cultivation and that restrict their use largely to grazing, woodland, or wildlife.

Physical conditions of soils in class VII are such that it is impractical to apply such pasture or range improvements as seeding, liming, fertilizing, and water control with contour furrows, ditches, diversions, or water spreaders. Soil restrictions are more severe than those in class VI because of one or more continuing limitations that cannot be corrected, such as (1) very steep slopes, (2) erosion, (3) shallow soil, (4) stones, (5) wet soil, (6) salts or sodium, (7) unfavorable climate, or (8) other limitations that make them unsuited to common cultivated crops. They can be used safely for grazing or woodland or wildlife food and cover or for some combination of these under proper management.

Depending upon the soil characteristics and local climate, soils in this class may be well or poorly suited to woodland. They are not suited to any of the common cultivated crops; in unusual instances, some soils in this class may be used for special crops under unusual management practices. Some areas of class VII may need seeding or planting to protect the soil and to prevent damage to adjoining areas.

Class VIII—Soils and landforms in class VIII have limitations that preclude their use for commercial plant production and restrict their use to recreation, wildlife, or water supply or to esthetic purposes.

Soils and landforms in class VIII cannot be expected to return significant on-site benefits from management for crops, grasses, or trees, although benefits from wildlife use, watershed protection, or recreation may be possible.

Limitations that cannot be corrected may result from the effects of one or more of the following: (1) Erosion or erosion hazard, (2) severe climate, (3) wet soil, (4) stones, (5) low-moisture capacity, and (6) salinity or sodium.

Badlands, rock outcrop, sandy beaches, river wash, mine tailings, and other nearly barren lands are included in class VIII. It may be necessary to give protection and management for plant growth to soils and landforms in class VIII in order to protect other more valuable soils, to control water, or for wildlife or esthetic reasons.

CAPABILITY SUBCLASSES

Subclasses are groups of capability units within classes that have the same kinds of dominant limitations for agricultural use as a result of soil and climate. Some soils are subject to erosion if they are not protected, while others are naturally wet and must be drained if crops are to be grown. Some soils are shallow or droughty or have other soil deficiencies. Still other soils occur in areas where climate limits their use. The four kinds of limitations recognized at the subclass level are: Risks of erosion, designated by the symbol (e); wetness, drainage, or overflow (w); rooting-zone limitations (s); and climatic limitations (c). The subclass provides the map user information about both the degree and kind of limitation. Capability class I has no subclasses.

Subclass **(e) erosion** is made up of soils where the susceptibility to erosion is the dominant problem or hazard in their use. Erosion susceptibility and past erosion damage are the major soil factors for placing soils in this subclass.

Subclass **(w) excess water** is made up of soils where excess water is the dominant hazard or limitation in their use. Poor soil drainage, wetness, high water table, and overflow are the criteria for determining which soils belong in this subclass.

Subclass **(s) soil limitations within the rooting zone** includes, as the name implies, soils that have such limitations as shallowness of rooting zones, stones, low moisture-holding capacity, low fertility difficult to correct, and salinity or sodium.

Subclass **(c) climatic limitation** is made up of soils where the climate (temperature or lack of moisture) is the only major hazard or limitation in their use.[8]

Limitations imposed by erosion, excess water, shallow soils, stones, low moisture-holding capacity, salinity, or sodium can be modified or partially overcome and take precedence over climate in determining subclasses. The dominant kind of limitation or hazard to the use of the land determines the assignment of capability units to the (e), (w), and (s) subclasses. Capability units that have no limitation other than climate are assigned to the (c) subclass.

Where two kinds of limitations that can be modified or corrected are essentially equal, the subclasses have the following priority: e, w, s. For example, we need to group a few soils of humid areas that have both an erosion hazard and an excess water hazard; with them the e takes precedence over the w. In grouping soils having both an excess water limitation and a rooting-zone limitation the w takes precedence over the s. In grouping soils of subhumid and semiarid areas that have both an erosion hazard and a climatic limitation the e takes precedence over the c, and in grouping soils with both rooting-zone limitations and climatic limitations the s takes precedence over the c.

Where soils have two kinds of limitations, both can be indicated if needed for local use; the dominant one is shown first. Where two kinds of problems are shown for a soil group, the dominant one is used for summarizing data by subclasses.

---

[8] Especially among young soils such as alluvial soils, although not limited to them, climatic phases of soil series must be established for proper grouping into capability units and into other interpretive groupings. Since the effects result from interactions between soil and climate, such climatic phases are not defined the same in terms of precipitation, temperature, and so on, for contrasting kinds of soil.

CAPABILITY UNITS

The capability units provide more specific and detailed information than the subclass for application to specific fields on a farm or ranch. A capability unit is a grouping of soils that are nearly alike in suitability for plant growth and responses to the same kinds of soil management. That is, a reasonably uniform set of alternatives can be presented for the soil, water, and plant management of the soils in a capability unit, not considering effects of past management that do not have a more or less permanent effect on the soil. Where soils have been so changed by management that permanent characteristics have been altered, they are placed in different soil series. Soils grouped into capability units respond in a similar way and require similar management although they may have soil characteristics that put them in different soil series.

Soils grouped into a capability unit should be sufficiently uniform in the combinations of soil characteristics that influence their qualities to have similar potentialities and continuing limitations or hazards. Thus the soils in a capability unit should be sufficiently uniform to (a) produce similar kinds of cultivated crops and pasture plants with similar management practices, (b) require similar conservation treatment and management under the same kind and condition of vegetative cover, and (c) have comparable potential productivity. (Estimated average yields under similar management systems should not vary more than about 25 percent among the kinds of soil included within the unit.)

OTHER KINDS OF SOIL GROUPINGS

Other kinds of interpretive soil groupings are necessary to meet specific needs. Among these are groupings for range use, woodland use, special crops, and engineering interpretation.

The range site is a grouping of soils with a potential for producing the same kinds and amounts of native forage. The range site for rangeland is comparable to the capability unit for cultivated land. The purpose of such a grouping is to show the potential for range use and to provide the basis for which the criteria for determining range condition can be established. The soils grouped into a single range site may be expected to produce similar longtime yields and respond similarly to alternative systems of management and to such practices as seeding, pitting, and water spreading.

Soils suitable for range but not for common cultivated crops may be placed in capability classes V and VI if they are capable of returning inputs from such management practices as seeding, fertilizing, or irrigating and in class VII if they are not. If these soils do not give economic returns under any kind of management when used for cultivated crops, pasture, woodland or range, they fall in class VIII.

Soil-woodland site index correlations are essential for interpreting the potential wood production of the individual soil units that are mapped.

Woodland-site indices are commonly developed for individual kinds of soils. Soil-mapping units can be placed in woodland groupings according to site indices for adapted species and other responses and limitations significant to woodland conservation. Such groupings do not necessarily parallel those for capability units or range sites; however, in some areas capability units may be grouped into range sites and woodland-suitability groups.

Rice has soil requirements unlike those of the common cultivated crops requiring well-aerated soils. Some fruits and ornamentals do not require clean cultivation. Therefore, these crops are not given weight in the capability grouping. Instead, special groupings of the soils for each of these crops are made in the areas where they are significant.

With a good basic table of yields and practices the soils can be placed in any number of suitability groups. Commonly, five groups—unsuited, fairly suited, moderately suited, well suited and very well suited—are sufficient.

Kinds of soil shown on the soil map are also grouped according to need for applying engineering measures including drainage, irrigation, land leveling, land grading; determining suitability as subgrade for roads; and constructing ponds and small dams. Such groupings may be unlike those made for other purposes.

CRITERIA FOR PLACING SOILS IN CAPABILITY CLASSES

Soil and climatic limitations in relation to the use, management, and productivity of soils are the bases for differentiating capability classes. Classes are based on both degree and number of limitations affecting kind of use, risks of soil damage if mismanaged, needs for soil management, and risks of crop failure. To assist in making capability groupings, specific criteria for placing soils in units, subclasses, and classes are presented here. Because the effects of soil characteristics and qualities vary widely with climate, these criteria must be for broad soil areas that have similar climate.

Capability groupings are based on specific information when available— information about the responses of the individual kinds of soil to management and the combined effect of climate and soil on the crops grown. It comes from research findings, field trials, and experiences of farmers and other agricultural workers. Among the more common kinds of information obtained are soil and water losses, kinds and amounts of plants that can be grown, weather conditions as they affect plants, and the effect of different kinds and levels of management on plant response. This information is studied along with laboratory data on soil profiles. Careful analysis of this information proves useful not only in determining the capability of these individual kinds of soil but also in making predictions about the use and management of related kinds of soil.

Basic yield estimates of the adapted crops under alternative, defined systems of management are assembled in a table. Where data are few, the estimates should be reasonable when tested against available farm records and studies of the combinations of soil properties.

Where information on response of soils to management is lacking, the estimates of yields and the grouping of soils into capability units, subclasses, and classes are based on an evaluation of combinations of the following:

1. Ability of the soil to give plant response to use and management as evidenced by organic-matter content, ease of maintaining a supply of plant nutrients, percentage base saturation, cation-exchange capacity, kind of clay mineral, kind of parent material, available water-holding capacity, response to added plant nutrients, or other soil characteristics and qualities.
2. Texture and structure of the soil to the depth that influences the environment of roots and the movement of air and water.
3. Susceptibility to erosion as influenced by kind of soil (and slope) and the effect of erosion on use and management.
4. Continuous or periodic waterlogging in the soil caused by slow permeability of the underlying material, a high water table, or flooding.
5. Depth of soil material to layers inhibiting root penetration.
6. Salts toxic to plant growth.
7. Physical obstacles such as rocks, deep gullies, etc.
8. Climate (temperature and effective moisture).

This list is not intended to be complete. Although the soils of any area may differ from one another in only a few dozen characteristics, none can be taken for granted. Extreme deficiencies or excesses of trace elements, for example, can be vital. Commonly, the underlying geological strata are significant to water infiltration, water yield, and erosion hazard.

Any unfavorable fixed or recurring soil or landscape features may limit the safe and productive use of the soil. One unfavorable feature in the soil may so limit its use that extensive treatment would be required. Several minor unfavorable features collectively may become a major problem and thus limit the use of the soil. The combined effect of these in relation to the use, management, and productivity of soils is the criterion for different capability units.

Some of the criteria used to differentiate between capability classes are discussed on the following pages. The criteria and ranges in characteristics suggested assume that the effects of other soil characteristics and qualities are favorable and are not limiting factors in placing soils in capability classes.

Arid and Semiarid, Stony, Wet, Saline-Sodic, and Overflow Soils

The capability-class designations assigned to soils subject to flooding, poorly or imperfectly drained soils, stony soils, dry soils needing supplemental water, and soils having excess soluble salts or exchangeable sodium are made on the basis of continuing limitations and hazards after removal of excess water, stones, salts, and exchangeable sodium.

When assessing the capability class of any soil the feasibility of any necessary land improvements must be considered. Feasible as used here means

(1) that the characteristics and qualities of the soil are such that it is possible to remove the limitation, and (2) that over broad areas it is within the realm of economic possibility to remove the limitation. The capability designation of these areas is determined by those practices that are practical now and in the immediate future.

The following kinds of soil are classified on the basis of their present continuing limitations and hazards: (1) Dry soils (arid and semiarid areas) now irrigated, (2) soils from which stones have been removed, (3) wet soils that have been drained, (4) soils from which excess quantities of soluble salts or exchangeable sodium have been removed, and (5) soils that have been protected from overflow.

The following kinds of soil are classified on the basis of their continuing limitations and hazards as if the correctable limitations had been removed or reduced: (1) Dry soils not now irrigated but for which irrigation is feasible and water is available, (2) stony soils for which stone removal is feasible, (3) wet soils not now drained but for which drainage is feasible, (4) soils that contain excess quantities of soluble salts or exchangeable sodium feasible to remove, and (5) soils subject to overflow but for which protection from overflow is feasible. Where desirable or helpful, the present limitation due to wetness, stoniness, etc., may be indicated.

The following kinds of soil are classified on the basis of their present continuing limitations and hazards if the limitations cannot feasibly be corrected or removed: (1) Dry soils, (2) stony soils, (3) soils with excess quantities of saline and sodic salts, (4) wet soils, or (5) soils subject to overflow.

Climatic Limitations

Climatic limitations (temperature and moisture) affect capability. Extremely low temperatures and short growing seasons are limitations, especially in the very northern part of continental United States and at high altitudes.

Limited natural moisture supply affects capability in subhumid, semiarid, and arid climates. As the classification in any locality is derived in part from observed performance of crop plants, the effects of the interaction of climate with soil characteristics must be considered. In a subhumid climate, for example, certain sandy soils may be classified as class VI or class VII, whereas soils with similar water-holding capacity in a more humid climate are classified as class III or IV. The moisture factor must be directly considered in the classification in most semiarid and arid climates. The capability of comparable soils decreases as effective rainfall decreases.

In an arid climate the moisture from rain and snow is not enough to support crops. Arid land can be classed as suited to cultivation (class I, II, III, or IV) only if the moisture limitation is removed by irrigation. Wherever the moisture limitation is removed in this way, the soil is classified according to the effects of other permanent features and hazards that limit its use and permanence, without losing sight of the practical requirements of irrigation farming.

Wetness Limitations

Water on the soil or excess water in the soil presents a hazard to or limits its use. Such water may be a result of poor soil drainage, high water table, overflow (includes stream overflow, ponding, and runoff water from higher areas), and seepage. Usually soil needing drainage has some permanent limitation that precludes placing it in class I even after drainage.

Wet soils are classified according to their continuing soil limitations and hazards after drainage. In determining the capability of wet areas emphasis is placed on practices considered practical now or in the foreseeable future. The vast areas of marshland along the seacoast or high-cost reclamation projects not now being planned or constructed are not classified as class I, II, or III. If reclamation projects are investigated and found to be feasible, the soils of the area are reclassified based on the continuing limitations and hazards after drainage. This places the classification of wet soils on a basis similar to that of the classification of irrigated, stony, saline, or overflow soils. Some large areas of bottom land subject to overflow are reclassified when protected by dikes or other major reclamation work. There are examples of these along streams where levees have been constructed. Land already drained is classified according to the continuing limitations and hazards that affect its use.

Needs for initial conditioning, such as for clearing of trees or swamp vegetation, are not considered in the capability classification. They may be of great importance, however, in making some of the land-management decisions. Costs of drainage, likewise, are not considered directly in the capability classification, although they are important to the land manager.

Toxic Salts

Presence of soluble salts or exchangeable sodium in amounts toxic to most plants can be a serious limiting factor in land use. Where toxic salts are the limiting factor, the following ranges are general guides until more specific criteria are available:

Class II—Crops slightly affected. In irrigated areas, even after salt removal, slight salinity or small amounts of sodium remains or is likely to recur.

Class III—Crops moderately affected. In irrigated areas, even after salt removal, moderate salinity or moderate amounts of sodium remains or is likely to recur.

Classes IV–VI—Crops seriously affected on cultivated land. Usually only salt-tolerant plants will grow on noncultivated land. In irrigated areas, even after leaching, severe salinity or large amounts of sodium remains or is likely to recur.

Class VII—Satisfactory growth of useful vegetation impossible, except possibly for some of the most salt-tolerant forms, such as some Atriplexes that have limited use for grazing.

Slope and Hazard of Erosion

Soil damage from erosion is significant in the use, management, and response of soil for the following reasons:

1. An adequate soil depth must be maintained for moderate to high crop production. Soil depth is critical on shallow soils over nonrenewable substrata such as hard rock. These soils tolerate less damage from erosion than soils of similar depth with a renewable substrata such as the raw loess or soft shale that can be improved through the use of special tillage, fertilizer, and beneficial cropping practices.

2. Soil loss influences crop yields. The reduction in yield following the loss of each inch of surface soil varies widely for different kinds of soil. The reduction is least on soils having little difference in texture, consistence, and fertility between the various horizons of the soil. It is greatest where there is a marked difference between surface layers and subsoils, such as among soils with claypans. For example, corn yields on soils with dense, very slowly permeable subsoils may be reduced 3 to 4 bushels per acre per year for each inch of surface soil lost. Yield reduction is normally small on deep, moderately permeable soils having similar textured surface and subsurface layers and no great accumulation of organic matter in the surface soil.

3. Nutrient loss through erosion on sloping soils is important not only because of its influence on crop yield but also because of cost of replacement to maintain crop yields. The loss of plant nutrients can be high, even with slight erosion.

4. Loss of surface soil changes the physical condition of the plow layer in soils having finer textured layers below the surface soil. Infiltration rate is reduced; erosion and runoff rates are increased; tilth is difficult to maintain; and tillage operations and seedbed preparation are more difficult.

5. Loss of surface soil by water erosion, soil blowing, or land leveling may expose highly calcareous lower strata that are difficult to make into suitable surface soil.

6. Water-control structures are damaged by sediments due to erosion. Maintenance of open drains and ponds becomes a problem and their capacity is reduced as sediment accumulates.

7. Gullies form as a result of soil loss. This kind of soil damage causes reduced yields, increased sediment damage, and physical difficulties in farming between the gullies.

The steepness of slope, length of slope, and shape of slope (convex or concave) all influence directly the soil and water losses from a field. Steepness of slope is recorded on soil maps. Length and shape of slopes are not recorded on soil maps; however, they are often characteristic of certain kinds of soil, and their effects on use and management can be evaluated as a part of the mapping unit.

Where available, research data on tons of soil loss per acre per year under given levels of management are used on sloping soils to differentiate between capability classes.

Soil Depth

Effective depth includes the total depth of the soil profile favorable for root development. In some soils this includes the C horizon; in a few only the A horizon is included. Where the effect of depth is the limiting factor, the following ranges are commonly used: Class I, 36 inches or more; class II, 20–36 inches; class III, 10–20 inches; and class IV, less than 10 inches. These ranges in soil depth between classes vary from one section of the country to another depending on the climate. In arid and semiarid areas, irrigated soils in class I are 60 or more inches in depth. Where other unfavorable factors occur in combination with depth, the capability decreases.

Previous Erosion

On some kinds of soil previous erosion reduces crop yields and the choice of crops materially; on others the effect is not great. The effect of past erosion limits the use of soils (1) where subsoil characteristics are unfavorable, or (2) where soil material favorable for plant growth is shallow to bedrock or material similar to bedrock. In some soils, therefore, the degree of erosion influences the capability grouping.

Available Moisture-Holding Capacity

Water-holding capacity is an important quality of soil. Soils that have limited moisture-holding capacity are likely to be droughty and have limitations in kinds and amounts of crops that can be grown; they also present fertility and other management problems. The ranges in water-holding capacity for the soils in the capability classes vary to a limited degree with the amount and distribution of effective precipitation during the growing season. Within a capability class, the range in available moisture-holding capacity varies from one climatic region to another.

Glossary

Alluvial soils Soils developing from transported and relatively recently deposited material (alluvium) with little or no modification of the original materials by soil-forming processes. (Soils with well-developed profiles that have formed from alluvium are grouped with other soils having the same kind of profiles, not with the alluvial soils.)

Available nutrient in soils The part of the supply of a plant nutrient in the soil that can be taken up by plants at rates and in amounts significant to plant growth.

Available water in soils The part of the water in the soil that can be taken up by plants at rates significant to their growth; usable; obtainable.

Base saturation The relative degree to which soils have metallic cations absorbed. The proportion of the cation-exchange capacity that is saturated with metallic cations.

Cation-exchange capacity A measure of the total amount of exchangeable cations that can be held by the soil. It is expressed in terms of milliequivalents per 100 grams of soil at neutrality (pH 7) or at some other stated pH value. (Formerly called base-exchange capacity.)

Clay mineral Naturally occurring inorganic crystalline material in soils or other earthy deposits of clay size—particles less than 0.002 mm. in diameter.

Deep soil Generally, a soil deeper than 40 inches to rock or other strongly contrasting material. Also, a soil with a deep black surface layer; a soil deeper than about 40 inches to the parent material or to other unconsolidated rock material not modified by soil-forming processes; or a soil in which the total depth of unconsolidated material, whether true soil or not, is 40 inches or more.

Drainage, soil (1) The rapidity and extent of the removal of water from the soil by runoff and flow through the soil to underground spaces. (2) As a condition of the soil, soil drainage refers to the frequency and duration of periods when the soil is free of saturation. For example, in well-drained soils, the water is removed readily, but not rapidly; in poorly drained soils, the root zone is waterlogged for long periods and the roots of ordinary crop plants cannot get enough oxygen; and in excessively drained soils, the water is removed so completely that most crop plants suffer from lack of water.

Drought A period of dryness, especially a long one. Usually considered to be any period of soil-moisture deficiency within the plant root zone. A period of dryness of sufficient length to deplete soil moisture to the extent that plant growth is seriously retarded.

Erosion The wearing away of the land surface by detachment and transport of soil and rock materials through the action of moving water, wind, or other geological agents.

Fertility, soil The quality of a soil that enables it to provide compounds, in adequate amounts and in proper balance, for the growth of specified plants, when other growth factors such as light, moisture, temperature, and the physical condition of the soil are favorable.

Field capacity The amount of moisture remaining in a soil after the free water has been allowed to drain away into drier soil material beneath; usually expressed as a percentage of the ovendry weight of soil or other convenient unit. It is the highest amount of moisture that the soil will hold under conditions of free drainage after excess water has drained away following a rain or irrigation that has wet the whole soil. For permeable soils of medium texture, this is about 2 or 3 days after a rain or thorough irrigation. Although generally similar for one kind of soil, values vary with previous treatments of the soil.

First bottom The normal flood plain of a stream, subject to frequent or occasional flooding.

Parent material The unconsolidated mass of rock material (or peat) from which the soil profile develops.

Permeability, soil The quality of a soil horizon that enables water or air to move through it. It can be measured quantitatively in terms of rate of flow of water through a unit cross section in unit time under specified temperature and hydraulic conditions. Values for saturated soils usually are called hydraulic conductivity. The permeability of a soil may be limited by the presence of one nearly impermeable horizon even though the others are permeable.

Phase, soil The subdivision of a soil type or other classificational soil unit having variations in characteristics not significant to the classification of the soil in its natural landscape but significant to the use and management of the soil. Examples of the variations recognized by phases of soil types include differences in slope, stoniness, and thickness because of accelerated erosion.

Profile (soil) A vertical section of the soil through all its horizons and extending into the parent material.

Range (or rangeland) Land that produces primarily native forage plants suitable for grazing by livestock, including land that has some forest trees.

Runoff The surface flow of water from an area; or the total volume of surface flow during a specified time.

Saline soil A soil containing enough soluble salts to impair its productivity for plants but not containing an excess of exchangeable sodium.

Series, soil A group of soils that have soil horizons similar in their differentiating characteristics and arrangement in the soil profile, except for the texture of the surface soil, and are formed from a particular type of parent material. Soil series is an important category in detailed soil classification. Individual series are given proper names from place names near the first recorded occurrence. Thus names like Houston, Cecil, Barnes, and Miami are names of soil series that appear on soil maps and each connotes a unique combination of many soil characteristics.

Sodic soil (alkali) Soil that contains sufficient sodium to interfere with the growth of most crop plants; soils for which the exchangeable-sodium-percentage is 15 or more.

Soil (1) The natural medium for the growth of land plants. (2) A dynamic natural body on the surface of the earth in which plants grow, composed of mineral and organic materials and living forms. (3) The collection of natural bodies occupying parts of the earth's surface that support plants and that have properties due to the integrated effect of climate and living matter acting upon parent material, as conditioned by relief, over periods of time.

A soil is an individual three-dimensional body on the surface of the earth unlike the adjoining bodies. (The area of individual soils ranges from less than ½ acre to more than 300 acres.)

A kind of soil is the collection of soils that are alike in specified combinations of characteristics. Kinds of soil are given names in the system of soil classification. The terms "the soil" and "soil" are collective terms used for all soils, equivalent to the word "vegetation" for all plants.

Soil Characteristic A feature of a soil that can be seen and/or measured in the field or in the laboratory on soil samples. Examples include soil slope and stoniness as well as the texture, structure, color, and chemical composition of soil horizons.

Soil management The preparation, manipulation, and treatment of soils for the production of plants, including crops, grasses, and trees.

Soil quality An attribute of a soil that cannot be seen or measured directly from the soil alone but which is inferred from soil characteristics and soil behavior under defined conditions. Fertility, productivity, and erodibility are examples of soil qualities (in contrast to soil characteristics).

Soil survey A general term for the systematic examination of soils in the field and in the laboratories, their description and classification, the mapping of kinds of soil, and the interpretation of soils according to their adaptability for various crops, grasses, and trees, their behavior under use or treatment for plant production or for other purposes, and their productivity under different management systems.

Structure, soil The arrangement of primary soil particles into compound particles or clusters that are separated from adjoining aggregates and have properties unlike those of an equal mass of unaggregated primary soil particles. The principal forms of soil structure are platy, prismatic, columnar (prisms with rounded tops), blocky (angular or subangular), and granular. Structureless soils are (1) single grain—each grain by itself, as in dune sand, or (2) massive—the particles adhering together without any regular cleavage as in many claypans and hardpans. ("Good" or "bad" tilth are terms for the general structural condition of cultivated soils according to particular plants or sequences of plants.)

Subsoil The B horizons of soils with distinct profiles. In soils with weak profile development, the subsoil can be defined as the soil below the plowed soil (or its equivalent of surface soil), in which roots normally grow. Although a common term, it cannot be defined accurately. It has been carried over from early days when "soil" was conceived only as the plowed soil and that under it as the "subsoil."

Surface soil The soil ordinarily moved in tillage, or its equivalent in uncultivated soil, about 5 to 8 inches in thickness.

Texture, soil The relative proportions of the various size groups of individual soil grains in a mass of soil. Specifically, it refers to the proportions of sand, silt, and clay.

Type, soil A subgroup or category under the soil series based on the texture of the surface soil. A soil type is a group of soils having horizons similar in differentiating characteristics and arrangement in the soil profile and developed from a particular type of parent material. The name of a soil type consists of the name of the soil series plus the textural class name of the upper part of the soil equivalent to the surface soil. Thus Miami silt loam is the name of a soil type within the Miami series.

Water table The upper limit of the part of the soil or underlying rock material that is wholly saturated with water. In some places an upper, or perched, water table may be separated from a lower one by a dry zone.

Water-holding capacity The capacity (or ability) of soil to hold water against gravity (see **Field capacity**). The water-holding capacity of sandy soils is usually considered to be low while that of clayey soils is high. It is often expressed in inches of water per foot depth of soil.

Waterlogged A condition of soil in which both large and small pore spaces are filled with water. (The soil may be intermittently waterlogged because of a fluctuating water table or waterlogged for short periods after rain.)

9: EFFECTS OF LAND CAPABILITY ON APPLE PRODUCTION IN SOUTHERN ONTARIO

L. J. P. Van Vliet[1], E. E. Mackintosh[2], and D. W. Hoffman[2]

[1]*Agriculture Canada, British Columbia Pedology Unit, 6660 N.W. Marine Drive, Vancouver, B.C. V6T 1X2, and [2]Department of Land Resource Science, University of Guelph, Guelph, Ontario N1G 2W1*

The effects of land capability on apple production were evaluated for 171 semi-dwarf trees (var. McIntosh on E.M. VII rootstocks) located in 19 orchards in Southern Ontario. Soil, climatic and management variables were analyzed using stepwise regression analysis. Approximately 82% of the yield variation was explained by 12 variables; climatic and management variables accounted for the largest portion of the variation. Most of the soil variables were related to soil drainage characteristics or water retention properties. Land capability class provided a reasonable prediction of potential apple yield. Average apple yield for classes 1 to 4 were 0.85, 0.71, 0.60 and 0.47 kg/cm², respectively. Subclass limits are proposed for each of the soil characteristics. The most productive lands consisted of soils with loamy sand to sandy loam solums underlain by medium to fine textured II C horizons. There was a poor correlation between apple yield and the lower categorical levels of soil classification, i.e. series and type.

Pour évaluer les effets de l'aptitude des terres sur la production des pommes, nous avons observé 171 arbres semi-nains (var. McIntosh sur E.M. VII) répartis entre 19 vergers du sud de l'Ontario. Le rôle des variables de sol, de climat et de gestion a été étudié par analyse de régression progressive. Environ 82% de la variation totale du rendement a pu être imputée à 12 variables, les éléments climatiques et culturaux en assumant la plus forte proportion. La plupart des variables pédologiques était reliée au drainage du sol ou à ses propriétés de rétention de l'eau. Le classement selon les aptitudes des terres s'est révélé être un assez bon outil de prédiction du rendement des pommes. Le rendement moyen obtenu pour les classes allant de 1 à 4 s'établissait dans l'ordre à 0.85, 0.71, 0.60 et 0.47 kg/cm². Les auteurs proposent l'établissement de limites de classes secondaires pour chacun des caractères pédologiques. Les terres les plus productives étaient celles dont le sol de surface allait du sable loameux au loam sableux et reposait sur un horizon IIC de texture moyenne à fine. Nous n'avons observé qu'une médiocre corrélation entre le rendement des pommes et les unités inférieures de la classification des sols, c.-à-d. la série et le type.

During the past two decades, the fruit-producing areas of Southern Ontario have come under increasing pressure from non-agricultural land uses. For example, about 2000 ha of high-producing tender fruit lands were lost to urbanization in Southern Ontario from 1962 to 1971 (Chudleigh 1972). The problem is even more acute when one analyzes the geographic relationships of Southern Ontario, particularly the coincidence of centers of urban expansion and high quality lands with climate and soil suitable for intensive fruit crop production.

From an area and production standpoint, apples are the major fruit crop grown in Ontario (Ontario Ministry of Agriculture and Food (OMAF) 1972). Krueger (1972) has reviewed the general production characteristics and geographic relationships for the apple industry in Canada. There are also some data available on marketing trends and costs of production for Ontario (Al-Haskim 1969). A number of workers have collected information on soil, climate, and cultural factors and studied their relationship to tree growth and apple production (Edelman 1962; Hoekstra and van Wallenburg 1969). However, there is little information that considers the broad interactions between land capability, yield, and economic returns that could form the basis for development of a land use policy for the fruit industry.

In Ontario, Mackintosh and Brown (1972) proposed a tentative Land Capability Classification for Tree Fruits based on an evaluation of soil, climatic, and management variables and apple yields. However, their work was limited to one experimental orchard using standard rootstocks. They used the same principles as the Soil Capability Classification for Agriculture (Department of Regional Economic Expansion (DREE) 1969), but reduced the total number of classes to five because classes 5 and 6 in the original Canada Land Inventory (CLI) only applied to non-arable crops; similar subclasses were also used following modifications according to the more specific requirements for fruit crops. Considerably more quantitative studies are required to test the proposed system over a wider range of biophysical environments and to determine land capability-yield relationships in order for rural planners and policy makers to use the information for land planning.

"Land capability" as used here is synonymous with the CLI term "soil capability," although the former term is preferred for semantic reasons. Climate and soil are explicit components in the definition of land (Vink 1975). Together with selected attributes of management, climatic and soil factors are used as the basis for classifying soil into the appropriate capability class in the Soil Capability for Agriculture Classification (DREE 1969). Hence, there are no inconsistencies in using the terms interchangeably, but "land capability" repre-

sents the more correct application of the term.

The objectives of this study were to assess the effects of soil, climatic, and management factors on apple production and hence to determine the relationship between land capability class and apple yield. The relationship between soil taxonomic units and yield was also investigated.

MATERIALS AND METHODS

Selection of Apple Trees

The study was performed in the Eastern Ontario and Georgian Bay fruit-growing regions during the 1972 growing season (Fig. 1). Using census information in conjunction with Regional Fruit and Vegetable Specialists, mature orchards growing apple variety McIntosh on East Malling (E.M.) VII semi-dwarf rootstocks were selected by stratified random sampling. These are the most widely planted rootstock-variety combinations in Southern Ontario (OMAF 1972, 1974). An average of nine apple trees from each of 19 orchards were chosen by simple random sampling to give a total of 171 trees (sampling units).

Climate

The orchards under investigation all occur in areas recognized as having optimum climates for apple production (Brown et al. 1968). This optimum climate is characterized by a mean May-September precipitation of 35–40 cm for adequate moisture supply, a mean annual frost-free period of between 150 and 160 days with more than 3700 mean annual growing degree days and a perennial crop growing season in excess of 210 days (Brown et al. 1968). Further, the presence of the Great Lakes contributes significantly to the ideal climate. In spring, the suppression of daytime temperatures near the shoreline delays blossoming which occurs later when there is little likelihood of a damaging night frost. This also results in extending the growing season into autumn. In addition, the Great Lakes have a moderating effect on winter temperatures.

Methodology

The method used to establish soil-climatic-management-yield relationships was similar to the site factor method for assessing biological productivity using regression analysis (Nix 1968). This method requires paired measurements at each sampling unit which consisted of

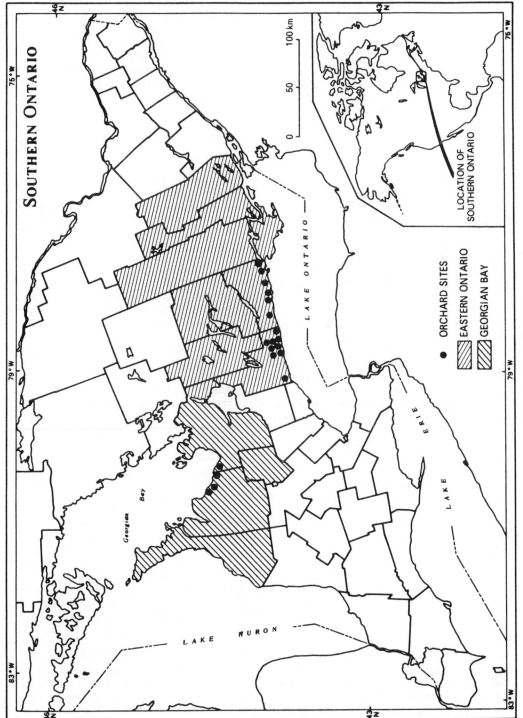

SOUTHERN ONTARIO

LOCATION OF
SOUTHERN ONTARIO

100 km

50

0

ORCHARD SITES

EASTERN ONTARIO

GEORGIAN BAY

LAKE ONTARIO

Georgian Bay

LAKE HURON

LAKE ERIE

Fig. 1. Location map.

183

apple yield, the response variable, as a function of certain soil, climatic, and management variables.

At all 171 sampling units, soil profiles were examined to a depth of 120 cm, routine soil profile descriptions were taken, and the approp-' riate soil series name assigned according to current definitions (Hoffman and Acton 1974). The geographic distributions of these soils in the respective regions are reported elsewhere (Gillespie and Richards 1954; Hoffman and Acton 1974). Soil samples from profile pits at 64 trees representing the major soil types over the 19 orchards were collected and analyzed for particle sizes and free carbonates.

The following variables were measured and recorded for each apple tree:

1. Apple yield:
Apple yield (for 1972) was expressed as weight per unit cross-sectional area (kg/cm^2) of the trunk at 45-cm height (yield values include windfall).

2. Soil factors:
– Depth of Ap and B horizons and depth to the top of the B, C, and IIC horizons in centimeters.
– Soil texture of Ap, B, C, and IIC horizons expressed as percent sand and percent clay. Hand textures were corrected using results of particle size analysis (McKeague 1976).
– Depth to free carbonates in centimeters and the calcium carbonate equivalent percentage (McKeague 1976).
– Soil drainage expressed as soil moisture class (Crown 1968). Seven orchards with tile drainage were assigned a soil moisture class rating equivalent to well drained soils.
– Slope (percent) measured with an Abney hand level.
– Land capability class based on the proposed Land Capability Classification for Tree Fruits (Mackintosh and Brown 1972).
– Soil type and series, using the Canadian system of soil classification (Canada Soil Survey Committee 1978) and related soil survey reports (Gillespie and Richards 1954; Hoffman and Acton 1974).

3. Climatic factors:
– Rainfall, expressed as accumulated centimeters for the two months periods May-June and July-August which were obtained from weather stations closest to the orchards.
– Aspect of the steepest slope at each sampling

unit where measured with a Brunton Compass to determine the azimuth from the magnetic north and then were corrected for true north.
– Altitude of each orchard (meter) obtained from 1:50 000 scale topographic maps.
– Orchard distance from Lake Ontario or Georgian Bay (kilometer) measured on 1:50 000 scale topographic maps.

4. Management factors:
– Tree density expressed as number of trees per hectare.
– Tree age (years).
– Amount of N, P, and K fertilizers applied in oxide form (kg/tree).
– Part-time or full-time apple grower, assigned value of 0 or 1 (a grower was classified as part-time if he spent less than 50% of his time growing apples in a commercial orchard).

Statistical Methods
To assess the effects of soil, climatic and management factors on apple production, the data were statistically analyzed using a stepwise multiple regression program. Because the regression analysis was performed for the purpose of obtaining equations that best described yield variation, the number of significant variables in the equation was of lesser importance. The significance at $P < 0.10$ was felt to be appropriate. The final selected equation was used as a tool for discerning relationships between the independent variables and apple yield rather than for yield prediction purposes.

Individual soil properties differ from tree to tree, whereas only one measure of climatic and management variables is available for each orchard. Thus, this study represents a case of "nested data," i.e. soil variables are "nested" within orchards (Daniel and Wood 1971). Analysis of nested data recognizes two distinct sources of yield variation, i.e. within-orchard variables (soil) and among-orchards variables (climate and management). Consequently, the selection of variables by regression analysis was performed separately for these two different sources of variation according to the methods described by Daniel and Wood (1971). Data for 64 of the 171 apple trees for which detailed soil information was measured and collected were used for the regression analysis. The final equation, used to describe the data, was selected by a combination of the following criteria: (a) R^2 value; (b) partial F values; (c) Cp value, which is the measure of total squared error (Daniel and Wood 1971), and (d) the examination of residuals to indicate the need for data transformations (Draper and Smith 1966). To determine the relative importance of the independent variables in relation to the dependent variable, the standard partial regression coefficients (b'_i) were computed to compare individual variables, since b'_i is independent of the original units of measurement (Steel and Torrie 1960).

Data collected for all the 171 apple trees were used to determine land capability-yield and soil taxonomic unit-yield relationships. A Student's *t* test was performed to analyze the results for differences in apple yields between soil types within soil series and Duncan's multiple range test was used to test for significant differences in yield between land capability classes and between soil series.

RESULTS AND DISCUSSION

Since only one year of yield data was used in this study, the limitations of the data base are obvious. To gain some perspective of the fruit-producing potential of 1972 relative to other years, mean apple yields for the 3-yr period 1971-1973 were compared using variety McIntosh from both fruit-growing districts (OMAF 1971, 1972b, 1973). The departure of 1972 apple yields from the 3-yr mean for the Georgian Bay and Eastern Ontario Regions were 3 and 8%, respectively. Thus, the year 1972 used in this study is considered to represent near normal yield conditions during this period.

Regression Analysis

The regression analysis was performed on data using 64 apple trees from 19 orchards. The effects of variation in yield among orchards were quantified by including 18 indicator (dummy) variables representing the 19 orchards. First, the within-orchard variables (soil variables) were analyzed by stepwise regression after all 18 dummy variables were forced into the equation. Dummy variables were used on the assumption that a correlation between soil variables and apple yield could be represented by a set of 19 straight lines with a common slope for each orchard (Daniel and

Wood 1971). Results of this analysis indicated that the dummy variables, together with five soil variables, i.e. capability class, soil moisture class, percent sand Ap horizon, depth to B horizon and percent sand IIC horizon, explained 85% ($R^2 = 0.85$) of the total variation in apple yield (Table 1). Of the 85%, 78% was accounted for by the dummy variables, which indicate an important orchard effect on apple yield.

Using the regression equation resulting from the within-orchard analysis, 19 apple yields were computed by substituting mean values from 64 observations for each of the five significant soil variables in the equation. The computed yield values, adjusted for among-orchard bias, were used as the dependent variables for developing an equation to describe the variations in yield among orchards that arise from climatic and management variables. The selected among-orchard equation, which accounted for 82% of the variability in yield, consisted of seven variables: altitude, distance from lakes, tree density, tree age, nitrogen added, potash added, and precipitation for July and August (Table 1). Before combining both equations into a final equation, soil variables were adjusted by subtracting its mean value, since mean values from 64 observations for each of the five significant soil variables were used in arriving at the among-orchard equation (Daniel and Wood 1971). The soil variables from the within-orchard equation were added to the among-orchard equation to form the following final equation:

$$Y = -0.63153 + 0.00158 \text{ (altitude)} + 0.03845 \text{ (distance)} + 0.00212 \text{ (density)} -0.03082 \text{ (tree age)} + 0.35413 \text{ (nitrogen)} + 0.14229 \text{ (potash)} + 0.03544 \text{ (precipitation July + August)} + 0.07701 \text{ (capability class} -2.96875) + 0.01857 \text{ (soil moisture class} - 24.35938) + 0.00241 \text{ (\% sand Ap horizon} - 54.87500) + 0.00210 \text{ (depth A horizon} - 31.93750) + 0.00227 \text{ (\% sand IIC horizon} - 12.54313).$$

The final equation, which includes the

Table 1. Results of stepwise regression analyses of apple yields (kg/cm^2) for selected soil, climatic and management variables significant at $P<0.10$

Variables	Coefficient	Standard error of estimate	Standard partial regression coefficient (b'_1)	R^2 value†
Variables from the among-orchards equation				
Constant	−0.63153			
Altitude	0.00158	0.00930	0.332	
Distance from lake	0.03845	0.01394	0.387	
Tree density	0.00212	0.00110	0.293	
Tree age	−0.03082	0.01547	0.332	0.82
Nitrogen	0.34513	0.07265	0.732	
Potash	0.14229	0.06001	0.359	
Precipitation July and August	0.03544	0.01185	0.477	
Variables from the within-orchards equation				
Capability class	0.07701	0.02121	0.459	
Soil drainage	0.01857	0.00767	0.237	
Sand % Ap horizon	0.00241	0.00153	0.186	0.85
Depth of A horizon	0.00210	0.00118	0.158	
Sand % IIC horizon	0.00227	0.00131	0.174	
Final equation combining within- and among-orchard variations				0.82

Analysis of variance for final equation with components of variance from regression analyses

Source	df	Mean square	F
Regression	7	0.10345	7.07²‡
Residuals	11	0.01464	
Among orchards	18	0.01038	
Within orchards	40	0.01434	

†Two R^2 values refer to separate regression analyses for within- and among-orchard variables required for "nested" data (Daniel and Wood 1971). The R^2 value of 0.85 for within-orchard variables included 18 dummy variables representing 19 orchards.
‡Significant at $P < 0.05$.

significant soil, climatic, and management variables, without among-orchard bias, accounted for 82% of the total variation in yield ($R^2 = 0.82$; Table 1).

Other equations including a different number and (or) types of soil, climatic, and management variables were rated almost as good in explaining yield variations. However, the final equation was selected according to the previously described criteria.

Soil, Climatic, Management – Yield Relationships

Standard partial regression coefficients (b'_1 values) were used to compare the relative importance of individual variables (Table 1). This comparison is only valid for either the within-orchard (soils) or among-orchard (climatic and management) variables, because the regression analyses were separately based on these two sources of variation.

Capability class, which represents the accumulative effects of a number of soil variables, stands out as the most important within-orchard variable (Table 1). This is followed by soil moisture class and three other soil variables, i.e. the sand content of the Ap and IIC horizons and depth to B horizon, which can also be considered as closely affecting the soil moisture regimes.

The emphasis on capability class is not surprising, because capability class by definition represents a grouping of soil variables affecting potential land productiv-

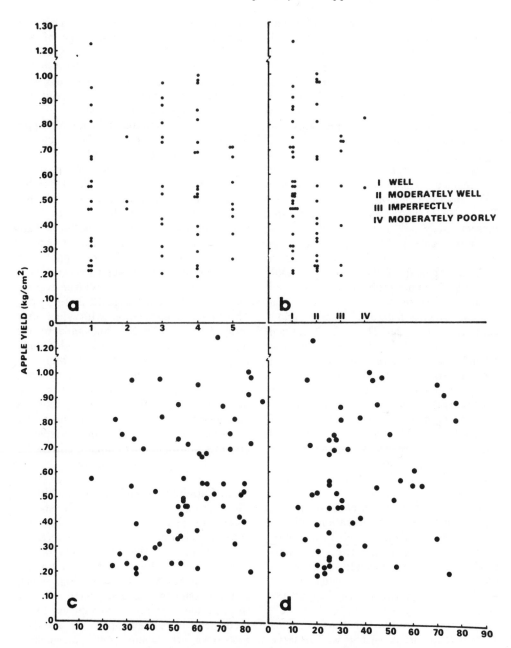

Fig. 2. Relationship between selected soil characteristics and apple yield (kg/cm²): (a) capability class, (b) soil drainage, (c) sand content of Ap horizon (%), (d) depth of A horizon (cm).

ity. The slight positive correlation between capability class and apple yield (Table 1, Fig. 2a) suggests increasing apple yield as the limitations become more severe. This points out the need for revising the subclass limits of the proposed Capability Classification for Fruit Trees (Mackintosh and Brown 1972) to accommodate apple trees grown on semi-dwarf rootstocks.

The sensitivity of fruit tree roots to high water table conditions has been well documented (Archibald 1966; Edelman 1952; Hoekstra and van Wallenburg 1969). The results of the regression analysis in the present study are consistent with these findings (Table 1, Fig. 2b). Further, the positive correlation of the sand content in both the Ap and IIC horizons with apple yield (Table 1) are probably related to soil drainage. The relationship between sand content in the Ap horizon and apple yield is depicted in Fig. 2c. Thus, the main soil variables correlated with yield are those related to soil moisture status. The one soil characteristic which is positively correlated with yield in this investigation and also in the pilot study (Mackintosh and Brown 1972) is the depth of the A horizon (depth to top of B horizon) (Fig. 2d). Presumably the high organic matter content of the Ap horizon improves soil structure, general fertility and water-holding capacity, which are generally conducive to higher yields.

Analysis of the between-orchard variables showed that nitrogen fertilization followed by potash fertilization were the most important management factors in apple production (Table 1). Application rates of both N and K in oxide form ranged between 0 and 1.8 kg/tree/yr with a mean N application of 0.58 kg/tree/yr and a mean K of 0.74 kg/tree/yr. The positive benefits from N and K fertilization are consistent with observations made by Archibald (1966) on their general deficiency in Ontario orchard soils. As well, many of the soils investigated are coarse-textured, ranging from sandy loam (SL) to loamy sand (LS).

Tree density as a management factor was positively correlated with yield. This was probably due to the small range of tree densities sampled in this study (168-272 trees/ha). Based on results of orchard studies in New York, Norton (1971) has suggested semi-dwarf tree populations of about 400 trees/ha for optimum apple yields.

Despite the optimum climate for apple production in the regions in which the orchards are located, it is evident that yield depression still occurs as orchards are located further away from the favorable climatic influence of the lakes and at higher altitudes (Table 1), even though the orchards investigated were all located within a 9 km distance of Georgian Bay or Lake Ontario.

Of the climatic variables, precipitation in the months of July and August was the most important variable (Table 1) with an average rainfall of 15.4 cm (range 12.2–19.2 cm). This positive correlation with yield may reflect low rainfall in 1972 but similar results were also observed in the 1971 pilot study involving Northern Spy and McIntosh varieties on Robusta rootstocks (Mackintosh and Brown 1972). This suggests that moisture supply during this period is particularly critical for maximizing yield. Therefore, it is an important variable to consider in formulating climatic criteria for selection of apple-producing lands.

Land Capability – Yield Relationships

The data analyses (Table 1, Fig. 2a) show a weak but positive relationship between capability class and yield. This is contrary to expectations and close inspection of the results (Fig. 2a) show that Classes 2 and 5 have a low number of observations which could account for the unexpected relationship. Further, the proposed subclass limits used here were developed for standard rootstocks. It would seem reasonable, therefore, to alter the depth criteria for the subclass limits in the proposed Capability Classification for Fruit Trees (Mackintosh and Brown 1972) to coincide with the more shallow-rooted nature of dwarf and semi-dwarf rootstocks. The proposed classifica-

Table 2. Proposed soil subclass limits for a "land capability classification for tree fruits"

Variable	Capability class				
	1	2	3	4	5
Drainage and texture	Well to moderately well drained	Well to moderately well drained	Imperfectly drained SL, SiL, and L.	Well to imperfectly drained CL-C-HvC.	All very poorly drained soils poorly drained
	SL, SiL and L.	SL, SiL, L and CL. Well to imperfectly drained coarse textured soils (SL-LS) over L-C IIC horizons at 60-100 cm	Well drained LS and S. Imperfectly drained S and LS over L-CL-C IIC horizons within 45-60 cm	Poorly drained S, LS, SL, SiL, L Rapidly drained LS and S	C and HvC. Rapidly drained gravels and coarse sands
Depth to soil impervious layers (cm)	>60	40-60	25-40	<25	<25
Depth to bedrock (cm)	>110	90-110	70-90	50-70	<50
CaCO$_3$ equiv. in C or IIC horizon	10-25%	10-25%	>25% or <10% within 70-100 cm of surface	>25% or <10% within 40-70 cm of surface	>40% or 0% within 40 cm of surface

tion was an initial attempt to evaluate land capability for tree fruit production. The system consisted of five classes: Classes 1–3 are capable of sustained production of fruit crops; Class 4 is marginal; and Class 5 is not capable of tree fruit production.

Following the revision of the soil subclasses according to Table 2, each of the 171 sampling units were re-evaluated and assigned to one of the five capability classes. The results of the analysis of variance test (Table 3) indicated significant yield differences at $P < 0.05$ between classes. There is also evidence that yield decreases with capability class. To determine if capability classes were significantly different from one another in yield, a Duncan's multiple range test was performed. This test revealed that

Table 3. Relationship between capability class and average apple yield for 171 trees

Capability class	Average yield (kg/cm^2)	Number of trees	Analysis of variance of apple yield data			
			Source	df	Mean square	F
1	.85 a	10	Among			
2	.71 a	40	classes	4	0.532	10.9*
3	.60 b	71				
4	.47 c	41	Within			
5	.41 c	9	classes	166	0.048	

a-c Different letters indicate statistically different means significant at $P < 0.05$. (Duncan's multiple range test).
*Significant at $P < 0.05$.

the mean apple yield for Class 3 land is significantly different from all the other classes (Table 3). No significant differences were observed between Classes 1 and 2 or Classes 4 and 5. For example, no significant difference was found between marginal land for apple production (Class 4) and land unsuitable for apple production (Class 5). The failure to adequately distinguish between yields in Classes 1 and 2, and Classes 4 and 5 is in part due to the low numbers of sampling sites in Classes 1 and 5. It may also reflect a further need to improve subclass limits in distinguishing the respective classes from 2 and 4.

Soil Taxonomic Unit – Yield Relationships

Soil taxonomic units at the lower categorical levels of soil classification, particularly the soil series and soil type, have been used as yield indicators for various crops (Hoffman 1976). In addition, soil series and type form part of the basis of the CLI soil capability classification for agriculture in Canada. Because of this connection between taxonomic and interpretive classifications of soils, the relationship between yield and taxonomic units was studied.

The soil types were identified at each of the 171 sites. To discover the relationships between apple yield and soil variables and to assess soil taxonomic information in tree fruit productivity investigations, analyses were performed on apple yields between soil types within series (Table 4) and between soil series (Table 5). The Student's t test was used at the soil type level.

In only three cases, i.e. Dundonald, Bookton and Berrien Series, were the yields of soil type within a series significantly different (Table 4). The significant differences were between sandy loam (SL) and loamy sand (LS) types. Furthermore, they all involved series that consisted of coarse-textured overburdens that were underlain by loam (L), clay loam (CL), clay (C) till within 1 m of the surface. Yields for the Bookton and Berrien LS soil types were greater than for the SL types, whereas these trends were reversed for the Dundonald Series. Thus, for these sites there seems to be no consistent relationship between soil type within a series and yield.

Table 4. Relationship between soil type† and apple yield

Soil series	Soil type	Sample size	Mean yield (kg/cm²)	SD (kg/cm²)	Significant at $P < 0.05$
Brighton	SL	6	.758	.338	NS‡
	LS	11	.603	.220	
Dundonald	SL	9	.792	.201	S§
	LS	4	.345	.133	
Edenvale	SL	6	.558	.207	NS
	LS	3	.403	.101	
Smithfield	L	8	.581	.302	NS
	SiL	3	.803	.297	
Schomberg	L	7	.724	.301	NS
	SiL	7	.507	.309	
Bookton	SL	3	.343	.135	S
	LS	5	.926	.076	
Berrien	SL	7	.527	.210	S
	LS	9	.741	.151	
Farmington	SL	7	.497	.139	NS
	C	2	.725	.219	

†For detailed descriptions, see Hoffman and Acton (1974) and Gillespie and Richards (1954).
‡NS denotes no significant differences (Student's t test).
§S denotes significant differences (Student's t test).

Table 5. Relationship between soil series† and apple yield

Soil series	Sample size	Mean yield (kg/cm²)	SD (kg/cm²)	Significant at $P < 0.05$
Bookton	9	.737	.308	c
Pontypool	8	.689	.227	a
Otonabee	10	.682	.236	a
Dundonald	13	.655	.279	a
Berrien	16	.648	.205	a
Brighton	18	.639	.272	a
Smithfield	12	.635	.291	a
Schomberg	15	.599	.309	a
Farmington	9	.548	.175	a
Percy	9	.524	.109	a
Edenvale	9	.507	.188	a
Norham	11	.470	.189	a
Wooler	4	.418	.137	a
Codrington	6	.415	.141	b

†For detailed descriptions, see Hoffman and Acton (1974) and Gillespie and Richards (1954).
a-c Different letters indicate statistically different means (Duncan's multiple range test).

Similarly, for the sites sampled, there is a very poor relationship between soil series and yield (Table 5). Only the Codrington and Bookton Series were statistically different from each other and from the remaining series investigated. The low lime to acid soils, the Codrington, Norham and Wooler Series, exhibited the lowest yields.

In the case of soil families or subgroups there was no discernible relationship. It is apparent that the categorical levels used in the Canadian System of Soil Classification (Canada Soil Survey Committee 1978) are generally poor indicators for predicting apple yields. This is likely because certain features of the land, such as slope and stoniness, are not used as differentiating criteria in determining taxonomic units whereas they are used in assessing land capability. Most of the 1:63 360 scale Ontario county soil surveys use the soil series, a taxonomic unit, as the mapping unit. Because of the poor relationship between taxonomic units and yield, use of such scale surveys for location of prime apple-producing lands will suffer from the same weaknesses.

CONCLUSIONS

The sampling program used for relating land properties to apple production recognized two sources of variation. These included soil properties, which represent within-orchard variations and climate and cultural practices, which vary among orchards. To accommodate these two distinct sources of variation the stepwise regression analysis was modified to a more suitable procedure required for "nested data" (Daniel and Wood 1971). Using this procedure, the final selected equation explained 82% of the variation in apple yield.

The among-orchard effects accounted for the highest proportion of the variance in apple yield which emphasize the importance of climatic and management factors in apple production. Moreover, it demonstrates a clear need to have more detailed climatic and management parameters included in future investigations. Most of the soil variables entering the equation were related to soil drainage characteristics or water retention properties. Available soil water storage capacity and air capacity were not measured in this study, but they too appear to be important variables warranting more detailed consideration.

It was found that the mean apple yield for Class 3 soils is significantly different from all other classes. No significant differences were observed between Classes 1 and 2 or 4 and 5. The low number of sampling sites, inadequate definitions of subclass limits and lack of measurement of all factors affecting yield can be cited as reasons for the lack of significant yield differences between some of the classes. The guidelines proposed for the various subclasses require more extensive testing for other fruit crops, and the subclass limits can be expected to change regionally.

The fact that a reasonable relationship exists between land capability class and yield suggests that for Southern Ontario the proposed subclass limits represent a good approximation for estimating the effects of soil characteristics on apple yields. Obviously a larger sample population is required to finalize yield potentials and productivity indices for each class. Nevertheless, the calculated productivity indices for Classes 1 to 4 (1.0, 0.84, 0.71 and 0.55, respectively) coincide reasonably well with those reported for a range of common field crops (Hoffman 1976). Therefore, it would appear a rationale exists for use of the information in local and regional planning of agricultural lands.

There was generally a poor relationship between yield and the lower categorical levels of soil classification, i.e. series and type.

Of the areas investigated, the most productive apple lands consisted of soils with less than one meter of SL-LS overburdens which are underlain by medium- to fine-textured IIC horizons. Apparently the poor water retention properties of coarse-textured soils are compensated for by the existence of impermeable stratigraphic or pedogenic layers at depths which create perched water conditions. The low lime and acid soils displayed the lowest yields.

ACKNOWLEDGMENTS

The authors wish to acknowledge Dr. R. J. Hines, Department of Statistics, University of Guelph, for advice and discussions on the statistical analyses. This project received financial assistance from Agriculture Canada Operating Grant #1043.

AL-HASKIM, M. 1969. Trends in the production and marketing of apples in Canada with special reference to Ontario. Farm Economics, Co-operatives and Statistics Branch, Ontario Department of Agriculture and Food, Toronto, Ont.

ARCHIBALD, J. A. 1966. Orchard soil management. Ontario Department of Agriculture and Food, Publication 457.

BROWN, D. M., MCKAY, G. A. AND CHAPMAN, L. J. 1968. The climate of Southern Ontario. Climatological studies. No. 5. Ont. Dept. of Transport. Meteorological Branch. The Queen's Printer, Ottawa, Ont.

CANADA SOIL SURVEY COMMITTEE. 1978. The Canadian system of soil classification. Agric. Can. Publ. 1646. Agriculture Canada, Ottawa, Ont.

CHUDLEIGH, E. L. 1972. Alternatives for the Ontario fruit industry. Report from study committee, Ontario Fruit Council.

CROWN, P. H. 1968. Some morphological features indicative of soil moisture. Unpublished M.Sc. Thesis, University of Guelph, Guelph, Ont.

DANIEL, C. and WOOD, F. S. 1971. Selection of variables in nested data. Pages 165–192 *in* Fitting equations to data. Wiley-Interscience (John Wiley and Sons, Inc.), New York, N.Y.

DEPARTMENT OF REGIONAL ECONOMIC EXPANSION. 1969. Soil capability classification for agriculture. Canada Land Inventory Report No. 2.

DRAPER, N. R. and SMITH, H. 1966. Applied regression analysis. John Wiley and Sons, Inc., New York, N.Y. 407 pp.

EDELMAN, C. H. 1962. Suitability of soils for horticultural crops and some related soil problems in the Netherlands. *In* Report of the 13th Int. Hortic. Congr., London. Vol. 1: 80–95.

GILLESPIE, J. E. and RICHARDS, N. R. 1954. Soil survey of Grey County. Ontario Soil Survey Report #17. Ontario Ministry of Agriculture and Food.

HOEKSTRA, C. and van WALLENBURG, C. 1969. Verslag van een proefplekken onderzoek bij appels, uitgevoerd van 1961-1964 op de Zuidhollandse eilanden. Stiboka report No. 718. Netherlands Soil Survey Institute, Wageningen, the Netherlands.

HOFFMAN, D. W. 1976. Soil capability analysis and land resource development in Canada. Pages 140–167 *in* G. R. McBoyle and E. Sommerville, eds. Canada's natural environment. Methuen Press, pp. 140–167.

HOFFMAN, D. W. and ACTON, C. J. 1974. The soils of Northumberland County. Ontario Soil Survey Report #42. Ontario Ministry of Agriculture and Food.

KRUEGER, R. R. 1972. The geography of the orchard industry in Canada. Pages 216–241 *in* R. M. Irving, ed. Readings in Canadian geography. Holt, Rinehart and Winston of Canada Ltd.

MACKINTOSH, E. E. and BROWN, D. M. 1972. Land capability classification for tree fruits. Unpublished data, University of Guelph, Guelph, Ont.

McKEAGUE, J. J. (Ed.). 1976. Manual on soil sampling and methods of analysis. Soil Research Institute, Agriculture Canada, Ottawa, Ont. pp. 212.

NIX, H. A. 1968. The assessment of biological productivity. Pages 78–88 *in* G. A. Stewart, Ed. Land evaluation. MacMillan, Melbourne.

NORTON, R. L. 1971. What you must know about high density plantings. Amer. Fruit Grower **91**(5): 14–16.

ONTARIO MINISTRY OF AGRICULTURE AND FOOD. 1971, 1972b, 1973. Seasonal fruit and vegetable reports. Toronto, Ont.

ONTARIO MINISTRY OF AGRICULTURE AND FOOD. 1972. 1971 fruit tree census. Part III. Apples. Toronto, Ont.

ONTARIO MINISTRY OF AGRICULTURE AND FOOD. 1974. Fruit and vegetable production in Ontario. Annual Summary. Toronto, Ont.

STEEL, R. G. D. and TORRIE, J. H. 1960. Principles and procedures of statistics. McGraw-Hill Book Co., Inc., Toronto, Ont. 481 pp.

VINK, A. P. A. 1975. Land use in advancing agriculture. Springer-Verlag, New York, N.Y.

Part V

Soil Survey Interpretation

Papers 10 and 11: Introductory Review

10 LINDSAY, SCHEELAR, and TWARDY
Soil Survey for Urban Development

11 BOUMA
*Soil Survey Interpretation: Estimating Use-Potentials of
a Clay Soil under Various Moisture Regimes*

As outlined in the introduction to this book, soil surveys are a recent phenomenon with most maps having been published since 1945. Such surveys along with their geological counterparts play a crucial role in providing national and international resource inventories. Paper 1 includes estimates of global soil survey coverage and concludes that about one fifth of the world's soils have been surveyed. Of course, as is emphasized, there is marked variation from continent to continent. The scale of mapping varies according to survey objectives. As scale becomes more detailed, sampling intensity has to increase with obvious cost implications. Dent and Young (1981) provide a very useful text describing the processes involved in soil survey. Table 1 demonstrates the relationships between survey scale, sampling intensity, mapping units, and purpose of survey. As can be seen from this table, soil series and their subdivisions, soil phases, are the mapping units at scales of 1:50,000 and larger. Soil series in the first instance are defined as taxonomic units according to profiles developed on similar parent materials and displaying similar horizon sequences in terms of properties and thickness. Soil phases are subdivisions of soil series according to such attributes as texture, slope, stoniness, wetness, and degree of erosion. These taxonomic units become the mapping units in soil survey. A target of 85% purity within individual mapping units may be set, but in practice only 50-60% is normally achieved. The purity of soil mapping units is of crucial relevance to soil map interpretations and most soil survey reports give no statistical information on variability. Though it is possible to express serious concern at the considerable occurrence of subdominant soils within individual soil mapping units, it is often the case that these other soils are closely allied in type to the named soil series.

The contents of a traditional soil survey report or memoir for a specific area can be summarized as follows:

1. General description of area
2. Climate and geology

Table 1. Soil survey scales and associated sampling intensities, mapping units and examples of applications

Typical scales	Mean distance between field observations at 1 per sq. cm	Examples of mapping units	Examples of applications
1:250,000	2.5 km	land systems	resource inventory at regional or national level
1:50,000	500 m	associations, series	project feasibility studies; regional land use planning
1:25,000 to 1:10,000	250 m 100 m	series, phases	agricultural advisory work, project planning, irrigation surveys
1:5,000	50 m	series, phases, individual properties	special purpose surveys, urban soil surveys

Source: From Dent and Young, 1981, p. 90

3. Soil parent materials
4. Methods of soil survey and classification
5. Systematic description of the soils for each series—representative profile descriptions, general descriptions of soil properties
   (This constitutes the bulk of the report.)
6. Vegetation
7. Land use—agriculture, forestry
8. Land use capability
9. Appendices of analytical data

The result is a tremendous body of information to complement the published soil map. The impression is frequently gained from reading older soil survey reports that the prime aim was always to produce a basic inventory of soils—a descriptive emphasis similar to the objectives of geological survey. As a qualification it should be said that the agricultural relevance in older reports is frequently highlighted. However, gone are the days when surveyors could spend considerable periods of time mapping the soils in particular areas with the aim of producing inventory-type soil survey memoirs. As Dent and Young (1981) stress, every effort should be made in the presentation of a report to make the information easily accessible and understandable. A soil survey is meant to be of use and the results have to be presented in an easily assimilable form. The older viewpoint was that the job of the surveyor was to produce the basic data and for users to interpret this information appropriate to their needs. The technical nature of traditional soil survey reports has proved to be a serious obstacle to such use and one response, as discussed in the preceding section, has been land capability assessment. Now there is an increasing tendency for soil surveyors to become much more involved with the interpretation of their results and this is reflected in a different style of soil survey reports.

The change in soil survey reports can be illustrated by selecting as an example the report on Madison County, New York, by Hanna (1981). On the inside cover and first page is a set of clear instructions on how to use the report. Guidance is given on the location of the area of interest to the user, the identification of soil map unit symbols, and how to extract relevant information about these soils. After a general introduction to the soils of the area, a description is given of each soil series with comments often given on agricultural, ecological, and recreational implications. Rectified aerial photographs act as the base to the soil maps published at a scale of 1:15,840. After the description of soil series, the use and management of soil are discussed with reference to crops and pasture, woodland management and productivity, wildlife habitat, recreation, and engineering. The user of the report can also consult tables to obtain estimates of yields for seven different crops for each map symbol. For areas of woodland, guidance is given in another table on management concerns (erosion hazard, equipment limitation, seedling mortality, and windthrow hazard), potential productivity, and suitable trees. Soils are also interpreted in terms of problems posed to camping areas, picnic areas, playgrounds, paths, and trails. Much attention is given to engineering interpretations—for example, the degree of problem posed to different types of building site development. The assessment of soils with reference to sanitary facilities merits separate attention. In another interpretation each soil is assessed in terms of suitability in providing roadfill, sand, gravel, and topsoil. The final part of the report gives analytical data (engineering, physical, and chemical), again for each soil. Shrink-swell potential, risk of corrosion, erosion factors, and soil moisture regimes are highlighted. This report for Madison County thus provides a demonstration of soil survey interpretation for a wide range of uses.

The topic of soil survey interpretation is well covered in the literature. A specialist theme is interpretation for irrigation projects, but this is excluded from present considerations. An early overview is given by Bartelli et al. (1966), and Bartelli (1978) has also written a more recent review. A special issue of *Geoderma* is devoted to nonagricultural applications (Simonson, 1974). Vold (1982) has edited a volume devoted to soil interpretations for forestry. A range of British soil survey applications is assembled by Jarvis and Mackney (1978). A text on the subject is written by Olson (1981), who has also produced a report dealing with engineering applications (Olson, 1973). It is instructive to list the types of soil survey applications covered in these publications.

1. Agriculture
    a. Suitability for specific crops including grassland
    b. Yield predictions
    c. Assessment of soils according to ease of cultivation
    d. Assessment of soil droughtiness
    e. Assessment of soil workability
    f. Assessment of erosion hazard

g. Soil suitability for direct drilling

h. Soil suitability for acceptance of slurry

2. Forestry
   a. Suitability for specific trees
   b. Yield predictions
   c. Assessment of specific hazards

3. Engineering
   a. Suitability as a source of topsoil
   b. Suitability as a water soakaway
   c. Assessment of corrosion hazard
   d. Assessment of shrink/swell potential
   e. Stability of foundations
   f. Predictions of soil problems for highway construction
   g. Interpretations for urban development
   h. Ratings for waste disposal in septic tanks, sewage lagoons, and sanitary landfill trenches

4. Recreation
   a. Suitability of soils for playing fields, parks and gardens, golf courses, camping sites, picnic areas, and footpaths
   b. Interpretation for general planning of national parks

5. Wildlife Habitat Conservation
   a. Identification of distinctive habitat conditions

The striking feature of this list is the diversity of applications. However, it must always be remembered that soil mapping units are assessed in terms of their suitability for any defined purpose; any interpretation is a spatial generalization and is not site specific. The accuracy of the assessment clearly depends on the initial scale and quality of the original soil survey. Soil survey interpretation for engineering purposes, for example, will never displace site investigations. Instead soil survey interpretations for engineering should be viewed as aiding the identification of potential problems at an early stage.

Paper 10 demonstrates how a detailed soil survey for the Mill Woods district of Edmonton, Canada, aided urban planning. The potential of soils for lawns and landscaping as well as for providing construction material is assessed. Emphasis is given in the engineering interpretation to evaluating the concrete corrosion hazard. The cost benefits of identifying such problems at an early stage of urban development are outstanding.

Critical to soil survey interpretation for any specific purpose is the specification of guidelines. As an example, Soil Survey Staff (1971) give details on interpreting soil survey data for engineering purposes. The specification of quantitative guidelines along with the computer-based storage of soil survey information opens up major possibilities for the computerization of soil survey interpretations. Olson (1981) describes the scheme as developed by the U.S. Soil Conservation Service (SCS). For "SCS Form 5," data are entered on physical, engineering, and chemical properties as well as upon interpretations for sanitary facilities, community development, source material (e.g., for topsoil, sand and gravel, etc.), water management, recreation, capability and predicted yields, woodland suitability, suitable windbreak species, wildlife habitat suitability, and potential native plant community. The tremendous advantage of such a computer-based approach is that information can be retrieved almost instantaneously and is available to any user as soon as it is entered. The person or agency that requests the information does not need to wait for the publication of a full soil survey report and then work through all the information. Instead the soil survey interpretations ought to be available much more quickly and in a form more specific to the needs of the user. The implication is that the development of computer-based information systems will increasingly make the publication of conventional soil survey reports redundant (see Part VI).

A quantitatively and dynamically based approach to soil survey interpretation is demonstrated in Paper 11. Bouma follows a distinguished Dutch tradition of soil survey interpretation, summarized by Davidson (1980). Bouma's investigation focuses attention on problems of clay soils along the Rhine. The nature and properties of these soils, as with many other soils in the Netherlands, are influenced to a marked extent by past and present management practices. As Bouma notes, temporal and spatial variations in soil moisture status, in part achieved by management strategies, result in swelling and shrinking and consequential changes in soil physical properties. He proposes the concept of identifying optimal management conditions as a means of predicting soil-use potentials. In essence he argues against the established approach of assessing land use limitations based on actual hydrological conditions in favor of evaluating land use with respect to potential conditions. Thus his paper concentrates upon measurement of actual conditions, the estimation of potential conditions using simulation models, and methods of achieving optimal conditions. In many ways the study by Bouma is more a project in land evaluation than one of soil survey interpretation. The implication is that the conceptual framework of soil survey interpretation will move toward the FAO *Framework for Land Evaluation.*

REFERENCES

Bartelli, L. J., 1978, Technical Classification System for Soil Survey Interpretation, *Advances in Agronomy* **30:**247-289.

Bartelli, L. J., A. A. Klingebiel, J. V. Baird, and M. R. Heddleston, eds., 1966, *Soil Surveys and Land Use Planning,* American Society of Agronomy, Madison, Wisconsin.

Davidson, D. A., 1980, *Soils and Land Use Planning,* Longman, London.

Dent, D., and A. Young, 1981, *Soil Survey and Land Evaluation,* George Allen and Unwin, London.

Hanna, W. E., 1981, *Soil Survey of Madison County, New York,* U.S. Department of Agriculture, Soil Conservation Service, Washington, D.C.

Jarvis, M. J., and D. Mackney, eds., 1979, *Soil Survey Applications,* Soil Survey Technical Monograph No. 13, Rothamsted Experimental Station, Harpenden.

Olson, G. W., 1973, Soil Survey Interpretation for Engineering Purposes, *FAO Soils Bulletin No. 19.*

Olson, G. W., 1981, *Soils and the Environment,* Chapman and Hall, New York.

Simonson, R. W., ed., 1974, *Non-agricultural Applications of Soil Surveys,* Elsevier, Amsterdam.

Soil Survey Staff, 1971, *Guide for Interpreting Engineering Uses of Soil,* U.S. Department of Agriculture, Soil Conservation Service, Washington, D.C.

Vold, T., ed., 1982, *Proceedings of the B.C. Soil Survey Workshop on Soil Interpretations for Forestry,* APD Technical Paper No. 6, Land Management Rept. No. 10, Ministry of Environment, Province of British Columbia, Victoria, B.C.

10: SOIL SURVEY FOR URBAN DEVELOPMENT*

J. D. Lindsay, M. G. Scheelar, and A. G. Twardy

Soils Division, Research Council of Alberta, Edmonton, Alberta, Canada

ABSTRACT

Lindsay, J.D., Scheelar, M.D. and Twardy, A.G., 1973. Soil survey for urban development. *Geoderma*, 10: 35–45.

As an aid to urban planning, a detailed soil survey is underway in the new Mill Woods district, City of Edmonton. Five soil associations – Ellerslie, Mill Woods, Argyll, Hercules, and Beaumont – are being mapped in the area. These soils represent the Chernozemic, Solonetzic, and Gleysolic Orders in the Canadian System of Soil Classification. Ellerslie and Beaumont soils are a good topsoil source and will support plant growth well. Argyll soils have poor surface drainage and being saline may present problems in lawn establishment and trafficability. The Mill Woods soils are intermediate between Ellerslie, Beaumont and Argyll associations. Hercules soils are poorly drained and may be saline; their suitability for landscaping purposes is limited.

From an engineering or construction standpoint, the soils in the Mill Woods area may present some problems related to shrink–swell potential and concrete corrosion. The Argyll, Mill Woods and Hercules soil associations are characterized by a relatively high sulfate content which represents a potential concrete corrosion hazard in the area.

The soil map also indicates areas of poorly drained soils which will require special engineering practices before development can be initiated.

INTRODUCTION

Historically, requests for soil information originated with individuals whose interests were related to the production of food, fibre or timber products. More recently, however, an increased awareness of the suitability or unsuitability of soils for other uses has become apparent. The unprecedented growth of urban communities expanding to new areas has resulted in requests for soil information concerning this particular alternate land use.

Recently, 6,000 acres of land were annexed adjacent to the City of Edmonton, Alberta, for urban expansion. According to the report of the City Planning Department (1971), this new community called Mill Woods will eventually accommodate 120,000 people and have a development time span of more than 20 years.

Development of the area began in 1970 and to assist with the planning, a high intensity (detailed) soil survey was carried out on 260 acres of land in that year. Subsequently, in 1971 and 1972, 500 and 320 acres, respectively, were mapped by soil survey.

City planners indicate the areas of developmental priority within the Mill Woods district and the soil-survey program is scheduled to provide information on the areas of immediate

---

* Research Council of Alberta, Contrib. No. 640.

concern. Each year a soil map and soil interpretation maps of topsoil suitability, potential concrete corrosion hazard and soil drainage are prepared.

This paper describes the methodology used in conducting the soil survey and presents some of the interpretations based on the morphological, chemical and physical properties' of the soils.

METHODS

The area to be mapped is carefully surveyed into a grid system in which stakes are established along lines spaced at 250-ft. intervals. This step ensures that adequate control is provided for soil mapping and soil sampling procedures. The aerial photographs used in the study are at a scale of 500 ft. to 1 inch (1:6,000).

A truck-mounted coring drill is used for the inspection of the soils. Cores, to a depth of 7 ft., are obtained at each of the staked sites in the grid system.

The soils are classified at each survey stake, using the cores, but sampled at only every second stake. Thus soil samples are obtained at 500-ft. intervals throughout the area.

In the laboratory, emphasis is given to the determination of water-soluble salts and electrical conductivity on a saturation extract, soil reaction (pH), particle size distribution, Atterberg limits, total nitrogen and total carbon.

RESULTS

Soils and surficial deposits

The soils of the area were mapped by Bowser et al. (1962) at a scale of 1 inch to 2 miles (1:126,000). This soil mapping was carried out as part of a basic data inventory program. Because of map scale, however, the information has limitations when used in the context of detailed urban planning. Consequently, to provide the planners with as much information as possible the soil map for the present study is published at a scale of 1 inch to 250 ft. (1:3,000).

The portion of the Mill Woods district soil mapped to date is developed primarily on fine-textured lacustrine clay. This area is part of Glacial Lake Edmonton (Bayrock and Hughes, 1962) which covered much of the Edmonton district during Late Pleistocene time. Soils developed from glacial till are of minor occurrence in the area. According to drill records (Hardy and Associates, 1971) the stratigraphic sequence of material is variable, but portions of the area consist of 12 ft. of lacustrine material over 10 ft. of clay loam till overlying bentonitic shales and sandstones of the Edmonton Formation.

Generally the topography of the area is fairly smooth with slopes seldom exceeding 2%. Low-lying depressional areas are a characteristic feature of the landscape.

The soils are mapped on a soil association basis. Each soil association is a group of related soil series developed on a particular parent material. The soil association, therefore, represents a combination of natural features including the kind of landscape, the surface color of the soil and the dominant soil textures.

The map units represent a portion or a segment of a soil association and are composed of one or more soil series. Different map units are separated on the basis of different proportions of soil series occurring within the association. These are indicated as being dominant or significant in the association.

The use of soil associations appears suited to this study because the fine divisions included in the soil classification system can be recognized, although in some cases their intimate occurrence in the landscape precludes delineation on the soil map. This is not regarded, however, as a shortcoming of the mapping procedure since most of the inseparable units, although significant from a classification standpoint, are not sufficiently different with respect to soil properties to affect their use for urban development.

Soils are classified according to the System of Soil Classification for Canada (Canada Department of Agriculture, 1970).

Significant and dominant subgroups of the various soil associations employed in the Mill Woods district are shown on the soil map legend (Fig.1). This map represents only a portion of the area covered by soil survey in the Mill Woods district.

The Ellerslie association consists of moderately well to imperfectly drained Chernozemic soils developed from lacustrine sediments. These soils are characterized by a thick dark colored, granular and friable Ah horizon. The B horizon is friable whereas the C is moderately calcareous and weakly saline. Soils of this association range in texture from silty clay to clay.

Soils of the Mill Woods association are moderately well to imperfectly drained Solonetzic soils developed from fine textured lacustrine material. They are usually found in areas of groundwater discharge where salts have been brought near the surface by a fluctuating water table. The Ah horizon of the Mill Woods soil is thinner than that of the Ellerslie association. They have a hard B horizon which becomes a sticky, gelatinous mass when wet. The soils are characterized by a high salt content in the lower portion of the profile.

The Argyll association is comprised of imperfectly drained alkaline Solonetz soils that are extremely dense and intractable. These impermeable soils have a thin Ah horizon overlying a dense B horizon. Significant amounts of soluble salts occur in the B and C horizons. The hard compact B horizon limits the penetration of water, air and roots. Argyll soils are developed from silty clay to heavy clay lacustrine deposits.

The Hercules association includes those soils that are saturated or are under reducing conditions continuously or during some period of the year. They are poorly and very poorly drained soils found in areas of groundwater discharge. An accumulation of relatively undecomposed peat occurs at the surface of some of these soils. Soluble salts may occur in all horizons of the Hercules soils which are developed from lacustrine silty clay and clay.

Beaumont soils are moderately well drained Chernozemic soils developed from loam to clay loam till. These soils are characterized by a thick, dark colored, granular and friable Ah horizon. The B horizon is friable whereas the C is moderately calcareous and weakly saline.

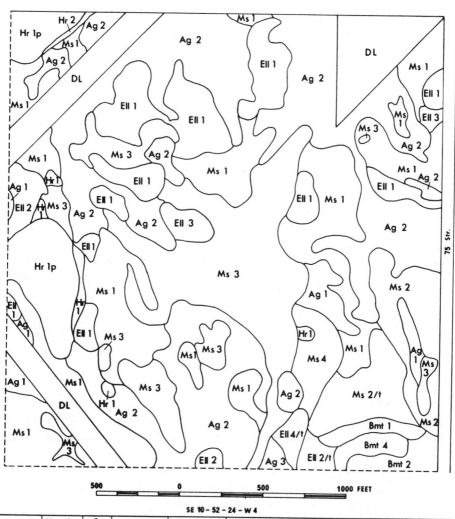

SE 10 – 52 – 24 – W 4

Association	Mapping Unit	% Slope	Order	Great Group	Dominant Subgroup	Significant Subgroup
Ellerslie	Ell 1	0 - 2	Chernozemic	Black	Eluviated Black	Orthic Black
	Ell 2	0 - 2			Solodic Black	Black Solod
	Ell 3	0 - 2			Gleyed Eluviated Black	
	Ell 4	2 - 5			Eluviated Black	Orthic Black
Mill Woods	Ms 1	0 - 2	Solonetzic	Solonetz and Solod	Black Solonetz	Black Solod
	Ms 2	0 - 2			Black Solod	Black Solonetz
	Ms 3	0 - 2			Gleyed Black Solonetz	Gleyed Black Solod
	Ms 4	2 - 5			Black Solod	
Argyll	Ag 1	0 - 2		Solonetz	Alkaline Solonetz	
	Ag 2	0 - 2			Alkaline Solonetz	Gleyed Alkaline Solonetz
	Ag 3	0 - 2			Gleyed Alkaline Solonetz	
Hercules	Hr 1	0 - 2	Gleysolic	Humic Gleysol	Orthic Humic Gleysol	
	Hr 2	0 - 2			Saline Rego Humic Gleysol	
Beaumont	Bmt 1	0 - 2	Chernozemic	Black	Eluviated Black	Orthic Black
	Bmt 2	0 - 2			Solodic Black	Black Solod
	Bmt 4	2 - 5			Solodic Black	Black Solod

p – peaty phase   DL – Disturbed Land   /t – overlying till

Fig.1. Soil map of a portion of the Mill Woods district.

Soil interpretations

From the basic soil survey data it is possible to make predictions of performance for the soils, based on soil morphology and associated soil physical and chemical properties. In the Mill Woods area there are two main uses for which the soils of the area will be required – lawns and landscaping, and as a construction material.

The data in Table I provide some indication of the suitability of the surface soils for landscaping. These data represent mean values for soil samples collected at some 116 sites in the area.

In descending order of topsoil suitability, the soil associations in the Mill Woods area can be ranked as Beaumont, Ellerslie, Mill Woods, Argyll and Hercules. This ranking is based on an evaluation of the Ah horizon in terms of organic matter content, total nitrogen content, water-soluble salt content, surface or internal drainage, texture, and permeability.

The Ellerslie and Beaumont associations have few properties that limit plant growth. The Argyll association, however, has fairly severe limitations because of its thin Ah horizon, relatively low organic matter content, moderate salinity, and low permeability. Rainwater tends to remain on the surface of these soils for relatively long periods to be removed only by evaporation. Such a phenomenon tends to result in the upward movement of salt-bearing groundwater (Cairns and Bowser, 1969). The soils of the Mill Woods association have moderate limitations for plant growth. They do not have the extremely undesirable physical and chemical properties of the Argyll association but at the same time the data indicate they are inferior to Ellerslie soils.

Areas of Hercules soils are poorly to very poorly drained. Such soils present vegetative rooting problems due to wetness. Also, salts have been brought near the surface by groundwater discharge which serves to further limit the suitability of these soils for landscaping and lawn establishment.

The Solonetzic soils, particularly those of the Argyll association, may present problems with respect to compaction and trafficability. These impermeable soils will puddle and compact under excessive pedestrian traffic at high moisture contents. School yards and

TABLE I

Mean and standard deviation values for some chemical and physical properties of the surface horizon (topsoil) of the soil associations in the Mill Woods district

Soil association	Thickness (cm)	pH	Organic matter (%)	Nitrogen (%)	Electrical conductivity (mmhos/cm)	Sulfate (%)	Texture
Ellerslie	24±9	6.4±0.2	12.2	0.69	0.4±0.1	0.00	silt loam
Mill Woods	17±5	6.4±0.1	11.2	0.59	1.1±0.4	0.02±0.07	loam
Argyll	12±4	6.2±0.4	8.7	0.49	1.5±0.8	0.03±0.04	clay loam
Hercules	22±11	6.8±0.1	10.9	0.67	2.0±1.7	0.06±0.03	clay loam
Beaumont	29±11	6.6	12.5	0.56	–	–	clay loam

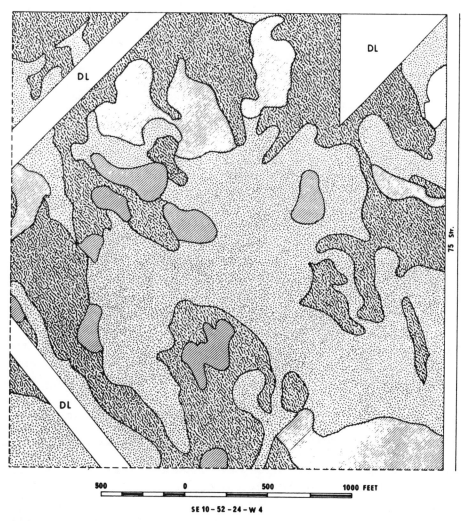

SE 10 – 52 – 24 – W 4

 Exellent

Fairly Good to Good

Poor

DL - Disturbed Land

Fig. 2. Soil suitability for landscaping.

playgrounds will be particularly susceptible to this type of problem.

In the Mill Woods area considerable care must be taken in preparing the land for land-scaping. Since subsoil salinity is characteristic of the Argyll, Mill Woods and Hercules soil associations, every precaution must be taken to ensure that the subsoil material is not left at the surface following construction. An interpretive soil map showing the suitability of the surface soils for landscaping purposes in a portion of the Mill Woods area is shown in Fig. 2.

TABLE II

Mean and standard deviation values for some chemical properties of the subsoil horizon (C) of the soil associations in the Mill Woods district

Soil association	pH	Electrical conductivity (mmhos/cm)	Sulfate (%)	m. equiv./litre		
				sodium	magnesium	calcium
Ellerslie	7.6±0.3	1.9±1.1	0.06±0.06	8.2±8.7	5.3±6.3	11.7±9.0
Mill Woods	7.6±0.2	4.3±2.0	0.22±0.14	33.9±29.4	15.8±11.0	20.4±7.5
Argyll	7.7±0.2	7.5±2.4	0.44±0.18	87.1±53.4	24.9±10.8	20.8±3.5
Hercules	7.6±0.3	4.7±2.9	0.24±0.20	41.4±38.7	18.5±19.0	17.0±7.3
Beaumont	7.7±0.3	1.7±1.2	0.04±0.05	8.9±14.3	3.9±4.1	10.3±10.0

From an engineering and construction standpoint, the soils in this area present a number of problems with regard to urban development. One major concern is the potential corrosion of concrete structures and underground conduits because of subsoil salinity. Some of the subsoil chemical properties of the soil associations are shown in Table II.

The mean sulfate content in the subsoil (C horizon) ranges from 0.04% in the Beaumont association to 0.44% in the Argyll association. Corresponding mean electrical conductivity measurements of a water extract from these soils are 1.7 and 7.5 mmhos/cm, respectively.

The principal soluble salt in the soils of the Mill Woods area is sodium sulfate, with magnesium sulfate and calcium sulfate also occurring to a significant extent. Pawluk and Bayrock (1969) and Swenson (1971) also report the dominance of these salts in some of the soils of the Canadian prairie region.

The *Concrete Manual* of the United States Bureau of Reclamation (1966) recognizes the following concrete corrosion categories:

Negligible attack: <0.10% sulfate in soil
Mild but positive attack: 0.10–0.20% sulfate in soil
Considerable attack: 0.20–0.50% sulfate in soil
Severe attack: >0.50% sulfate in soil

Using the above standards as a guideline, the potential corrosion hazard associated with the soil associations in the Mill Woods area ranges from negligible to mild in the Beaumont and Ellerslie associations, mild to considerable in the Mill Woods association, considerable to severe in the Argyll association, and considerable in the Hercules association.

Swenson (1971) has outlined in some detail the precautions that should be taken where concrete structures are to be placed in a sulfate soil environment. Such measures include the following: use of sulfate-resisting cement, a low water-cement ratio, high cement content, air-entrainment, waterproof coatings, drainage facilities, and special reinforcing cover.

An interpretive soil survey map showing the various areas of potential concrete corrosion in a portion of the Mill Woods area is shown in Fig.3.

Physical properties of the soil are of special interest to engineers because they affect design, construction, and maintenance of structures. In the Mill Woods area a number of sites were sampled specifically for engineering tests. The results of the analyses are shown in Table III.

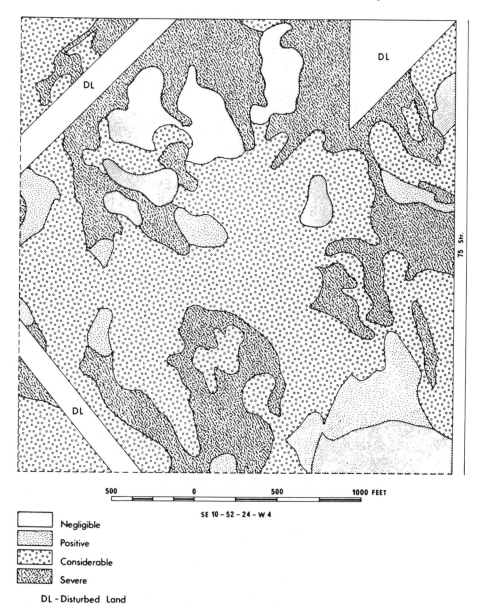

Negligible

Positive

Considerable

Severe

DL - Disturbed Land

Fig.3. Potential concrete corrosion hazard of the soil associations.

Since a major portion of the Mill Woods area mapped to date is mantled to a depth of at least 7 ft. with lacustrine clay, the soil associations differ very little in so far as the engineering data are concerned. The exception is the Beaumont association which is developed from till rather than lacustrine material. The subsoils of the Ellerslie, Mill Woods, Argyll, and Hercules associations usually are classified as CH in the Unified System and A-7-6 in the AASHO system of classification, whereas the Beaumont association is CL and

TABLE III

Engineering test data for the subsoil (C horizon) of representative soil profiles of the soil associations from the Mill Woods district

Soil associa- tion	Depth from surface (cm)	Per cent passing sieve							Per cent smaller than				Liquid limit	Plastic- ity index	Activ- ity No.	Textural classification		
		1 in.	3/4 in.	5/8 in.	No. 4	No. 10	No. 40	No. 200	.05 (mm)	.005 (mm)	.002 (mm)	.001 (mm)				AASHO	Unified	USDA
Ellerslie	50–100	100	100	100	100	100	96	70	69	48	38	34	43	21	0.6	A7-6	CL	SiC
	100–150	98	98	98	97	97	97	86	83	66	43	38	53	26	0.5	A7-6	CH	SiC
Mill Woods	50–100	100	100	100	100	100	99	94	93	79	61	51	66	37	0.6	A7-6	CH	SiC-HC
	150–225	100	100	100	100	100	100	96	95	78	52	41	60	33	0.6	A7-6	CH	SiC-HC
Argyll	90–140	100	100	100	100	100	98	88	87	74	65	62	64	39	0.6	A7-6	CH	SiC-HC
	165–225	100	100	100	100	100	96	74	72	54	40	33	61	34	0.9	A7-6	CH	SiC
Beaumont	63–180	100	100	100	100	99	94	72	70	42	33	28	34	12	0.4	A6	CL	CL
	180–250	100	100	100	100	99	93	68	67	40	32	29	33	13	0.4	A6	CL	CL

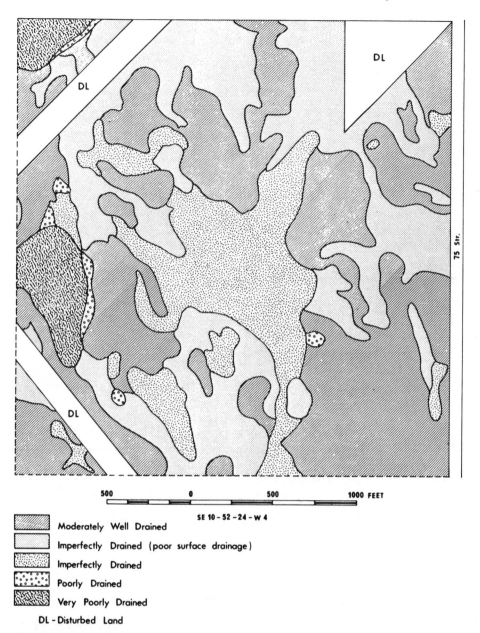

Fig.4. Drainage classes of the soil associations.

A-6. Such material, particularly the lacustrine sediments, is characterized by a high content of plastic clays. Arshad (1966), in a study of the soils of this area, indicates montmorillonite as the dominant clay mineral with illite and kaolinite next in abundance. Montmorillonite is an expansible clay and soils characterized by this clay mineral have a high shrink—swell potential and are subject to fairly large volume changes with change in moisture content.

The area of poorly drained soils, the Hercules soil association, is of similar texture to other soils of the area but wetter. These soil areas have water tables near the surface and may present problems in bearing strength and drainage for structures. A map of a portion of the Mill Woods district showing the various soil drainage classes is shown in Fig.4.

Special engineering practices are required in the poorly drained areas where artificial drainage, use of piling or addition of fill material may be required before construction can be initiated.

CONCLUSIONS

Requests for detailed or high intensity soil surveys are rapidly increasing. Such surveys can be used for planning a wide assortment of facilities ranging from homes and industrial plants to schools and playgrounds. The cost-benefit ratio of such surveys has been estimated at 1 to 100 (Klingebiel, 1966).

The information provided by the soil survey of the Mill Woods district of Edmonton has aided in the formulation of construction practices, particularly in regard to the specifications for the type of concrete to be used in the area. At the same time new home owners benefit from the soils information in that recommendations can be made with regard to the preparation of the soils for lawns and landscaping.

It should be mentioned, however, that soil survey information is not meant to eliminate the need for deep borings for specific structures. The erection of high-rise towers and large buildings will require on-site investigation; the soil survey, however, aids in determining where the deep borings should be made and where the buildings should be sited.

REFERENCES

Arshad, M.A. and Pawluk, S., 1966. Characteristics of some solonetzic soils in Glacial Lake Edmonton basin of Alberta, II. Mineralogy. *J. Soil Sci.*, 17 (1): 8 pp.

Bayrock, L.A. and Hughes, G.M., 1962. Surficial geology of the Edmonton District, Alberta. *Res. Counc. Alta. Prelim. Rep.*, 62-6: 40 pp.

Bowser, W.E., Kjearsgaard, A.A., Peters, T.W. and Wells, R.E., 1962. Soil survey of Edmonton sheet (83-H). *Alta. Soil Surv. Rep.*, 21: 66 pp.

Cairns, R.R. and Bowser, W.E., 1969. Solonetzic soils and their management. *Canada Dept. Agric. Publ.*, 1391: 23 pp.

Canada Department of Agriculture, 1970. *System of Soil Classification for Canada.* Canada Dept. of Agriculture, Queen's Printer, Ottawa, 249 pp.

City of Edmonton Planning Department, 1971. *Mill Woods, a Development Concept Report Prepared on Behalf of the Civic Administration,* 56 pp.

Hardy, R.M. and Associates, 1971. *Edmonton Public Schools Foundation Investigation, Grace Martin Elementary School, Mill Woods Development,* 14 pp.

Klingebiel, A., 1966. Cost and returns of soil surveys. *Soil Conserv.*, 32 (1): 3–6.

Pawluk, S. and Bayrock, L.A., 1969. Some characteristics and physical properties of Alberta tills. *Res. Counc. Alta. Bull.*, 26: 72 pp.

Swenson, E.G., 1971. Concrete in sulphate environments. *Canadian Building Digest, Division of Building Research, National Research Council of Canada*, 136: 4 pp.

United States Bureau of Reclamation, 1966. *Concrete Manual.* United States Department Interior, Bureau of Reclamation, 7th ed., 642 pp.

11: SOIL SURVEY INTERPRETATION: ESTIMATING USE-POTENTIALS OF A CLAY SOIL UNDER VARIOUS MOISTURE REGIMES

J. Bouma

Netherlands Soil Survey Institute, P.O. Box 98, 6700 AB Wageningen, The Netherlands

ABSTRACT

Bouma, J., 1981. Soil survey interpretation: estimating use-potentials of a clay soil under various moisture regimes. Geoderma, 26:165—177.

Current Dutch soil survey interpretation emphasizes assessment factors which independently define key aspects of soil behaviour under actual conditions. For grassland these are: moisture-supply capacity, bearing capacity and drainage status. Practical questions focus on how actual limitations can be overcome. Computer simulation techniques, to be focused on the individual assessment factors, are needed to answer these questions. Soil survey and morphology data were used in this context to: (1) select experimental sites; (2) modify physical monitoring procedures; (3) derive simulation models for swelling soils with macropores; (4) develop simple field methods for characterizing basic physical soil properties and their regional variability, and (5) use soil maps for extrapolating the obtained interpretations.

Future soil survey reports should ideally contain basic physical data and the possible ranges for the different assessment factors, expressed by simulation as a function of water management. Basic data include hydraulic conductivity, moisture retention, bearing capacity and drainage rate. The latter two were characterized in this study by new field methods. Possible ranges differ for the different assessment factors. For example, an inadequate moisture supply capacity in the growing season can be completely compensated by raising the water table, by sprinkler irrigation or by a combination of both methods. The presented simulation offers a quantitative analysis. The inadequate bearing capacity and drainage status can be compensated for only partly by lower water-table levels in winter and spring.

INTRODUCTION

Non-calcareous basin clay soils along the Dutch part of the Rhine river are exclusively used as meadows and pastures. They offer management problems. Originally these soils occurred in very poorly drained backswamps (De Bakker, 1979). Soil conditions were improved by tile drainage which lowered the water table (Van Hoorn, 1960). Still, many problems remain. Drains often do not work properly. This is thought to be due to either the low vertical saturated hydraulic conductivity (K_{sat}) of the clay above the drain, resulting in perched water tables, or to a low K_{sat} of soil surrounding the tile drains. Mechanization of farming operations causes compaction of surface horizons, leading to ponding of water. Also, lower levels of the water table during the growing season, which are associated with improved drainage, result in a drop of the water supply capacity. This, in turn, has convinced many farmers of the necessity for sprinkler irrigation. Their questions as to optimal sprinkling intensities and quantities cannot be answered adequately because soil moisture regimes of clay soils are difficult to characterize. Problems are due to processes of swelling and shrinkage which continuously change pore geometry and the associated physical properties.

Management problems, mentioned above, can only be analysed by a multidisciplinary team, which includes soil scientists. The soil survey specialist will be interested in the regional distribution of the soil and he will try to assess soil suitability for a variety of uses. In doing so, he must base his judgement on actual soil conditions which are strongly affected by soil and water management. But management practices have been different locally and characterization of differing *actual* conditions, though relevant, may be less effective than definition of *optimal* conditions and of management practices which are needed to realize those conditions. The latter approach, which focuses on practical questions of farmers and planners, defines soil-use-potentials.

Though attractive, the procedure described goes considerably beyond the usual expertise of the soil survey specialist. The three year study to be discussed here deals with these problems by analysing the optimal soil moisture regime for a Dutch clay soil. These clay soils have moderate limitations for use as grassland due to wet conditions and a slow start of growth in spring and a limited moisture supply capacity in summer.

Particular emphasis will be on use of soil survey information in such a project and on the development of an innovative system of soil survey interpretation which emphasizes use-potentials rather than use-limitations.

SOIL SURVEY INTERPRETATION IN THE NETHERLANDS

A new system for soil survey interpretation is now being used in The Netherlands which defines assessment factors (Haans and Van Lynden, 1978; Haans, 1979). These describe key aspects of soil behaviour, to be characterized independently, as follows.

The *drainage status* describes prevalent moisture conditions in the surface soil and is currently characterized by the average highest level of the groundwater table in spring (Van Heesen, 1970). The *bearing capacity* describes the penetration resistance of the soil surface as measured with a penetrometer. This resistance is, for any given soil, a function of the soil moisture content. The *internal drainage* describes the vertical K_{sat} of the upper metre of soil, and the *moisture supply capacity* defines the amount of water (to be obtained by computer simulation) which is available to the plants in a 10% dry year. This is a year with an evapotranspiration surplus (i.e. rainfall deficit) which has a statistical probability of being exceeded only once in every ten years.

The assessment factors are currently used to characterize *actual* hydrological conditions. They are combined into different suitability classes, which have been discussed by Haans (1979). Assessment factors can also be used to characterize *potential* conditions to be realized by different types of management or profile modifications. In fact, questions of farmers, county-agents and planners often focus on use-potentials. In others words, how can the different assessment factors be improved by management if they are currently considered to be inadequate?

Determination of assessment factors for *actual* conditions can be based on on-site observations and on contacts with local farmers and extension experts. More difficult is the prediction of *potential* conditions for which no experience exists. Field experiments will often be too expensive. Computer simulation may then be the only alternative. This involves an expression of physical processes in terms of mathematical equations with variables and constants that can be obtained by independent measurements (e.g., Feddes and Van Wijk, 1976; Feddes et al., 1978; Hillel, 1977; De Laat, 1980; Bouma et al., 1980a). Simulation models represent strong generalizations of reality. They have to be validated by comparing calculated and measured data for actual conditions in a given year. Once validated, a model can be used for prediction purposes.

Each assessment factor being distinguished is a direct function of the soil moisture regime, which has, therefore, a key function in the discussion of assessment factors for both actual and potential conditions. Computer simulation of the soil moisture regime is used to define the assessment factors as a function of different types of water management. Optimization techniques are necessary to derive the best practical system of water management. This is needed because individual assessment factors may be associated with conflicting management procedures. For example, lowering of the water table may improve bearing capacity and drainage status, but the moisture supply capacity may be reduced.

The discussion so far has centered on the application of the Dutch system of soil survey interpretation. The concepts used, however, are in agreement with the FAO system, even though some terms are defined differently (FAO, 1976). In this context, assessment factors correspond with land qualities. The land-utilization type (FAO, 1976; Beek, 1978) can be characterized as follows: (1) the soils discussed are exclusively used as meadows and pastures for intensive dairy farming using farms of 20–50 ha and 2.5 cows per ha; (2) chemical fertilizers are applied at high rates, to the effect that physical, rather than chemical limitations are relevant for land use, and (3) the applied technology is of the highest level and includes major capital investment. In fact, management problems, as discussed in this paper, do not result from lack of proper technology but from questions as to how it should be used.

The term "soil" rather than "land" is used in the Dutch interpretation system. The term "land" characterizes the physical environment including climate, relief, soils, hydrology and vegetation, but excluding economic and social aspects (FAO, 1976). Only relatively small regional differences are found in the Dutch climate. The land is mostly flat, and hydrology and vegetation are being studied by many other experts. The role of the soil scientist in such a multidisciplinary context (which is typical for a highly industrialized country) is being discussed in this paper.

PHYSICAL METHODS

Research is focused on the separate assessment factors and characterizes: (1) actual conditions; (2) potential conditions, and (3) optimal water management.

Several physical methods had to be developed to allow a satisfactory research program. Emphasis is on field methods to avoid disturbances which are often associated with sampling in clay soils (e.g., Bouma, 1981).

Water-table levels are needed for the *drainage status* and the *moisture supply capacity*. Levels were measured in perforated plastic pipes with a length of 2 m and a diameter of 2 cm. In accord with the studies of Domhof et al. (1965), shallow perforated tubes and piezometers with a length of 50 cm were used to investigate the occurrence of perched water tables (Soil Science Society of America, 1978). At four locations a series of tensiometers was placed at 10 cm depth intervals. Readings were made using transducer technology. Neutron moisture meters were used to obtain corresponding moisture contents.

Drainage status was characterized by measuring the drainage rate of the surface soil in spring following wetting to negative pressure heads near saturation of approximately −20 cm. The soil surface on a plot of 4 m² was covered with a plastic sheet to avoid evapotranspiration and pressure heads at 5 cm below surface were measured during two weeks with six tensiometers. Water-table levels at the experimental site were at 1 m below surface. A simulation model was used to predict the drainage rate as a function of the level of the water table. Measured values were used to validate the model.

Bearing capacity was measured at different times to obtain a range of moisture conditions, using a penetrometer with a cone of 1 cm². Pressure heads were measured simultaneously at the same locations with tensiometry at 5 cm below surface. At each location 25 penetrometer values and 6 values for the pressure head were obtained. Median values were used for further interpretations. The relation between compaction and infiltration rate was evaluated by measuring the infiltration rate into tracks made by a tractor, which travelled over soil with different moisture content. The weight of the tractor was 3130 kg, the speed 10 km/h. Tensiometry was used to measure the pressure head in soil before compaction. Small infiltrometers with a surface area of 50 cm^2 and a height of 7.5 cm were used to measure the infiltration rate in and next to the track (Falayi and Bouma, 1975). In addition, infiltration rates at the soil surface into compacted and uncompacted soils were determined by using large infiltrometers with a surface area of 680 cm^2 and a height of 10 cm (Dekker and Bouma, 1978).

The column method for measuring vertical K_{sat} was used to characterize *internal drainage* (Bouma et al., 1979). The K_{sat} of soil surrounding the drain was measured with a new technique which uses a block of soil carved out in situ around the drain, allowing outflow from the drain which occurs in the middle of the block. The block is covered with gypsum and K_{sat} of soil above and below the drain is measured by turning the block and by exposing and covering infiltrative surfaces (Bouma et al., 1981).

Calculation of the *moisture supply capacity* requires data on rooting depth, moisture retention and hydraulic conductivity. Weather conditions and levels of the water table during the growing season are needed as boundary conditions (De Laat, 1980; Bouma et al., 1980b). Rooting depths were observed in pits and were defined as the level above which 80% of all roots were present. Moisture retention curves were obtained by standard desorption techniques. Hydraulic conductivity curves were obtained by the column method (K_{sat}); the crust test for $h = 0$ cm to $h = -30$ cm (e.g., Bouma, 1977, p. 47) and the hot-air method for $h = -30$ cm to $h = -16,000$ cm (Arya et al., 1975). The hot-air method (the name of which is being proposed here for communication purposes) is particularly suitable for clay soils because the short experimental period does not allow formation of large cracks, which form during a slow drying process. Slow drying occurs when the instantaneous profile method is applied. Then, cumulative evaporation increases rather than decreases with time, thus not allowing K calculations.

Application of flow theory to clay soils offers serious problems because the porous medium is not stable due to swelling and shrinkage. This has significant effects on the soil moisture regime, as will be shown later. Formation of vertical cracks up to the soil surface induces preferential downward flow of water to the subsoil. This process has been called "short-circuiting" (Bouma and Dekker, 1978). The magnitude of short-circuiting as a function of the initial moisture content of the soil and rain intensity and duration is measured by applying rain to undisturbed large cores (Bouma et al., 1978). These measurements indicate that heavy and very heavy rains are most likely to short-circuit. Their amount is estimated and natural rainfall is then reduced by this estimate (Bouma and De Laat, 1981).

Formation of horizontal cracks upon drying of clay soil will strongly hamper upward flow of water from the water table to the root zone. The K curve obtained with the hot-air method is representative for the peds but not for the entire soil. To obtain a representative K curve for *upward* flow, a new in-situ technique was devised which estimates the relative surface area of horizontal cracks as a function of the pressure head in the soil. Several blocks of soil with a range of pressure heads are carved out in situ and covered with gypsum. After turning the blocks on their sides, a methylene blue solution is percolated through them, and this stains continuous cracks. Each hot-air K value, which corresponds with one of the pressure heads in the blocks, is reduced proportionally to the observed stained areas (Bouma and De Laat, 1981). Thus the effect of horizontal cracks on upward flow is characterized.

RESULTS AND DISCUSSION

Actual conditions

Two major use limitations characterize actual hydraulic conditions. The first one is ponding of water at the soil surface in winter and spring. This had been attributed to: (1) surface compaction; (2) a low vertical K_{sat} of the clay above the drains, which was thought to result in perched water tables; (3) clogging of the drainpipes; (4) a low K_{sat} of soil around the drainpipe. These four aspects will now be analysed.

Surface compaction, due to grazing cattle or soil traffic under wet conditions may result in ponding of water. Infiltration rates at the soil surface in compacted soil were less than 1 cm/day, whereas the non-compacted soil averaged 20 cm/day (Dekker and Bouma, 1978).

Measurement of the vertical K_{sat} of soil between 20 and 80 cm below surface at 40 locations showed relatively high values which averaged 55 cm/day, thus not allowing formation of perched water tables (Bouma et al., 1979).

The observed surface ponding of water (in uncompacted soils) was not due to a low K_{sat} but to clogging of the drains. The ponded water disappeared rapidly after cleaning of the drains when the water table was low (Bouma et al., 1979). Soil around the drainpipe, as measured at twelve locations, had high K_{sat} values averaging 10 m/day (Bouma et al., 1981). These values are sufficiently high to allow good functioning of the drains.

Observations of a free water surface in shallow perforated pipes (Domhof et al., 1975) did not indicate the presence of perched water tables, as was initially assumed, but, rather, that preferential movement of water occurred along the faces of unsaturated peds. This water flowed first into the perforated pipes and then moved slowly into the surrounding, unsaturated peds. During this time, the presence of a perched water table is suggested. Piezometers at the same level, however, did not contain water and tensiometers indicated negative pressure heads, whereas a deep water table was observed in a deep borehole (Bouma et al., 1980c). Perched water tables in clay soils with peds should, therefore, not be observed in shallow, perforated pipes.

The second major use-limitation is a limited moisture-supply capacity during the growing season, as calculated with a computer simulation model (De Laat, 1980; Bouma et al., 1980a). Calculations for a growing season of 150 days were validated for 1979. Results were only satisfactory when the effects of vertical and horizontal cracking were taken into account (Bouma and De Laat, 1981). The moisture-supply capacity was lower than potential evapotranspiration. It can be increased by either raising the water table (which increases the upward flow of water to the root zone) or by sprinkler irrigation. The latter is now being widely applied by farmers. Optimal water table levels and sprinkling intensities need to be defined to allow selection of the best procedure.

Potential conditions

Potential conditions will be discussed separately for three assessment factors. The validated simulation model was used to calculate the *moisture supply capacity* for different levels of the water table for statistically expressed climatic conditions. The difference between potential evapotranspiration and the calculated evapotranspiration, as shown in Table I, equals the amount of water which should be added to the soil during the growing season to achieve potential evapotranspiration.

TABLE I

Calculated differences between potential and actual evapotranspiration (mm) for various constant levels of the water table in three years with different frequencies of occurrence [*1]

Depth to water table (cm)	Differences between potential and simulated actual evapotranspiration (mm)		
	Frequency of occurrence (%)		
	10% (E_{pot} = 470 mm)	20% (E_{pot} = 450 mm)	50% (E_{pot} = 440 mm)
50	0	0	0
60	34	5	0
70	109	74	14
80	154	115	50
90	180	144	76

[*1] The differences are equivalent to the amount of sprinkler irrigation which is needed to achieve potential evapotranspiration.

The simulation model for the soil moisture regime can be applied for an entire year, rather than for the growing season alone. Thus, pressure heads in the surface soil can be predicted during the wet seasons for various weather conditions. The *bearing capacity* was determined as a function of the pressure head by field measurements (Fig. 1, left section). A penetrometer value of $5 \cdot 10^5$ Pa (which corresponds here approximately with $h = -90$ cm) has been suggested as a critical value which separates adequate from inadequate conditions in terms of bearing capacity (Schothorst, 1970). In addition, compaction by a tractor wheel reduced the infiltration rate from 100 cm/day

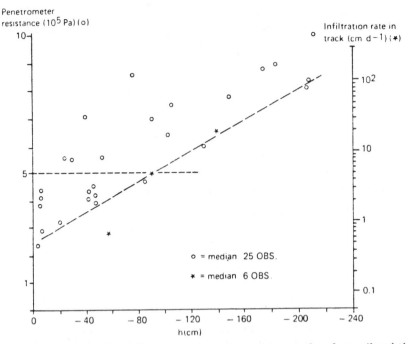

Fig. 1. The relationship between penetrometer resistance of surface soil and the pressure head (o). The observation period covered two months (left side of figure). The right side of the figure shows the relationship between the infiltration rate into a wheeltrack, as measured with an infiltrometer, and the pressure head in surface soil *before* compaction (*). The average infiltration rate in not compacted soil next to the tracks was 100 cm/day.

in uncompacted soil to very low levels at $h = -70$ cm and to also lower, but acceptable levels when compacted at $h = -100$ cm and $h = -150$ cm (Fig. 1, right section). Selection of a "critical" pressure head of −90 cm, which can be derived from both types of measurements, allows calculation of the number of days in different years when the bearing capacity is adequate (Wind, 1976; Feddes and Van Wijk, 1976). This aspect is not further explored in this paper. Here, the critical pressure head is used to derive the minimal level of the water table in the wet period of the year. Lack of evapotranspiration implies hydraulic equilibrium where the pressure head at every depth is equal to the height above the water table. Equilibrium is not reached, however, as long as rainwater flows towards the water table. The natural drainage rate is therefore important. Curves obtained for a (covered) clay soil with a water table at 1 m below surface (Fig. 2) show that drainage is very slow and that equilibrium conditions are unlikely to occur in the wet season because new rain is likely to fall before equilibrium has been reached. The curves of Fig. 2 are, in combination with the level of the water table, a measure of the *drainage status*.

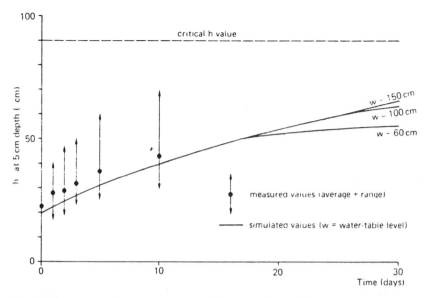

Fig. 2. The pressure head at 5 cm depth below surface during a 30-day period of drainage. The field plot was covered with plastic during the measurement to avoid evapotranspiration. Measurements and simulations were made for a constant water table depth of 100 cm below surface. Simulations were also made for water table levels of 60 cm and 150 cm below surface.

Lowering the water table below the equilibrium level will have very little effect toward increasing the drainage rate of the surface soil, thereby improving bearing capacity and drainage status. This is demonstrated by simulation results for water table levels at −60 cm and −150 cm below surface. The drainage rate increases only very slightly at deeper water table levels (Fig. 2). Evapotranspiration, and possibly occasional freezing in winter, are the main mechanisms for drying of surface soils.

Creating optimal conditions

Actual use limitations can be overcome only in part by water management procedures. Lack of significant evapotranspiration in late fall, winter and early spring results in relatively wet conditions in the surface soil which are associated with inadequate bearing capacity and drainage status. The water level in the ditches should be below drain level at approximately 100 cm below the soil surface in the period cited to at least induce equilibrium conditions which are associated with adequate bearing capacity. Soil traffic and cattle grazing should therefore be strongly restricted when conditions are wet, (h> −90 cm), particularly in late fall and early winter, because compaction may then result in a long period of ponding which will damage the grass crop. Cracking of soil, as a result of freezing or drying due to evapotranspiration, rapidly restores the infiltration capacity of the soil. In The Netherlands compaction in March is therefore, in principle, less damaging than compaction in November. A deep water level in the ditches has the advantage that the drains can be easily cleaned. This type of maintenance is essential for proper functioning of drains.

The inadequate moisture-supply capacity can be improved by a combination of sprinkler irrigation and raising the water table. Economical and technical considerations determine which of the combinations of Table I is the most attractive one. Sprinkler irrigation, as currently applied, often uses water inefficiently. Up to 50% of the water applied may flow beyond the root zone due to short-circuiting. Column studies suggest that each separate application of water should not exceed 15 mm. The sprinkling intensity may vary, but each application should be separated from the next by at least an hour (Bouma et al., 1978).

Recommended management procedures should consider the long-term effects of any suggested measure. Research was specifically initiated to investigate this aspect. Tile drainage resulted in a favorable *increase* of the vertical K_{sat} over a period of 20 years (Bouma et al., 1979). Also, raising of the water levels in the ditches during 15 consecutive summers had, apparently, not resulted in a decrease of K_{sat} around the drains (Bouma et al., 1981). The long-term effects are therefore considered to be favorable.

PROSPECTIVE SOIL SURVEY INTERPRETATIONS

Soil survey interpretations should focus increasingly on use-potentials and on the means to achieve them. The soil survey specialist must therefore more than ever communicate with specialists in other fields, such as soil physicists, hydraulic engineers, economists, cropping specialists and simulation experts. This is particularly true when dealing with a highly developed, intensive agricultural system. In the present study the soil survey contribution in this multidisciplinary team consisted of: (1) selecting experimental field sites, following interpretations of the soil map; (2) defining soil structure and its effect on on-site physical monitoring (here: improved measurement procedure for the water-table level); (3) defining independent procedures, based on soil morphology, which modify input data for simulation models, so as to make them suitable for use in swelling clay soils with macropores; (4) initiating applied field research to evaluate the regional variability of basic physical properties (here: vertical K_{sat}; K_{sat} around drains and short-circuiting phenomena). In this context, several new techniques had to be developed in cooperation with soil physicists. These were also used to predict the long-term effect of suggested management procedures (here: changes in K_{sat} following drainage), and (5) using the soil map to extrapolate data obtained. In this regard, computer maps may be valuable (Bouma et al., 1980b)

Traditionally, the soil survey specialist has integrated diverse aspects of soil and landscape. This particular function is much needed now as various disciplines, which deal with soil and its many uses, become increasingly specialized. Means must be found to integrate generalized levels of knowledge of the diverse disciplines, mentioned earlier. When that can be accomplished, realistic impressions of soil use potentials can be obtained. Next, how should these be presented in future soil survey reports?

A distinction can be made between basic soil characteristics on the one hand, and those that depend on boundary conditions of the hydrological system in terms of the climate and of water table fluctuations on the other. The *first* category covers hydraulic conductivity, moisture retention, drainage rate (as measured in this study) and the relation between penetration resistance (or the infiltration rate into a wheel track) and the pressure head. These soil characteristics require laboratory or on-site measurements. They are currently not presented in soil survey reports but they should be in the future. Attempts should be made to relate these key characteristics to data which are routinely assembled during soil survey, such as texture, structure, bulk density and organic matter content.

The *second* category covers the assessment factors, which vary as a function of climatic conditions. They correspond, in fact, with land qualities as described by FAO (1976). The moisture-supply capacity can be expressed for various dry years, as already discussed. The bearing capacity and drainage status can be expressed in terms of the number of days in which a specified critical pressure head is exceeded in a given year (e.g., Wind, 1976).

Assessment factors should be analysed separately. They form the core of the interpretation system. Optimization techniques are necessary to develop an overall management scheme which integrates the sometimes contradictory requirements imposed by the different assessment factors. Optimized management schemes, however, should not necessarily be parts of future soil survey reports. Instead, the *possible* ranges of the separate factors should be presented as a function of different management procedures. These ranges will be characteristically different for different soils. A specific example of this approach was presented in Table I for the moisture supply capacity. Instead of one particular system of management, a realistic range of possibilities is given. The user is offered a choice rather than a judgment.

The presentation of data of the first and second category is focused on engineers and hydrologists, who work at a technically advanced level. Using these data, they will better be able to make correct management decisions. There will, however, also remain a future need for the conventional forms of interpretation in terms of relative suitabilities, which are useful for land-use planning purposes. Then, the specific characterization of the assessment factors, as discussed, will allow better definitions of the suitability classes to be distinguished.

ACKNOWLEDGEMENTS

Some of the soil physical measurements were made by Mr. L.W. Dekker. The simulation data for soil drainage were developed by Dr. Ch. Belmans, both at the Netherlands Soil Survey Institute. Installation and use of tensiometers were based on procedures developed at the Institute for Land and Water Management Research in Wageningen. Helpful comments by Dr. J.C. F.M. Haans are gratefully acknowledged.

REFERENCES

Arya, L.M., Farrell, D.A. and Blake, G.R., 1975. A field study of soil water depletion patterns in presence of growing soybean roots, I. Determination of hydraulic properties of the soil. Soil. Sci. Soc. Am. Proc., 39: 424—430.

Beek, K.J., 1978. Land evaluation for agricultural development. ILRI publ. 23, Wageningen, 333 pp.

Bouma, J., 1977. Soil survey and the study of water in unsaturated soil. Soil Surv. Pap. 13. Soil Surv. Inst. Wageningen, 107 pp.

Bouma, J., 1981. Soil morphology and preferential flow along macropores. Agr. Water Manage. (in press).

Bouma, J. and Dekker, L.W., 1978. A case study on infiltration into dry clay soil, I. Morphological observations. Geoderma, 20: 27—40.

Bouma, J., Dekker, L.W. and Wösten, J.H.M., 1978. A case study on infiltration into dry clay soil, II. Physical measurements. Geoderma, 20: 41—51.

Bouma, J., Dekker, L.W. and Haans, J.C.F.M., 1979. Drainability of some Dutch clay soils: A case study of soil survey interpretation. Geoderma, 22: 193—203.

Bouma, J. and de Laat, P.J.M., 1981. Estimation of the moisture supply capacity of some swelling clay soils in The Netherlands. J. Hydrol., 49: 247—259.

Bouma, J., de Laat, P.J.M., Awater, R.C.H.M., van Holst, A.F., van Heesen, H.C. and van de Nes, Th.J.M., 1980a. Use of soil survey data in a simulation model for predicting regional soil moisture regimes. Soil. Sci. Soc. Am. J., 44: 808—814.

Bouma, J., de Laat, P.J.M., van Holst, A.F. and van de Nes, Th.J.M., 1980b. Predicting the effects of changing soil moisture regimes for soil survey interpretation. Soil Sci. Soc. Amer. J., 44: 797—802.

Bouma, J., Dekker, L.W. and Haans, J.C.F.M., 1980c. Measurement of depth to water table in a heavy clay soil. Soil Sci., 130: 264—270.

Bouma, J., van Hoorn, J.H. and Stoffelsen, G.H., 1981. The hydraulic conductivity of soil adjacent to tile drains in some heavy clay soils in The Netherlands. J. Hydrol., 50: 371—381.

De Bakker, H., 1979. Major Soils and Soil Regions in The Netherlands. Pudoc, Wageningen, and Junk, Den Haag, 203 pp.

Dekker, L.W. en Bouma, J., 1978. Relaties tussen de vertikale verzadigde doorlatendheid van enige komkleigronden en het voorkomen van plasvorming. Cult. Tech. Tijdschr., 18 (3): 126—143.

De Laat, P.J.M., 1980. Model for unsaturated flow above a shallow water table, applied to a regional sub-surface flow problem. Pudoc, Wageningen, Agric. Res. Rep., 895, 126 pp.

Domhof, J., Haans, J.C.F.M. and Knibbe, M., 1965. Measuring of ground water levels in soils with slowly permeable layers. Boor Spade 14: 151—163 (Dutch, with English summary).

Falayi, O. and Bouma, J., 1975. Relationships between the hydraulic conductance of surface crusts and soil management in a Typic Hapludalf. Soil Sci. Soc. Amer. Proc., 39: 957—963.

FAO, 1976. A framework for land evaluation. FAO Soils Bull., 32: 87 pp.

Feddes, R.A. and van Wijk, P.L.M., 1976. An integrated model approach to the effect of water management on crop yield. Agric. Water Manage., 1: 3—21.

Feddes, R.A., Kowalik, P.J. and Zaradny, H., 1978. Simulation of field water use and crop field. Simulation monograph. Pudoc, Wageningen, 189 pp.

Haans, J.C.F.M. (Editor), 1979. De interpretatie van bodemkaarten. Stichting voor Bodemkartering, Wageningen. Rapport 1463, 221 pp. (in Dutch).

Haans, J.C.F.M. and van Lynden, K.R., 1978. Assessment factors as an aid for interpreting soil surveys. Int. Congr. Soil Sci., Edmonton, Canada, 11th, 1: 71 (abstract).

Hillel, D.I., 1977. Computer simulation of soil water dynamics. Int. Developm. Res. Centre, Ottawa, 320 pp.

Hoogmoed, W.B. and Bouma, J., 1980. A simulation model for predicting infiltration into cracked clay soil. Soil Sci. Soc. Am. J., 44: 458—462.

Schothorst, C.J., 1970. De draagkracht van graslandgronden. In: Bodemkunde: Cursus V. Opleiding Landbouwkundig Personeel. Min. Landb. Visserij, Deel 3: 745—769 (in Dutch).

Soil Science Society of America, 1978. Glossary of Soil Science Terms. Madison, Wisc., 36 pp.

Van Heesen, H.C., 1970. Presentation of seasonal fluctuation of the water table on soil maps. Geoderma, 4 (3): 257—279.

Van Hoorn, J.W., 1960. Ground-water flow in basin clay soil and the determination of some hydrological factors in relation with the drainage system. Versl. Landbk. Onderz., 66.10, Pudoc, Wageningen, 136 pp. (in Dutch with English summary).

Wind, G.P., 1976. Application of analog and numerical models to investigate the influence of drainage on workability in spring. Neth. J. Agric. Sci., 24: 155—172.

Part VI

Land Information Systems

Papers 12, 13, and 14: Introductory Review

12A   BURROUGH
*Computer Assistance for Soil Survey and
Land Evaluation*

12B   BURROUGH
*Postscript: Computer Assistance for Soil Survey and
Land Evaluation*

13   VAN KUILENBURG et al.
*Accuracy of Spatial Interpolation between Point Data
on Soil Moisture Supply Capacity, Compared with
Estimates from Mapping Units*

14   GILTRAP
MIDGE, a Microcomputer Soil Information System

A phenomenon of the 1980's has been the emergence of information technology. This development has come about through the availability of low-cost computer systems that have large storage capacities, along with software packages for database management, computer graphics, and quantitative methods of data analysis. In essence information technology is the phrase used to describe computer-based techniques of data storage, retrieval, processing, and presentation. Applications are widespread in business, industry, and commerce; the revolution is now being applied to libraries whereby catalogues and abstracting sources are being replaced by information systems far more flexible and fast compared to older methods. Land evaluation has as its core the assessment of land for land use planning purposes and requires the assessment of those land attributes deemed relevant to the land use. Thus the storage and processing of data are central to land evaluation and the consequences of the information technology revolution are to be expected in this subject area. As already discussed in Part V, the older approach to soil survey reports was the presentation of an enormous amount of basic data in soil maps and associated reports. The following papers illustrate some of the developments and applications in land informtion systems since, without doubt, this is the most exciting theme in land evaluation.

A land information system should not be viewed solely as an efficient technique of data storage and retrieval, but also as a means of evaluating such data for specific questions. According to this interpretation, land evaluation can also be integral to land information systems. Beckett (1984) discussed the types of questions a soil informtion system (SIS) can be designed to answer, and these can be broadened for a land information system (LIS). Four types of questions (based on Beckett, 1984, p. 102) can be recognized:

1. What are the values of specific properties at one or more points in the landscape?
2. Given these properties, is it possible to grow particular crops success-fully or to construct buildings? Related to this, what land improvements are necessary in order for certain crops to be grown?
3. Where are there areas with individual properties within defined ranges, for example, clay <20%, slope <5%, and mean annual rainfall <1000 mm?
4. Where are there areas suited for growing particular crops?

These questions not only demonstrate the nature and scope of a LIS, but also indicate the types of information necessary for such a system. A clear distinc-tion should be made between the fundamental or raw data as generated by field survey, field monitoring, remote sensing imagery, and laboratory analysis, and the interpretative results which clearly depend upon assumptions and models that are liable to be modified or replaced.

A. FUNDAMENTAL DATA
Point data
1. Values of individual variables as determined at specific points in land-scapes, for example, elevation, slope angle, soil pH, cation exchange capacity, and so forth.
2. Category data, e.g., vegetation/land use type, mean annual precipita-tion class, soil class.

Areal data

Delimitation of areas deemed to be homogeneous according to defined criteria, for example, free soil survey method and soil mapping units, landscape ecological mapping and landscape ecological units.
1. Input of this information either on a cell-by-cell basis, or by digitizing the original maps.
2. Compilation of a data bank on these spatial units, for example, crop yields, forestry yield classes.

B. INTERPOLATED DATA
Values of individual land properties for points or areas predicted using a spatial interpolation method, for example, regression model, trend surface analysis, kriging.

C. LAND EVALUATION
1. Land use requirements of individual land use types.
2. Models to assess ecological suitability of points, or areas for these land use types, based on specified assumptions.
3. Models to assess economic suitability of points or areas for these land types, based on specified assumptions.

The newcomer to land information systems is confronted by many problems, but one difficulty is the pace of change, due mainly to the ever-changing availability of low-cost minicomputers and microcomputers. The scope of the subject and the diversity of approaches can be appreciated by reading the papers resulting from the International Society of Soil Science (ISSS) meetings of the Working Group on Soil Information Systems (Bie, 1975; Moore and Bie,

1977; Sadovski and Bie, 1978; Burrough and Bie, 1984). The papers from the symposium "Resource Information Systems" held as part of the Eleventh Congress of the International Society of Soil Science meeting in 1978 also present a comprehensive view of the subject at that time (McCormack, Moore and Dumanski, 1978). A more recent review is given by Burrough (in press).

At the national and international levels, any land information system has to use large main-frame computers. An example is the Canada Soil Information System (CanSIS), which is described by Dumanski, Kloosterman, and Brandon (1975). CanSIS stores data in a structured hierarchical manner using files, records, and modules. Files are held under the following headings:

Soil names (listing of all soil names, used in correlation)
Soil description (for storing soil survey records)
Soil data (site and analytical data from sampling points)
Soil cartography (digitized soil maps)
Administrative/geographic file (digitized map data, e.g., boundaries of pro-
   vinces, municipalities, climate, etc.)
Performance/management (productivity data on agriculture and forestry)
Land degradation (information on erosion, pollution)

In their review of soil information systems in Canada, the United States, and Australia, McCormack, Moore, and Dumanski (1978) conclude that CanSIS is the most thoroughly integrated computerized system of the three countries. Although land evaluation is not integral to the system, the underlying assumption is the importance of soil data to planning. CanSIS is also closely allied to the Canada Land Data System (CLDS) managed by the Lands Directorate of Environment Canada (Thie, Switzer, and Chartrand, 1982).

In the United States, an Integrated Resource Information System (IRIS) is under development and Bluhm, Carlis, and Decker (1984) provide a progress report. The provision of readily accessible natural resource information is mandated in the Soil and Water Resources Conservation Act of 1977. The background to this was the continued concern over soil erosion and land degradation. A major difficulty in creating the database for IRIS results from the lack of standardization, the variability, and the magnitude of information generated by soil surveys over the last 35 years. Bluhm, Carlis, and Decker (1984) outline the logical data structure for the soil information; the user must know either the series name or the soil interpretation record, though specification of location and soil descriptive properties will generate a listing of all soil series in the area that fit the conditions. In a short guest editorial to the journal *Soil Survey and Land Evaluation,* Valentine (1983) suggests that the next step forward with computer-based soil information systems is the abandonment of soil series and their mapping units; instead, data ought to be stored about polygons. These can be grouped together as appropriate for specific purposes, and maps and tables of selected properties can easily be produced.

Paper 12 by Burrough provides an excellent introduction to the use of computers in soil survey and land evaluation. He begins by outlining the advantages and disadvantages of main-frame, mini-, and micro-computers for this research. The storage of data is of crucial concern and he stresses the benefits of combining databases with geographic information systems. In recent years major improvements have been made in computer graphics, as demonstrated by Burrough, who concludes by posing ten questions to any organization considering the use of computers in soil survey and land evaluation. In a postscript to his original paper, Burrough summarizes developments in computer hardware and software over the period 1982-1985. His note emphasizes the pace of change and makes the important observation that priority should now be given to the available software for an information system rather than to hardware. This is a clear reflection of the reasonable cost of the larger microcomputers.

An example of using a microcomputer for producing soil interpretive maps is given by Cunningham, Petersen, and Sacksteder (1984). They used an IBM PC microcomputer with 576 K of memory. Soil maps for a trial area in Pennsylvania were digitized and data files were developed for the mapping units. Programs were then written for a wide variety of interpretations with all functions being menu-driven. A map can be created on the screen from data files in less than 20 seconds, and there is virtually instantaneous redisplay of a previously created image. The power and potential of such a system are most impressive, but it must be remembered that the quality of the output is dependent on the original soil survey. The other critical issue, as already discussed, is the validity of using mapping units for the prediction of such a wide range of properties or interpretations.

For an alternative approach to a land information system, reference can be made to the study in the Netherlands by Burrough (1980). This research in the Netherlands Soil Survey Institute involved the modification of commercially available software. As already indicated in Part II, there is a strong tradition in the Netherlands of using landscape ecological information as an input to planning at all levels. The aim of the project as reported by Burrough (1980) is limited to processing data pertaining to the visible aspects, structure, and content of the landscape. Three categories of information are defined: (1) point data (e.g., windmill); (2) line data (e.g., line of poplar trees); (3) areal data (e.g., a pine plantation). Thus the system had to cope with the storage of point, line, and polygon data in terms of location and descriptive attributes. Much of the paper is devoted to the modifications made to the Computervision CADDS-3 software package. One essential modification was the provision of interactive digitizing facilities to enable the input of point, line, and areal symbols. The resultant system, besides being a very efficient technique for providing maps specific to user requirements, has the potential for landscape classification and simulation.

The purpose of any land information system, as already stated, is the prediction of land properties or land suitability for specific land uses at specified locations. A land information system is a predictive tool like any conventional map though it has enormous advantages of flexibility and efficiency. Central to any LIS must be spatial prediction. It is a problem also faced by other environmental sciences such as geology whereby spatial predictions have to be made on the basis of field and laboratory analysis from sampled sites. One geostatistical technique that has been applied to geological and soil data is kriging. A set of papers exploring soil applications is given by Burgess and Webster (1980a, 1980b), Webster and Burgess (1980), Burgess, Webster and McBratney (1981), and McBratney and Webster (1983). In essence kriging is a technique based on the theory of regionalized variables for predicting the values of variables at points or within small areas. This is possible only if the spatial pattern in the soil property of interest is first established. Kriging thus offers the possibility of being incorporated into a land information system in order to predict the values of soil properties at nonsampled points. The important question thus arises as to the accuracy and efficiency of this technique compared to other geostatistical methods as well as to prediction using soil mapping units as the framework. This is the topic examined in the project reported by Van Kuilenburg et al. (Paper 13).

This Dutch team selected a very small study area (2 km × 2 km) in Gelderland, and produced a conventional soil survey map at a scale of 1:10,000 with site data collected at 530 random survey borings and 661 test borings. Concern was limited to soil moisture supply capacity. Interpolation of values was done using proximal, weighted average and kriging techniques, which are described in the paper. Comparison of the root mean squared errors indicated that the weighted average and kriging technique produced very similar results, and furthermore these results were better than those from the proximal method. The results of prediction using the soil map are of particular interest. The authors conclude that with a small increase in sampling intensity, the root mean squared error of moisture supply capacity would only be 10% higher than that from the weighted average and kriging techniques. The results from the study confirm the validity of a soil survey map as a basis for spatial prediction. Furthermore, soil survey maps can be used for predicting patterns in a wide range of variables.

Paper 14 by Giltrap demonstrates how kriging can be integrated with a soil information system developed in New Zealand called MIDGE (map image display generator). Giltrap emphasizes the benefits of such an approach in terms of not losing information through taxonomic generalization (the conventional approach using soil mapping units). The original field-sampled sites may be randomly distributed, and kriging results in the prediction of values at points occurring on the intersections of the grid. The MIDGE system can then process and display this information in a variety of forms—distribution of individual properties, prediction of mimina and maxima, superimposition of images, and so forth. The linkage of composite maps with predictive performance models has the potential for leading to very sophisticated land information systems.

REFERENCES

Beckett, P. H. T., 1984, Soil Information Systems: The Problem of Developing a Capacity of Reappraising Data for Single Purposes, in *Soil Information Systems Technology,* P. A. Burrough and S. W. Bie, eds., Pudoc, Wageningen, pp. 102-111.

Bie, S. W., ed., 1975, *Soil Information Systems,* Proceedings of the Meeting of the ISSS Working Group on Soil Information Systems, Pudoc, Wageningen.

Bluhm, G., J. Carlis, and G. Decker, 1984, Going Database in IRIS: A Status Report, in *Soil Information Systems Technology,* P. A. Burrough and S. W. Bie, eds., Pudoc, Wageningen, pp. 31-40.

Burgess, T. M., and R. Webster, 1980a, Optimal Interpolation and Isarithmic Mapping of Soil Properties. I. The Semi-variogram and Punctual Kriging, *Jour. Soil Sci.* **31:**315-331.

Burgess, T. M., and R. Webster, 1980b, Optimal Interpolation and Isarithmic Mapping of Soil Properties. II. Block Kriging, *Jour. Soil Sci.* **31:**333-341.

Burgess, T. M., R. Webster, and A. B. McBratney, 1981, Optimal Interpolation and Is-arithmic Mapping of Soil Properties. IV. Sampling Strategy, *Jour. Soil Sci.* **32:**643-659.

Burrough, P. A., 1980, The Development of a Landscape Information System in the Netherlands, Based on a Turn-key Graphics System, *Geo-processing* **1:**257-274.

Burrough, P. A., and S. W. Bie, eds., 1984, Soil Informtion Systems Technology, *Proceedings of the Sixth Meeting of the ISSS Working Group on Soil Information Systems,* Pudoc, Wageningen.

Cunningham, R. L., G. W. Petersen, and C. J. Sacksteder, 1984, Microcomputer Delivery of Soil Survey Information, *Jour. Soil and Water Conserv.* **39:**241-243.

Dumanski, J., B. Kloosterman, and S. E. Brandon, 1975, Concepts, Objectives and Structure of the Canada Soil Information System, Canadian *Jour. Soil Sci.* **55:**181-187.

McBratney, A. B., and R. Webster, 1983, Optimal Interpolation and Isarithmic Mapping of Soil Properties. V. Co-regionalization and Multiple Sampling Strategy, *Jour. Soil Sci.* **34:**137-162.

McCormack, D. E., A. W. Moore, and J. Dumanski, 1978, A Review of Soil Information Systems in Canada, the United States, and Australia, *Symposia Papers, 11th Congress International Society of Soil Science,* vol. 3, pp. 143-158.

Moore, A.W., and S. W. Bie, eds., 1977, Uses of Soil Information Systems, *Proceedings of the Australian Meeting of the ISSS Working Group on Soil Information Systems,* Pudoc, Wageningen.

Sadovski, A. N., and S. W. Bie, eds., 1978, Developments in Soil Information Systems, *Proceedings of the Second Meeting of the ISSS Working Group on Soil Information Systems,* Pudoc, Wageningen.

Thie, J., W. A. Switzer, and N. Chartrand, 1982, *The Canada Land Data System and Its Application to Landscape Planning and Resource Assessment,* paper presented at the Internat. Symposium on Landscape Information Systems, March 9-10, 1982, Wissenschaftszentrum, Bonn-Bad Godesberg.

Valentine, K., 1983, Guest Editorial: Another Way of Doing Things, *Soil Survey and Land Evaluation* **3:**29-30.

Webster, R., and T. M. Burgess, 1980, Optimal Interpolation and Isarithmic Mapping of Soil Properties. III. Changing Drift and Universal Kriging, *Jour. Soil Sci.* **31:**505-524.

12A: COMPUTER ASSISTANCE FOR SOIL SURVEY AND LAND EVALUATION

P. A. Burrough

Abstract The equipment and some present uses of computing in the handling of soil data are reviewed. The use of computers has implications for the collection and structure of environmental data. It also opens possibilities for statistically-based survey of soil patterns as an alternative to time-consuming conventional soil survey where the soil properties of interest cannot be mapped by interpretation of surface features.

For potential new users of computing, guidance is offered on some problems and present costs of computer-based soil information systems.

The computer, the data base management system and automated cartography have taken their place beside the environmental scientist's more traditional tools of auger, spade, laboratory analysis and air photo interpretation. Although the growing body of (largely younger) soil scientists using the computer is a testimony to its acceptance (just as in any other modern discipline) the computer and all that goes with it has not been accepted without some doubts and hard thinking. There are several reasons for this. The first is that soil science is a relatively young, highly complex, and in many respects a largely qualitative science that has often defied quantitative research. Only recently, through the application of statistical methods and modelling studies has serious quantitative study of soil variability, soil water movement or soil-plant interaction been possible. In spite of recent important developments (Beek 1978, Brinkman and Smyth 1973) land evaluation largely remains a qualitative discipline, though rapid strides are being made (eg. Centre for World Food Studies 1980, Buringh 1980).

A second reason has been that until recently computers were expensive, unfriendly beasts which operated via mountains of punched cards or paper tape. The results of their operations were piles of paper 'print out'. They were a daunting prospect for any researcher trying to solve a complex problem, particularly if this was spatial or graphic in nature.

Against these objections there was a real need to reduce the masses of soil data that were being collected all over the world to standard and manageable proportions; to reduce labour-intensive tasks, such as map production; and to obtain a more quantitative understanding of the soil and our environment. It is greatly to the credit of all the scientists who have worked in this field for the last ten years that these aims are now largely within our reach. It is particularly in those aspects of computing devoted to graphics and visual communication where huge advances have been made, allowing very rapid, interactive manipulation of all sorts of spatial data (eg. Whitted 1982).

Department of Regional Soil Science, Agricultural University, Wageningen, The Netherlands. Peter Burrough is secretary to the International Society of Soil Science working group on soil information systems

We can break down the problem of providing good computer services for soil scientists into a number of sections:

> computer hardware
>
> computer software
>
> data structure and data base management
>
> automated mapping
>
> spatial analysis and statistical mapping.

The following brief analysis of these topics is designed for the soil scientist who is as yet unfamiliar with the scope of these fields, and to help him, should he be in the position of having to manage a project requiring the use of computer services, to avoid expensive mistakes and to profit from past experience.

COMPUTER HARDWARE

The advent of mass-storage disc drives, micro-chips and on-line interactive communication have totally revolutionised computing. Punch cards are almost a phenomenon of the past, having been largely replaced by on-line, interactive data entry to the computer for storage on magnetic media such as disc or tape. As soil scientists, we do not need to concern ourselves with the details of computer architecture, nor do we need to know how computers work. Like the purchaser of a car, however, we should have some idea of the range of products in the market, how much they can do and will cost, and whether they will meet our needs. At least, we should know how to distinguish between micro-computers, mini-computers and main-frames.

Mainframe computers are large, complex and expensive. They used to be the only kind of computer and are used by large organisations who need to cope with masses of data, often in very standard ways. Modern time-sharing main-frame computers allow many users (c. 50-150) to work with them simultaneously. They have large memories and fast computing speeds. Mainframes are used in banks, airline booking offices, universities, government tax offices, large businesses and research institutes to provide central computing facilities for many users.

Because mainframes are so large and costly, they are often tailored to a particular broad class of computing that may make them less than ideal as host for a soil information system. Sometimes this is because of non-technical restrictions imposed by the way the computer centre, or the peripherals (line printers and other apparatus) are organised. Even though the computer may be suitable, the presence of certain peripherals such as plotters or specially-designed line-printers can be essential for your soil information system (cf. Webster et al 1979).

Mini-computers are much smaller and cheaper than main-frames, yet linked to mass-storage devices such as high-speed replaceable disc drives, they can provide very powerful computing for a small number of interactive users (up to 10). Mini computers are used in almost all of the independent 'turn-key' graphic design and mapping systems currently available (e.g. Bie 1980, Burrough 1980). Although slower in absolute computing speeds than their big sisters, the fact that they are usually dedicated to a given job means that as far as the user is concerned they may be more suitable than a main frame.

Micro-computers are the smallest of the range, though the boundaries between them and pocket calculators on the one hand, and minis on the other is becoming increasingly difficult to define. In their simplest form, the 'household' or 'games' computer, they can be linked to a domestic television and cassette recorder. The more sophisticated and flexible models can be linked to replaceable 'floppy-disc' drive memories that provide enough room to store at least all the data from 2000 soil profiles for easy access. Micro-computers can function as independent systems, or they can be used as 'intelligent' terminals to allow data to be passed to larger computers. They are currently being used in the agricultural world for budgeting and stock control on larger farms and in computer graphics. Because of their power, small size and light weight they would form an excellent basis for a soil or land evaluation information system that could be carried by all travelling experts.

COMPUTER SOFTWARE

In spite of the development of many attractive, easy to use computer languages such as PASCAL, PL1, APL and many more, FORTRAN remains the dominant scientific programming language used for commerical soil information systems running on main-frame and mini-computers. BASIC is almost universal on the micro-computers. In syntax and structure BASIC resembles FORTRAN; the essential difference is that while FORTRAN is always translated into computer-usable code before the program can be run, BASIC commands on the least sophisticated microcomputers are translated one at a time. This restriction causes BASIC programs to operate much more slowly than their FORTRAN equivalents and could prove a stumbling block to operating a soil information system of any complexity on certain types of a micro-computer.

FORTRAN is an old computer language and, from a programmer's point of view, has many shortcomings. These seem to be outweighed by the advantages of standardisation, portability of programs, and the fact that almost every main-frame and mini will be capable of supporting it. But the user should watch out, for there are many non-standard dialects of FORTRAN that can only be used on a particular type of computer. Usually a FORTRAN program will require some modifications to be run on another machine, but there have been instances where the dialect dependence of a program package has been so great that transference has been impossible. BASIC and other languages also suffer from hardware-specific dialects. One need not apologise for thinking that this electronic version of the Tower of Babel has been created for the advantage of the computer manufacturers and suppliers to lock users into a particular system. As far as computer users are concerned, non-standardisation is an expensive headache.

DATA BASE MANAGEMENT SYSTEMS (DBMS)

The DBMS is a computer program for organising the data in the computer's memory. Usually several kinds of operation are recognised, such as data input, data output (printing results on paper or screen), editing and updating, sorting, merging and retrieval. All this sounds straightforward until one realises that the efficiency of the system depends on the structure of the data. This is where soil scientists should become interested, because the structure that they perceive or impose on their soil data directly affects the choice of operation of the DBMS.

Bie et al (1977) showed how different data structures, and hence different DBMS strategies were needed to allow efficient management of various kinds of geological data. The subject of the 'ideal' DBMS design to meet soil data requirements is still one of hot debate (Cormack and Moore 1981) because of the repercussions on how data must be organised, and indeed on the way soil and land are perceived by soil scientists.

Bie et al (1977) recognised three basic data base structures: hierarchical systems, network systems and relational models. As with geological data, soil data may have a particular structure that can be better matched by one or other of these data base structures. For example, soil profile data are usually structured into a set of layers known as soil horizons. Soil profiles may be grouped into soil series and soil series into soil families. Here we have an example of the familiar hierarchical structure. So long as all our data handling follows this hierarchy the organisation of the DBMS is easy.

Now, let us consider the relation between a given soil profile and some aspects of the landscape, such as parent material and land use. In a hierarchical system, should we so arrange the data structure so that the parent material is recorded for every profile, or should we group the profiles (and the soil series) according to parent material?

soil series
↕
profile
↕
parent material, land use
↕
horizons

parent material
↑
land use
↕
profile
↕
horizons

If we want to use land use as a means of retrieving the data on the parent material, series and profiles, how should that be organised? Which method will be most efficient, which will save most computer time and space? Clearly, if every profile must have both a parent material and a land use code the total amount of data to be stored and searched is much greater than if the series are grouped by parent material. In these situations, a cross-referencing, or network structure might be more appropriate, in which land use and parent material could reference each other and the soil data without having a strict hierarchical relation.

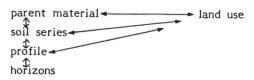

Relational data base models extend the principles of cross-referencing seen in networks to data structures based on row and column tables (eg N Soil sites - rows - with M soil properties - columns - measured at each site)

In the simplest form of cross-referencing, known as the linear model, the data structure reflects a tabular presentation of the user's data. If the data sets are small and the user can remember how different files can be linked, the linear model provides an easy method of access. Such a system would almost inevitably be chosen for a small information system based on a micro- or even a mini computer and would be suitable for project management of moderate size on mainframe. More complex data, and larger data sets can be handled more efficiently (at the cost of a much more complex DBMS) by more complex versions of the tables in which not only row and column links within tables, but also links between tables can be maintained and searched.

Many DBMS's have been developed and are being used in soil science, e.g. G-EXEC (Jeffrey et al 1975) CANSIS (Dumanski and Kloosterman 1975), POSEIDON (van der Driessche 1975), DASCH (Voss 1981), FORDATA (Smith, 1981). While the first DBMSs were usually associated with non-spatial data (soil profiles, plot yields etc.) current trends are to combine these data with geographic data in geographic information systems. According to some authorities in this field, not only soil, but other environmental and socio-economic data should be included as well, to make the data base as useful as possible to as many as possible. There are important consequences here for data standardization and quality control.

AUTOMATED MAPPING

The development of SYMAP and related lineprinter maps demonstrated the value of the computer in geographical studies but these first attempts to automate mapping were little appreciated by most soil scientists and cartographers. There were at least two reasons.

First, the lineprinter maps were graphically inelegant. Even when the problem of non-square characters had been overcome by using either non-square grid cells, or specially developed lineprinters (only available for certain periods at some main-frame computer centres - Webster et al 1979), these grid-cell, or raster maps failed to charm those of us used to the elegance, exact scales and sheet art of the usual full colour thematic soil map. The second problem was that the size of the line printer cell (1/10 x 1/6 inch), coupled to current computer memory sizes and speeds, effectively limited the size of area that could be handled and its spatial resolution. Nevertheless, lineprinter maps were, and still are, greatly used, particularly in landscape planning (eg. Steinitz 1979) and to produce a range of interpretative maps from a basic soil survey (eg. Rogoff 1982).

In contrast to the raster map described above, the normal thematic soil map is built up of polygons, or areas surrounded by boundaries. Although far fewer data are needed to describe a polygon for a given level of spatial resolution than would be necessary in a raster system, the computerization of the thematic, polygon map has proved a difficult and often expensive business (eg. Burrough 1980). In principle, it is not difficult to break down the soil map into a series of lines (boundaries) linked to form the soil polygons that are described by a name or code. Neither does it take much computer space to store the associated coordinates in vector form (i.e. as linked coordinate pairs having place and direction), and these can be directly entered into the computer by digitizing. Clever programs are required however, to link all these lines and names into a logical network that actually allows one to do more with the digitised map than merely display it on a screen or redraw it. Until recently, polygon maps had to be drawn on expensive, slow, flat-bed or drum plotters: sometimes light beams are used to draw the results accurately on film or microfiche, because the pen plotter has the great drawback that the quality of its product is determined ultimately by the contact between the tip of the pen and the paper.

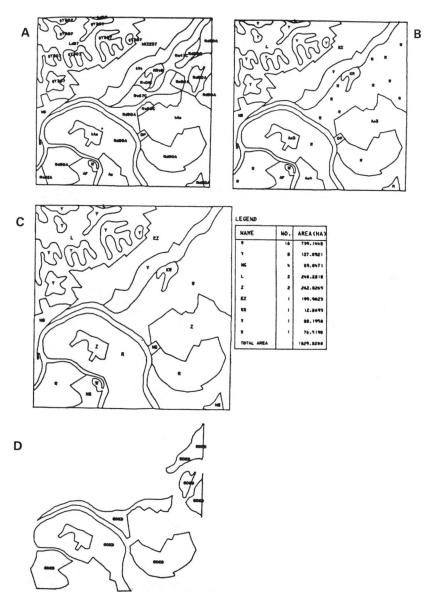

Figure 1. Data manipulation with computer maps

A) Digital form of part of a 1:50 000 Soil series map. The soil codes give information about parent material, profile development, drainage status and groundwater level. Each part of the code can be handled separately or together.

B) Selection from A) showing the soil pattern at the soil family level (W = water, A-codes are associations, OP and NG are disturbed and unmapped areas, respectively)

C) Interactively-improved version of B) with automatically generated legend showing number of occurrences and areas.

D) Automatic land classification map produced by reclassification and selection operations. Courtesy Netherlands Soil Survey Institute, Wageningen

Why digitize maps at all? The first reason was to try to make map production more efficient (cf. Johnson 1975). Another, more interesting reason is that digitized maps are much more flexible than their printed brothers: given sufficient information about land capability, land qualities, socio-economic constraints, etc., (all of which can be linked to the digitized map data base via the soil polygon codes) one can extract and manipulate the map data to produce maps tailor-made to users' requirements, including simulating the effects of land use decisions.

All the published 1:50 000 soil maps of the Netherlands have now been digitized. Figure 1 shows a series of simple manipulations of the basic soil map data made with a geographic information system (Burrough 1980, van Kuilenburg et al 1981). Only a small map fragment is shown as an example, but the system is fully operational and has been in use for some years for making selection maps, a variety of user-specified classifications and for landscape simulation modelling for soil, landscape and geological mapping (Burrough and de Veer 1980).

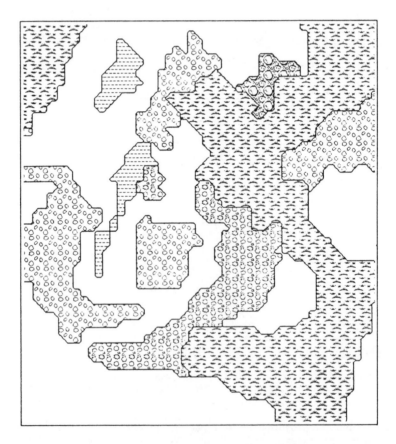

Figure 2. Australia's "Regional and Urban Planning System," aids town planners in the evaluation of land use. Shaded thematic maps are produced with a Digital Equipment PDP 11/40 computer and a Versatec 11 inch printer/plotter. Matrix plotters allow very fast production of thematic maps. Typically, a whole map can be printed in a few minutes. Colour printing is only possible via lithography, but the ease with which descriptive shading can be chosen allows production of very evocative maps (Courtesy Versatec Corporation, De Meern, The Netherlands).

The ease with which data can be extracted from soil maps suggests that not only can data be manipulated in terms of the original polygon structure of the map, but that different polygonal structures can be overlaid to create new maps. This sounds an obvious and simple method to combine information from different sources, and has indeed been done by planners for years. In practice, polygon overlay is not so simple, because of the large number of small, meaningless polygons that can be created through the less than perfect alignment of boundaries. The problem has been solved by the ODYSSEY system of polygon overlay, available from Harvard Laboratory for Computer Graphics 1978, for relatively small sets of polygons (100-300) but many logical and procedural problems remain. In contrast, in grid-cell or raster mapping, the overlay problem does not arise. Every grid-cell on one thematic map has a 1 to 1 location with a grid-cell on another thematic map. Overlay is then a problem of deciding how to compute a new grid-cell value from the others. This is easy to program and easy to use, and is consequently the method that has been used in many simple but effective geographic information systems (e.g. IMGRID - Laboratory for Computer Graphics 1978). Moreover, this format is also used by many remote-sensing systems, making data comparisons very easy indeed.

Because raster overlay is so easy, most modern systems using a polygonal data base first convert the polygons to a raster format for the overlay, and then convert it back again afterwards. This will result in some loss of resolution but the gain in time and intelligibility of the results makes it well worthwhile. Polygon-to-raster conversions are also done when data are to be plotted by a matrix or dot printer (Figure 2). These are excellent compromises between the advantages of the raster format and the accuracy of pen plotters. Unlike the crude lineprinter graphics, matrix plotters can have a resolution of 200 dots per inch. They have few moving parts and large maps can be plotted in only a few minutes. Plotting times are not dependent on map complexity either, and the availability of graphic symbols means that informative, shaded, thematic maps can be quickly produced. This is in contrast to a pen-plotter, where shading is usually a very time-consuming operation.

SPATIAL ANALYSIS AND STATISTICAL MAPPING

Modern techniques of spatial analysis and statistical mapping, widely developed and applied in other fields such as mineral exploration, groundwater hydrology and meteorology are also gaining ground in soil survey (e.g. Burgess and Webster 1980). These methods have advantages over conventional mapping procedures whenever the nature of the soil attribute to be mapped cannot readily be ascertained from external features of the landscape such as landform or air-photo appearance. Many landscapes have a complex history of development and it can be important for both scientific and practical reasons to discover the scales of soil variation present before committing oneself to any given mapping program (cf. Nortcliff 1978). For example, Burrough and Stoffelsen (in preparation) working in a part of the eastern Netherlands, used spatial analysis methods to reveal important short-distance subsoil patterns in a Pleistocene boulder clay landscape. The boulder clay had since been covered by layers of late-Pleistocene aeolian sand that totally obscured the sub-surface features occurring within 40-140cm below the surface. This reconnaissance study, which required only 2½ days field work for 64 profile descriptions and 2½ days computer analysis and reporting, provided necessary information for the groundwater hydrological studies that were the main object of research. Given the scale of the soil variations found, very detailed (and thus expensive) conventional surveys would have been needed to reveal the nature of the soil pattern of this area.

In areas such as these where external features cannot be relied upon to map soil patterns by conventional techniques, mapping by interpolation may be appropriate. The technique of kriging (Burgess and Webster 1980) has many attractive features, including the important one of estimating the errors of the interpolated values probabalistically. This method requires much computing, including the availability of computer-graphics to plot the resulting maps.

Multivariate analysis techniques, such as principal component analysis, are really only possible with computers, but they can be very valuable for revealing how the soil varies spatially as a multi-variate phenomenon (Front cover). Linked to spatial analysis techniques, they can be a valuable tool in the research phase of soil survey (Dent and Young 1981).

TABLE 1 Approximate costs (US $) of Computer hardware and software

Hardware	Cost(US $x10^3$)	Comment
16-bit mini computer	15–100	Cost varies with type, memory and 'extras'
Micro computer	2–25	Cost ranges from hobby computers to robust, reliable machines from leading manufacturers
80 M word fixed disc memory	40–60	Price varies according to peripherals and computer
Floppy disc drive	1–15	Price varies with capacity and quanlity
Plotters-flatbed	2–500	Depends on size, plot quality, type of drawing instrument (pen, light beam), with or without own computer
Matrix plotters	5–50	Depends on size, vector-raster translation firmware etc.
Digitizers	8–30	Depends on size, accuracy and type
Terminals	1–5	Varies from printer type to screens, width of carriage, cost of telephone modems etc
Software packets		Yearly renewal
Statistical package for the Social Sciences	approx 20	approx. 10
DBMS systems	20–50	10–15
Graphics systems	1–50	3–10
Micro systems	5–10	

N.B. Cost quoted is only an indiction of actual costs. The author is not responsible for prices asked by any manufacturer.

GETTING STARTED

Although many industrial nations have had access to soil information systems for several years, there are organizations in many lands that are still contemplating computerization. Before beginning they would do well to learn of the experience gleaned over the last ten years by the Institutes and related organisation that have supported the International Society of Soil Science Working Group on Soil Information Systems. In particular, any organisation contemplating introducing computer assistance for soil survey and land evaluation should consider seriously at least the following ten questions.

1. Identify your problems carefully, what do your customers expect of your organisation, and will a computer help provide the service they need?
2. How much money have you for investment and operation? (See Table 1)
3. Have you trained staff at your disposal for running computer hardware/software or for the strict organisation of the job that efficient use of a computer requires?
4. Are you aiming at country-wide systems or single-project systems?
5. How much data, and what kinds of data will you have to process at any one time?
6. What is the structure of your data? Will you have to interface with other types of data that may possibly have a different organisation?
7. What quality of graphical output can you afford, and what quality will your staff and clients accept?
8. Have you the necessary physical support facilities such as stable electricity supplies, air conditioning and low humidity rooms?
9. Can you collect data of reasonable quality that are worth the investment of a computer system?
10. What existing systems can you make use of? Can you acquire them in a modular way allowing the gradual build-up of a comprehensive computing system. How permanent are these systems, and how dependent will you be on a particular company or supplier for support when things go wrong or become obsolescent?

The most critical is likely to be problem of trained staff, because even in the current times of economic depression computer personnel seem to be eagerly sought after, and few of these have experience in agriculture or geography. Although scientists from developing countries working in fields such as cartography or remote sensing may receive training at home or abroad in using the computer, there is to my knowledge nowhere where soil scientists and specialists in land evaluation can receive a similar schooling, except on the job. It is time we made a start.

ACKNOWLEDGEMENTS

The author wishes to thank all participants of the Working Group on Soil Information Systems, conceived at the I.S.S.S. Congress in Moscow in 1974 and launched in Wageningen by Dr. J. Schelling and Dr. S. W. Bie of STIBOKA. This article is based on the experience of all those who have taken part in the international meetings (Wageningen 1975, Canberra 1976, Sofia 1977, Purdue 1980, Canberra 1980, Paris 1981) and contributed to the published proceedings (Bie 1975, Moore and Bie 1977, Sadovski and Bie 1978, Baumgardner 1980, Moore et al 1981, Girard et al 1981).

REFERENCES

Baumgardner, M. (1980) Proceedings International Symposia on Machine Processing of Remotely Sensed Data, Soil Information Systems and Remote Sensing and Soil Survey. L.A.R.S. Purdue University, West Lafayette, Indiana

Beek, K.J. (1980) Land Evaluation for Agricultural Development. ILRI, Wageningen 333 pp.

Bie, S.W. (1975) Soil Information Systems, Proceedings of the Meeting of the ISSS Working Group on Soil Information Systems, Wageningen. PUDOC, Wageningen 87 pp.

Bie, S.W. (1980) Computer-assisted soil mapping, in The Computer in Contemporary Cartography ed D.R.F. Taylor. Wiley 123-149

Bie, S.W., R.W. Bowen, K.G. Jeffery, M.Lenci and G.M. Martin (1977) Relevant Data Structures. COGEODATA Working Group on Data Structures and Data Management. Netherlands Soil Survey Institute, Wageningen 53 pp.

Brinkman, R. and A.J. Smyth (1973) Land Evaluation for Rural Purposes Publ. 17. ILRI, Wageningen 116 pp.

Burgess, T.M. and R. Webster (1980) Optimal interpolation and isarithmic mapping of soil properties. J. Soil Science 31, 315-342

Buringh, P. (1980) A comparison of three methods for supplying physical data on crop production for agricultural development planning. Working Paper SOW-80-3, Centre for World Food Studies, Wageningen 26 pp.

Burrough, P.A. (1980) The development of a Landscape Information System in the Netherlands. Geoprocessing 1, 257-274

Burrough, P.A. and A.A. de Veer (1980) Cartographic Processes, in The CAD/CAM Handbook ed. C. Machover and R.E. Blauth. Computervision Corporation, Bedford

Centre for World Food Studies (1980) The model of physical crop production Res. Rep. SOW-80-5. Centre for World Food Studies, Wageningen 31 pp.

Cormack, R.S. and A.W. Moore (1981) Modelling of land resource data for computer storage and retrieval. In A.W. Moore et al. 1981

Dent, D.L. and A.Young (1981) Soil Survey and Land Evaluation. Allen and Unwin, London, 57-63

Driessche, R. van der., A. Gracia Gomez, A.M. Aubry and A. Giey (1978) POSEIDON in Sadovski and Bie 1978

Dumanski, J., B. Kloosterman and S.E. Brandon (1975) Concepts, objectives and structure of the Canada Soil Information System. Can. J. Soil Science, 181-187

Girard, M. (1981) Proc. ISSS Workshop on Soil Information Systems, Paris 1981. Institut National Agronomique, Paris

Jeffrey, K.G., E.M. Gill, S. Henley and J.M. Cubitt (1975) G-EXEC System User's Manual. Atlas Computing Division, Chilton, England

Johnson, C.G. (1975) The role of automated cartography in soil survey. in Bie 1975, 48-53

Kuilenburg, J.van., B. Bunschoten, P.A.Burrough and J.Schelling, (1981) The digital soil map scale 1:50 000 of the Netherlands, in Girard, M. (editor) 1981 Sols no. 5 73-86

Laboratory for Computer Graphics and Spatial Analysis (1978) IMGRID - An Information Manipulation System for Grid Cell Data Structures. ODYSSEY - a polygon overlay manipulation system. Laboratory for Computer Graphics and Spatial Analysis, Harvard

Moore, A.W. and S.W. Bie (1977) Uses of soil information systems Proc. Australian Meeting of the ISSS Working Group on Soil Information Systems, Canberra, 1976. PUDOC, Wageningen 103 pp.

Moore, A.W., B.C. Cook and L.G. Lynch (1981) Information systems for soil and related data. Proc. 2nd Australian Meeting of the ISSS Working Group on Soil Information Systems, Canberra, 1980. PUDOC, Wageningen 161 pp.

Nortcliff, S. (1978) Soil variability and reconnaissance soil mapping. J. Soil Science, 29, 404-419

Rogoff, M.J. (1982) Computer Display of Soil Survey Interpretations using a Geographic Information System, Soil Survey and Land Evaluation, 2,2 37-41

Sadovski, A.N. and S.W. Bie (1978) Developments in Soil Information Systems. Proc. 2nd Meeting of the ISSS Working Group on Soil Information Systems. Varna/Sofia, 1977. PUDOC, Wageningen 113 pp.

Smith, J.L. (1981) A tutorial introduction to FORDATA. In Moore et al 1981

Steinitz, C. (1979) Simulating alternative policies for implementing the Massachusetts scenic and recreational rivers act: the North River demonstration project. Landscape Planning 6, 51-89

Voss, H.H. (1981) Soil Data; capture, handling and display using the system DASCH. in Girard, M. (editor) sols no. 4 97-100

Webster, E.R., T.R. Harrod, S.J. Staines and D.V. Hogan (1979) Grid sampling and computer mapping of the Ivybridge area, Devon. Technical monograph no. 12 Soil Survey of England and Wales, Harpenden 64 pp.

Whitted, T.(1982) Some recent advances in Computer Graphics. Science 215, 767-774

12B: POSTSCRIPT: COMPUTER ASSISTANCE FOR SOIL SURVEY AND LAND EVALUATION

P. A. Burrough

Since this article [Paper 12A] was first published, there have been considerable technological developments that have made some of the original statements about the computer hardware and software out of date. This postscript summarizes the main developments that have occurred from 1982-1985, and indicates some directions in which trends are going.

HARDWARE DEVELOPMENTS

The power/price ratio of computers has continued to improve, with microcomputers having an internal memory of up to 1 Mbyte linked to a Winchester (or fixed disk) of 10-35 Mbytes becoming almost commonplace. These systems are small (the size of a small suitcase) and reasonably priced ($5,000-$20,000 depending on type and exact configuration). While microcomputers are becoming based on the 16-bit word, 32-bit micro systems are now being sold. 32-bit systems are now a general standard for the minicomputers used for automated mapping and database management. The advantages of the 32-bits are that coordinates can be represented to more significant digits, arithmetic can be carried out more quickly and easily, and integers are no longer limited to the ± 32000 possible on the 16-bit integer machines.

Data output devices have also improved in quality and price. High-resolution color screens with the ability to display almost any desired color combination are now generally available. Though the systems with the highest resolution (c. 1200×1024 pixels per 19-inch screen) are still very expensive, there are many good alternatives to be found. Matrix plotters can now plot in color (but they are expensive). Simple color ink-jet plotters can be purchased from around $1,000 upwards that allow eight or more separate color combinations. High-quality film printing of remotely sensed imagery is possible, but the hardware is expensive.

SOFTWARE DEVELOPMENTS

For many developments in environmental computing and geographical information systems, FORTRAN is being partially replaced by PASCAL and other languages.

These comments were written expressly for this volume.

FORTRAN-77 includes a number of PASCAL-like statements and has much easier data input and output capabilities than were possible in earlier versions. There is a welcome trend toward standardization of software so that programs written in a standard version of a language on one machine can be transferred easily to another. This trend toward standardization has manifested itself in the personal computer world with the production of personal computers that are fully compatible with the IBM-PC under the operating system MS-DOS. On larger machines there are trends toward using operating systems such as UNIX that allow software to be operated in a machine-independent way, as long as they conform to the UNIX standards. Inevitably, some manufacturers have produced nonstandard versions of UNIX, thereby defeating its purpose! For graphics software, the development of the Graphics Kernel System (GKS) has meant that programs can be written without having to pay attention to the requirements of particular devices. These are operated using their own assembler or hard-wired programs, which can be interfaced directly with the GKS programs.

DATABASE MANAGEMENT, AUTOMATED MAPPING, AND SPATIAL ANALYSIS: THE DEVELOPMENT OF GEOGRAPHICAL INFORMATION SYSTEMS

There have been considerable developments in integrating systems for manipulating spatial data that contain information about position and about nonspatial attributes, such as land use, soil type, and so on. These integrated systems are called geographical information systems (GIS) and comprise modules for entering spatial data from maps, scanners, and field surveys. The database includes information about their spatial type (point, line, or area); the way they are represented — as lines or polygon outlines (VECTORS) or as arrays of cells (RASTERS); and associated nongraphic properties. Besides having routines for extracting data from the database and sending them to output devices such as screens and plotters, GIS have a wide range of data analysis capabilities. These include not only methods for reclassifying existing data but also for spatial modeling and for simulating the possible impacts of proposed changes in the landscape. Instead of regarding the land resource inventory as a static source of information, many GIS make it possible to use the digital database as a test bed for development ideas so that the user can explore the possible consequences of a given line of action before mistakes are irretrievably made in the landscape itself. There is much work to be done here in exploring the potential of these new tools in land evaluation, and the reader is referred to works by Steinitz and Brown (1981), Teicholz and Berry (1983) and Burrough (in press). Of particular importance is the need to train people the world over how these new and powerful tools for resource analysis can and should be used to best effect.

TRENDS

The main trends are clear: computer hardware is increasing in power and declining in price. Computer software is expensive because of the highly skilled manpower required and the current shortage of people with the correct skills. Computer packages are now very much easier to use than was the case a few years ago because people are no longer prepared to accept that they need to know how a program has been written in order to enter data or to compute a result. An organization contemplating buying a GIS should be more concerned about a software package that meets their requirements than about the hardware on which it runs.

The price of deluxe systems remains high, but there is an increasing number of small GIS products that are suitable for small databases that run on the larger microcomputers. Public awareness and acceptance of these systems is increasing, but there is a tremendous need to ensure that the proper training is available at all levels from management to field scientists so that the powers being made available can be used to their greatest benefit.

REFERENCES

Burrough, P. A., (in press), Principles of Geographical Information Systems for Land Resource Assessment. Oxford University Press, Oxford.

Steinitz, C. and H. J. Brown, 1981, A computer modelling approach to managing urban expansion. *Geo-Processing* **1**(4):341-376.

Teicholz, E. and B. J. L. Berry, 1983, Computer Graphics and Environmental Planning. Prentice-Hall, Englewood Cliffs, New Jersey.

13: ACCURACY OF SPATIAL INTERPOLATION BETWEEN POINT DATA ON SOIL MOISTURE SUPPLY CAPACITY, COMPARED WITH ESTIMATES FROM MAPPING UNITS[1]

J. Van Kuilenburg, J. J. De Gruijter, B. A. Marsman, and J. Bouma[2]

The Netherlands Soil Science Survey Institute, P.O. Box 98, 6700 AB Wageningen, The Netherlands

Three interpolation techniques were applied to point data on soil moisture supply capacity in a 2 km × 2 km area of cover sand in the eastern part of The Netherlands. The interpolation techniques are: Proximal, Weighted Average and Kriging; survey points used for interpolation were stratified random, with an average density of 1.5 per ha. The Root Mean Squared (RMS) Error of these techniques, as estimated from an independent statistical sample, was 37, 29 and 29 mm, respectively, whereas the moisture supply capacity in the area ranged from 50 to 240 mm. Profile descriptions at the same survey points were used to make a soil map (scale 1 : 10 000), the mapping units of which were delineated in the field. Using the means of these mapping units as estimates for points in the area would e.g. have led to an RMS Error of 32 mm if the means were estimated from an additional random sample of 5 profile descriptions per mapping unit or 0.4 per ha. This lower efficiency, compared with Weighted Average and Kriging, should be weighed against the advantage of the soil map of being a basic document that can be directly used for various purposes.

INTRODUCTION

Detailed soil maps are widely used to help determine soil suitabilities for a variety of uses within a region. These suitabilities are based on soil survey interpretations for particular soil types which are assumed to be representative of mapping units, as defined by the legend of the soil map. The soil surveyor determines the soil type and the delineations of the mapping units. By necessity, his work is based on a limited number of observed profiles

---

[1] Contribution from The Netherlands Soil Survey Institute, P.O. Box 98, 6700 AB Wageningen (The Netherlands).
[2] Head Computer Dept., Soil Survey Inst.; Statistician, Inst. TNO for Mathematics, Information Processing and Statistics; Soil Scientist; and Head Soil Physics Dep., respectively.

and on an interpretation of landscape features. This procedure has therefore a subjective character.

Mapping units usually include soils which do not fit the description of the legend: the so-called "impurities". In addition, soil properties usually also vary within the pure part of mapping units. Recent studies on variation within mapping units have raised the question of how suitable these units are as a basis for soil survey interpretations. This question is relevant because automated derivation of assessment factors and suitabilities from profile data, and automated interpolation between profiles are now technically and economically within reach.

This study focuses on the problem of choosing between mathematical interpolation techniques and delineation of mapping units in the field for estimating soil properties at given points in an area. Attention will be confined to one soil property: the soil moisture supply capacity. This is a crucial assessment factor for many soil survey interpretations in The Netherlands, where there is a precipitation deficit in the growing season (Bouma et al., 1980b).

The purpose of this study is: (1) to evaluate and compare the accuracies of three interpolation techniques when applied to profile data on soil moisture supply capacity, and (2) to compare these accuracies to that achieved by using data of the mapping units of a soil map.

MATERIALS AND METHODS

Soils and soil map

The study area was a 2 km × 2 km square in a rural landscape developed on cover sand, near the village of Laren in the province of Gelderland, The Netherlands. Its location is indicated in Fig.1. As built-up parts were excluded, the study area measured 359 instead of 400 ha. A soil map of the study area was made using a scale of 1 : 10 000. Its mapping units were delineated in the field by interpretation of landscape features. To obtain comparable results, the same profile data were used both for the soil map and for the mathematical interpolations. The profile data are in this case field estimates of basic soil properties, obtained by borings at randomly selected locations with a density of 1.48 per ha. The sampling scheme is discussed in the section "Interpolation techniques".

Some major properties of the soil types in the study area and their classification according to Soil Survey Staff (1975) are presented in Table I. More detailed information is presented by De Bakker (1979). All soils had a sand fraction with a median size value between 150 and 155 μm. The soil map has 30 different mapping units, which are defined in terms of one of the nine soil types and the fluctuation of the groundwater level during the year (e.g. Van Heesen, 1970). This fluctuation is expressed in classes of the average highest (GHG) and lowest (GLG) groundwater levels (see Table II). For

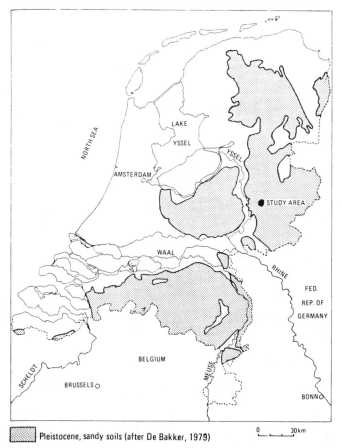

Pleistocene, sandy soils (after De Bakker, 1979)

0   30 km

Fig.1. Location of the study area within the Pleistocene sandy soils of The Netherlands.

clarity, two separate maps are presented in Figs.2 and 3. The soil map in Fig.2 shows only the soil types and the map of Fig.3 shows only the groundwater classes. Normally, both types of maps are combined into one.

Moisture supply capacity

The moisture supply capacity (to be abbreviated hereafter as MSC) is defined as the amount of moisture that can be supplied by the soil to a crop in a 10 per cent dry year. This is a relatively dry year with an evapotranspiration surplus (= rainfall deficit) in the growing season from April 15th to September 15th, that has a probability of being exceeded only once in 10 years (Rijtema, 1971). Moisture absorption is usually schematically represented to include a fraction which is absorbed within the root zone and a fraction which is absorbed at the lower boundary of the root zone. Water rises to this level by upward unsaturated flow from the water table. The lower

TABLE I

Soil types in the study area, characterized by soil classification and average values of some major soil properties

Code soil map	Classification	Percentage of:						Rooting depth (cm)
		org. matter (10 cm below surface)	silt	clay	org. matter (70 cm below surface)	silt	clay	
Hn33	Typic Haplaquods; fine sand	6.8	12	3	1.5	10	2	45
Hn35	Typic Haplaquods; loamy fine sand	6.0	19	3	1.5	15	2	50
cHn33	Plaggeptic Haplaquods; fine sand	6.5	15	3	2.0	12	2	60
cHn35	Plaggeptic Haplaquods; loamy fine sand	7.5	19	3	3.0	15	2	60
EZ35	Plaggepts; loamy fine sand	8.0	20	3	5.0	17	2	60
pZg35	Typic Humaquepts; loamy fine sand	7.0	20	3	1.0	15	2	70
fkZn35	Typic Psammaquents; loamy fine sand*	5.0	25	9	1.0	15	2	55
pZn33	Weakly spodic Humaquepts; fine sand	6.0	12	3	1.0	9	2	40
pZn35	Weakly spodic Humaquepts; loamy fine sand	6.0	19	3	1.0	12	2	45

*With bog iron ore.

TABLE II

Groundwater classes defined in terms of average highest (GHG) and average lowest (GLG) groundwater levels (cm below surface)

Groundwater class	GHG	GLG
III	0—40	80—120
III*	25—40	80—120
V	0—40	>120
V*	25—40	>120
VI	40—80	>120
VII	80—140	>120
VII*	> 140	>140

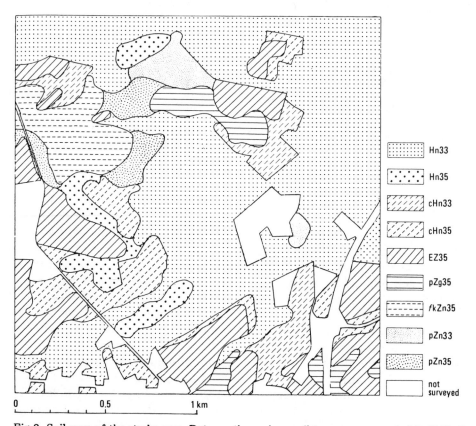

Fig. 2. Soil map of the study area. Data on the various soil types are presented in Table I.

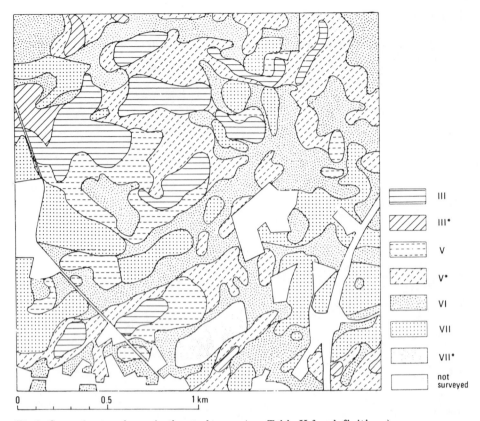

☰	III
⧄	III*
┅	V
⧄	V*
░	VI
⋯	VII
▢	VII*
▢	not surveyed

0   0.5   1 km

Fig.3. Groundwater classes in the study area (see Table II for definitions).

boundary of the root zone is the level above which approximately 80% of the roots occur (Rijtema, 1971). The MSC can be calculated with a computer simulation model which requires moisture retention data for the root zone and the subsoil, and hydraulic conductivity data for the subsoil. Necessary boundary conditions of the flow system are formed by climatic data and data on water table fluctuations (De Laat, 1980; Bouma et al., 1980a,b). Calculations of the MSC are made for each boring. They are based on field estimates of the water table fluctuation, the thickness of the root zone, soil textures, bulk densities and organic-matter contents of the various soil horizons. The latter three characteristics are used to predict moisture retention and hydraulic conductivity data, as discussed by Bouma et al. (1980a). The most recent version of the simulation model (De Laat, 1980) was not available when the calculations, as cited here, were made. The calculation procedure, as such, is, however, not essential to the discussion in this paper. The crucial point is that data from each boring were used to calculate the MSC with a well-defined, consistent and reproducible procedure.

Interpolation techniques

Three interpolation techniques were compared with respect to accuracy. For this purpose two sets of borings were available: a set of random survey borings and a set of random test borings. In the analysis the geographical coordinates of each boring were used, together with its calculated MSC value. Survey and test set form two mutually independent, stratified random samples with (apart from some dropping out), respectively, 9 and 11 randomly located borings per stratum. The same strata were used for both samples, namely squares of 250 m X 250 m. Thus, in total, there were 530 random survey borings and 661 test borings, resulting in average densities of 1.48 and 1.84 per ha, respectively.

The three techniques were successively applied, so that for each test boring an interpolated MSC value was obtained, using the calculated MSC values of the random survey borings in the neighbourhood of that test boring. The difference between the calculated and the interpolated MSC value for a given test boring was treated as the error made by the interpolation technique in question at that point in the area. From these individual errors the Mean Squared Error of each interpolation technique was estimated by the usual estimation procedure for stratified random samples (see e.g. Cochran, 1977). The design of this experiment is roughly similar to that used by Braile (1978), although that author compared other interpolation techniques in other circumstances.

The interpolation techniques can be characterized as follows, in order of increasing sophistication.

Proximal. By this method the value of the nearest survey boring is taken as the interpolated value for a given test boring. The method is simple and cheap. No explicit weighting is carried out, because only one value is used.

Weighted Average. By this method (see e.g. Davis, 1973) the interpolated value for a test boring is calculated as a weighted average of the values of the nearest survey borings. The weighting function can be any function which decreases with distance. Both the number of neighbouring values and the exact form of the weighting function can be chosen. In this study the values of the ten nearest survey borings were used, with weights proportional to the inverse of the squared distance from the test boring.

Kriging. Here the interpolated value for a test boring is also a weighted average of the values of survey borings in the neighbourhood. The difference with the previous technique is that with Kriging the weights are explicitly chosen so that each interpolated value is an unbiased estimate with minimum variance, i.e., with smallest possible expected error. The Kriging technique is a result of the statistical theory of regionalized variables, developed by G. Matheron and coworkers (Matheron, 1971). An introduction to

Kriging can be found in David (1977) and, with more mathematical detail, in Olea (1975). Other applications to soil data have been reported by Giltrap (1978) and Burgess and Webster (1980).

Mathematically, the weights of the n survey borings in a neighbourhood of a test boring are found by solving the following system of $n + 1$ linear equations:

$$\sum_{j=1}^{n} a_j \gamma_{ij} + \mu = \gamma_{i0} \qquad\qquad (i = 1, \ldots, n)$$

$$\sum_{j=1}^{n} a_j = 1$$

(1)

where a_j is the weight of the jth neighbouring boring, μ is a Lagrange multiplier, and γ_{ij} is the semi-variance between the ith and jth boring, the test boring being indexed by $j = 0$. As indicated hereafter, the semi-variances in these equations can be estimated from the available data, so that only the n weights and μ remain as unknowns. Now the system of equations can be solved.

The semi-variances represent the spatial correlations in the area. For two points i and j the correlation is defined as:

$$\gamma_{ij} = \frac{1}{2} E \{z(x_i) - z(x_j)\}^2$$

where E denotes expectation and $z(x_i)$ the studied variable (here MSC) at location x_i. With the simple Kriging technique used here, it is assumed that the values at points in the area can be described by a stationary random process. This implies that γ_{ij} is the same for each pair of points with the same difference in location. It may therefore be written as a function of this difference only:

$$\gamma(h) = \frac{1}{2} E \{z(x) - z(x + h)\}^2$$

Note that in the present case the difference h is a two-dimensional vector like x, that can be represented by a distance and a direction component.

The function $\gamma(h)$ has been estimated by averaging the squared difference between MSC values of pairs of test borings, after sorting these pairs into classes defined in terms of distance and direction. It appeared that γ dit not clearly depend on direction, so the averages were pooled over all directions. This resulted in a two-dimensional variogram, i.e., a graph of semi-variance versus distance $|h|$ (Fig.4), to which the "spherical model" was fitted:

$$\gamma(|h|) = c_0 + c \left\{ \frac{3|h|}{2a} - \frac{|h|^3}{2a^3} \right\} \qquad \text{for } 0 < |h| \leqslant a$$

(2)

$$\gamma(|h|) = c_0 + c \qquad\qquad \text{for } |h| > a$$

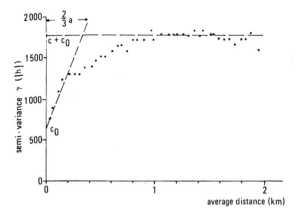

Fig.4. Variogram of Moisture Supply Capacity in the study area, to be used for the Kriging technique. The dotted lines were drawn to obtain estimates of the constants c, c_0 and a of the spherical variogram model (2).

The three parameters a, c_0 and c were estimated from the variogram as shown in Fig.4: a = 0.6 km, c_0 = 600 mm^2 and c = 1200 mm^2. These parameters have a useful descriptive meaning. Parameter a denotes the distance beyond which two points are practically uncorrelated; it is called the "range". Parameter c_0 denotes the so-called "nugget-effect" (from gold mining), representing variability among samples at the shortest possible sampling distance. The sum $c_0 + c$ is called the "sill" and denotes the semi-variance of uncorrelated points. Once these parameters were determined the semi-variance of any pair of borings could be calculated by substituting their mutual distance in (2).

As mentioned before, a system (1) of $n + 1$ equations had to be solved for each interpolation, with n denoting the number of survey borings in a neighbourhood of the test boring. To avoid a large amount of unnecessary computation, this number had to be as low as possible, yet high enough to avoid loss of accuracy. As with the Weighted Average technique it was decided to use the ten nearest borings; preliminary analysis showed that using more would have given almost the same results.

Proximal, Weighted Average and Kriging are of increasing complexity and demand increasing computer time. The number of computer operations depends primarily on the number of neighbouring points carried along in the interpolation. With Proximal the number of operations is lowest. With Weighted Average the number of operations increases linearly, and with Kriging the number increases at least quadratically.

RESULTS AND DISCUSSION

Data exploration

The variation among the MSC values calculated for all random test and survey borings is shown in the frequency diagram of Fig.5. The distribution

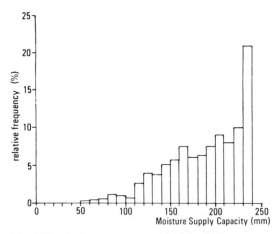

Fig.5. Frequency diagram of Moisture Supply Capacity calculated for 1191 random survey and test borings.

is highly skewed. The MSC class occurring most frequently is that of 230– 240 mm, which equals the potential evapotranspiration in a 10% dry year. Obviously, the MSC cannot exceed this maximum value. So the skewness indicates that in a relatively large part of this area the soil can supply all the moisture that is needed by the plants in a 10% dry year.

Information on the spatial distribution of the MSC values is not provided by Fig.5. This aspect is shown in Fig.6, which indicates locations and MSC values for all test borings. This map suggests a general spatial continuity of the data and does not obviously conflict with the assumption underlying the Kriging technique (David, 1977). The spatial distribution is also re- flected in Fig.7. This shows frequency and average distance for 25 classes of the absolute values of differences in MSC of pairs of nearest test borings. It indicates, for example, that 25% of the adjacent borings differs less than 5 mm in MSC, whereas less than 1% differs more than 110 mm. Although many adjacent borings have small differences in MSC, a substantial percentage of the neighbouring values differ largely. Fig.7 shows that larger distances between borings also tend to correspond with larger differences in MSC; the same tendency had already been observed in the variogram (Fig.4) for a larger range of distances.

Data exploration thus demonstrates the considerable spatial variability of MSC even at short distances in the study area. This phenomenon is reflected

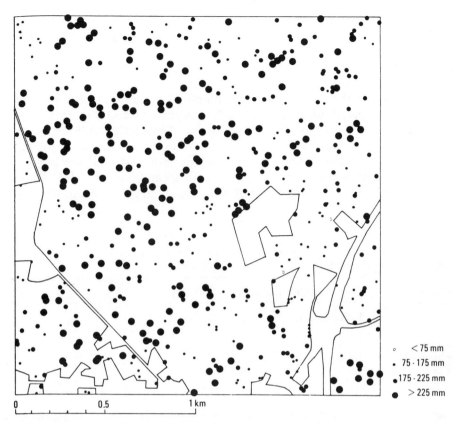

Fig.6. Locations and Moisture Supply Capacities of 530 random survey borings.

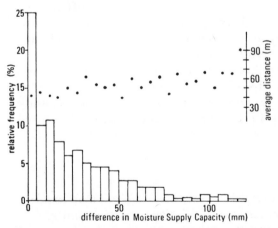

Fig.7. Frequency of differences in Moisture Supply Capacities and average distance for 25 classes of differences in Moisture Supply Capacity between 661 random test borings **and** their nearest neighbours.

by the results of the various interpolation techniques as will now be discussed.

Interpolation

As mentioned in the preceding paragraph on interpolation techniques, an estimate of the Mean Square Error of each interpolation technique was calculated together with the standard deviation of this estimate. From each estimate and its standard deviation, the 95% confidence limits were calculated for the Mean Square Error. Square root transformation of these limits resulted in 95% confidence intervals for the Root Mean Squared (RMS) Errors as given in Table III. The RMS Error of both Weighted Average and Kriging

TABLE III

Root Mean Squared Error of three techniques used to interpolate calculated Moisture Supply Capacities of random survey borings (1.48 per ha)

Interpolation technique	95% Confidence interval of RMS Error	
	lower limit (mm)	upper limit (mm)
Proximal	36.4	36.9
Weighted Average	29.2	29.7
Kriging	28.9	29.4

turned out to be about 29.1 mm, that of Proximal is 36.6 mm. As assessed with the Student test on the mean of the pairwise differences between squared errors, all three RMS Errors differ significantly at the $1^0/_{00}$ level and decrease in the order: Proximal, Weighted Average, Kriging. The difference in accuracy between Kriging and the relatively simple Weighted Average technique can, however, be neglected in practice. Further simplification by using the Proximal technique leads to substantially larger errors.

One weakness of the Weighted Average technique, which is avoided in Kriging, is that possible clusters of survey points are weighted too heavily. Due to the stratification, however, such clusters do not occur in this study. This is probably the main reason for the relatively good result of Weighted Average in this instance.

Use of the soil map

Estimates of MSC cannot be derived directly from the soil map as its mapping units are not defined in terms of MSC. Each mapping unit as delineated on the map could, however, be used as a more or less homogeneous stratum, the mean MSC value of which might be taken as an estimate for any point within that unit.

The rationale of this approach is that in both defining and delineating the mapping units one attempts to divide the area into parts that are as homogeneous as possible with respect to primary soil properties. Because MSC is related to these properties, the mapping units may also be expected to have a degree of homogeneity with respect to MSC. The success of the approach depends, of course, on the degree of homogeneity actually attained, and on the accuracy with which the means of the units are estimated. The former is completely determined by the quality of the map, whereas the latter varies with the effort spent on collecting profile data. These two components are therefore dealt with separately.

The homogeneity of one mapping unit with respect to MSC can be numerically expressed as the standard deviation of MSC within that unit. Similarly, the homogeneity of the map as a whole can be expressed as the standard deviation within all units of that map, conceptually obtained by pooling all individual deviations from the means of the respective units. This standard deviation has been estimated (as the square root of the pooled variance within units) from the calculated MSC values of the 661 random test borings. The estimate turned out to be 29 mm. This result implies that if the true mean MSC of each mapping unit could be used as the estimate for any point within that unit, that estimate would have the same RMS Error (29 mm) as interpolation by Weighted Average or Kriging.

In practice, the true means are unknown, and will have to be estimated with limited accuracy, which adds an extra error to the 29 mm. The size of this extra error will depend on the estimation procedure followed. Various procedures are possible, for instance:

(a) construct a "modal" soil profile description for the mapping unit and calculate its MSC;

(b) select one or more "representative" profile descriptions from those that were made within the unit, and calculate their mean MSC;

(c) calculate the MSC for each of the profile descriptions also used for delineating, and calculate their mean;

(d) calculate the MSC for each of the profile descriptions in a statistical sample not used for delineating, and calculate their mean.

It is beyond the scope of this paper to go into the relative merits of these procedures. It should be noted, however, that procedure (d) is especially interesting in the context of this study because it is the only one which enables the accuracy to be objectively quantified beforehand. For instance, if a simple random sample of n profiles is taken from a mapping unit, then the variance $s^2(\bar{x})$ of the estimated mean $\bar{x}$ equals $s^2(x)/n$, where $s^2(x)$ denotes the variance of the property concerned. If $\bar{x}$ is also used as the estimate for any profile in the unit, the Mean Squared Error of that estimate equals $s^2(x) + s^2(x)/n = s^2(x)(n + 1)/n$, so the RMS Error equals $s(x)\sqrt{(n + 1)/n}$. For an "average" unit of the present soil map, having a standard deviation of 29 mm and 22 test borings, this would result in an RMS Error of 29.7 mm. With a more realistic sample size of 5 borings, for instance, the RMS Errors would be 31.9 mm. The same values would apply to the map as a whole if these sample sizes were allocated to each unit. In general, it will be possible to achieve some reduction of these values by using a more efficient sampling strategy than simple random, and by more efficient allocation of sample sizes to units, taking their area and standard deviation into account. The standard deviations of the largest mapping units of the soil map are presented in Table IV; they appear to range between 6.6 and 38.3 mm. The RMS Error would differ accordingly from unit to unit.

TABLE IV

Areas and standard deviation of Moisture Supply Capacity of the largest mapping units, estimated from 661 random test borings

Code soil map	Groundwater class	Area (%)	Standard deviation (mm)
Hn33	III	2.8	14.4
Hn33	V	3.7	22.4
Hn33	V*	16.3	34.4
Hn33	VI	19.0	36.8
Hn33	VII	4.3	38.3
Hn35	V	3.5	14.0
cHn33	VI	3.0	27.0
cHn35	VI	6.6	33.2
EZ35	VII	11.4	26.0
EZ35	VII*	2.0	15.0
fkZn35	III	3.1	15.2
fkZn35	III*	2.3	6.6
pZn35	V	1.6	12.1

In conclusion, an extra sampling effort of e.g. 5 random borings on average in each of the 30 mapping units to estimate their mean MSC, would increase the sampling density by 28%, and lead to an expected RMS Error which is 10% higher than that of Weighted Average and Kriging. This difference in efficiency should be weighed against the advantage of the soil map as being a multiple-purpose document. The map as such gives a comprehensive overview of many soil properties simultaneously and can serve as a basis for various soil survey interpretations.

One difficulty not yet mentioned is that of observational errors. The calculated MSC values not only reflect variations present in the area, they also contain errors due to the fact that the MSC values were calculated from field estimates. These errors are present in both survey and test data, and have affected the results. As no reliable information about the magnitude of these errors was available, however, it was not possible to make appropriate corrections. If the observational errors in the calculated MSC values were independently distributed with zero mean and equal variance, then they would have raised the variogram by that variance. We do not know how this affects the optimality of the Kriging interpolations. Similarly, the observational errors will have increased the estimated RMS Errors and standard deviation within mapping units. The authors expect this increase to be less than 3 mm.

The results of this study can only be generalized to situations with a similar type of variability and with a similar pattern of observation points. The conclusions, of course, remain limited to the survey method and interpolation techniques included in this experiment.

ACKNOWLEDGEMENTS

The authors wish to express their thanks to Dr. P.A. Burrough and Dr. J. Schelling of The Netherlands Soil Survey Institute for their useful comments to an earlier draft of this paper.

REFERENCES

Bouma, J., De Laat, P.J.M., Awater, R.C.H.M., Van Holst, A.F., Van Heesen, H.C. and Van de Nes, Th.J.M., 1980a. Use of soil survey data in a simulation model for predicting regional soil moisture regimes. Soil Sci. Soc. Am. J., 44: 808—814.

Bouma, J., De Laat, P.J.M., Van Holst, A.F. and Van de Nes, Th. J.M., 1980b. Predicting the effects of changing water-table levels and associated moisture regimes for soil survey interpretations. Soil Sci. Soc. Am. J., 44: 797—802.

Bouma, J., 1981. Soil Survey Interpretation: estimating use-potentials of a clay soil under various moisture regimes. Geoderma, 26: 165—177.

Braile, L.W., 1978. Comparison of four random to grid methods. Comput. Geosci., 4: 341—349.

Burgess, T.M. and Webster, R., 1980. Optimal interpolation and isarithmic mapping of soil properties, 1. The semi-variogram and punctual kriging. J. Soil Sci., 31: 315—331.

Cochran, W.G., 1977. Sampling Techniques. Wiley, New York.

David, M., 1977. Geostatistical Ore Reserve Estimation. Elsevier, Amsterdam.

Davis, J.C., 1973. Statistics and Data Analysis in Geology. Wiley, New York.

De Bakker, H., 1979. Major soils and soil regions in The Netherlands. Pudoc, Wageningen/ Junk, Den Haag.

De Laat, P.J.M., 1980. Model for unsaturated flow above a shallow water tabel, applied to a regional sub-surface flow problem. Pudoc, Wageningen, Agric. Res. Rep., 895.

Giltrap, D.J., 1978. Mathematical Techniques for Soil Survey Design. Doct. thesis, Univ. Oxford.

Matheron, G., 1971. The theory of regionalized variables and its applications. Cah. CMM Fasc., 5 (ENSMP, Paris.)

Olea, R.A., 1975. Optimal mapping techniques using regionalized variable theory. Series on spatial analysis, 2. Kans. Geol. Surv., Lawrence.

Rijtema, P.E., 1971. Een berekeningsmethode voor de benadering van de landbouwschade ten gevolge van grondwateronttrekking. ICW, Wageningen, ICW Nota 587 (in Dutch).

Soil Survey Staff, 1975. Soil Taxonomy: a Basic System of Soil Classification for Making and Interpreting Soil Surveys. Soil Conserv. Serv., USDA. Agric. Handbook, 436. Washington, DC, 754 pp.

Van Heesen, H.C., 1970. Presentation of seasonal fluctuation of the water table on soil maps. Geoderma, 4: 257—279.

14: MIDGE, A MICROCOMPUTER SOIL INFORMATION SYSTEM

D. J. Giltrap

Soil Bureau, Department of Scientific and Industrial Research, Private Bag, Lower Hutt, New Zealand

Summary

MIDGE (map image display generator) is a microcomputer-based map display and manipulation system which gives a powerful data retrieval system for soil or other land-based information. Because it is implemented on a low-cost microcomputer (currently an LSI 11/2) MIDGE does not require access to large computer facilities or central databases.

MIDGE accesses maps stored on floppy discs in a run-length coded grid format. These maps may be displayed at any scale on a colour VDU (Intercolor 8001G). The storage format allows storage of quite detailed maps in files of 10 kbytes or less so that a large number of single-factor maps of any area can be stored on a single disc.

Maps may be overlaid to produce composites and this allows sophisticated land interpretation. As an example, maps showing predicted pastoral productivity, and a suitability classification based on seasonal production patterns have been generated from basic soil and climatic data. Any users of the system can create interpretive classifications to meet their own requirements and generate the resulting maps from basic land information.

The basic maps used by MIDGE should ideally be produced by interpolation from point data but there is no technical problem in using data from other sources (e.g. digitized soil maps). In general, however, single-factor maps generalized from soil maps appear to be less detailed than similar maps interpolated directly from point observations. Conventional soil maps can also be produced by interpolation and can be displayed with MIDGE.

MIDGE allows a series of maps of the same area with same legend to be stacked in a single file. This facility can be used to store distribution maps for different soil classes or to store means, minima and maxima (based on interpolation errors) for particular soil properties. This gives the user access to information not usually available at all from conventional soil maps.

Because MIDGE is a self-contained low-cost system, it can be used directly by land-information users (e.g. farmers, land planners). These users then have access to a very much larger body of information than could be displayed on a single hard-copy map, how ever sophisticated the information system used to produce that map may have been.

Introduction

Modern techniques of processing soil survey data and of land evaluation have generated a need for more powerful cartographic information systems than can be provided by traditional maps. A major
advance in soil survey technology is the capture and subsequent
retrieval of basic soil properties (as determined at a single site)
for land evaluation. This avoids the potentially serious information losses associated with taxonomic generalization and allows
much more detailed land evaluation.

The simplest technique for storing and mapping individual soil
properties is the grid survey (Rudeforth, 1975). In this technique,
survey observations are at the intersections of a regular grid.
Maps may then be drawn on a line printer or by other means (e.g.
grid to vector conversion) based on the actual soil properties observed at each point. An alternative technique is the polygon survey where the landscape is subdivided into a number of polygons
taken to be uniform and the properties of the soils occurring in
each unit are recorded. This technique resembles conventional soil
mapping and the polygon format is used in a number of land information systems (Van Berkel & Eyles, 1981 ; Tomlinson, 1967). In practice, however, it is often impossible to subdivide a landscape into a manageable number of polygons without considerable generalization (i.e. the polygons are markedly varied in at least some
properties). Similarly a grid survey often gives an adequate degree
of detail only where a large number of grid cells are used thus
imposing an unrealistic burden on the soil surveyor who must characterize the soils at each grid cell.

These problems may be overcome by interpolation procedures (de
Gruijter & Bie, 1975). With these procedures, survey observations
may be at random sites (or at the surveyor's convenience) and the
observed properties are then interpolated mathematically to 'target
points' on an arbitrarily fine grid. The interpolated grid data
may then be mapped in exactly the same way as for a grid survey. A
particular interpolation technique that has recently attracted
interest in soil science is 'kriging' (Burgess & Webster, 1980;
Yost et al., 1982; Giltrap, 1983a). This method gives a theoretically optimum (minimum standard error) solution and also gives a
separate estimate of standard error for each interpolated point.
Kriging requires substantially more computer time than other interpolation techniques but it has been shown (Giltrap, 1981) that it
can be applied routinely to soil surveys for a comprehensive range
of soil properties with computer costs that are small compared to
total survey costs. With this approach, large numbers of single-
factor soil maps may be routinely generated by soil survey.

As soil survey organizations have acquired the capacity to generate
(and retrieve) large collections of soil data, there has been an
increase in the information requirements for modern land-use man-

agement and planning. Land evaluations are required to be increasingly specific and related to particular land-uses. Ideally land
evaluation maps should give quantitative predictions of yields of
particular crops and responses to particular management practices.
Such maps should also give some indication of their reliability
and of the entent of land variability over small areas. The resulting demands on a land information system cannot be met by traditional printed maps.

The 'cartographic' information discussed above cannot easily be
handled by standard database management systems, which are designed to store and retrieve information about discrete enumerated
objects. The 'object domain' of cartographic information is a continuous set of points on the earth's surface and, retrieval requests will often relate to points other than those at which data
has been collected.

It is possible to make cartographic data fit the conventional database concept by arbitrarily dividing the landscape into polygonal
regions and then treating these regions as discrete objects. This
approach, however, leads to problems of cartographic generalization
and ensuing information loss. Furthermore geographic relationships
between polygons (e.g. contiguity) may be poorly handled and separate programs are often needed for graphical output or for specifying requested search areas (which may not correspond to polygon
boundaries).

Alternatively the landscape may be represented by a regular array
of grid points. In order to achieve reasonable resolution, however,
a large number of grid points will be needed. This leads to database management problems if we attempt to use individual grid
cells as the basic entities in a database. It is also very unlikely
that a user would wish to retrieve data on the individual grid
cell (e.g. obtain listing of all grid cells with attributes in a
specified range). The grid cells will, in fact, be used only to
represent a continuous geographic surface with output presented
either as a map or as a summary of total areas possessing particular combinations of attributes.

We may more appropriately treat the complete arrays of grid cell
attribute values as internal computer representations of the spatial distribution of attributes across a continuous surface and
treat these distributions as the basic entities in a database.
O'Callaghan & Graetz (1981) refer to this as image-based storage.
In practice, image-based systems lead to small simple databases
(albeit with large complex records) and database management systems
turn out to be unnecessary.

The MIDGE system

The MIDGE (map image display generator) system was developed at
this laboratory to provide a map display and manipulation system
capable of exploiting the amount of data produced by the applica-

tion of geostatistical techniques to soil surveys (Giltrap, 1983b) and of using modern predictive models to construct land evaluation maps from basic soil properties. MIDGE provides interactive map display on a low-cost colour VDU and is designed to operate on stand-alone microcomputers. The full map-processing capabilities of the system are thus available to any land-use decision maker for a modest capital outlay. This contrasts with systems implemented on large central computers, where the end-user of the land information has access only to some form of computer printout (e.g. computer-plotted map).

MIDGE is currently implemented on an LSI 11/2 microcomputer with 64 kbytes RAM and dual 500 kbyte floppy disc drives using an Inte-colour 8001G VDU as the terminal console. As the programs are written in FORTRAN, it should be relatively easy to implement MIDGE on any other microcomputer of comparable capacity. The individual map images are stored as run-length encoded grids in floppy disc files. The run-length encoded format gives substantial data compression and quite detailed map images (200×200 pixels or more) can be stored in files of less than 10 kbytes. A single floppy disc can thus hold many thematic map images for any given area.

The MIDGE display is formed from colour patterns, which are formed by printing a character in one of eight possible colours on a different background colour. This restricts the resolution of the display to that of the normal character on the 8001G screen (48 rows by 80 columns) but makes it easy to identify unambiguously a large number (> 50) of distinct units. This contrasts with both vector format displays and conventional image display systems, which give greater resolution but poorer 'readability' for maps with many units. In practice, the limited resolution is not serious as MIDGE allows 'zoom' and 'pan' functions to look at specific parts of the image in greater detail. The maximum detail that the MIDGE display can resolve is limited only by the resolution of the stored image. This is typically about 200×200 pixels but much greater detail (1000×1000) may be used where the quality of the basic data warrants it.

The MIDGE display is constructed from the stored image by mapping each character position in a fixed (37×49) window on the screen to the closest corresponding stored image pixel and drawing the colour pattern of the appropriate unit. The remainder of the screen is used to display the map legend and title, the current display scale and a statistical summary of unit areas. The display is manipulated by a set of single-letter commands with possible numeric arguments (e.g. the command S10000 sets the display scale to 1 : 10 000). These commands are supplemented by simple keystroke operations for cursor movement across the map display and colour pattern definition.

MIDGE files may contain several map images of a single land surface provided that these images share a common legend. This helps avoid file proliferation by keeping groups of related images together.

Examples of groups of images that could be stored together in this
way include
- maps of a single soil property (e.g. pH) measured at different
depths;
- maps of predicted cash return for a range of alternative land
uses;
- maps of seasonal (or monthly) soil moisture deficit (or any other
temporally varying land property;
- percentage distribution maps for soil classes or vegetation types.
A simple one letter command is available to step (or jump) through
the images stored in a multi-image file.

Probably the most powerful facility MIDGE possesses, however, is
the ability to overlay two or more images to produce a new composite image. For simple overlaying, the composite map is produced
pixel by pixel by classifying the combinations of units in the
source images for the appropriate pixel. MIDGE can also produce
overlaid images from source images defined on different grids from
each other or from the composite image. This facility can be used
to 'compose' images of neighbouring areas into a single large image.

The classification of the combination of source image units is
interactive. The computer displays the combinations actually found
and the user keys in the composite unit numbers. The user is then
prompted for the new map title and unit descriptors and the composite map image is then displayed and stored. This approach means
that no provision need be made for combinations of source units
which do not occur in practice.

The applications of map overlay extend far beyond the simple exercise of simultaneously displaying more than òne image. Because the
combinations are reclassified, a wide range of predictive models
may be used to generate land evaluation maps from basic land properties. Several examples of this will be given in the following
section. The classification may be used with a single-source image
to alter isarithm intervals. An initial isarithmic map may be
stored with very fine intervals (up to 255 classes) and these
classes may be grouped as required.

Examples of use

MIDGE has been used to display map images generated by geostatistical techniques from current soil surveys. The overlay technique
has been used to generate predictive land evaluation maps based on
soil and climatic properties.

In a survey of the urban environs of Masterton, described by Giltrap (1981), a wide range of basic soil properties (e.g. soil
thickness, depth to particular layers, soil colour and texture at
specified depth intervals, were kriged from observed points to a
regular grid. These grids were transferred to the MIDGE system for
display and manipulation. In this area, the most important properties for assessment of agricultural potential were thought to be

available moisture storage capacity and drainage. Available water storage was estimated from the thickness of the various layers within the root zone and the particle size distribution of these layers. Drainage was represented by the average abundance of orange mottles in the root zone. Because these images were produced by kriging, it was possible to produce error maps for them and mean, minimum (mean - s.d.) and maximum (mean + s.d.) images were produced for each property and stored in multi-image files.

These water storage capacity and mottle abundance images were over-laid and the resultant classes reclassified to give a composite map in which the soil properties were expressed as land limitations (none, slight, moderate or severe). The resulting map resembled conventional land-suitability maps in general format. Good visual separation of the classes was obtained with a total of 16 units. The composite map was easily produced and any required classification of the units could have been used.

Water balance calculations were performed for the various available water classes and used as inputs to a range of predictive models. A simple model estimated the (water-limited) summer grass production from the ratio of actual to potential evapotranspiration. An image showing this prediction was generated by reclassifying the available water map. In this survey climate was constant; has a larger area been involved, available water would have been overlaid with appropriate climatic maps. The resulting image gave an apparently good general representation of the pattern of summer productivity and showed that summer production over the landscape varied by a factor of about 2.

A more sophisticated model may consider production for all four seasons. Evidence based on production trials (unpublished work) suggests that pasture production in any season can be predicted from radiation, soil and air temperature and actual evapotranspiration. A pastoral suitability classification has been set up on the basis of these relationships. This classification takes account of the seasonal variation and annual reliability of production as well as the total mean annual potential production. A map image of these classes was constructed on MIDGE by combining the available water storage with the relevant climatic data.

MIDGE has also been used to display and manipulate images of conventional soil maps. The simplest way to do this is to digitize a soil map and convert from vector to grid format. In a recent soil survey, geostatistical techniques were used to generate soil maps from point observations. These techniques led to an interpolated grid array with probability estimates for each possible soil class at each grid cell. A soil map was generated from this grid by simply allocating each grid cell to the class with highest probability (i.e. simple legend). Alternatively, had particular combinations of probabilities occurred over extensive areas, these areas could have been mapped to a complex unit.

With MIDGE, however, it is possible to store the complete probability map for each class in a single multi-image file. This enables the user to display the (probable) distribution for any class (or combination of classes). In particular, minor classes that are never dominant and hence are not shown on a conventional map can be displayed as required. The same technique could presumably also be used for other complex nominal data (e.g. vegetation types).

Conclusions

A microcomputer-based system for map-image display and manipulation has been developed. This system has been shown to be suitable for sophisticated land evaluation with large amount of information derived from geostatistical processing of soil survey data. The data compression achieved by run-length encoding in the image files means that microcomputer systems (using floppy discs) have adequate capacity to hold all the information likely to be required for any given application. Because the map image is treated as the basic entity of data, large database management systems are not required and hence the system is not dependent on links to larger computers.

Because the image is interactively generated, a very large number of different images are available to the user. This means that new techniques for displaying map information are available. One example of this that has been demonstrated is the use of multi-image files to store distribution maps for each possible soil class as opposed to the traditional soil map, which shows only the dominant class at each point. Another example is the display of statistical ranges (mean, minimum and maximum) for isarithmic maps rather than just the mean.

The generation of new images by overlay has been demonstrated and the reclassification of overlaid units has been used to generate land-evaluation maps based on predictive performance models. This opens the way to sophisticated land-use planning as more detailed land information and better models of how this data relates to land performance become available. Even where such information is not available, however, MIDGE or other similar systems can contribute to the better use of whatever data is available by providing a clear simple display of land properties to the end-user of this information. Because of the low (and falling) cost of microcomputer systems, MIDGE can be made available to many land-information users in developing or developed countries and not just a few large institutions.

References

Burgess, T.M. & R. Webster, 1980. Optimal interpolation and isarithmic mapping. I. The semi-variogram and punctual kriging. J. Soil Sci. 31: 315-331.
Gruijter, J.J. de & S.W. Bie, 1975. A discrete approach to automated mapping of multivariate systems. Proc. Int. Cartos. Ass. Com. III. Enschede. p. 17-28

Giltrap, D.J., 1981. A practical application of spatial interpolation for the rapid production of a wide range of special purpose soil maps. In: Information systems for soil related data. Proceedings of the second Australian meeting of the ISSS workshop on soil information systems, Canberra, Australia, 19-20 February 1980. (Eds A.W. Moore, B.G. Cook & L.G. Lynch). Pudoc, Wageningen. pp. 73-82.

Giltrap, D.J., 1983a. Computer production of soil maps. I. Production of grid maps by interpolation. Geoderma 29: 295-311.

Giltrap, D.J., 1983b. Computer production of soil maps. II. Interactive map display. Geoderma 29: 313-325.

O'Callaghan, J.F. & R.D. Graetz, 1981. Software for image-based information systems: its application to integrating Landsat imagery and land tenure data for rangeland management. In: Information systems for soil and related data. Proceedings of the second Australian meeting of the ISSS workshop on soil information systems. Canberra, Australia, 10-20 February 1980. (Eds A.W. Moore, B.G. Cook & L.G. Lynch). Pudoc, Wageningen, pp. 64-72.

Rudeforth, C.C., 1975. Storing and processing data for soil and land use capability surveys. J. Soil Sci. 26: 155-168.

Tomlinson, R.F., 1967. An introduction to the geo-information system of the Canada land inventory. Canadian Dept. of Forestry and Rural Development. 23 pp.

Van Berkel, P.R. & G.O. Eyles, 1981. The New Zealand resource inventory database for the national soil and water conservation organisation. In: Information systems for soil and related data. Proceedings of the second Australian meeting of the ISSS workshop on soil information systems. Canberra, Australia, 19-20 February 1980. (Eds A.W. Moore, B.G. Cook & L.G. Lynch). Pudoc, Wageningen. pp. 104-121.

Yost, R.S., G. Uehara & R.L. Fox, 1982. Geostatistical analysis of soil chemical properties of large land areas. II. Kriging. Soil Sci. Soc. Am. J. 46: 1033-1037.

Part VII

Rating Indices and Yields

Papers 15 Through 18: Introductory Review

A rating index implies the assignment or calculation of some score for land conditions. At the simplest, a surveyor might scan a landscape and categorize individual fields as either very suitable, suitable, or unsuitable for agriculture. Assessment of land capability following one of the schemes as described in Part IV would give a much more rigorous and objective result, but again the ultimate rating is expressed using an ordinal scale. The derivation of a specific rating index using an interval scale can be achieved by the measurement of component variables, and then an overall score is obtained by incorporating these into a formula. This method is called the parametric approach. An alternative approach is to calculate rating indices on the basis of land performance, for example, using crop yield data. The aim of this section is to present a number of papers that demonstrate these two fundamental approaches: inductive rating indices from land properties and deductive rating indices from yield data. The topic is reviewed by Huddleston (1984) who summarizes the various approaches in the United States toward developing numerical ratings as an input to land use planning, equalization of land values, and tax assessments.

The notion of being able to rate a site on a scale—say, from 0-100—is highly attractive, although, as will become apparent, there are substantial problems to be solved in achieving this. In theory land attributes are defined, measured, and scored, and the component values are fed into an equation to determine the overall index. Different types of equations can be used and can be summarized as follows:

Additive (e.g., $I = A + B + C + D$)
Multiplicative e.g., $I = A \times B \times C \times D$
Complex function e.g., $I = A \times \sqrt{(B \times C \times D)}$

where I stands for overall rating index and A, B, C, D, represent values or ratings of component variables. Examples of these approaches are given by Riquier (1974), McRae and Burnham (1981) and Huddleston (1984).

With the additive approach, the score of many variables can be added up to give an overall index. The additive process, especially if many variables are included, means that the effect of any very high or low scoring component is relatively small. In practice, the presence of one major constraint may well be sufficient to exclude a range of land use options however favorable the other variables may be. An index based on addition would not highlight such a problem. Nevertheless additive systems have been developed and tested. For example, an additive system has been used in Germany since the 1920s whereby each field is assessed to aid taxation; Weiers and Reid (1974) and McRae and Burnham (1981) provide details. A sophisticated rating system using a similar framework has been developed for Iowa (Fenton et al., 1971). Yield information is a critical input whereby soils and weather conditions are first assessed in terms of suitability for growing corn. Areas with the most favored conditions are given a Corn Suitability Rating (CSR) of 100. The guidelines specify a range of slope and precipitation factors each with component ratings; deviations from ideal land conditions are assessed by subtracting the component ratings from the ideal CSR score of 100. Fenton (1975) describes how each soil mapping unit in Iowa is assigned a CSR and the results are shown to produce an equitable assessment of land for taxation purposes.

In multiplicative systems, the presence of one very low score has a considerable effect on the overall result. This may well be deemed correct on the basis of the principle of limiting factors. A consequence of multiplication is that the numerical range of scores is much greater compared to scores derived by addition. The best-known multiplicative system was developed by Storie in California. The original Storie Index Rating (SIR) was obtained by multiplying ratings for character of soil profile, texture of surface soil, and modifying factors such as drainage, slope, or alkalinity (Storie, 1933). The system has been gradually revised over the years with slope being introduced as a separate factor, with more classes of soil profile development, and with slight changes in scores for component variables (Storie, 1976). The system has been widely modified and applied; for example, Leamy (1974) describes how it has been used in New Zealand to aid farm valuation assessment.

Paper 15 in this section provides an interesting comparison of the U.S. Department of Agriculture (USDA) Land Capability Classification with the Storie Index Rating. The stimulus to this project by Singer was the need to define prime agricultural land in California. Implementation of legislation designed to protect prime agricultural land is obviously dependent upon the clear identification of such land. For his investigation, Singer selected eight study areas for which he then determined the extent of land in capability classes I and II, as well as the extent of land with SIR scores in the ranges 60-79.9 and 80-100. Much of the paper is devoted to a detailed comparison of the two assessment systems, and, broadly speaking, the results are similar. Singer stresses that both systems were not developed with the specific objective of defining prime agricultural land. The flexibility of the Storie system is emphasized, though difficulties arise in identifying particular limiting factors as is done in the capability scheme. The ultimate test of these systems in defining prime agricultural land should be the strength of relationship between crop yield and economic return on land proposed to be in this category.

The calculation of a rating index using a complex function allows the combination of arithmetic and multiplicative operations. The number of ways by which an index can be expressed as a complex function of three or more variables is infinite. Unless crop response to environmental conditions can be predicted on theoretical grounds, statistically derived relationships between yields and rating indices have to be used. An analogous situation is with a nonlinear regression problem whereby a computer program tests many functions to determine which one gives the best correlation. Similar calibration is necessary with complex functions as used to predict rating indices. The best-known complex function was proposed by Clarke (1951, 1971). It is used to obtain a score for a soil profile: for each horizon, scores for texture and depth are multiplied and then added for the complete profile before being multiplied by a drainage factor to produce the overall profile value. It is a simple method and Clarke (1951) demonstrates that the results give a good indication of soil quality by establishing a close correlation with wheat yield.

McRae and Burnham (1981) list 15 advantages and disadvantages of parametric systems. Among the advantages are: (1) Once a rating is defined as a function of specific attributes, its determination becomes straightforward, quantitative, and consistent. (2) Ratings are measured on an interval (or continuous) scale, which makes the calculation of average figures for farms or fields an easy operation; furthermore, such a scale is preferred to an ordinal one if the rating is to be used for taxation purposes. (3) The approach is flexible: if sensible results are not obtained, then changes can be made to the included variables and their mathematical association.

Some disadvantages that can be highlighted include: (1) There is a danger that a parametric system can be taken to give an objective measure; in fact, there is a high degree of subjectivity involved in the selection of variables and how the function is expressed. (2) A crucial problem is interaction of factors and how combinations affect land use or crop yield. (3) Ratings developed and tested in one area for a specific crop may have to be redefined for application in other localities.

An interesting and alternative approach to the quantitative rating of land for specific crops is given by Schreier and Zulkifli in Paper 16. In their study in British Columbia, the first step was the development of a database on soil properties for soil mapping units. A subset of properties considered important to individual crops was then selected before factor and cluster analysis were executed. As a result groupings of similar soils with respect to these defined attributes were recognized and could be tested with reference to productivity data in order to provide agricultural capability ratings. Details of the approach as applied to raspberry cultivation are given by Schreier (1983). The following properties were considered important to this crop: drainage, texture of main surface horizon, available water storage capacity in main surface horizon, organic matter content in the main surface horizon, depth to pore size discontinuity, texture of the main horizon responsible for pore size discontinuity, and available water storage capacity of the main horizon. Cluster analysis on these data for 24 soil series gave 8 soil management groups. Of course the identification of natural groupings remains an academic exercise until it is demonstrated that such groupings indicate varying degrees of suitability of soils for raspberries.

Schreier (1983) carried out such tests using information on land capability and yield data derived from farm interviews and was therefore able to grade soil series as either well suited, moderately suited, or poorly suited for raspberry cultivation. He obtained additional confirmation of the groupings by examining the changing spatial occurrence of raspberries. Most of the production was located on the soils categorized as well suited. The approach by Schreier (1983) as demonstrated in Paper 16 is more satisfactory in many ways than the use of simple parametric rating indices, in that properties relevant to specific crops are first defined to allow the recognition of groups of soils similar with respect to these properties. The results are tested by reference to actual occurrence and yield. However, for an area where such a calibration is not possible, the better strategy would be to devise a suitability classification based on known land use requirements.

The last two papers in this section are particular case studies, with Paper 17 concerned with rating land for tree growth and Paper 18 with soil potentials for urban land uses. An economic concern in many west European countries is the magnitude of timber import bills: there is much need to expand areas under forest. This is always a highly controversial issue, but rational policy formulation is possible only if predictions on yield from different land areas are made. Such predictions can be estimated only after actual relationships between forest yield and land conditions have been established. An extensive literature exists on this topic. As one example, Van der Poel (1976) relates growth indices of beech (*Fagus sylvatica*) to a wide range of topographic and soil variables as measured in his study area in Luxembourg. This study demonstrates the importance of parent materials with the growth of beech being more successful on sandstone rather than on marls. For a contrasting type of tree, reference can be made to the study by Mashimo (1974) who was concerned with testing a site index for Japanese cedar (*Cryptomeria japonica*), one of the major tree species for planting in Japan. An actual site index was measured and compared with an estimated one based on geological, topographic, and soil attributes. The result was a high multiple correlation coefficient (0.963), thus supporting the validity of the index.

Paper 17 also makes use of regression analysis to aid the prediction of forest productivity, focusing on Scots pine (*Pinus sylvestris*) grown in two forests in northeast Scotland. The paper describes how yield was estimated using a range of methods. Data on a range of topographic, shelter, climatic, and soil conditions were then obtained so that multiple regression analysis could be used to predict tree growth indices. One very important result from this project is the difference for the two areas in established relationships between tree growth and site factors. The authors imply that extreme caution needs to be used when any attempt is made to apply established relationships between yield and site characteristics from one area to another. To account for this, the authors stress the variability of the upland environment. In their conclusion, they suggest that better results could be achieved by selecting landscape areas of greater overall homogeneity. They propose that this could be achieved by the use of a landscape ecological approach—in particular, land facets (see Part II).

Paper 18 could have been included in Part V (Soil Survey Interpretation), but it is reproduced in this section given its aim of describing a system for rating soils for urban uses. The key component in the derivation of the soil potential index is the relative costs of applying treatments or management practices to cope with soil limitations. Rogoff et al. selected Windsor Township in Michigan to develop ratings for septic tank operation, streets and roads, sewered homes with and without basements, and excavations for water supply. The paper describes how the authors collected information on measures that could be applied to correct or control soil limitations for these five land uses. All the information was stored in a natural resource inventory system, which incorporated a Resource Analysis Package; the latter allowed the calculation of soil potential ratings for the five land uses. The approach is an interesting contrast to the one reported in Paper 16, which used cluster analysis to determine groupings. In the Michigan study, an ideal set of circumstances was defined for specific land uses and then the distance in n-dimensional space was determined from actual points to this ideal one. This distance, after normalization, was taken as the soil potential index. Four classes of soil potential for the various land uses were then determined, aided by another statistical package designed to select optimal class intervals. The results were presented through computer-generated interpretative maps. The Michigan study demonstrates a sophisticated approach to the assessment of soil ratings.

In conclusion, it is interesting to note that the early rating systems as introduced in California and Germany are still in use. To a large extent this is because they have become widely adopted and they produce sensible results. Only a relatively small number of more sophisticated rating indices have been subsequently developed. Of particular concern is the need to have flexibility whereby the variables and their weightings can be changed according to specific land use requirements. Emphasis now seems to be on defining such requirements and measuring how well specific land conditions match these needs. This is the philosophy central to the FAO *Framework for Land Evaluation* as already discussed.

REFERENCES

Clarke, G. R., 1951, The Evaluation of Soils and the Definition of Quality Classes from Studies of the Physical Properties of the Soil Profile in the Field, *Jour. Soil Sci.* **2:**50-60.

Clarke, G. R., 1971, *The Study of Soil in the Field,* Clarendon Press, Oxford.

Fenton, T. E., 1975, Use of Soil Productivity Ratings in Evaluating Iowa Agricultural Land, *Jour. Soil and Water Conserv.* **30:**237-240.

Fenton, T. E., E. R. Duncan, W. D. Schrader, and L. C. Dumenil, 1971, *Productivity Levels of Some Iowa Soils,* Iowa State Univ. Sci. and Technology, Agricultural and Home Economics Experiment Station and Coop. Ext. Serv. Spec. Rep. No. 66.

Huddleston, J. H., 1984, Development and Use of Soil Productivity Ratings in the United States, *Geoderma* **32:**297-317.

Leamy, M. L., 1974, *An Improved Method of Assessing the Soil Factor in Land Valuation,* New Zealand Soil Bureau Scientific Report No. 16, Department of Scientific and Industrial Research, Wellington, New Zealand.

McRae, S. G., and C. P. Burnham, 1981, *Land Evaluation,* Oxford University Press, Oxford.

Mashimo, Y., 1974, Estimation of Forest Stand Growth by Quantification of Soil Conditions and Environment Factors, *10th Trans. Internat. Congress of Soil Sci.* **6:**50-55.

Riquier, J., 1974, A Summary of Parametric Methods of Soil and Land Evaluation, *FAO Soils Bull.* **22:**47-53.

Schreier, H., 1983, Soil Survey Data for Land Use Planning: A Case Study of Raspberry Cultivation in British Columbia, *Jour. Soil and Water Conserv.* **38:**499-503.

Storie, R. E., 1933, *An Index for Rating the Agricultural Value of Soils,* California Agricultural Experimental Station Bulletin No. 556.

Storie, R.E., 1976, *Storie Index Soil Rating,* Univ. of California Division of Agricultural Science Spec. Pub. No. 3203.

Van der Poel, P. W., 1976, Influence of Environmental Factors on the Growth of the Beech, *Catena* **3:**203-214.

Weiers, C. J., and I. G. Reid, 1974, *Soil Classification, Land Valuation, and Taxation. The German Experience.* Centre for European Agricultural Studies, Wye College, Ashford, Kent.

15: THE USDA LAND CAPABILITY CLASSIFICATION AND STORIE INDEX RATING: A COMPARISON

Michael J. Singer

ABSTRACT—Definitions of prime agricultural land often start with a soil rating or land capability classification system. The U.S. Department of Agriculture's Land Capability Classification (LCC) and the Storie Index Rating (SIR) are two soil rating systems used in California as part of the legal definitions of prime agricultural land. Although similar, the two systems differ in the soil properties rated, rating methods, and weighting of soil criteria. The systems are not interchangeable. Class I soil mapping units in eight soil survey reports have an average SIR of 91.3. Class II units have an average SIR of 68. A few mapping units with an SIR greater than 60 have LCC ratings of III, IV, and VI. Methods of rating available water-holding capacity, slope, salinity, and climate account for most differences in the LCC and SIR ratings. Productivity functions for various cropping systems need to be combined with these two rating systems to determine more quantitatively what is prime agricultural land.

PRIME agricultural land, its definition, and its preservation have become major topics of concern. Some researchers attempt to explain the loss of agricultural land in terms of social, political, and economic factors (3). Others consider the acreages of land in various uses relative to the world's food production potential (7). Several recent articles discuss means of retaining land in agriculture (4, 14).

Economist Philip Raup (13), in a recent

Michael J. Singer is an assistant professor in the Department of Land, Air, and Water Resources, University of California, Davis, 95616.

editorial, asked the fundamental question, "What is prime land?" Raup proceeded to enumerate three alternatives for defining prime agricultural land. His third alternative was to grade land by the physical characteristics of soil and climate, but he cautioned against using the U.S. Department of Agriculture's Land Capability Classification (LCC) as the single determinate of prime agricultural land.

In California, as in other states, there have been numerous attempts to pass legislation that would involve the state in agricultural land preservation. One successful effort produced the California Land Conservation Act, now over 10 years old. Its successes and failures are well known (7).

California's 1977-1978 legislative session saw eight bills and one concurrent resolution dealing with agricultural land preservation introduced.[1] In each of these proposals the technical classification of soils by one or more capability classification systems was used as one definition of prime agricultural land.

My purpose here is to examine two classification systems used in part for the legal definition of prime agricultural land in California. I will consider their similarities and differences, explore some of the consequences of these differences, and suggest where soils research might improve the usefulness of the systems in answering the question: What is prime agricultural land?

Two Classification Systems

The two systems are the LCC (*10*) and the Storie Index Rating (SIR) (*16*). LCC places soils in eight classes (I through VIII), depending on the limitations to agricultural use imposed by soil properties and climate. Thirteen criteria (*17*) are considered: effective soil depth, surface layer texture, permeability, drainage class, available water-holding capacity, slope, erosion hazard, flooding hazard, salinity, alkalinity, toxic substances, frost-free season, and climate indices (ET_p and $4ET_a$). A soil is considered Class I until it fails to meet any one criterion. It is then placed in the next lower class (more limitations) and subsequent classes until it meets all the criteria in a particular class. Factors are not weighted, and the value of each criterion [for example, a 100-cm (40-in) effective depth is required for Class I and II soils] was chosen on the basis of its effect on the soil's manageability.

SIR, developed in California in the 1930s, is used to classify soils on the basis of pedologic characteristics and their usefulness to agriculture (*16*). A soil is judged on four factors: A, B, C, and X. Factor A, a profile development factor, rates a soil on its degree of development. A young alluvial soil with no textural B horizon and no impediment to roots would rate 100. An old alluvial soil with a strongly developed clay pan would rate between 40 and 80, depending on the depth to the clay pan. Factor B rates surface texture. Factor C rates slope. Factor X rates several properties, including drainage, salinity and alkalinity, fertility, acidity, erosion, and microrelief.

[1]AB222 Warren, AB293 Boatwright, AB437 Perino, AB1625 Fazio, AB1900 Calvo, SB193 Zenovich, SB975 Dunlap, SB1003 Garamendi, and ACR11 Calvo.

Figure 1. Location of eight study areas in California.

A soil is rated from 0 to 100 for each of the four factors (or subfactor within factor X). The ratings are then multiplied to give a single rating between 0 and 100. For example, a soil might rate A = 95, B = 100, C = 80, X = 95. The SIR for the soil is (.95 x 1 x .8 x .95) x 100 = 72.

Both systems are used in California legislation to define prime agricultural land. The California Land Conservation Act uses Class I and II land and SIR's of 80 to 100 to define prime agricultural land. Other California legislation defines prime agricultural land using various soil quality levels as measured by the two systems.

Study Methods and Sites

I selected for study eight areas in California with modern published soil survey reports (Figure 1). The areas represent a cross section of soils and land uses.

In California a published soil survey area covers an entire county, a part of one

county, or portions of several counties. Each soil survey contains LCC and SIR ratings for the mapping units. I tabulated these ratings from the published reports, then analyzed their similarities and differences.

The Antelope Valley area covers .4 million hectares (1 million acres) in Los Angeles, Kern, and Ventura Counties. The soil survey report, published in 1970 (*18*), identified the soils in the area as Entisols, Inceptisols, Aridisols, Mollisols, Vertisols, and Alfisols. A wide range of field, orchard, and specialty crops is grown under irrigation in the area.

Adjacent to the Antelope Valley area is the Ventura area. The soil survey report, covering .2 million hectares (549,000 acres), was also published in 1970 (*5*). Soils include Entisols, Inceptisols, Mollisols, Vertisols, and Alfisols. Ventura County is a rapidly urbanizing area that faces many land use planning problems. Lemons, avocados, strawberries, celery, fresh flowers, and flower seed are the major crops.

I used two soil survey reports from the San Joaquin Valley in my study. The eastern Fresno area report (*8*), issued in 1971, covers .5 million hectares (1.1 million acres). Fresno County is among the nation's leading counties in the production of field, seed, fruit, and nut crops. The soils mapped include Entisols, Inceptisols, Mollisols, Vertisols, and Alfisols.

The eastern Stanislaus area in the east central portion of California's Great Valley covers about .2 million hectares (475,000 acres). This area's soil survey report was published in 1964 (*2*). Irrigated field crops, orchard crops, and beef cattle are the area's major agricultural commodities. The same soil orders were mapped in this area as in the eastern Fresno area.

Yolo County is in the southern part of the Sacramento Valley. The county's soil survey report, published in 1972 (*1*), en-

Table 1. Land area and area in Classes I and II, SIR 60 to 79.9 and SIR 80 to 100 for eight soil survey report areas in California.

Study Area	Total Area (ha)	Area of Class I and II (ha)	Area of SIR 60-79.9 (ha)	Area of SIR* 80-100 (ha)	No. Mapping Units
Antelope Valley	423,458	166,329	80,176	131,886	149
Eastern Fresno	449,208	173,218	78,369	111,436	373
Eastern Stanislaus	192,596	72,150	45,678	44,141	219
Shasta County	419,175	29,522	32,029	8,298	239
Sierra Valley	83,004	0	8,433	0	85
Sonoma County	409,277	34,961	15,872	9,638	259
Ventura County	222,294	60,000	28,427	29,015	135
Yolo County	268,013	101,018	48,562	39,120	105
Total Area	3,467,024	637,199	337,548	373,535	1,564
Percent of total area	100	25.8	13.7	15.1	

*The area of SIR 60-70.9 and 80-100 does not equal the area of Classes I and II because of land in Classes III, IV, and VI with an SIR greater than 60 and land in Class II with an SIR less than 60.

compasses a land area of .3 million hectares (662,000 acres), most of which is in agriculture. The soils are in the same five orders as in the eastern Stanislaus and eastern Fresno areas. Irrigated row crops (tomatoes and sugar beets) are common, as are field crops (sorghum, wheat, barley) and orchard crops (apricots, almonds, walnuts).

The soil survey report for the Shasta County area, at the north end of the Sacramento Valley, covers .4 million hectares (1 million acres). It was published in 1974 (9). Less than 3 percent of the area's land is in cultivated agriculture. Timber, brush, and rangeland occupy the remainder. Ultisols, Entisols, Inceptisols, Mollisols, Vertisols, and Alfisols are the soils mapped in this area.

The Sierra Valley area soil survey report, published in 1975 (15), includes parts of Sierra, Plumas, and Lassen Counties in northeastern California. This area is the smallest (.1 million hectares or about 205,000 acres), least populated, and has the least cultivated land of any area in my study. Soils mapped in the area are Entisols, Inceptisols, Aridisols, Mollisols, and Alfisols.

Sonoma County is located on the coast north of San Francisco. The soil survey report, published in 1972 (11), identifies six soil orders in the county: Entisols, Inceptisols, Mollisols, Vertisols, Ultisols, and Alfisols. The county's .4 million hectares (1 million acres) of land is in forest, range, and cultivated cropland. The county provides an interesting study area because of the combination of high-value crops (wine grapes), recreation, rangeland, and timber.

Table 1 summarizes each area by LCC and SIR.

Classification System Comparisons

LCC I

The LCC and SIR are different in approach and calculation but rate soil properties similarly. The results, therefore, correspond fairly well (Table 2). No Class I land rates below 60 in SIR, and 94 percent of that land has a SIR greater than 80. The average SIR for all Class I land is 91.3 (Table 3).

I expected these results because most soil scientists agree that deep, level, well-drained soils with medium textures and no

rooting restrictions are the least limiting for most agricultural crops. A few mapping units rated less than 80 because of coarse surface texture or slope are given lower ratings in SIR than in LCC. No distinction is made in SIR between irrigated and nonirrigated land use. Thus, a slope of 3 percent rates 95 under SIR but is Class I (nonirrigated) or Class II (irrigated) under LCC.

LCC II

SIR varies widely relative to Class II land. An SIR greater than 80 does not correspond well at all with Class II (Tables 2 and 3). Only 27 percent of the Class II land has an SIR greater than 80. Seventy-four percent of the Class II mapping units has an SIR greater than 60; the overall average is 68 (Table 3).

The broad distribution of SIR within Class II is due to differences in values assigned to soil properties. I can demonstrate this by examining how some characteristics of individual soil mapping units are rated and by examining the Class II soils with SIR's less than 60.

Hanford sandy loam, a deep alluvial soil, has an SIR of 95 and is Class IIe-4

Table 2. Number of soil mapping units in Classes I, II, III, IV, and VI with SIR's between 80 and 100, 60 and 79.9, and less than 60 for eight study areas in California.

Study Area	Class I			Class II				Class III				Class IV			Class VI
	SIR 80-100	SIR 60-79.9	Total	SIR 80-100	SIR 60-79.9	SIR <60	Total	SIR 80-100	SIR 60-79.9	SIR <60	Total	SIR 80-100	SIR 69-79.9	Total	SIR 60-100
Antelope Valley	13	1	14	20	11	4	35	5	10	15	30	2	1	3	1
Eastern Fresno	21	3	24	19	26	29	74	0	25	73	98	0	1	1	0
Eastern Stanislaus	15	0	15	14	24	6	44	1	16	38	55	0	2	2	0
Shasta County	8	0	8	7	21	5	33	0	6	25	31	0	1	1	0
Sierra Valley	0	0	0	0	0	0	0	0	11	7	18	0	1	1	1
Sonoma County	6	0	6	1	13	18	32	0	5	27	32	0	1	1	0
Ventura County	7	0	7	12	16	6	34	0	5	15	20	0	0	0	0
Yolo County	9	1	10	2	16	4	22	0	7	12	19	0	0	0	0
Number in total area	79	5	84	75	127	72	274	6	85	212	303	2	7	9	2
Percent of total	94	6	100	27	46	27	100	2	28	70	100	22	78	100	100

Table 3. Average SIR for each LCC in eight study areas in California.

Study Area	Class I		Class II			Class III			Class IV			Class VI
	SIR 80-100	SIR 60-79.9	SIR 80-100	SIR 60-79.9	SIR <60	SIR 80-100	SIR 60-79.9	SIR <60	SIR 80-100	SIR 60-79.9	SIR <60	SIR 60-100
Antelope Valley	94.3	68.0	88.2	69.8	52.5	88.4	69.2	48.1	90.5	69.0		64.0
Eastern Fresno	90.7	73.3	88.3	68.1	42.1	-	69.9	38.0	-	62.0		-
Eastern Stanislaus	94.1	-*	84.7	69.1	50.8	85.0	68.7	38.8	-	70.0		-
Shasta County	94.5	-	87.6	67.8	52.8	-	64.2	40.9	-	62.0		-
Sierra Valley	-	-	-	-	-	-	68.5	50.3	-	62.0		69.0
Sonoma County	90.3	-	81.0	67.3	49.5	-	64.6	39.3	-	62.0		-
Ventura County	93.7	-	87.6	68.9	51.5	-	67.6	44.7	-	-		-
Yolo County	89.8	-	81.0	68.6	47.0	-	65.3	40.9	-	-		-
SIR average	92.5	-	87.1	68.5	47.1	87.8	68.2	40.4	90.5	65.3		66.5
SIR average for class†	91.3		68.0			49.1			70.9			

*- indicates no mapping units in this class.

†These are weighted averages calculated as: $\sum_{area\ 1}^{8} \dfrac{\text{no. of mapping units on area} \times \text{average SIR for area}}{\text{total mapping units in class}}$

Table 4. Mean SIR by subclass and unit for Class II soils and numbers of each unit with SIR less than 60.

		Class II													
		Subclass e				Subclass w			Subclass s						
	Unit	1*	3	4	5	2	3	5	0	1	3	4	5	6	7
No. with SIR < 60		9	2	1	6	14	0	1	0	0	3	1	14	21	0
Total no. mapping units in capability unit		68	10	6	7	60	11	1	7	2	25	29	16	33	6
Percent with SIR < 60		13	20	17	86	23	0	100	0	0	12	3	88	64	0
Average SIR for unit		75.8	60.6	75.0	50.9	66.9	71.1	46.0	71.3	69.0	70.6	80.0	45.6	50.0	75.3
Average SIR for subclass		72.2				67.2			64.0						

*Principal soil property or limitation: 0 = coarse sandy or very gravelly substrata limiting to root penetration and moisture retention; 1 = potential or actual wind or water erosion hazard; 2 = drainage or overflow hazard; 3 = slowly or very slowly permeable subsoils or substrata; 4 = coarse or gravelly textures; 5 = fine or very fine textures; 6 = salinity or alkalinity sufficient to constitute a continuing limitation or hazard; 7 = stones, cobbles, or rocks sufficient to interfere with tillage.

because its available water-holding capacity is too low to meet Class I requirements. Factor B (surface texture) for the Hanford soil is given a 95 because of coarse texture. This is the only soil property in the case of Hanford soil that is rated below 100 by SIR. As the surface texture becomes finer or coarser than loam, SIR declines. LCC rates available water-holding capacity for the profile directly, while SIR considers it indirectly by rating surface texture and profile development. Hanford coarse sandy loam (IIs-4) has an SIR of 80, and Hanford gravelly sandy loam (IIs-4) has an SIR of 70 because of coarse surface texture. SIR gives a range of values for the three soil mapping units due to this weighting of surface texture, while all soils are in the same class, subclass, and unit within LCC.

SIR also penalizes salinity, alkalinity, and wetness, resulting in a range of ratings. The Grangeville series in Fresno County has a IIw-2 (drainage) or IIs-6 (salinity) rating in LCC for an irrigated land use. Its rating under SIR ranges from 48 for a saline-alkali phase with a high water table to 60 if the soil has a high water table and no saline or alkali problem to 72 if it is saline and alkali but has no high water table.

One or several criteria may place a soil in Class II or lower classes in LCC. Capability class does not indicate if the soil has a single or multiple limitations. SIR reflects multiple limitations as a result of the numerical reductions for each limitation. The Fresno series that is both saline and wet thus has a lower rating than the same series with only one limitation.

One disadvantage of SIR is that the specific limitation(s) is (are) not obvious as with the LCC subclass and unit designations, unless the soil survey report enumerates the values for factors A, B, C, and X. The Sonoma County soil survey report provides a good example of this.

SIR rates both Blucher loam (IIw-2 irri-gated) and Dibble clay loam (IIIe-3 irri-gated) at 65. Blucher loam is a somewhat poorly drained basin soil with stratified silt and clay substratum. Its only limitation is a high water table, shown clearly by the IIw-2 (2 represents drainage or overflow) rating. Dibble clay loam is an upland soil with a thick B2t horizon at 66 cm (26 in) and sandstone bedrock at 152 cm (60 in). Its SIR is reduced from 100 by the slope (5-9%), depth to clay B2t, and erosion hazard. The rating accounts for all three (A = 85, B = 100, C = 85, X = 90).

The LCC rating of IIIe-3 shows that erosion and slow subsoil permeability are the major problems. Making unit designations universal could improve the LCC system. Unit "3" represents slow subsoil permeability in California, but it may indicate another limitation elsewhere.

The two systems also rate effective soil depth differently. A 102-cm (40-in) effective soil depth, sufficient for Class I and II ratings, might rate as low as 40 in the A factor of SIR if a hard pan exists at 122 cm (48 in). This raises the question of why some criteria were established. A 102-cm depth may be the optimum depth for many crops, and perhaps soil depths of less than 100 cm should lower LCC ratings, but testing of this criterion and others in both systems is needed. One advantage of SIR is that soil depth is rated on a scale of 0 to 100. This permits some flexibility in the rating scheme, but these ratings have not been validated. The question of why any one soil depth gets rated in a particular way cannot be answered.

Comparisons between Class II soils by subclass and unit and their average SIR illustrates the different criteria and weightings used in the two systems (Table 4). SIR varies widely within each subclass, particularly the "s" (soil limitation) subclass. The IIe subclass includes four capability units with an overall SIR of 72.2. Only one of the units (e-5) has a majority

of the mapping units with an SIR less than 60, and 20 percent of the subclass mapping units have an SIR less than 60. Those soils with IIe-5 ratings and SIR's less than 60 are predominantely well-drained Vertisols on level to gently sloping landscapes. Clay surface textures rate 50 to 60 in the B factor. Slopes to 8 percent, a drainage class poorer than well drained, or microrelief can reduce the rating to between 40 and 50. In California this low rating is justified because of the difficulty in managing Vertisols for crops other than pasture, rice, or dryland grain crops.

Nine of the 68 IIe-1 mapping units have an SIR less than 60. The properties of these units vary widely, but all have combinations of properties that reduce their SIR to less than 60. Several have well-developed B2t horizons that reduce their A factor value and gravelly surface textures that reduce their B factor value. These properties, combined with a slope of less than 8 percent, result in an SIR less than 60.

In subclass IIw the mapping units are in three capability units. Fifteen of the 72 mapping units (21%) have an SIR less than 60. Fourteen of these units are in unit IIw-2 (w-2 represents wetness-drainage or overflow hazard). Drainage and overflow are rated in the X factor of SIR. Their values vary widely, ranging from 100 for well-drained soil to 10 for a badly water-logged soil. Most of the w-2 units are somewhat poorly drained, thus earning a low (40-80) X-factor rating. These low ratings, combined with less than desirable surface textures, result in overall ratings less than 60. Some IIw-2 ratings are as low as 39.

Only one mapping unit has a rating of IIw-5 (5 represents fine or very fine textures), and it is less than 60. This fact and the fact that 88 percent of the mapping units with IIs-5 ratings have an SIR less than 60 illustrate that the presence of fine textures in surface soils and subsoils and the effects of these fine textures on other soil properties (primarily drainage) are more severely rated in the SIR system than in the LCC system.

Subclass IIs contains 118 mapping units with an average SIR of 64.0. Thirty-three percent of these mapping units have an SIR less than 60. Most are IIs-5 and IIs-6 units.

Salinity or alkalinity is the major limitation in IIs-6 soils. SIR rates salinity or alkalinity problems more severely than LCC (Table 4). Soils affected slightly by salinity or alkalinity problems earn an X-factor rating between 60 and 95. The system does not define "slight" quantitatively (16). However, those soils are included in which the growth of most fruits and vines is curtailed but in which the effect on field crops is minimal. LCC drops a soil to Class II with slight alkalinity and a salinity less than 8 mmhos/cm at 25°C. A soil with moderate alkalinity and a salinity less than 16 mmhos/cm may be Class III. The same soil earns an X-factor rating of 30 to 60.

These low ratings, plus the effect of slight reductions in other factors, produce very low SIR values on some Class IIs-6 soils. One example comes from the eastern Fresno area soil survey report, where a Pond sandy loam (IIs-6) has an SIR of 15. This alluvial soil has a strongly developed Bt horizon starting at 20 cm (8 in) in the typical profile. It is somewhat poorly drained and affected slightly by salt and alkali. This combination of properties reduces the SIR drastically but allows the LCC to remain IIs-6.

LCC III

A few soils have SIR's greater than 60 but fall in Classes III, IV, and VI. Thirty percent of the Class III soils have SIR's greater than 60, most between 60 and 80 (Table 2).

A majority (51%) of the Class III mapping units that have an SIR greater than 60 have IIIe-1 and IIIs-4 ratings. SIR does not explicitly consider available water-holding capacity, and many soils that are Class IIIs-4 because of their low available water-holding capacity are rated only on surface texture by SIR. This may reduce the rating by no more than 10 to 20 points, leaving some mapping units with ratings greater than 60.

Many IIIe-1 mapping units are in slope classes of 8 to 15 percent or 0 to 8 percent, which places them in Class III. These broad slope classes make use of LCC difficult. Irrigated Class I soils must have slopes less than 2 percent, Class II less than 5 percent, and Class III less than 9 percent. A soil mapping unit with a 0 to 8 percent

slope phase thus includes three capability classes. Consideration should be given to narrowing the slope classes. This problem occurs in SIR, but the slope ranges in SIR are broader (0-2, 3-8, 9-15%) than in LCC. In general, SIR rates moderate slopes (<15%) less severely than LCC.

SIR does not consider climate as LCC does. Several Class III mapping units rate 90 to 100 because SIR does not rate length of growing season and potential or actual evapotranspiration.

LCC IV, VI

A very small number of soils in Classes IV and VI have an SIR greater than 60. These are soils on slopes greater than 15 percent that fall into Classes IV and VI (irrigated) but have no other problems. SIR thus gives them 100 for the A, B, and X factors and 80 to 95 for the C factor. A few soils are gravelly. They fall into Class IVs-0 because of their low available water-holding capacity. One mapping unit is Class IV because of poor drainage, and one is Class VI because of climate.

Implications of Differences

Differences between the two systems do not indicate that one system or the other is necessarily better or that either classification is wrong. Obviously, though, there are major differences in what soil properties each system evaluates and how the properties are weighted.

While parallel, the two systems are not identical and should not be used interchangeably. In using either system to define prime agricultural land, careful consideration must be given to these differences. Neither system was developed to classify prime agricultural land, and an interpretation of either one for this purpose may extend the system beyond its intended use. Both systems were developed to group soils with similar management problems for interpretive purposes. Both do that well.

Flexibility in SIR makes it a valuable tool for land use planners and soil scientists. Weightings can reflect a particular set of soil conditions. For example, the A factor permits a range of values that reflect rooting depth. The index can thus be calibrated to the state's needs.

A major disadvantage of SIR is the problem of identifying the limiting factors that are signified by class, subclass, and unit symbols in LCC. This can be overcome by including a tabulation of A, B, C, and X values in soil survey reports that use SIR.

Major management decisions in agriculture and several California laws related to

agricultural land preservation are being based wholly or in part on SIR or LCC. Both systems should be tested more. It would be useful to know the relationship between crop yields, energy and water use efficiencies, and economic returns (12) on soils with different capability ratings. Work is urgently needed also to insure that the values used in the ratings represent reality rather than arbitrary divisions.

REFERENCES CITED

1. Andrews, Wells F. 1972. *Soil survey of Yolo County, California*. Soil Cons. Serv., U.S. Dept. Agr., Washington, D.C. 102 pp.
2. Arkley, Rodney J. 1964. *Soil survey of the Eastern Stanislaus area, California*. Soil Cons. Serv., U.S. Dept. Agr., Washington, D.C. 160 pp. and maps.
3. Barron, James C., and Thomas E. Dickinson. 1975. *Social, economic, and institutional constraints affecting production and the reservation of agricultural land in the USA*. Agr. Environ. 2: 147-163.
4. Collins, Richard C. 1976. *Agricultural land preservation in a land use planning perspective*. J. Soil and Water Cons. 31(5): 182-190.
5. Edwards, Ronald D., Daniel F. Rabey, and Richard W. Kover. 1970. *Soil survey of the Ventura area, California*. Soil Cons. Serv., U.S. Dept. Agr., Washington, D.C. 148 pp. and maps.
6. Hannah, A. E. 1975. *Land and food: An appraisal*. J. Soil and Water Cons. 30(6): 264-267.
7. Hansen, David E., and Seymour I. Schwartz. 1976. *Prime land preservation: The California Land Conservation Act*. J. Soil and Water Cons. 31(5): 198-204.
8. Huntington, Gordon L. 1971. *Soil survey of the Eastern Fresno area, California*. Soil Cons. Serv., U.S. Dept. Agr., Washington, D.C. 323 pp. and maps.
9. Klaseen, T. A., and D. K. Ellison. 1974. *Soil survey of the Shasta County area, California*. Soil Cons. Serv., U.S. Dept. Agr., Washington, D.C. 160 pp. and maps.
10. Klingebiel, A. A., and P. H. Montgomery. 1961. *Land capability classification*. Agr. Handbook No. 210. Soil Cons. Serv., U.S. Dept. Agr., Washington, D.C. 21 pp.
11. Miller, Vernon C. 1972. *Soil survey of Sonoma County, California*. Soil Cons. Serv., U.S. Dept. Agr., Washington, D.C. 188 pp. and maps.
12. Patterson, G. T., and E. E. Mackintosh. 1976. *Relationship between soil capability class and economic returns from grain corn production in southwestern Ontario*. Can. J. Soil Sci. 56: 167-175.
13. Raup, Philip M. 1976. *What is prime land?* J. Soil and Water Cons. 31(5): 180-182.
14. Schwartz, S. I., and D. E. Hansen. 1975. *Two methods for preserving agricultural land at the urban fringe: Use-value assessment and transferable development rights*. Agr. Environ. 2: 165-180.
15. Sketchley, Harold R. 1975. *Soil survey of Sierra Valley area, California, parts of Sierra, Plumas, and Lassen Counties*. Soil Cons. Serv., U.S. Dept. Agr., Washington, D.C. 121 pp. and maps.
16. Storie, R. Earl. 1964. *Handbook of soil evaluation*. Univ. Calif., Berkeley. 225 pp.
17. U.S. Department of Agriculture, Soil Conservation Service. 1975. *Guide for placing soils in land capability classification in California*. Davis, Calif. 5 pp.
18. Woodruff, George A., William J. McCoy, and Wayne B. Sheldon. 1970. *Soil survey of the Antelope Valley area, California*. Soil Cons. Serv., U.S. Dept. Agr., Washington, D.C. 187 pp. and maps. □

16: A NUMERICAL ASSESSMENT OF SOIL SURVEY DATA FOR AGRICULTURAL MANAGEMENT AND PLANNING

H. Schreier and M. A. Zulkifli

This paper demonstrates how soil survey data, selected climatic indices and numerical techniques can be used to arrive at soil interpretations relevant to management and planning. Numerical cluster analysis, applied to soil survey data, is used to obtain soil management groups. These are then related to land use and performance data to arrive at quantitative suitability assessments. Agricultural suitability is emphasized in the present case, but the method can also be used to arrive at management groups and suitability ratings for other land uses. Since the assessments are quantitative, they can form a basis for economic analysis and will facilitate management decisions.

SOIL SURVEY APPLICATIONS

General soil surveys have been carried out for much of the populated area in the western world, but the use of the survey data has been less than its potential. It appears that many users find the information provided by general soil surveys too general, outdated, or in a form not readily useful and understandable for decision making in management and planning or for economic assessments (Young, 1973; Miller, 1978; Beckett and Bie, 1978).

Originally soil surveys were narrowly defined and were aimed primarily at providing information relating to agricultural management. In recent years the non-agricultural uses of soil survey data have been increasing, particularly with regard to urban planning, engineering, waste disposal and recreation (Beatty et al., 1979; Davidson, 1980; McCormack and Johnson, 1982). These users demand more sophisticated and specific soil information which would include knowledge of the accuracy and variability of the survey, alternatives which would overcome limitations, and most of all more detailed interpretations. Often such interpretations cannot readily be made from traditional soil survey data and require knowledge of other soil parameters and historical information on soil performance and behaviour.

Continuous urban growth and increasing demands for natural resources have created pressure on the land resources even in Canada. The problem is particularly apparent when dealing with land quality near urban centres. Land use decisions are being made without taking into consideration the national or regional impact, the scarcity of certain types of land, and long term consequences and options for multiple and renewable use. Decisions are being made on the basis of purely economic or political considerations with only a very shallow look at the biophysical data base. To some extent this is the result of problems relating to the form and availability of the biophysical data.

Dept of Soil Science, University of British Columbia, Vancouver, B.C. V6T 1W5, Canada

METHOD

Numerical methods were applied to soils data from the Lower Fraser Valley, the most important agricultural area in British Columbia. 103 different soils were classified using factor and cluster analysis. In order to demonstrate how raw data that is already available can be analysed and applied, use was intentionally made of data from existing published soil surveys. The resulting soil groups were then related to climate and soil productivity for various crops.

Table 1. Soil and site parameters used for soil data bank

PARAMETERS	UNITS	TOP HORIZON >10 cm THICK	HORIZON RESPONSIBLE FOR PORE SIZE DISCONTINUITY
1 Texture	Classes 0-14	✓	✓
2 Parent Material	Classes 1-12	✓	✓
3 CEC	meq 100 g^{-1}	✓	✓
4 Carbon content	%	✓	✓
5 Structure	Classes 1-8	✓	✓
6 Consistency	Classes 1-4	✓	✓
7 Hue	Classes 1-4	✓	✓
8 Value	Classes 1-5	✓	✓
9 Chroma	Classes 1-6	✓	✓
10 Water holding capacity	Classes 1-7	✓	✓
11 Depth to horizon	cm	✓	✓
12 Depth of organic layer	cm	✓	✓
13 Drainage	Classes 1-6	At modal site	
14 Salinity	mS cm^{-1}	At modal site	

(for parameter 12: At modal site)

Soil survey and climatic data

Quantitative and categoric data for all modal soils mapped in the Langley-Vancouver map area (Luttmerding, 1980) were placed in a computer data file. Of the many soil and site parameters listed in the soil survey report, 25 were initially chosen for the analysis (Table 1). They can be divided into site parameters, parameters in the top horizon (>10cm in depth), and parameters relating to the horizon responsible for pore size discontinuity. Three criteria were used in the parameter selection: 1. soil parameters had to be fairly permanent and not readily altered by management (this eliminated such soil chemical parameters as N, P, K, Ca and acidity); 2. they had to be important in influencing productivity; 3. the parameters had to be variable to be good indicators. The parameters listed in Table 1 were selected as a result of a factor analysis and from consultation with literature sources such as Sakar et al. 1966, Whyte 1976, and Beek 1981.

The climatic capabilities for each modal soil were determined on the basis of the Agricultural Climatic Capability Map (Coligado, 1980) which relied on the following climatic indices: 1. Frost-free period (consecutive days above O$^{\circ}$C); 2. moisture deficit or surplus (difference between total precipitation and total potential evapotranspiration from May 1st to September 30; (3) effective growing degree days (average accumulated departure of 1°C of the daily mean temperature above 5°C). This divided the soils into the three climatic capability classes provided in Table 2.

Table 2. Definition of climatic capability for agriculture in study area

AGRICULTURE CLIMATIC CAPABILITY CLASS	EGDD	FFP	CMS/PE ratio
1	825	150	0.34
2	736-825	120-150	0.35-0.55
3	650-735	100-119	0.56-0.75

EGDD Effective growing degree days above 5°C.

FFP Frost-free period in days.

CMS/PE Climatic moisture surplus (mm)/potential evapotranspiration (mm).

Numerical techniques

The soil was analysed using factor and cluster analysis techniques. Factor analysis (Cattel, 1965) is a method which describes complex inter-relationships between many parameters in terms of the smallest number of factors. This determines which parameters are correlated and how much each factor contributes to the total variance, and thus facilitates the selection of parameters used for the subsequent grouping with cluster analysis. Cluster analysis is a process by which the degree of similarity between units is determined using a multi-parameter data base. The average distance cluster analysis described by Ward (1963) was used and the similarity between soil types in terms of physical and chemical properties was measured using n-dimensional distances determined via the Pythagorean Theorem and matrix algebra. The computer program which was used is described by Patterson and Whitacker, 1982.

Productivity data

As noted by Odell (1958) it is difficult to obtain accurate yield data for any one soil and each acquisition method has significant advantages and disadvantages. Young (1973, 1978) noted that among western farmers there are relatively small differences in management, and in order to be competitive efforts have to be made to optimize management techniques and to use superior cultivation practices. As a consequence, differences in management are probably more pronounced in growing different crops and cultivating different soils. Productivity data from different soils and crops were obtained from three sources: farm interviews, research trials and experts' estimates.

One hundred farmers, identified by the B.C. Ministry of Agriculture personnel as top producers, were interviewed in all parts of the test area. Records were established in terms of farm location, size, type of soils cultivated, soil and crop management practices, and yields for most of the crops grown in the valley. Research trial data were only available from one station covering two crops on one soil series. To verify the farm yield data a comparison was made between the actual farm yield and yield estimates made by a team of agricultural experts in the valley in 1975. Out of seven crops examined, good relationships between actual and estimated yields were obtained for corn, maize, potatoes, and grain crops. Actual farm yields were slightly higher than the experts' estimates for beans and peas, while the reverse occurred for raspberry and strawberry yields. The farm interviews provided productivity data for 50 different soil series and 45 soil complexes.

Table 3. Parameters and class units used for analysis

Texture Classes

0	Organic
1	Heavy Clay
2	Clay
3	Silty Clay
4	Sandy Clay
5	Clay Loam
6	Silty Clay Loam
7	Sandy Clay Loam
8	Silt
9	Silt Loam
10	Loam
11	Sandy Loam
12	Loamy Sand
13	Sand
14	Gravelly Sand

Parent Material Classes

1	Colluvium
2	Outwash
3	Alluvium
4	Aeolian
5	Lacustrine
6	Glacio-Lacustrine
7	Glacial Till
8	Glacio-Marine
9	Marine
10	Igneous Bedrock
11	Sedimentary Bedrock
12	Organic

Available Water Holding Capacity

1	very high	0.20 cm cm^{-1}
2	high	0.17 cm cm^{-1}
3	mod. high	0.15 cm cm^{-1}
4	moderate	0.12 cm cm^{-1}
5	mod. poor	0.10 cm cm^{-1}
6	poor	0.08 cm cm^{-1}
7	very poor	0.05 cm cm^{-1}

Drainage Classes

1	rapid
2	well
3	mod. well
4	imperfect
5	poor
6	very poor

Depth of Organic Layer

cm

Depth to Pore Size Discontinuity

cm

Organic Matter Content
%

Salinity
mS cm^{-1}

RESULTS

Prior to determining the degree of similarity amongst the 103 modal soils in the study area a parameter selection was made via factor analysis and from literature sources. This is listed in Table 3. The following nine parameters were found to be essential for separating the soils in the study area: drainage, texture-S (surface horizon >10cm thickness), texture-D (horizon responsible for pore size discontinuity), parent material, available water holding capacity, depth of organic layer, organic matter content, depth to pore size discontinuity and salinity. The horizon responsible for pore size discontinuity was selected where major textural and structural changes occurred within each modal profile. Drainage is a qualitative and inferred property and can be altered by management. It was included in this study due to lack of more precise measurements on infiltration and percolation rates. Also in many cases soil surveyors in Canada tend to select the modal soil profile within a mapping unit at an undisturbed location, ignoring the fact that cultivated areas within the unit might have very different soils due to the influence of management. Since almost all modal soils in the study area reflect natural conditions, drainage was included so as to be able to compare natural soil conditions. However, other more precise measurements relating to drainage should be used wherever available. Survey data on percent coarse fragments was incomplete and thus could not be included in the analysis.

The subsequent grouping of soils with cluster analysis was accomplished in a two-step process indicated in Table 4. First the degree of similarity amongst soils was determined on the basis of drainage, texture-S, texture-D and parent material. This provides the first level of discrimination of six basic groups (A-F). Each group was then further separated by cluster analysis using combinations of the following parameters: water holding capacity, depth to pore size discontinuity, depth of organic layer, organic matter content, salinity and texture. In this way 25 soil management groups were extracted from the cluster dendrogram and each group contains soils which are similar in the majority of parameters used in the grouping process. A schematic illustration of the results is provided in Figure 1 and a summary of the conditions at level 1 is provided in Table 5.

The validity of the soil management groups was examined in four ways:

(1) Statistical significance within and between soil groups

To show that the individual soil groups are indeed unique a Mann Whitney U-Test (Siegel 1956) was used to compare the parameters within and between each group. The parameters which are significant discriminators at level 1 are given in Figure 2 and in all subsequent tests at level 2 a significant difference between soil groups was observed in a least one of the parameters used for the grouping. The individual soil groups therefore differ significantly from one another.

(2) Relationships between soil groups and genetic soil classification

The genetic soil classification at the subgroup level (CSSC 1978) was tabulated for each individual soil and soil group. As can be seen from Table 6, a fairly good separation was obtained. All soils in Groups A, B and D are Podzols, Luvisols, Brunisols and Regosols, while Groups C, E and F are dominated by Gleysols and Organic soils. Not more than four different subgroups were represented in each cluster group.

(3) Relationship between soil groups and agricultural capability

For each modal soil location, agricultural capability classes based on the Canada Land Inventory Scheme (McCormack 1976) were determined. Both the unimproved and improved ratings (Kent and Cotic 1982) were listed in Table 6. The numbers refer to the capability classes (1-7) and the letters related to the limiting factors or capability subclasses. Again, a fairly good separation was obtained between the cluster groups and only in one of the 25 groups did the capability range over a four class interval (Group E3). In 20 of 25 cases the capability range was less than or equal to two capability classes. Also the subclasses indicate that drought is the main limiting factor for Group A while excess water was the main limitation for soils in Groups C to F.

(4) Relationships between soil groups and productivity data

Crop yields were summarized in Table 7 for each level 2 soil group. Based on data from 100 interviews of top farmers it quickly became evident that not all soil groups were used for cultivation of all crop types. This implies that some soils are unsuited for a specific crop or they are not utilized because of tradition, lack of agricultural infrastructure, socio-economic reasons or insufficient density in interview data. Given the many factors that influence productivity data, statistical yield differences between all soil groups would not be expected but, as can be seen from Table 7, the yields of cauliflower, beans and raspberries are sensitive to differences in soil conditions. Other crops such as potatoes, peas, strawberries and maize are less sensitive and it appears that management overrides soil differences.

Table 4 Process used in grouping modal soils into management units

SOIL MANAGEMENT GROUP	PARAMETERS USED TO DIFFERENTIATE BETWEEN SOILS AT LEVEL 1	SOIL MANAGEMENT SUB GROUPS	PARAMETERS USED TO DIFFERENTIATE BETWEEN SOILS AT LEVEL 2
A		A_1-A_4	Water holding capacity Texture-D Parent Material
B		B_1-B_4	Water holding capacity Texture-D Depth to pore size discontinuity
C		C_1-C_4	Organic matter content Texture-D Parent Material
D	Texture-S Texture-D Drainage Parent Material	D_1-D_2	Drainage Water holding capacity Depth to pore size discontinuity Texture-D
E		E_1-E_5	Water holding capacity Texture-D Organic matter content Salinity
F		F_1-F_6	Texture-S Depth to pore size discontinuity Organic matter content Water holding capacity Salinity

Texture-S = Texture of surface horizon > 10cm in depth

Texture-D = Texture of horizon responsible for pore size discontinuity

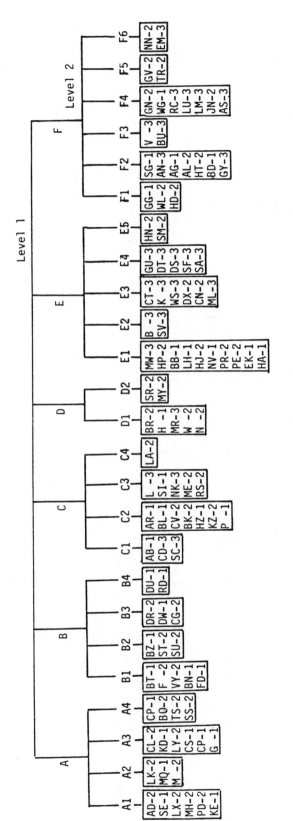

Level 1: Based on drainage, texture-S, texture-D, and parent material
Level 2: Based on one of the following parameters : depth to pore size discontinuity, depth of organic layer,
         water holding capacity, organic matter content, drainage, texture, and salinity.
Level 3: Based on climatic capability classes for agriculture, classes 1-3.

Letters = Soil series identifications
Numbers = Climatic capability classes

Figure 1. Soil management groups derived via cluster analysis.

291

Table 5 Soil conditions of soil management groups at level 1

NO OF SOIL CLUSTER GROUP	SOIL SERIES INCLUDED	DRAINAGE CATEGORY	CODE	TEXTURE-S CATEGORY	CODE	TEXTURE-D CATEGORY	CODE	PARENT MATERIAL DOMINANT CATEGORY	CODE	SOIL ORDERS INCLUDED IN GROUP
A	19	rapid to mod. well	1-3	silt loam sandy loam Sand	9-13	sandy loam sand gravelly sand	11-14	outwash alluvium aeolian	2-8	Podzols Luvisols Brunisols Regeosols
B	13	mod. well to imperfect	3-4	silt loam	9-11	silt loam sandy loam sand gravelly sand	9-14	outwash alluvium lacustrine glacial till	2-7	Podzols Luvisols Brunisols
C	17	poor to very poor	5-6	clay loam sandy clay loam loam	5-10	clay sandy clay silty clay loam	2-6	alluvium glacio-marine marine	3-9	Gleysols
D	7	mod. well to imperfect	3-4	clay loam sandy clay loam sand	5-13	heavy clay sandy clay silty clay loam	1-6	glacio-marine marine	8-9	Podzols Luvisols
E	25	poor to very poor	5-6	silty clay loam clay loam loam loamy sand	6-12	silt loam sandy loam sand	9-13	alluvium lacustrine	3-5	Gleysols
F	22	poor to very poor	5-6	organic heavy clay silty clay	0-3	organic silty clay silt loam	3-13	alluvium organic	3-13	Gleysols Organic Soils

Table 6. Soil classification and capability ratings of soil management groups.

SOIL GROUP	# OF SOIL SERIES	GENETIC CLASSIFICATION	AGRICULTURAL CAPABILITY RATINGS	
			UNIMPROVED	IMPROVED
A1	6	Orthic Humo-Ferric Podzol	2 (A)	1
A2	3	Eluviated Eutric Brunisol	1-2(A)	1
A3	6	Orthic Humo-Ferric Podzol Eluviated Dystric Brunisol Orthic Regosol Brunisolic Gray Luvisol	3-4(A,P,F)	2-4(A,P,F)
A4	4	Orthic, Duric, and Ortstein Humo Ferric Podzol Orthic Regosol	3-5(A,P,F)	2-4(A,P,F)
B1	5	Gleyed Sombric Brunisol Gleyed Eluviated Melanic Brunisol Gleyed Gray and Gray-Brown Luvisol	2 (W)	1
B2	3	Duric Ferro-Hunic Podzol	3-4(P,A,T,P)	2-4(T,P,A)
B3	3	Gleyed Ferro Humic Podzol Gleyed Ortstein Humo Ferric Podzol Gleyed Eluviated Melanic Brunisol	2-3(A,W,D)	1-2(A,D)
B4	2	Orthic Humo Ferric Podzol	2 (A,T)	1-2
C1	3	Humic Luvic Gleysol Orthic Humic Gleysol	4 (W,D)	3 (D,W)
C2	7	Rego Humic & Orthic Humic Gleysol Humic Luvic Gleysol	3-4(W,D)	2-3(W,D)
C3	5	Humic Luvic Gleysol Rego & Orthic Humic Gleysol	3-5(W,D,I)	2-4(W,D,I)
C4	1	Humic Luvic Gleysol	3 (W,D)	2 (W,D)
D1	5	Gleyed Podzolic Gray Luvisol Gleyed Eluviated Melanic Brunisol Gleyed & Luvisolic Humo-Ferric Podzol Podzolic Gray Luvisol	2 (W,D,A)	1-2(W,D)
D2	2	Gleyed Ortstein Humo Ferric Podzol	2-3(W,D,A)	1-2(A,D)
E1	10	Orthic and Rego Humic Gleysol Rego Gleysol	3-4(W,A,D)	2-3(W,A,D)
E2	2	Rego & Rego Humic Gleysol, saline phase	5 (W,N)	3-4(N,W)
E3	5	Orthic & Rego Gleysol Rego Humic Gleysol	2-5(W,D)	1-3(W,D)
E4	6	Orthic Humic Gleysol, saline phase Rego Gleysol, saline phase	3-4(W,N)	2-3(W,N)
E5	2	Rego & Orthic Gleysol	3 (W,A,F)	2 (W,F,A)
F1	3	Gleyed Gray Luvisol Orthic & Rego Humic Gleysol	3-4(W,D)	2-3(W,D)
F2	5	Orthic & Rego Gleysol, peaty phase	4-6(W,I,D)	3-5(W,I,D)
F3	2	Rego Gleysol, saline and peaty phases	4-5(W,N)	3 (W,N)
F4	9	Ferric Mesisol & Humisol	05 (W,F)	03-04(W,L)
F5	2	Typic Fibrisol	06-07(W,F)	03-04(W,L)
F6	2	Rego & Rego Humic Gleysol (org. stratification)	4 (W)	2-3(W,N)

* Agricultural capabilities of modal soil profiles (classes 1-7) based on Canada Land Inventory (CLI), McCormack 1976 and improved CLI-ratings by Kenk and Cotic (1982).

Letters refer to limiting factors:

A = Aridity   N - Salts
D = Undesirable structure   P = Stoniness
F = Low fertility   T = Topography-slope
I = Inundation flooding   W = Excess water

Table 7. Crop yields in relation to soil management groups.

CLUSTER GROUP	# OF FARMS (n)	AREA (ha)	POTATOES RANGE	POTATOES x̄	CAULIFLOWER RANGE	CAULIFLOWER x̄	BEANS RANGE	BEANS x̄	PEAS RANGE	PEAS x̄	RASPBERRIES RANGE	RASPBERRIES x̄	STRAWBERRIES RANGE	STRAWBERRIES x̄	CORN RANGE	CORN x̄
A1	14	315	ND		9-16	13	10-12	11	5	5	8-12	11	10-12	11	ND	54
A2	5	25	ND		ND		15	15	5-6	5	ND		ND		48-56	56
A3	8	141	ND		12	12	15	15	5-8	6	10	10	10-11	11	56	
A4	5	28	40	40	11	11	ND		ND		ND				47	47
B1	28	357	36	36	ND		12-15	14	5-8	6	ND		11	11	43-69	51
B2	–		ND		ND		ND		ND		ND		ND		ND	
B3	2	12	ND		11-12	11	ND		ND		ND		11	11	ND	
B4	3	21			9-12	10	10-15	13	5	5	10-11	10	11-12	11	56	56
C1	1	51	36	36	ND		ND		ND		ND		ND		51	
C2	11	247	ND		ND		13		5-8	6	ND		ND		42-72	53
C3	9	422	34-36	35	11	11	7-11	9	5-6	5	ND		11	11	34-49	40
C4	–		ND		ND		ND		ND		ND		ND		ND	
D1	2	8	45	45	11	11	ND		ND		9	9	11	11	ND	
D2	1	8	40	40	ND		ND		ND		ND		11	11	ND	
E1	5	46	ND		9	9	10	10	ND		8-10	9	10-12	11	45-56	49
E2	3	72	ND		11		NO	7	ND		ND		10-12	12	ND	
E3	27	579	34-72	41	8-9	9	8-11	10	4-8	6	ND		6-11	10	34-63	48
E4	29	1258	28-5	45	ND		7-11	10	5-6	6	ND		7-11	9	34-63	47
E5	6	870	ND		8-11	9	12	12	4-8	6	8-11	9	5-11		58	58
F1	2	13	ND		ND		ND		ND		ND		ND		47	47
F2	7	99	ND		ND		ND		6-8	7	ND		ND		47-67	55
F3	18	259	27-56	40	ND		8-10	9	5-6	6	ND		9-11	10	36-56	48
F4	34	714	27-56	39	9	9	10	10	ND		ND		8-12	10	45-67	51
F5	1	6	ND		ND		ND		ND		ND		ND		56	56
F6	12	175	45	45	ND		ND		ND		ND		ND		47-56	50

n = # of farm interviews for productivity data base   ND = None of the interviewed farmers grew the specific crop

area = Cultivated area covered by farm interviews (ha)

Although only a few of the yields were found to be statistically different between the soil groups, some general trends were clearly evident. Cauliflower, beans and raspberries showed higher yields in the coarser-textured and better-drained soils (A1-4) and lower average yields were observed in the D-F soil groups. Raspberries, which are particularly sensitive to poor drainage, showed a slight decrease in average yields from A to E with no data for groups C and F. Indeed none of these latter soils are cultivated for raspberries because they are unsuited and the management input needed to arrive at average yields would be considerable. Although the yield differences are small and variable, the overall trend shows that the soil groups are useful in terms of determining management problems and suitability.

Figure 2. Results of significance test of soil management groups at level 1

SOIL CLUSTER GROUPS

B	C	D	E	F	
DRAINAGE	DRAINAGE TEXTURE-S TEXTURE-D	DRAINAGE TEXTURE-D	DRAINAGE TEXTURE-S	DRAINAGE TEXTURE-S TEXTURE-D PARENT MATERIAL	A
	DRAINAGE TEXTURE-S TEXTURE-D	TEXTURE-D	DRAINAGE	DRAINAGE TEXTURE-S PARENT MATERIAL	B
		DRAINAGE PARENT MATERIAL	TEXTURE-D	TEXTURE-S PARENT MATERIAL	C
			DRAINAGE TEXTURE-D	DRAINAGE TEXTURE-S PARENT MATERIAL	D
				DRAINAGE TEXTURE-S	E

TEXTURE-S = SURFACE TEXTURE

TEXTURE-D = TEXTURE OF HORIZON RESPONSIBLE FOR PORE SIZE DISCONTINUITY

RESULTS OF MANN-WHITNEY U-TEST AT $\alpha = 0.05$

DISCUSSION

A quantitative relationship between soil groups and yield cannot be expected because management plays a significant role and, in many cases, soil problems can be overcome by appropriate management practices. This is evident when comparing the yield data for potatoes, peas, strawberries and maize, where no trends were observed and where average yields showed small overall variation. However, the scheme does provide a basis for management input in that the properties of each soil group are similar and each group is unique. Consequently different management practices should be used to arrive at the average yields. We assume that the top farmers are using the most appropriate management technique in order to arrive at the average yields indicated in Table 7.

The yield data provides a standard of actual production values for each soil group and this provides a good basis for economic assessments. Recommendations for optimum soil management can then be derived from the farmers, extension personnel, and economists and their consensus on the best management practice for a specific soil can then be extended to all other soils in the same soil management group.

The method developed in this study provides a good sorting mechanism for large numbers of soil survey data. The programmes are relatively easy and inexpensive to run and can be applied to standard soil survey data. A two-level grouping was found to be useful because direct clustering based on all parameters did not produce soil groups which were entirely unique due to compensating factors in the multidimensional array. Also not all parameters are of equal importance; a hierarchy has certain thresholds and the same parameters should not be used to separate the hierarchy at all levels.

Finally it would be possible to further separate the 25 soil management groups into three subclasses on the basis of agricultural climatic capability. The number accompanying the soil series abbreviations in Figure 1 indicates the climatic subclass for a particular soil. Indeed one would expect a difference in yields for crops growing on the same soil but in different climatic subclasses, and this could be used as a guideline for suitability assessments. Soils in climatic capability class 1 should be better suited than the same soil in class 2 or 3 but unfortunately this study could not demonstrate this trend on the basis of the yield data available, partially because it is almost impossible to obtain reliable yield data for every soil series in a soil survey mapping area.

CONCLUSIONS

(1) Advantages of using numerical techiques: Different soils can be sorted into groups based on physical and chemical parameters. The method is simple, rapid and flexible and allows the use of different soil parameters at different levels in the grouping hierarchy. In the present study drainage, texture and parent material were used for a first level separation and water holding capacity, depth to pore size discontinuity, organic matter content, depth of organic layer, salinity and texture were used for a second level grouping. These parameters are the most critical for management in the study area but parameter emphasis can readily be altered to suit conditions in other areas.

(2) Significance of soil management groups: The soil management groups obtained in this study are unique in terms of their overall chemical and physical properties. Soil members in any one group have properties which are similar and consequently should be managed in a similar fashion. The validity and usefulness of the soil groups were proven by using significance tests and by relating the soil groups to soil classifications, agricultural capability ratings and yield data.

Relationship between soil groups and yields proved to be useful for cauliflower, beans and raspberries which showed a trend from higher to lower average yields moving from soil group A to F. Other crops did not show significant yield variations between soil groups and this is attributed to management which in many cases can override deficiencies and differences in soil conditions. The method of separating soils and relating them to yield is most useful because it provides a guideline for economic assessment and suitability rating without having to derive complex quantitative cause and effect relationships.

ACKNOWLEDGEMENTS

This research has been funded by B.C. Science Council Grant 22. Data and information for the project were provided by members of the B.C. Ministry of Agriculture (P. Bertrand, C. Wood) and the B.C. Ministry of the Environment, Terrestrial Studies Branch (H. Luttmerding and Dr. M. Sondheim). The help and assistance of Ms T. D. Nguyen, Department of Soil Science, U.B.C., are gratefully acknowledged.

REFERENCES

Beatty, M.T, Petersen, G.W. and Swindale, L.S. 1979 Planning the uses and management of land. Am. Soc. Agronomy Ser. 21. Soil Sci. Soc. of Am. Inc.

Beckett, P.H.T. and Bie, S.W. 1978 Use of soil and land system maps to provide soil information in Australia. Div. of Soils, Tech. Paper 33. CSIRO

Beek, K.J. 1981 From soil survey interpretations to land evaluations. Part 2. From the present to the future. Soil Survey and Land Evaluation 1: 18-25

Canada Soil Survey Committee 1978 The Canadian system of soil classification. Canada Dept. of Agriculture

Cattel, B. 1965 Factor analysis - introduction to essentials. Biometrics 21: 190-215

Coligado, M.C. 1980 Climatic capability maps for agriculture. Air Management Branch 926/SE. Ministry of Environment, Victoria, B.C.

Davidson, D.A. 1980 Soils and land use planning. Longman

Kenk, E. and Cotic, I. 1982 Land capability for agriculture in British Columbia. Tech. Paper, Terrestrial Studies Branch, Ministry of Environment, Victoria, B.C.

Luttmerding, H.A. 1980 Soil of the Langley-Vancouver Map area. R.A.B. Bulletin 18. Ministry of the Environment

McCormack, D.E. and Johnson, R.W. 1982 Soil potential for on site sewage disposal in Leon County, Florida. Soil Survey and Land Evaluation, 2: 2-8

Miller, F. 1978 Soil survey under pressure: the Maryland experience. J. Soil and Water Conservation 33: 104-111

McCormack, R.J. 1976 The Canada Land Inventory. Land capability for agriculture. CLI - Lands Directorate

Odell, R.T. 1958 Soil survey interpretation - yield predictions. Soil Sci. Soc. Am. Proc. 2: 157-160

Patterson, M. and Whitacker, R. 1982 UBC - C Group hierarchical cluster analysis. Univ of British Columbia Computer Center

Sarkar, P.K., Bidwell, O.W. and Marcus, L.F. 1966 Selection of characteristics for numerical classification of soils. Soil Sci. Soc. Am. Proc. 30: 269-272

Siegel, S. 1956 Nonparametric Statistics. McGraw Hill, N.Y., 116-127

Ward, J. 1963 Hierarchical grouping to optimize an objective function. Am. Stat. Ass. 58: 236-274

Whyte, R.O. 1976 Land and Land Appraisal. J.W. Junk Publ.

Young, A. (1973) Soil survey procedure in land development planning. Geogr. J. 138: 53-64

Young, A. (1978) Recent advances in the survey and evaluation of land resources. Progr. in Phys. Geogr. 2: 462-479

17: THE PREDICTION OF SCOTS PINE GROWTH IN NORTH-EAST SCOTLAND USING READILY ASSESSABLE SITE CHARACTERISTICS

A. Cook, M. N. Court, and D. A. MacLeod

Department of Soil Science, University of Aberdeen

Summary

The growth of Scots pine was measured at 214 0·01 ha sample plots in two areas in west Aberdeenshire, Strathdon and Ballater, with similar physical environments. The following site variables were assessed, some from available maps and aerial photographs and others from single site visits: rainfall, altitude, slope, aspect, geomorphic shelter, soil parent material, major soil group, vegetation type and topographic position. Regression equations to predict growth were computed for each locality and those derived from Strathdon were tested at Ballater to assess the feasibility of extrapolation. At Ballater local yield class could be predicted with an accuracy of ±0·9 m³/ha/annum, but at Strathdon the level of prediction (±1·8 to 2·7 m³/ha/annum) is too low to be of practical significance. Extrapolation of the Strathdon equations to Ballater results in a gross overestimate of yield class, which is attributed to wide differences in growth: site factor relationships between the two areas. It appears that the high inherent variability of the Scottish uplands precludes the development of predictive equations of sufficient accuracy which can be applied over a reasonably extensive area. A physiographic approach to land evaluation may be more relevant to the needs of forestry.

Introduction

Widespread use has been made of regression analysis for the prediction of forest productivity. The technique was developed for the assessment of forest site productivity by Coile (1935) in North America and its further development has been reviewed by Coile (1952), Ralston (1964) and Rennie (1963). It has been successfully used by Page (1970) for the prediction of the growth of Sitka spruce (*Picea sitchensis* (Bong.) Carr.), Douglas fir (*Pseudotsuga taxifolia*, Rehd.) and Japanese larch (*Larix Kaempferi* (Lambert) Carriere).

The method involves the derivation of regression equations between paired measurements of tree growth and site variables, which are then used to predict growth in areas that are either unplanted or where the stands are too young to be measured directly. Site variables may be essentially qualitative or quantitative in nature. For example, soil series, physiographic and vegetation classes fall into the first category: these constitute the basis of mapping systems whereby the landscape is divided into units which are relatively homogeneous and before they can be used in regression equations they must be expressed in quantitative terms (see "Statistical analysis" section). Variables falling into the second category consist of specific attributes of the environment, which are quantitatively measured. Recorded data can be used directly in regression analysis, so that subjective evaluation is eliminated. A difficulty in their application to site mapping is that the delineation of their spatial distribution is laborious and time-consuming unless they are closely correlated with features discernible on the land surface such as vegetation and topography.

In the present study an evaluation has been mad of the practical application of regression analysis to the prediction of Scots pine (*Pinus sylvestris* L.) growth in north-east Scotland. Scots pine was selected for study on account of the distribution of measurable stands over a fairly wide range of environmental conditions in north-east Scotland. The selection of site variables was based in the first instance on their significance for pine growth as deduced by Adu (1968) in the Upper Don Basin, west Aberdeenshire. Since detailed expensive methods of land evaluation are rarely justified for even moderately extensive forms of land use like forestry, variables such as soil nutrient levels, which require intensive sampling (Blyth, 1974) and laboratory analysis, have not been considered. Preference has been given to variables which could be assessed by interpretation of existing topographic, soil and geological maps and aerial photographs and by single site visits. With these criteria in mind four qualitative variables (soil parent material, major soil group, vegetation type and topographic position) and five quantitative ones (rainfall, altitude, slope, aspect and geomorphic shelter) were chosen.

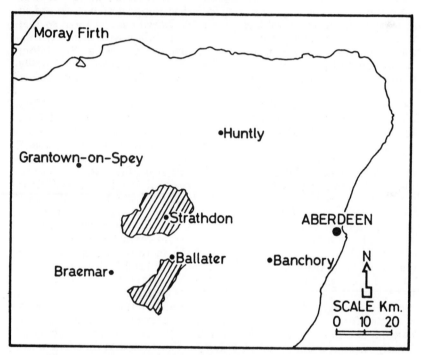

Fig. 1   Location of the experimental sites at Ballater and Strathdon.

Experimental sites were located in two areas: (i) Strathdon in the Upper Don Basin and (ii) Ballater, some 15 km to the south in the Dee Valley

(Fig. 1). The ranges of physiographic and climatic conditions and geological formations are similar in the two areas. Regression equations were developed in each area for various tree growth indices. To test the feasibility of developing growth prediction equations to cover extensive areas of north-east Scotland, the Strathdon equations were applied to Ballater and the accuracy of prediction assessed. A comparison has been made of the influence of the selected site variables on growth in the two areas.

The Derivation of Growth Prediction Equations
TREE GROWTH MEASUREMENTS

Within each area 82 circular 0·01 ha plots were established. In addition, data obtained by Adu (1968) from 50 sites in Strathdon were utilised. Plots were located so as to cover the full range of site factors and to achieve as far as possible an even distribution over this range. Plots were sited on uniformly sloping ground to minimise variation and well away from plantation margins. Stands suffering from damage, disease or obvious understocking were avoided. The sampled stands ranged in age from 17 to 62 years, all having reached closed canopy stage so that the trees were considered to have reached equilibrium with their environment. Unthinned plots numbered 56 at Ballater and 95 at Strathdon. Fertilisation and ploughing had not been carried out except incidentally on former agricultural land that had been surface cultivated before afforestation.

At each plot General Yield Class (G.Y.C.) and Local Yield Class (L.Y.C.) were estimated. For the latter, three values were obtained from (i) dominant breast height quarter-girth, L.Y.C. (b.h.q.g.), (ii) total basal area for unthinned plots only, L.Y.C. (b.a.), and (iii) local volume tables* based on volume:basal area relationships for unthinned Strathdon plots only, L.Y.C. (l.v.t.). All these indices, apart from the last, are derived from yield tables representing average regional conditions and their limitations for growth estimation at the local level should be recognised (Susmel, 1966). In consequence, mean annual height increment (m.a.h.i.) and mean annual volume increment (m.a.v.i.), the latter based on the Strathdon local volume tables, were also used to characterise growth.

From Table 1 it is seen that in Strathdon there is an increase in the estimate of yield from G.Y.C., based only on height, through L.Y.C. (b.a. and b.h.q.g.) based on combinations of height and radial growth. The greater volume estimates given by indices incorporating radial growth arise from the higher basal area:top height ratios that are associated with the stunted form of tree growth characteristic of regions of high exposure (Malcolm and Studholme, 1972). G.Y.C. based only on top height thus seriously underestimates timber volume. The fact that L.Y.C. values based on local volume tables, and hence considered the most accurate measure of timber production, are significantly higher than other L.Y.C.

* The tables were compiled and kindly made available by the Department of Forestry, University of Aberdeen.

values indicates that in areas of high exposure, such as the north-east Highlands, standard Production Class curves do not make sufficient corrections to G.Y.C. measurements. An additional cause for the observed differences between G.Y.C. and L.Y.C. indices results from the lower

TABLE 1

MEANS AND STANDARD DEVIATIONS (S.D.) OF THE VARIOUS ESTIMATES OF YIELD CLASS

Yield Class*	Strathdon		Ballater	
	Mean	S.D.	Mean	S.D.
G.Y.C.	7·5	1·8	7·7	2·3
L.Y.C. (b.a.)	8·6	3·5	7·1	3·7
L.Y.C. (b.h.q.g.)	9·2	2·8	7·8	3·1
L.Y.C. (l.v.t.)	11·9	2·8		

* For explanation of abbreviations see text.

than average stocking rates found at Ballater and Strathdon. In the standard method of determining total basal area trees of girth less than 10 cm are ignored. A consequence of the lower stocking level is that for a unit area of an unthinned stand fewer trees are ignored, resulting in a higher estimate of total basal area and L.Y.V. (b.a.) (M. S. Philip, personal communication). The lower standard deviation of G.Y.C. may be a reflection of the greater sensitivity of radial growth to environmental conditions.

At Ballater L.Y.C. (b.a.) gives the lowest estimate, otherwise the trend is similar to Strathdon. There is no obvious explanation for the low mean value of L.Y.C. (b.a.). This index is especially low for sample plots on the very exposed Pannanich Hill, where special environmental effects may be operating.

It has often been suggested that tree girth and volume are sensitive to stocking density, which could obscure the influence of environmental factors. A positive correlation ($r=0.216*$) was found between density and L.Y.C. (b.a.) at Strathdon, but there is no evidence to suggest that height growth is influenced by density. In order to take account of its effect on growth, density was included in the regression analysis. At Ballater only, significant correlations were observed between age and G.Y.C. ($r=0.274*$) and L.Y.C. (b.h.q.g.) ($r=0.284**$). These correlations are thought to arise from the negative association of age with altitude and aspect due to initial planting on more favourable sites and not from an independent effect on growth.

ASSESSMENT OF QUANTITATIVE VARIABLES

Geomorphic shelter was calculated as the sum of the skyline angles in the eight principal compass directions. A weighted value was also calculated to allow for prevailing wind direction by doubling the five angles from north through west to south. Aspect was expressed on two scales: (i) from 0° at N to 180° at S measured through E or W, (ii) from 0° at E to 180° at W measured through N or S. The first permits an evaluation of the effect on tree growth of aspect along an E-W axis.

The large number of plots precluded the setting up of individual rain gauges, and rainfall data were obtained by interpolation of existing rainfall maps (Birse and Dry, 1970).

ASSESSMENT OF QUALITATIVE VARIABLES

Profile pits were excavated to determine soil parent material and major soil group.

Vegetation communities have been used by Anderson (1961) to assess forestry potential in Scotland, and an attempt was made to identify the original vegetation occurring on the forest plots. Recourse was made to evidence from (i) 1:10,560 (1869) and 1:25,000 (1941) Ordnance Survey maps, (ii) aerial photos taken in 1954, (iii) forest records and local knowledge and (iv) present day ground vegetation. From this information the plots were assigned to the following vegetation classes: former arable land and improved pasture, rough pasture, grass heath, basic grass heath, and heather moorland.

Topographic position was assessed from examination of contour maps and aerial photos and field observations. Six classes were recognised: valley floor, spur, hill top, and lower, middle and upper slope.

STATISTICAL ANALYSIS

Prediction equations for each tree growth index were derived by multiple regression analysis, all nine site variables being included in the analysis. Some workers, such as Page (1970), have assigned scores to the constituent classes of each qualitative variable based on their estimated influence on growth. To avoid the high bias involved in this approach the following procedure was adopted in the present study. For each of the four qualitative variables a given category was assigned a value of 1 if present at a sample plot, and 0 if absent. As a result of this procedure some of the classes became linearly dependent. To eliminate these and other dependencies arising from the discarding of plots, in which all the necessary variables for a particular regression analysis had not been measured, a preliminary program was run to determine a set of linearly independent qualitative variables by Gaussian elimination.

Comparison of Growth Prediction Equations for Strathdon and Ballater

Examples of the predictive equations developed for the Strathdon and Ballater growth variables are shown in Table 2. Predicted and measured values of G.Y.C. are compared in Fig. 2. From Table 3 it is seen that the percentage variation accounted for by regression equations at Strathdon is only moderate; the accuracy of prediction of yield class lies within the range 1·8 to 2·7 m³/ha/annum. For forest management purposes the confidence limit should not exceed the 2 m³/ha/annum yield class interval of the management table (Hamilton and Christie, 1971). The percentage

TABLE 2

COMPARISON OF REGRESSION EQUATIONS FOR G.Y.C. (m³/ha/annum)

	Strathdon		Ballater	
	Independent variable	Coefficient	Independent variable	Coefficient
	Altitude (ft)	-0·005	Altitude (ft)	-0·003
			Rainfall (inches/annum)	0·009
Major soil group:	brown earth	1·16	brown earth	0·17
Major soil group:	iron podzol	1·00	iron podzol	0·06
Major soil group:	peaty podzol	0·24	peaty podzol	0·32
Vegetation:	heather moorland	1·78	heather moorland	-1·11
Vegetation:	grass-heath	1·49	grass-heath	0·52
Vegetation:	rough pasture	2·03		
Vegetation:	arable-improved pasture	2·94		
Vegetation:	flush grass	1·16		
Parent material:	mixed basic/acid drift	-0·40	hornblende schist	2·10
Parent material:	basic rocks	-0·64	mica schist	2·01
Parent material:	mica schist	-1·27	mixed basic/acid drift	3·06
Parent material:			acid rocks	1·55
Topographic position:	hill top	0·23	upper slope	1·05
Topographic position:	middle slope	0·01	middle slope	1·90
Topographic position:	valley floor	0·40	lower slope	1·53
Topographic position:	spur	0·30	valley floor	-1·41
Topographic position:			spur	1·02
	Unweighted geomorphic shelter (°)	0·03	Weighted geomorphic shelter (°)	0·04
	Aspect (°) E or W of N	-0·15	Aspect (°) E or W of N	0·01
	Aspect (°) N or S of E	-0·002	Aspect (°) N or S of E	0·005
	Slope (°)	-0·02	Slope (°)	-0·04
	Constant	9·84	Constant	4·70
	% Variance accounted for	49·2	% Variance accounted for	59·2
	% Significance	0·1	% Significance	0·1

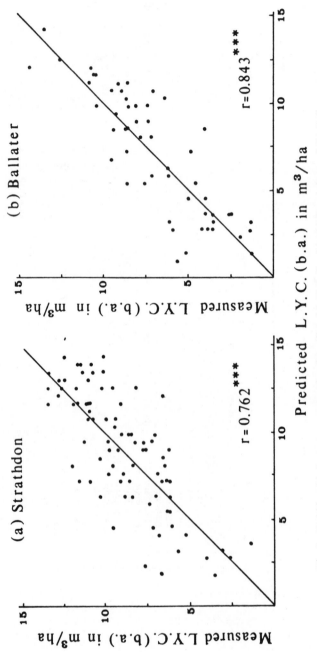

Fig. 2   Relationship between measured and predicted L.Y.C. (b.a.) in (a) Strathdon and (b) Ballater.

variation accounted for at Ballater is considerably higher, particularly in the case of L.Y.C. (b.a.), which can be predicted with an accuracy of 0·9 m³/ha/annum.

TABLE 3

% VARIATION ACCOUNTED FOR BY REGRESSION EQUATIONS

Tree growth index	Strathdon	Ballater
Mean annual height increment	58·5	62·7
Mean annual volume increment	65·0	
G.Y.C.	56·1	59·2
L.Y.C. (b.a.)	58·0	71·1
L.Y.C. (b.h.q.g.)	56·5	57·3
L.Y.C. (l.v.t.)	55·6	

The dissimilarity between the equations for the two areas is highlighted when the Strathdon equations are used to predict growth at Ballater. The predictive power of the equations is very low, the percentage variance accounted for being 32·7 for G.Y.C., 27·9 for mean annual height increment and negligible for L.Y.C. (b.a.). The slopes of the regression lines show that for the first two indices growth is underestimated throughout the sampling range. For the more sensitive index, L.Y.C. (b.a.), the predicted value is a gross overestimate.

TABLE 4

CORRELATION COEFFICIENTS BETWEEN TREE GROWTH AND QUANTITATIVE VARIABLES

Quantitative Variable	G.Y.C.		L.Y.C. (b.a.)	
	Strathdon	Ballater	Strathdon	Ballater
Rainfall		−0·298**		−0·001
Altitude	−0·565***	−0·464***	−0·304***	−0·070
Shelter unweighted	0·377***	0·492***	0·300***	0·327**
weighted	0·309***	0·519***	0·234**	0·399***
Aspect E or W of N	0·024	0·214	0·125	0·204
Aspect N or S of E	0·031	−0·344**	0·020	−0·294**
Slope	0·126	0·048	0·184*	−0·030

*: p=0·05
**: p=0·01
***: p=0·001
Sample size is 132 at Strathdon and 82 at Ballater.

Tree Growth—Site Factor Relationships

It is clear that the relationships between tree growth and site factors, upon which the regression equations are based, are quite different for the two areas, despite their close proximity and environmental similarity. To investigate the differences in these relationships, correlation coefficients between quantitative variables and growth indices have been calculated (Table 4). This type of analysis, however, is of limited value for qualitative variables. An alternative approach is to assign standard values to the independent variables in the regression equations to obtain a predicted growth rate. By altering the value of one variable while keeping the others constant the influence of this variable on growth for each area can be assessed. This method has the advantage over correlation analysis that account is taken of association between variables.

QUANTITATIVE VARIABLES

In order to obtain meaningful predictions the standard values used in the regression equations were chosen so as to obtain a combination of values which could occur within the landscape of both areas. Likewise the values substituted for the standards also met this requirement. Where a variable has been characterised differently at Ballater, the standard has been chosen so as to be equivalent to the Strathdon standard as far as possible. Thus, for an unweighted shelter of 40° at Strathdon, a weighted value of 65·4° was calculated for Ballater, assuming eight equal skyline angles.

TABLE 5

EFFECT OF CHANGES IN QUANTITATIVE VARIABLES ON PREDICTED
G.Y.C. AND L.Y.C. (b.a.) AT STRATHDON AND BALLATER

Values assigned to quantitative variable*		G.Y.C.		L.Y.C. (b.a.)	
		Strathdon	Ballater	Strathdon	Ballater
Rainfall (in)	35		9·0		12·4
	45		9·1		11·6
Altitude (ft)	1000	9·2	9·0	14·4	12·0
	1400	7·2	7·9	13·0	12·5
Shelter (°) { unweighted	40	9·2	9·0	13·0	12·0
{ weighted	65·4				
{ unweighted	80	10·2	11·5	14·4	17·4
{ weighted	130				
Aspect E or W of N (°)	0	8·9	7·6	11·4	6·3
	180	9·2	9·0	13·0	12·0
Aspect N or S of E (°)	0	9·2	7·9	12·5	8·1
	180	8·9	8·7	11·8	10·2
Slope (°)	5	9·2	9·0	13·0	12·0
	15	9·0	8·6	12·5	9·9

* For each variable the first value is the standard used in regression equations.

The results obtained for G.Y.C. and L.Y.C. (b.a.) illustrate the different effects of the quantitative variables in the two areas (Table 5).

ALTITUDE—The decrease in growth with increasing altitude is more marked in Strathdon than Ballater. In Strathdon all seven growth indices show a highly significant negative correlation with altitude compared with three out of five at Ballater. The slight increase in L.Y.C. (b.a.) with elevation at Ballater may be due in part to the higher radial:height growth ratio associated with stunted tree form in exposed situations (Cook, 1971).

GEOMORPHIC SHELTER—Increasing geomorphic shelter results in a marked increase in growth, particularly in radial growth. The more pronounced effect at Ballater is thought to account for the lower significance of elevation in this area. Weighting shelter values to take account of prevailing wind direction gives higher correlation coefficients at Ballater but not at Strathdon.

ASPECT—South-facing slopes are more favourable than north-facing ones, the effect being greater at Ballater. Growth is slightly lower on westerly aspects facing the prevailing wind direction at Strathdon. The reverse appears to be true for Ballater, but since westerly aspect has already been taken into account by weighting geomorphic shelter it cannot be interpreted from the results that west-facing slopes support better growth. In fact, strong negative correlation coefficients were found between growth and westerly aspect (Table 4).

SLOPE—In both areas predicted growth rate is greater on gentler slopes.

QUALITATIVE VARIABLES

In calculating predicted growth rates only combinations of qualitative variable categories which actually occur within the experimental areas were used. The standard values were selected so that as many categories as possible could be compared whilst maintaining constant values for other variables. In certain cases, however, it has been necessary to alter the standard values due to the non-occurrence of some combinations of variables. Thus, gley soils are associated only with flush grass; alluvial soils always occur below and podzols above 300 m. In such cases it is not possible to attribute changes in predicted growth solely to one variable. The predicted growth indices are shown in Table 6.

PARENT MATERIAL—In Strathdon there is a general trend for growth to decrease in the order:

basic > mixed > acid > serpentine

The high growth rates observed on alluvium and glacio-fluvial deposits are attributed to their sheltered position at low altitude (for which allowance has been made in selecting standard values) and their high fertility associated with their agricultural history. The exact cause of the poor growth on the Strathdon serpentine is not settled but according to the studies of Kilic (1976) it is mainly due to severe phosphorus deficiency coupled with high pH, high exchangeable magnesium:calcium ratios and possibly some toxic effects of nickel and chromium. In the stands on serpentine growth is very erratic so that the number of measurable trees per plot is reduced, resulting in extremely low total basal area values. At Ballater the differentiation between parent materials is much less marked, but growth is again lowest on serpentine.

TABLE 6

EFFECT OF CHANGES IN QUALITATIVE VARIABLES ON PREDICTED G.Y.C. AND L.Y.C. (b.a.)

B: Ballater only   S: Strathdon only

Qualitative Variable Category	G.Y.C.		L.Y.C. (b.a.)	
	Strathdon	Ballater	Strathdon	Ballater
Patent Material				
Glacio-fluvial sand and gravel (S)	8·9		8·8	
Alluvium (S)	8·5		9·0	
Basic	6·2	7·1	9·1	9·8
Mica schist, mixed basic-acid drift	6·5	7·0	7·9	11·8
Acid	5·6	6·5	5·9	9·4
Serpentine	3·9	5·9	1·6	6·5
Major Soil Group				
Alluvial soil (S)	8·5		9·0	
Brown earth	6·1	6·6	9·1	9·3
Iron podzol	5·9	6·5	7·9	8·2
Peaty podzol (B)		7·0		8·1
Gley	4·3	7·5	4·9	9·4
Lithosol (B)		6·4		7·2
Magnesian soil	3·8	5·4	1·7	5·9
Original Vegetation				
Arable/improved pasture (S)	8·9		11·9	
Rough pasture (S)	8·0		12·0	
Heather moorland	7·7	7·6	11·6	9·5
Grass-heath	7·4	8·2	9·4	10·0
Flush grass	4·5	8·1	4·8	9·9
Basic grass-heath	3·9	5·9	1·6	6·5
Topographic Position				
Valley floor (S)	8·5		9·0	
Lower slope	6·2	9·1	7·1	9·8
Middle slope	6·8	7·4	9·6	10·4
Upper slope	6·1	9·1	6·6	9·3
Hill top	5·8	8·4	5·6	8·8
Spur	6·1	7·4	6·6	8·7

MAJOR SOIL GROUP—The best growth at Strathdon occurs on alluvial and brown earth soils followed by iron podzols, gleys and magnesian soils. In sharp contrast, gleys are most favourable at Ballater. The Strathdon gleys have a uniform dull grey subsoil indicating that strongly anaerobic conditions prevail throughout the year. In the Ballater profiles, however, ochreous colours with well developed mottling are prominent suggesting better drainage conditions. Furthermore, *Molinia caerulea* (L.) is present and often dominant on the Ballater gleys, whereas it is absent from the Strathdon plots, being replaced by *Deschampsia caespitosa* (L.). The contrast in vegetation is attributed to a higher degree of lateral drainage associated with flushing at Ballater enabling tree roots to extend to greater depths.

ORIGINAL VEGETATION—The lowest rates found on flush grass and basic grass-heath at Strathdon correspond to the low values found on gleys and magnesian soils which are associated with these vegetation types (Table 6). At Ballater, on the other hand, the good growth found on flush grass is in agreement with the values predicted for gley soils.

TOPOGRAPHIC POSITION—At Strathdon valley floor sites on alluvium show the highest predicted growth. In both areas the higher values found on middle slopes in comparison to lower ones may be due to the lower incidence of frost damage and freer drainage. Upper slope, hill top and spur positions maintain a lower ranking even when adjusted for altitude and shelter.

Discussion

This investigation of regression analysis using variables, which can be evaluated from maps, aerial photos and single site visits, has shown that it is not possible to predict tree growth with sufficient accuracy and precision for practical purposes by extrapolating predictive equations developed for one area to an adjacent area with apparently similar climate, topography and geology. The failure of the predictive equations is attributed mainly to differences in the relationships between growth and site factors between the two areas arising from the high spatial variability of the upland environment. In particular, altitude, geomorphic shelter and the development of gley morphology differ markedly in their relationship to tree growth at Ballater and Strathdon.

Rennie (1963) deprecated the use of undifferentiated terms, such as soil texture and humus type, in soil-site studies and recommended their replacement with causal factors of physiological importance. The variables used in this study have been chosen mainly because of their ease of assessment and it is worth considering how the selection and characterisation of variables might improve growth prediction.

Where soil maps are available, soil series could replace major soil group. Toleman and Pyatt (1974) have found, however, that while major soil groups are very relevant to silvicultural problems, many of the finer distinctions separating soil series are unimportant. Jones (1971) also found that there was little advantage in using soil series instead of major soil groups in the evaluation of grassland productivity in Strathdon. Moreover, the use in the present study of parent material in conjunction with major soil group should have the same effect as separation at the series level.

The high variation in growth found on soils grouped together as gleys indicates the inadequacy of the present soil classification system in characterising drainage conditions. It is clearly important to distinguish between saturation with stagnant and flush water, and further work is required to permit a fuller interpretation of soil aeration from profile morphology.

Apart from a broad characterisation of rainfall, it has not been possible to include climatological parameters. However, altitude and geomorphic shelter have been found to be strongly correlated with temperature and wind exposure respectively in Strathdon (Adu, 1968; Jones, 1971).

Although the use of quantitative variables, especially those of causal significance as recommended by Rennie (1963), might reasonably be expected to lead to an improvement in prediction, recent studies in north-east forests indicate that the improvement achieved does not justify the extra cost and effort involved. Adu (1968) measured 86 climatic, topographic and soil parameters in Strathdon and derived regression equations containing 18 variables which explained 71% of the variation in Scots pine growth. The accuracy of prediction is little better than that achieved in the present study (D. Low, personal communication). Blyth (1974) has also demonstrated the limited value of regression analysis for predicting Sitka spruce growth in the north-east Highlands. Such low predictability is attributed to the high spatial variability exhibited by most soil and climatic parameters.

It is concluded that with the land evaluation technology currently available the inherent variability of the upland environment precludes the development of regression equations that are sufficiently accurate and precise for them to be applied over a reasonably extensive area. Instead of the parametric approach to land evaluation a more realistic solution would appear to be offered by physiographic analysis, in which the landscape is subdivided on physiographic criteria into units known as facets. Within these units soil, climatic and hydrological conditions show a reasonable degree of uniformity such that tree growth and silvicultural requirements are sufficiently uniform to be of practical value to the forest manager. A preliminary evaluation by Papamichos (1973) suggests that the comparative speed and low cost of this method make it better suited than regression analysis to land evaluation for moderately extensive purposes such as forestry.

Acknowledgements

We are indebted to the late Mr A. L. P. S. Wallace of Candacraig and the Conservator of the East (Scotland) Conservancy of the Forestry Commission for permission to establish experimental sites; to Professor J. Tinsley for his valuable criticism of the manuscript. One of us (A.C.) was supported by a S.R.C. studentship.

References

Adu, S. V. (1968): *Studies of land capability assessment for Scots pine in Strathdon.* Ph.D. Thesis, University of Aberdeen.

Anderson, M. L. (1961): *The selection of tree species. An ecological basis for site classification for conditions found in Great Britain and Ireland.* 2nd ed. Oliver & Boyd, Edinburgh.

Birse, E. L. and Dry, F. T. (1970): *Assessment of climatic conditions in Scotland, I. Based on accumulated temperature and potential water deficit.* The Macaulay Institute for Soil Research.

Blyth, J. F. (1974): *Land capability assessment for forestry in North-east Scotland.* Ph.D. Thesis, University of Aberdeen.

Coile, T. S. (1935): Forest classification: classification of forest types with special reference to ground vegetation, *J. For.* **36**, 1062-1066.

Coile, T. S. (1952): Soil and the growth of forests. *Adv. Agron.* **4**, 329-398.

Cook, A. (1971): *Assessment of tree growth in north-east Scotland by computer analysis of soil and site data.* Ph.D. Thesis, University of Aberdeen.

Hamilton, G. J. and Christie, J. M. (1971): *Forestry management tables (metric).* For. Comm. Booklet, No. 34, H.M.S.O. London.

Jones, R. J. A. (1971): *Interactions of soil, climate, altitude, aspect and fertiliser treatment on grass production in the Upper Don Basin, Aberdeenshire.* Ph.D. Thesis, University of Aberdeen.

Kilic, N. (1976): *Factors affecting the growth of* Picea sitchensis *(Bong) Carr. and other conifers on serpentinitic soils near Strathdon, Aberdeenshire.* Ph.D. Thesis, University of Aberdeen.

Malcolm, D. C. and Studholme, W. P. (1972): Yield and form in high elevation stands of Sitka spruce and European larch in Scotland. *Scott. For.* **26**, 298-308.

Page, G. (1970): Quantitative site assessment: some practical applications in British Forestry. *Forestry* **43**, 45-56.

Papamichos, N. (1973): *The evaluation of a physiographic approach in forest capability assessment.* Ph.D. Thesis, University of Aberdeen.

Ralston, C. W. (1964): Evaluation of forest site productivity. *Int. Review For. Res.* **1**, 171-201.

Rennie, P. J. (1963): Methods of assessing forest site capacity. *Comm. For. Review,* **42** (4), 316-317.

Susmel, L. (1966): Les techniques de l'evaluation du potential de la station dans les climates temperes. *6th World For. Congr.* **2**, 1386-1387.

Toleman, R. D. L. and Pyatt, D. G. (1974): Site classification as an aid to silviculture in the Forestry Commission of Great Britain. *10th Commonwealth Forestry Conference, 1974.* pp 1-20.

18: COMPUTER-ASSISTED RATINGS OF SOIL POTENTIALS FOR URBAN LAND USES

Marc J. Rogoff, Eckhart Dersch, Delbert L. Mokma, and Eugene P. Whiteside

ABSTRACT: A set of techniques that would help prepare soil potential ratings for urban land uses and communicate these interpretations to soil survey users was tested in Windsor Township, Eaton County, Michigan. A systematic procedure was employed to numerically rate a soil's potential for five different urban land uses. Results indicated that by applying different corrective measures to soils with severe limitations the amount of suitable land for these uses could potentially be increased in Windsor Township. The introduction of new, innovative technologies to overcome these soil hazards invites serious questions regarding the impact on a region's land use regulations.

FOR more than two decades soil interpretations have followed a general procedure of rating soils by limitations (2, 3, 8, 10). A three-class system is commonly used, employing the terms "slight," "moderate," or "severe" to indicate a sequence of increasing limitations or problems that require solution before the soils can be used for the purpose indicated (11).

Information provided by soil limitation ratings is useful to sketch in broad perspective the magnitude of soil problems that users can expect. However, these ratings do not necessarily indicate suitability. Some limiting soil properties may not absolutely restrict certain land uses although they may limit soil performance. Some of these limitations can be corrected, while others cannot.

As the use of soil survey reports by professionals and laymen alike has increased, there has been an increase in requests for soil scientists to provide detailed and more quantitative predictions of soil behavior. Simply providing individual, colored factor-maps from interpretive tables in soil survey reports is no longer sufficient to fulfill the needs of sophisticated user groups (6). The number of potential users of soil survey information continues to grow as many states embark upon accelerated soil mapping programs. Past methods of presenting soil interpretations must change

if soil scientists are to meet the increasing needs of this larger audience.

By the early 1970s, many state offices of the Soil Conservation Service (SCS) were receiving requests for information regarding the suitability of soils for nonagricultural land uses and the measures and costs involved in overcoming soil limitations. At the same time, there was greater recognition by those involved in soil interpretations within the National Cooperative Soil Survey that their method of rating soils by limitations no longer fulfilled the information needs of many users (5, 9, 12). A concerted effort began about 1970 to develop a new concept of soil survey interpretations focusing on the suitability of a soil or its potential after measures to overcome limitations, relative to other soils in an area, have been applied. A guide for preparing soil potential ratings was published in April 1978 after nearly three years of interdisciplinary review (1, 11).

Our research sought to build upon the framework of these guides by developing a set of computer-assisted procedures that would help prepare soil potential ratings for several urban land uses. We report here our experiences in Michigan to test these procedures in Windsor Township of Eaton County.

Study area

Windsor Township is located west of Lansing. A modern soil survey report had recently been published for the area (4), and Michigan State University had developed a computer-based natural resource informatin system for the township.

The study area's landscape is primarily the result of glaciation during the Wisconsin Age, which ended in Michigan 10,000 to 12,000 years ago. The flat to gently undulating surface in Windsor Township was formed when stagnant or constantly reced-

ing ice slowly melted, leaving behind g[...] cial debris covering the landscape with[...] thick mantle of glacial drift.

About 75 percent of the township [...] devoted to agriculture. More than half [...] planted to crops and tilled annually. Th[...] lands are subject to increasing urban pr[...] sures from an expanding Lansing met[...] politan community.

Preparation of soil potential ratings

For purposes of our study, we defin[...] "soil potential" as the relative quality [...] suitability of a soil for a particular la[...] use, using the most recent, acceptable tec[...] nology, in comparison with soils in Eat[...] County (7). We employed a systema[...] procedure to rate a soil's potential nume[...] cally for several different urban land u[...] in the county. In deriving this "soil pote[...] tial index," we considered the relative co[...] of applying feasible treatments or mana[...] ment practices to overcome soil limitatio[...] and the limitations remaining after the[...] corrective measures had been applied.

Land uses and soil properties. We p[...] pared soil potential ratings for the follo[...] ing land use categories: (a) septic ta[...] filter fields for on-site waste disposal, [...] residential streets and roads, (c) residen[...] dwellings with sanitary sewers and ba[...] ments, (d) residential dwellings with sa[...] tary sewers and without basements, a[...] (e) excavations for residential waterlin[...] In selecting these five nonagricultural la[...] uses, our intention was to illustrate seve[...] different types of urban land uses that h[...] been closely identified with site conside[...] tions for residential home construction [...] the Lansing metropolitan area and t[...] also have slightly different physical [...] quirements.

As a next step we developed an ope[...] tional definition for each of these land u[...] and prepared rating criteria for their ev[...] uation. Our definitions set forth the pre[...] conditions and assumptions under whi[...] the soil potentials would apply. We th[...] developed evaluation guides for each la[...] use, listing the important soil, site, a[...] other factors affecting soil performance [...] the intended use. These were modifi[...] from existing guide sheets in the Natio[...] Soils Handbook, Section 400 (11).

Marc J. Rogoff, an environmental and land use planner with Battelle Memorial Institute, Columbus, Ohio 43201, was formerly a graduate research assistant in the Department of Resource Development at Michigan State University. Eckhart Dersch is a professor of resource development, Delbert L. Mokma is an assistant professor of crop and soil sciences, and Eugene P. Whiteside is emeritus professor of crop and soil sciences at Michigan State University, East Lansing 48824. Published as Michigan Agricultural Experiment Station Journal Article No. 9370.

Table 1. Soil limitations and corrective measures used for five land uses in Eaton County, Michigan.

Limitations	Specific Corrective Measures	On-Site Waste Disposal	Roads and Streets	Dwellings with Basements	Dwellings without Basements	Residential Waterlines
		Land Use Categories				
Corrosivity	Wrap pipe					X*
Depth to rock	Excavate rock			X		X
	Sand mound	X				
Excess humus	Excavate peat and muck		X	X	X	X
Floods	Add fill to raise grade		X	X	X	
	Waterproof basement			X		
Low strength	Increase pavement thickness		X			
	Reinforce slab				X	
Percs slowly	Increase filter field size	X				
	Sand mound	X				
Wetness	Waterproof basements			X		
	Areawide surface drainage			X	X	
	Add fill to raise grade		X	X	X	
	Drainage of footing			X	X	
	Drainage of slab			X	X	
	Dewater trench					X
	Serial distribution	X				
Steep slope	Cuts and fills		X	X	X	
	Tamp backfill by hand					X
	Thrust blocking and anchoring					X

*An X indicates that the corrective measure is used for the specified land use.

Data collection. Our next task was to assemble data on local corrective measures, if any, that could be applied to overcome specific soil limitations, their relative costs, and limitations that might continue after these treatments are applied. A thorough literature review helped identify construction designs and development costs needed to overcome soil limitations. We also interviewed representatives from trade associations and individual contractors as well as state, regional, and local governmental agencies to obtain pertinent information. Construction cost data were derived from nationally known reference texts or averages of actual case studies supplied by local contractors and adjusted for prices of materials and labor in the Lansing area in 1979.

We also estimated what continuing limitations there might be after designs or treatments had been installed to correct soil hazards. A three-class system, using the terms, "slight," "moderate," and "severe," indicated the severity of these limitations. The rating of a given soil in such a system signifies the degree to which soil hazards have been corrected or overcome by special construction designs or treatment. In general terms, the rating also represents a prediction of the costs and levels of maintenance required for upkeep of these special treatments.

Assignment of these qualitative ratings to each soil was made with the assistance of technical experts familiar with the construction and maintenance difficulties encountered with each particular urban land use.

Computer input and processing. We entered the data collected in our study into an existing natural resource inventory system for Windsor Township. This data bank contains an extensive file of soils and natural resource data assembled previously by the Remote Sensing Project at Michigan State University using a 10-acre (4.05 hectare) dot grid overlayed onto several different factor maps. A computer software system called RAP (Resource Analysis Package) assisted in the retrieval, manipulation, and analysis of these spatially encoded data (*13*).

With the aid of a multidimensional scaling option available in RAP, we generated soil potential ratings for the five land use categories. Briefly, this scaling technique consisted of establishing an n-space, where n is the number of factors in the analysis. The numerical value of each factor establishes a point for it in this n-space. The Euclidian distance between that point and a point representing an optimum condition set for a soil potential was defined as the soil potential index. The resulting interpoint distance were normalized to cover the conventional range of 0 to 100. The index was then inverted so that soils with the highest soil potential would have large numbers, while those with the lowest soil potential would have small numbers. Each

Table 2. Corrective measures and their costs for on-site waste disposal in Eaton County, Michigan.

Corrective Measures	Cost/Dwelling* (1978 $)
Increase in filter field size	
0-11 minutes per inch, percolation rate	700-900†
11-25 minutes per inch, percolation rate	900-1,200
26-45 minutes per inch, percolation rate	1,200-1,600
46-60 minutes per inch, percolation rate	1,600-2,000
Slope design	
6-12 percent slopes	50-350
12-18 percent slopes	350-550
18-25 percent slopes	550-850
Sand mound design	
0- 6 percent slopes	2,600-2,800
6-12 percent slopes	2,800-3,200
Holding tank	2,000-4,000

*Costs are based on water use for a three bedroom, single-family dwelling, estimated at 75 gallons per person per day with washer and garbage disposal unit.
†Range of study averages.

component of a soil complex (map unit) was rated separately with the final rating of the entire unit determined by multiplying the rating of each by its estimated areal extent in the map unit and tallying these index values.

These index values permitted us to assign each soil to one of four qualitative classes of soil potential—"excellent," "good," "fair," and "poor." We then employed a computer grouping program called JENKS to select statistically optimal class intervals for grouping soils into each of these four rating classes. Soil potential ratings for each land use category were then entered into computer disk storage for subsequent analysis. A computer mapping program available in RAP was then used to construct computer-generated interpretive maps illustrating soil potentials and limitations for each of the five land uses.

Study results

Soil limitations and corrective measures. During the course of the interviews we compiled a list of specific corrective measures used in the study area to overcome

certain soil limitations for the five different land uses (Table 1). We also summarized the corrective measures likely to be needed and their costs at mid-year 1978 for on-site waste disposal in Eaton County (Table 2).

Corrective measures and continuing limitations. In cooperation with local governmental officials as well as private contractors, we identified the recommended engineering designs to overcome soil limitations for different soils in the county for the five urban land uses. As an illustration of this information, table 3 lists soil factors affecting use for on-site waste disposal, recommended designs to overcome these limitations for representative soils, a statement of each soil's overall potential, and the kind of limitations remaining after these designs are installed.

There are two feasible alternatives presently used in the study area to supplement conventional septic tank filter field systems. These are mound systems and sewage holding tanks. Alternate systems, such as composting toilets that have been developed for handling home sewage, have

had little evaluation in the Lansing metropolitan area. Consequently, we did not consider these approaches to on-site waste disposal, although they may prove feasible in the future.

Costs for on-site waste disposal. Table 4 presents the estimated costs of applying the different corrective measures to overcome soil limitations of representative soils for on-site waste disposal in Eaton County. These are general estimates in 1978 dollars and are not intended to eliminate the need for cost estimating by local contractors on a site-by-site basis. The dollar figures are the mean of the range in costs from table 2.

The average initial costs of installing corrective measures on different soils for home sewage disposal in the county ranged from $800 to $3,000. These data clearly indicate the need for additional investment and alternative systems for adequate sewage disposal in soils with severe limitations. Soils with slight limitations (e.g., Boyer loamy sand, 0 to 6 percent slopes) required an initial investment of $800 to $1,050 for installation of conventional septic tank-

Table 3. Soil potential ratings, recommended designs to overcome soil limitations, and continuing limitations of selected soils for on-site waste disposal in Eaton County, Michigan.

Soil Mapping Unit	Limitations and Restrictions	Soil Potential and Corrective Measures	Continuing Limitations
Boyer loamy sand, 0 to 6 percent slopes	Slight:	Excellent: Conventional septic tank filter field, small field	Slight: Possible pollution of shallow ground water supplies by effluent
Capac loam, 0 to 3 percent slopes	Severe: Wetness, percs slowly	Poor: Holding tank	Severe: Cost of hauling sewage high, continual monitoring of liquid level in tank, water use restrictions
Cohoctah fine sandy loam, frequently flooded	Severe: Wetness, floods	Poor: Holding tank	Severe: Cost of hauling sewage high, continual monitoring of liquid level in tank, water use restrictions
Marlette loam, 2 to 6 percent slopes	Moderate: Percs slowly	Good: Conventional septic tank filter field, large field	Slight
Marlette loam, 6 to 12 percent slopes	Moderate: Percs slowly, slope	Good: Conventional septic tank filter field, large field, serial distribution	Slight
Marlette loam, 12 to 18 percent slopes	Severe: Slope	Fair: Conventional septic tank filter field, large field, serial distribution	Moderate: Occasional surfacing of effluent downslope
Marlette loam, 18 to 25 percent slopes	Severe: Slope	Fair: Conventional septic tank filter field, large field, specially designed for improved serial distribution	Severe: Occasional surfacing of effluent downslope, maintain vegetative cover to prevent erosion
Sebewa loam	Severe: Wetness, flooding	Poor: Holding tank	Severe: Cost of hauling sewage high, continual monitoring of liquid level in tank, water use restrictions
Winneshiek silt loam, 0 to 3 percent slopes	Severe: Depth to bedrock	Fair: Septic/mound system for soil shallow to bedrock	Moderate: Maintenance of pump system, possibility of failure, power costs

Table 4. Soil limitations and estimated costs of applying different corrective measures for on-site waste disposal in Eaton County, Michigan.

Soil Map Unit	Soil Limitation	Initial Cost (1978 $)	Corrective Measures
Bixby loam, 0 to 3 percent slopes	Slight	800	Conventional system
Boyer loamy sand, 0 to 6 percent slopes	Slight	800	Conventional system
Boyer loamy sand, 6 to 12 percent slopes	Moderate	1000	Conventional system
Brady-Bronson sandy loams, 0 to 3 percent slopes	Severe	2700	Mound system
For Bronson part see Bronson series			
Bronson series	Moderate	800	Conventional system
Mapped only in a complex with Brady soils			
Capac loam, 0 to 3 percent slopes	Severe	3000	Holding tank
Cohoctah fine sandy loam, frequently flooded	Severe	3000	Holding tank
Edwards muck	Severe	3000	Holding tank
Hillsdale sandy loam, 2 to 6 percent slopes	Slight	1050	Conventional system
Hillsdale sandy loam, 6 to 12 percent slopes	Moderate	1250	Conventional system
Kibbie fine sandy loam, 0 to 3 percent slopes	Severe	2700	Mound system
Lenawee silty clay loam, depressional	Severe	3000	Conventional system
Marlette loam, 2 to 6 percent slopes	Moderate	1800	Conventional system
Marlette loam, 6 to 12 percent slopes	Moderate	2000	Conventional system
Marlette loam, 12 to 18 percent slopes	Severe	2250	Conventional system
Marlette loam, 18 to 25 percent slopes	Severe	2500	Conventional system
Metamora-Capac sandy loam, 0 to 4 percent slopes	Severe	2700	Mound system
For Capac part see Capac series			
Tuscola fine sandy loam, 0 to 4 percent slopes	Severe	2700	Mound system
Wasepi sandy loam, bedrock variant, 0 to 3 percent slopes	Severe	2700	Mound system
Winneshiek silt loam, 0 to 3 percent slopes	Severe	2700	Mound system

Table 5. Proportionate extent and approximate acreage of soils classified by soil limitations and potentials for on-site waste disposal in Windsor Township, Eaton County, Michigan.*

Degree of Soil Limitation	Excellent		Good		Fair		Poor		Unrated		Total	
	%	Acres	%	Acres	%	Acres	%	Acres	%	Acres	%	Acres
Slight	4.2	968	—		—		—		—		4.2	968
Moderate	1.4	323	37.0	8525	—		—		—		38.4	8848
Severe	—		2.5	576	9.9	2281	43.2	9953	—		55.6	12810
Unrated	—		—		—		—		1.8	415	1.8	415
Total	5.6	1291	39.5	9101	9.9	2281	43.2	9953	1.8	415	100.0	23040

*Calculations are based on 2,304 cells, 10 acres per cell, in Windsor Township.

disposal systems, while those soils with moderate limitations (e.g., Marlette loam, 2 to 6 percent slopes) required an expenditure of $1,000 to $2,000 to install similar systems. Initial costs for soils with severe limitations (e.g., Marlette loam, 12 to 18 percent slopes; Winnishiek silt loam, 0 to 3 percent slopes, etc.) were higher, ranging from $1,250 to $3,000.

In addition to the higher installation costs, alternative systems, such as mound systems or holding tanks, are necessary on many of these soils (Table 3). These systems require increased maintenance and monitoring relative to conventional home waste disposal systems.

Table 5 shows the percentage and approximate acreage of soils in Windsor Township with different degrees of limitation for home sewage disposal. The calculations are based on the number of cells in each category (slight, moderate, severe, unrated) in the township. According to the information in this table, 968, 8,848, and 12,810 acres have slight, moderate, and severe limitations for on-site sewage disposal, respectively. This total acreage ac-

counts for 98.2 percent of the land area in the township (22,625 acres). The remaining acreage (415) is water and borrow land left unrated.

These data indicate that 42.6 percent of the land (9,816 acres) in the township has slight or moderate limitations for on-site sewage disposal and is therefore suitable for use of conventional septic tank-soil absorption systems, while more than half of the land area, 55.6 percent, has severe soil restrictions for these systems.

With the advent of new technologies to overcome or treat severe soil limitations, significant changes can occur in the acreage of land suitable for nonagricultural land uses. Table 5 shows the proportionate extent and approximate acreage of soils in Windsor Township classified according to their potentials for home sewage disposal. As indicated by the totals at the bottom of the table, 1,291, 9,101, 2,281, and 9,953 acres have excellent, good, fair, and poor potential, respectively. But, over 11 percent of the 12,810 acres of land in the township having severe soil limitations for on-site sewage disposal has good or fair soil

potential for this land use. That assumes modifications of conventional systems and mound systems are installed. This is a significant increase, 32 percent or 2,857 acres, in the land suitable for on-site waste disposal in the township.

This additional area has either soil permeability rates and depth to seasonally high water tables or restrictive subsoil horizons presently adequate for mound systems, or soil slope gradients acceptable for specially engineered conventional septic tank-absorption systems with serial distribution of effluent.

Conclusions

Our investigation was designed to develop procedures by which ratings of soil potential can be generated, stored, and displayed in computer-drawn interpretive maps. The techniques and analytical results developed and illustrated by the pilot study in Windsor Township exhibit practical usefulness and applicability as planning and educational tools that may help improve land use decisions by both private and public resource developers.

By applying different corrective measures to soils with severe limitations for urban uses (e.g., on-site waste disposal), the land suitable for these uses may potentially be increased in Windsor Township. Land thought to be unsuitable for urban development may now be available, provided certain corrective measures are applied to overcome soil hazards. Urban growth can thus take place in areas where development was not planned previously. The introduction of new, innovative technologies to overcome these soil hazards invites serious questions about the impacts on a region's land use regulations.

REFERENCES CITED

1. Bartelli, L. J. 1975. *Soils survey interpretations—a look ahead.* In Proc., Nat. Work Planning Conf., of Nat. Coop. Soil Survey. Soil Cons. Serv., Washington, D.C.
2. Bartelli, L. J., A. Klingebiel, J. Baird, and M. Heddleson, eds. 1966. *Soil surveys and land use planning.* Soil Sci. Soc. Am., Madison, Wisc.
3. Butler, K. S., B. H. McCown, and W. A. Gates. 1977. *Use of a computer-based resource data system to evaluate on-site waste disposal alternatives.* J. Soil and Water Cons. 32(5): 214-219.
4. Feenstra, J. E., et. al. 1978. *Soil survey of Eaton County, Michigan.* U.S. Govt. Printing Office, Washington, D.C.
5. McCormack, D. E. 1974. *Soil potentials: A positive approach to urban planning.* J. Soil and Water Cons. 29(6): 258-262.
6. Miller, R. P. 1978. *Soil survey under pressure: The Maryland experience.* J. Soil and Water Cons. 33(3): 104-111.
7. Rogoff, M. J. 1979. *A computer-assisted approach for preparing ratings of soil potential for urban land use management.* Ph.D. diss. Mich. State Univ., East Lansing.
8. Simonson, R. W., ed. 1974. *Nonagricultural applications of soil surveys.* Elsevier Scientifics Pub. Co., New York, N.Y.
9. Slusher, D. F., W. L. Cockerham, and S. D. Mathews. 1974. *Mapping and interpretation of histosols and hydraquents for urban development.* In A. R. Aandahl [ed.] *Histosols: Their Characteristics, Classifications, and Use.* Soil Sci. Soc. Am., Madison, Wisc. pp. 95-109.
10. Soil Survey Staff, Soil Conservation Service, 1967. *Guide for interpreting engineering uses of soils.* U.S. Dept. Agr., Washington, D.C.
11. Soil Survey Staff, Soil Conservation Service, 1978. *National soils handbook.* U.S. Dept. Agr., Washington, D.C.
12. Taff, H. A. 1972. *Use of soil information in resource planning.* In Proc., 27th ann. mtg. Soil Cons. Soc. Am., Ankeny, Iowa. pp. 15-19.
13. Tilmann, S. E. 1978. *Resource analysis program: User's guide to RAP.* Remote Sensing Project, Mich. State Univ., East Lansing. □

Part VIII

Land Evaluation and Planning

Papers 19 and 20: Introductory Review

The objective of land evaluation is to provide an assessment of land that is incorporated into planning, management, or conservation decisions. The entire subject is focused on the ultimate application of results. Land evaluation is an applied science, and, as has been already demonstrated, land evaluation projects integrate the management and assessment of environmental information with economic and social analysis. Emphasis has been given in preceding parts to presenting an array of papers that demonstrate the wide range of techniques and approaches to land evaluation. Attention now turns in this last section to an examination of how projects in land evaluation can be integrated with subsequent planning processes. As will become apparent, there is an increasing trend toward the fusion of the evaluation and planning processes.

Paper 19 demonstrates how a soil capability analysis aids land use planning decisions for the Ottawa urban fringe. The investigation by Dumanski, Marshall, and Huffman begins by describing how soil landscape units were mapped using an ecological approach. The Canada Land Inventory system of capability assessment for agriculture was modified to give greater detail on degree of limitation. It is argued that the data on these limitations are important to other biological as well as nonagricultural uses. Figure 2 in this paper is a good demonstration of a filter approach to this information whereby class I and II agricultural soils and areas posing serious problems to construction were sifted out in order to indicate localities suitable for urban expansion. Several maps (Figs. 3-9) indicate the distributions of specific limitations—namely wetness, variation in drainage, inundation relative to biological growth, topography, bedrock, stoniness, natural fertility, soil structure, and droughtiness. The practical implications of these limitations are discussed with respect to agriculture and constructional activities. In the final analysis, areas suitable for urban expansion are identified and related to the planning needs of the region. Comparison is made with the Ottawa-Carleton official plan and recommendations for urban expansion are proposed for specific localities. The merits of this Canadian study are its very clear approach, the presentation of results in a set of maps, and the specific planning implications that emerge from the investigation.

The results from the study should easily be incorporated into the planning process for this urban region.

Paper 20 is a detailed case study with a very different objective—a land evaluation project in a small area of Jamaica with the aim of aiding a smallholders settlement scheme as part of a land-reform program. As stated by Andriesse and Scholten, quantitative land evaluation can make an important contribution in settlement schemes where land use options need to be identified and decisions are necessary on minimum farm sizes. The paper begins by giving an introductory description of the study area (Burnt Ground settlement scheme), which, by tradition, had been under pasture. The aim of the land evaluation was to determine an equitable method of subdividing the land to ensure that individual farmers could achieve viable incomes. The whole approach was based on the FAO *Framework for Land Evaluation* with emphasis being given in the first instance to the selection of land utilization types (LUTs). A wide variety of factors were taken into account in selecting LUTs ranging from government policy to available agricultural skill. Inputs and outputs for the three selected LUTs were then estimated in order to predict maximum productivity per hectare, minimum farm size, and total labor requirement. The requirements of each LUT were specified and matched with actual land conditions as determined by a soil survey. Consideration was given to limitations posed by slope, effective depth, stoniness, rock outcrops, flooding, and soil acidity. In this manner land capability classes and subclasses were decided for the soil mapping units for each of the three LUTs. In the final stage in the analysis, minimum farm sizes were predicted for each LUT using productivity estimates for each capability class. Thus it was possible to determine the necessary farm sizes to produce target farm incomes. An example of results from the evaluation is presented in a detailed map (Fig. 6) which shows the distribution of proposed dairy pastures, backyard gardens, and areas of bush to be reforested.

This Jamaican study demonstrates the benefits of shaping a land evaluation exercise to the particular needs of an area. Furthermore, the results are taken beyond the stage of evaluating the suitability of areas for a number of alternative LUTs. Instead the investigation progressed into landscape planning with a proposal for farm types, farm layout and size, and general land use patterns. The authors rightly claim the central place that soil information can take in land capability assessment for planning purposes. Their study bridged the gap between simply assessing the capability of land and proposing a land use plan. It would be interesting to know the extent to which their plan has been adopted.

A frequent complaint by land evaluation scientists is that their results are not properly incorporated into land use planning decisions. One solution is for investigators, as demonstrated in Papers 19 and 20, to present their results in a form that can be easily understood by nonspecialists; also there is much merit, as shown in Paper 20, for specific plans to be proposed. A starting point is achieved in this fashion and the plan can be shaped to take other considerations into account. The Land Resources Development Centre (LRDC), a United Kingdom government agency concerned with many land evaluation issues in developing countries, places great importance on how they present their reports to ensure maximum use. The importance of communication between land evaluation scientist and client is emphasized by Smyth (1981). According to Smyth, one LRDC project in the Tabora region of Tanzania made use of local

Swahili names for soil terms in order to aid local understanding; information is also given on soil classification using international systems, but this information is given in an appendix to the report. However great the temptation to use sophisticated and complex techniques, land evaluation scientists must guard against presenting their results in too technical a manner.

Much emphasis has been placed in this book on describing techniques that yield results of value to land use planning and management. It is unfortunate that there is often a lack of integration of the evaluation and planning processes. It is only with settlement, land reallocation, or irrigation schemes that such integration is achieved. The Jamaican study (Paper 20) is one example of an investigation that incorporated planning priorities into the approach. Nevertheless, there is much room for developing techniques for integrating evaluation and planning procedures. To indicate the potential of this theme, reference is made in the remaining part of this review to recent Canadian and Australian advances.

In a review of land classification techniques as used in Canada, Flaherty and Smit (1982) stress the importance of being able to assess land resources with regard to alternative sets of conditions and goals. They argue ". . . for a more comprehensive and integrated approach to the analysis of land use planning issues than that facilitated by land classification schemes alone" (Flaherty and Smit, 1982, p. 330). Subsequent papers by Smit et al. (1983) and Smit et al. (1984) demonstrate such an integrated approach with reference to food production potential in Ontario. The Land Evaluation Project Team at the University of Guelph has developed a land evaluation model for Ontario (LEM 2). This model uses systems analysis in order to present a number of evaluations using a range of scenarios. Full details of LEM 2 are given by Smit (1981*a*). Information on constraints must first be incorporated into LEM 2; this includes data on resource, agricultural land use, urban land use, and forestry land use constraints. The aim of LEM 2 is to determine the land use flexibility that is possible within given constraints. A number of objective functions are then introduced to select minimum possible allocations of land use activity for each area. In summary LEM 2 is an interactive, user-oriented system comprising the following five major components: (1) data management, (2) the generation of scenarios, (3) the solution algorithm, (4) the generation of evaluation measures, and (5) the production of maps. It is an elegant and sophisticated system and the interested reader should consult the report by Smit (1981*a*) for details. An outline of the system is also given by Smit (1981*b*).

The publication by the Guelph Land Evaluation Project Team demonstrates LEM 2 with respect to food production in Ontario (Smit 1981, *a*). This is done under three scenarios: (1) a base scenario reflecting land supply, productivity, and demand conditions in 1976; (2) a modest growth scenario assuming food production targets based on a provincial population of 11 million and the maintenance of current trading patterns; and (3) a substantial growth scenario incorporating similar needs to those in scenario 2 but with most agricultural produce being generated within Ontario. The results indicate the variation in importance of climatic and land type areas for different land uses under the three scenarios. This integral approach to land evaluation has tremendous potential for influencing broad-scale, long-term land use planning. The flexibility of the approach is enormous in that a variety of possible outcomes can be presented to the decision makers according to the nature of defined assumptions and scenarios.

The long tradition of land evaluation research in Australia by CSIRO was introduced in Parts II and III, and attention turns now to an approach by the Division of Water and Land Resources as developed since the mid-1970s. The Australian system is known as SIRO-PLAN and it is described as a step-by-step recipe for carrying out environmental planning exercises (Baird, 1983; Cocks et al., 1983). Central to the approach is the specification of a set of guidelines that express the outlooks and objectives of the interest groups for whom the plan is being produced; the task of SIRO-PLAN, therefore, is to identify land uses or land management strategies that best satisfy the stated guidelines. Baird (1983) describes five essential requirements for carrying out a SIRO-PLAN project and it is instructive to summarize these.

1. Land uses: The starting point should be clear statements on project objectives and these are expressed as a set of land uses considered to be the key issues.

2. Guidelines: This stage involves achieving agreement with interested groups concerning policies or guidelines that ought to apply in the allocation of land use. Baird (1983) describes five types of guidelines, ranging from exclusion ones (certain land uses not to be considered), to preference ones (areas where certain land uses are to be encouraged).

3. Mapping units: A decision needs to be made at an early stage on the mapping units, and, once determined, these units control the resolution of the ultimate published plan. These units should conform to the land areas on which decisions are to be made.

4. Data collection: This is not a blanket operation but rather one guided by the decisions of the preceding three stages. The data are obviously compiled according to mapping units.

5. Importance weights: These weights indicate a client's or community's preference for each of the stated guidelines. Thus SIRO-PLAN integrates such personal or political assessments into the system.

The final and most crucial part of the analysis involves the combination of these importance weights with component ratings to produce an overall suitability score. A computer program called LUPLAN has been developed to implement SIRO-PLAN (Ive and Cocks, 1983; Ive, 1984). A linear programming approach is adopted to produce suitability scores for each land use in every mapping unit. The land use with the highest score is proposed as the most preferred strategy. The LUPLAN package is available in Microsoft BASIC (version 5.01) so that it can be operated on a range of microcomputers. A user's manual with demonstration output is written by Ive (1984).

The Australian SIRO-PLAN, like the Canadian LEM 2 system, marks a significant advance in land evaluation. It has been applied to around 30 projects, with half of these concerned with local government planning, and the remainder with the planning of parks, reserves, and forests (Cocks et al., 1983). Its particular attribute is the facility for incorporating policy statements into the evaluation process though this could also be achieved in the Canadian system by specifying different scenarios. The dominant emphasis in SIRO-PLAN is to produce land use solutions for land planning areas. Criticisms might be made about having to categorize in a generalized way environmental attributes for fairly large areas, but ultimate planning decisions are necessary on such blocks of land. For example, an area of land might display quite a marked variation in relief and soil conditions, yet a decision on whether to afforest or not may be required. Perhaps there is need with SIRO-PLAN to include measures of environmental variability for land units. Such variability can be as important as average conditions in terms of selecting land uses.

This concluding review and the two papers in this final section demonstrate that the philosophy and techniques of land evaluation have been revolutionized since the time when research was limited to resource inventory. The two outstanding trends over the last decade have been the development of techniques to yield results that can be incorporated into land planning decisions, and the built-in flexibility of evaluation systems so that outcomes can be proposed for any land use or defined set of circumstances. Computers have played a key role in permitting such developments. But however rigorous or relevant, the results of land evaluation will be used only if there is clear perception by politicians and decision makers of their value. Thus land evaluation scientists have the continuing responsibilities of not only improving their methodologies but also convincing the public at large about the importance of incorporating their research findings into decisions about land. In many ways the latter is the greater challenge.

REFERENCES

Baird, I. A., 1983, SIRO-PLAN and Its Interpretation of the Planning Process, in *Environmental Planning, SIRO-PLAN and the Rural Land Evaluation Manual,* I. A. Baird, P. T. Compagnomi, J. R. Davis, and J. R. Ive, eds., Tech. Memorandum 83/17, CSIRO Institute of Biological Resources, Division of Water and Land Resources, Canberra, pp. 28-42.

Cocks, K. D., J. R. Ive, J. R. Davis, and I. A. Baird, 1983, SIRO-PLAN and LUPLAN; An Australian Approach to Land Use Planning. 1. The SIRO-PLAN Land Use Planning Method, *Environment and Planning B: Planning and Design* **10:**331-345.

Flaherty, M., and B. Smit, 1982, An Assessment of Land Classification Techniques in Planning for Agricultural Land Use, *Jour. Environ. Manage.* **15:**323-332.

Ive, J. R., 1984, *LUPLAN: Microsoft BASIC, CP/M User's Manual,* Tech. Memorandum 84/5, CSIRO Institute of Biological Resources, Division of Water and Land Resources, Canberra.

Ive, J. R., and K. D. Cocks, 1983, SIRO-PLAN and LUPLAN: An Australian Approach to Land Use Planning. 2. The LUPLAN Land Use Planning Package, *Environment and Planning B: Planning and Design* **10:**347-355.

Smit, B., 1981a, *Procedures for the Long-term Evaluation of Rural Land,* CRD Publication No. 105, University School of Rural Planning and Development, University of Guelph.

Smit, B., 1981b, Prime land, land evaluation and land use policy, *Jour. Soil and Water Conserv.* **36:**209-212.

Smit, B., S. Rodd, D. Bond, M. Brklacich, C. Cocklin, and A. Dyer, 1983, Implications for Food Production Potential of Future Urban Expansion in Ontario, *Socio-Economic Planning Sci.* **3:**109-119.

Smit, B., M. Brklacich, J. Dumanski, K. B. MacDonald, and M. H. Miller, 1984, Integral Land Evaluation and Its Application to Policy, *Canadian Jour. Soil Sci.* **64:**467-479.

Smyth, A. J., 1981, *Strategy for Technical Assistance in Soil Survey and Interpretation: Experience of the Land Resources Development Centre, U.K.,* paper presented at the National Work Planning Conference, April 6-10, 1981, Washington, D.C.

19: SOIL CAPABILITY ANALYSIS FOR REGIONAL LAND USE PLANNING — A STUDY OF THE OTTAWA URBAN FRINGE

J. Dumanski[1], I. B. Marshall[2], and E. C. Huffman[1]

[1]*Land Resource Research Institute, Agriculture Canada, Ottawa, Ontario K1A OC6 and* [2]*Lands Directorate, Fisheries and Environment Canada, Hull, Quebec, K1A OH3*

A procedure is outlined for analyzing soil data for regional land use planning. Maps of basic land factor limitations are illustrated for the Ottawa urban fringe, and each map is evaluated for biological and nonbiological uses. The major land factors relative to urbanization are used along with other data to derive an urban "suitability" map. Results are compared to the regional development plan for the area.

L'auteur expose une méthode d'analyse de données pédologiques à des fins d'aménagement régional du territoire. Il fournit des cartes illustrées des classes d'aptitudes des terres pour la région périphérique d'Ottawa, chaque carte étant évaluée en fonction des utilisations biologiques et non biologiques. Les principaux facteurs pédologiques relatifs à l'urbanisation sont utilisés avec d'autres données pour établir une carte urbaine "d'aptitude." Les résultats sont comparés au plan d'aménagement régional de la région.

The conversion of rural land for urban expansion has been very rapid in the last two decades. In the United States between 1967 and 1975 approximately 9.1 million hectares were converted from cropland to urban and water uses. Of these about 3.2 million hectares (0.4 million hectares per year) were prime farmland (Schmude 1977). Comparable figures for Canada between the years 1966 and 1971 indicate that about 84 000 ha (16 700 ha per year) were converted from rural to urban uses. Seventy-six percent of this area was farmland and 63% comprised the top three soil capability classes (Gierman 1977). Nowland and McKeague (1977) have projected a further conversion of 800 000 ha for Ontario and Quebec between now and the year 2000 if current rates of urbanization are maintained.

These and similar figures have prompted much public and scientific debate but their true implications are difficult to estimate. Gibson (1977) recently reviewed some of the social, environmental and economic implications of the question, but it is likely that the debate will continue well into the future. Concern on the possibility of land misallocation in the rural-urban fringe has prompted renewed interest in soil survey information for these areas in Canada.

Knowledge of the physical characteristics of land is fundamental to rational land planning and this became very apparent with the advent of master planning in the regional municipality of Ottawa-Carleton. Large-scale development programs created the need for new and more sophisticated land data, including topography, soil conditions, drainage and tract size. Most such demands could be satisfied by conducting a modern soil survey, but until recently the only data available were those published in 1944 at 1:126 720 based on mapping 202 000 ha in one season without the aid of aerial photography (Hills et al. 1944). Because the old survey could no longer meet current planning needs, a resurvey at 1:25 000 was begun (Marshall et al. 1979). The objectives of the resurvey were to develop a landscape approach to soil survey applicable to large-scale mapping, and an interpretive scheme for urbanization. This paper reports on part of the findings.

The term "land" has physical and social connotations including those of space, nature, location, property and capital. Also, it is considered as a production factor, a consumer good or commodity and a source of pleasure and recreation (Brinkman and Smyth 1973). As used in this paper, land is considered as the physical entity, and is defined as embracing the atmosphere, the soil and underlying geologic material, the hydrology and vegetation which are on, above or below a specific area of the earth's surface.

General Features of the Area
The Ottawa Valley has a humid climate with a mean annual air temperature of 5.4°C, mean annual precipitation of about 82 cm and average snowfall of 230 cm. The growing season precipitation averages about 39 cm and degree days above 5°C average 1830.

Primarily the area consists of level to very gently undulating, poorly drained plains associated with marine and estuarine deposits. Where these are covered by thick, sandy materials, the surface is shaped into dunes and other forms typical of wind action. Till materials usually exist as shallow veneers and blankets overlying bedrock highs, but elongated, ridged drumlins occur in certain areas.

Poorly drained Gleysolic soils on level and very gently sloping land occupy by far the largest portion of the area, but imperfectly and well drained Brunisolic soils occur on sloping terrain of knolls and ridges. Limited areas of well drained Podzolic soils are found in sandy deposits.

Data Collection and Analysis
Refined systems of soil mapping and land capability assessment were used in the 1978 study. Land conditions were mapped using the categorical soil mapping system described by Marshall et al. (1979) and shown in Fig. 1. Central to this system are soil landscape units which are subdivisions of landforms and soil parent materials, themselves subdivisions of broad pedoclimatic areas (due to the nature of the physiography and the generally small size of the survey area only one pedoclimatic area was recognized.) The landscape units are made up of one or several soil components, each occupying set positions in, and defined proportions of, the landscape unit. This system is similar but not identical to the biophysical land classification system (Jurdant et al. 1975), and it differs from normal Ontario soil survey procedures by focussing on landscape as well as soil features.

Each soil landscape unit consists of a collection of discrete characteristics or properties that vary continuously or discontinuously over the landscape. Due to the complexity of these, as well as the nature of their variation, use-related interpretations require an interpretive scheme. A form of the soil capability scheme for agriculture, similar to that devised for the Canada Land Inventory (1965) was developed for this purpose. In this scheme differentiae at the class level were those of the C.L.I. system, but subclasses were based on land factor limitations of three degrees of severity: major, moderate and minor. These were made approximately equivalent by equating one major land factor limitation to two moderate and to four minor. (Land factor limitations are similar to capability subclasses, but they are quantitatively defined. This new term was introduced in an attempt to circumvent the agricultural bias inherent in the capability subclass. Land factors can be basic or derived; this is explained in subsequent sections.) The resulting system, while remaining with seven capability classes and nine subclasses, allowed for more detailed evaluations of individual areas. A series of maps was prepared illustrating the distribution and severity of

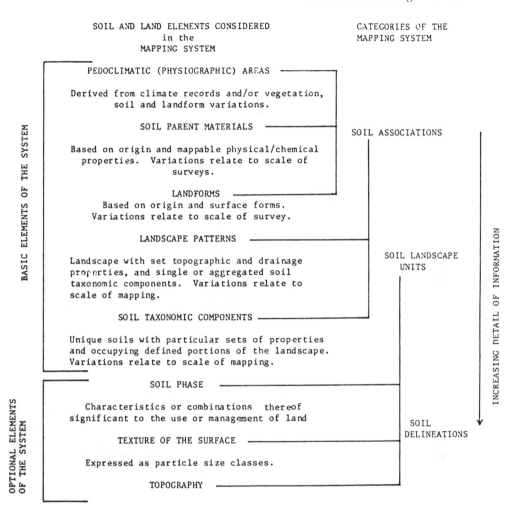

Fig. 1. Categories and elements of the soil mapping system employed in the survey. Note that the optional elements listed are supplementary to the basic elements, and are those that were considered to be particularly important in the area mapped.

land factor limitations in the area. Criteria for each degree of severity are shown on the legend for each respective factor.

The soil-capability class is a rating of land quality specific to field crop agriculture. The subclass, on the other hand, is a listing of kinds and severity of land factor limitations present in an area. By focussing on the definitions of the land factors and the respective degrees of severity, a user can extrapolate the capability map to other biological but non-agricultural uses, as well as to non-biological uses. Land factors, such as susceptibility to inundation, rockiness, stoniness, steep slopes, drainage variability and natural soil drainage, are fundamental to many non-biological uses such as housing sites, playgrounds, effluent disposal systems, septic tanks, highways and pipelines. Such uses are affected only slightly, or not at all, by soil-specific factors such as poor structure, low fertility and droughtiness. But these factors, along with others, can play major roles in biologically oriented uses such as reforestation, landscaping, playground maintenance and recreation planning.

To illustrate the capacity to extrapolate from the capability map, a map was prepared defining general areas "suitable" for urban expansion. The procedure used was to progressively eliminate from the map those physical land factors most serious to construction (major wetness, moderate and major rockiness, major topography), as well as Class 1 and 2 agricultural soils, organic soils and soils with peaty surface horizons (inundation), and areas of gravel. This collection of factors was used to represent hazardous, excessively costly or "socially desired" situations, as far as possible with the information at hand. Areas remaining were considered to be "suitable" for urbanization.

Certain of the factors (gravel and peaty soils) were not shown adequately on the capability map and had to be derived directly from the soils map. Areas of gravel and high quality agricultural soils represent resources that should be protected. Factors which could not be obtained from a soil map, such as airport noise zones, land tenure, the presence of services and the spring floodline, were not used.

RESULTS

A schematic, condensed version of the soil capability map for agriculture is shown in Fig. 2. This shows that the best soils (Class 1 and 2) are located in the Richmond Plain, in the plain bisected by the Rideau River, near Orleans and Leitrim, and in a small area southwest of Carlsbad Springs. Of the area south of the National Capital Commission (NCC) greenbelt, approximately 42% of the land area is Class 1 and 2 for agricultural uses, 37% is Class 3 and 4 and 14% is Class 5, 6, 7 or organic and of no use to commercial agriculture other than as pasture. An earlier report (Dumanski 1976), indicated that most of the planned urban expansion will take place on Class 1 and 2 land in spite of the fact that over 50% of the

study area is of moderate to low capability for agriculture and could be used for housing, thus saving the best agricultural land.

Table 1 and Figs. 3–9 show the extent and distribution of the 9 basic land factors considered in this study. Land factors can be basic or derived. Basic land factors are those properties that are easily measured in the field, such as slope and rockiness, and whose effect on a use is generally singular. Derived land factors, such as slope stability and frost heave potential, are determined by considering several land factors at the same time. This concept is similar to land qualities and land characteristics as explained by Brinkman and Smyth (1973). The single most extensive land factor limitation in the area is "wetness" (Fig. 3), affecting 57% of the land surface to varying degrees. This factor is complicated by the factors of "soil drainage variability" (Fig. 4) and "inundation" (Fig. 5). Wetness is due to high water tables whereas drainage variability is due to topographic conditions.

The wetness condition affects agricultural, as well as most non-agricultural uses, and costs of improvements are often very high. However, large-scale, community-sponsored drainage schemes, whereby costs of individual projects are amortized against the project as a whole, have proven successful in the past and may offer a possible solution. Such projects generally provide efficient control of soil moisture and water tables, particularly where outlets are available and where tile, rather than surface drainage, is feasible. An extreme wetness condition, shown by the factor inundation, generally cannot be economically improved.

The land factor "topography" or steep slopes is shown in Fig. 5. This factor affects about 20% of the area to varying degrees and is important primarily as it relates to slope stability and water erosion. Slopes of major significance cover approximately 7% of the area, primarily as eroded ravines and scarps along the major rivers and creeks. Such slopes are dangerous for urban development

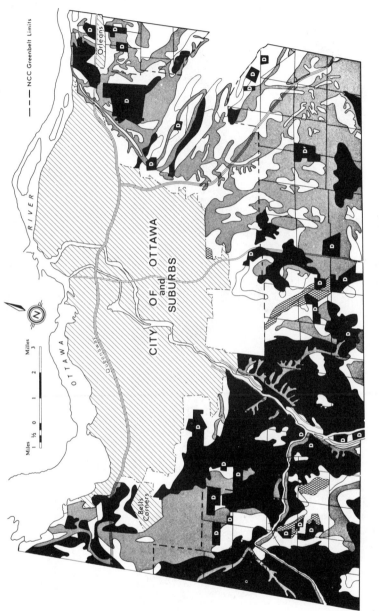

LAND AREAS "SUITABLE" FOR URBAN EXPANSION

A - Soils of Class 1 and 2 Capability for Agriculture

L - Soils with Significant Physical Limitations (R,R',W,T')

O/I - Organic and Inundated Soils

G - Gravel Deposits

D - Disturbed Land

Areas without major physical restrictions to construction.

Fig. 2.   Soil capability for agriculture.

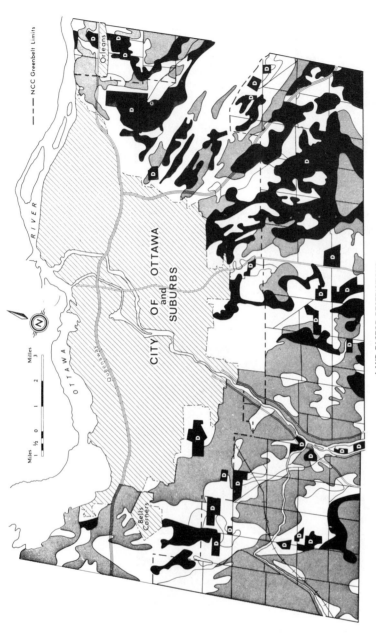

LAND FACTOR RESTRICTIONS

WETNESS

W' – Major - excessive wetness generally due to ponding, seepage, or impermeable subsoil. May cause suffocation and winter kill of plants

W – Moderate - wetness or poor to very imperfect drainage on flat to gently sloping land. Often on clay land or over impervious subsoil

w – Minor - periodic wetness or imperfect drainage on sloping land. Mainly on lower slopes of till ridges

☐ Disturbed Land

▨ **D** Disturbed Land

Fig. 3. Land factor restrictions — Wetness.

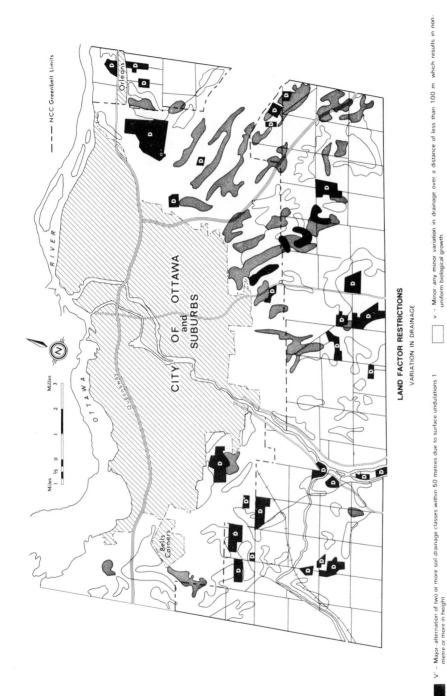

LAND FACTOR RESTRICTIONS

VARIATION IN DRAINAGE

V¹ – Major alternation of two or more soil drainage classes within 50 metres due to surface undulations 1 metre or more in height

V² – Moderate alternation of drainage of one soil drainage class over a distance greater than 50 m . on undulations of less than 1 m . in height

v – Minor -any minor variation in drainage over a distance of less than 100 m . which results in non-uniform biological growth

☐ Disturbed Land

Fig. 4. Land factor restrictions — Variations in drainage.

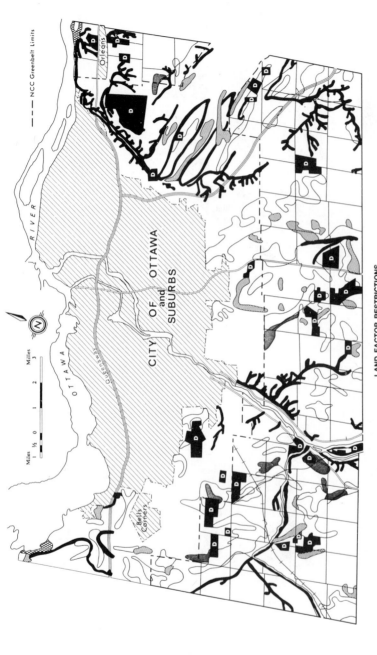

LAND FACTOR RESTRICTIONS

INUNDATION° RELATIVE TO BIOLOGIC GROWTH

I' – Major - frequent land flooding of extended duration (> 5 days)

I – Moderate - occasional overflow of short duration (< 5 days) causing high water tables of extended duration (> 5 days)

i – Minor - occasional, brief inundation (1 day) with very high water table. Affects only deep rooted plants.
° – This does not consider spring flooding of the Jock, Rideau and Ottawa Rivers

Disturbed Land

TOPOGRAPHY

T' – Major - short slopes (< 100m.) steeper than 9%, which affect the use of machinery and which require protection against water erosion.

T – Moderate-short slopes (< 100 m) less than 9%, which interfere slightly with the use of machinery and which require some protection against water erosion.

t – Minor - slopes of 3 to 6% which do not interfere with machinery but may result in slight water erosion and/or non-uniformity in moisture distribution and plant growth.

Fig. 5. Land factor restrictions — Inundation relative to biologic growth. Topography.

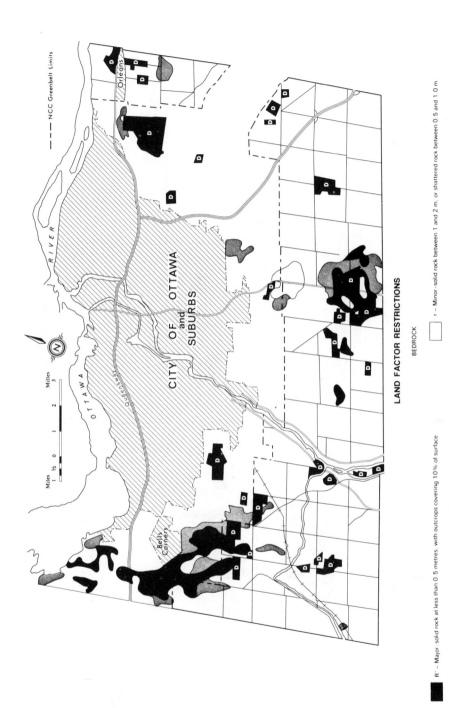

LAND FACTOR RESTRICTIONS

BEDROCK

▮ R' – Major- solid rock at less than 0 5 metres. with outcrops covering 10% of surface

▮ R – Moderate- solid rock between 0 5 and 1 0 m. with outcrops covering < 10%. or shattered rock (shale.
▨ schist) between 0 3 and 1 0 m. with outcrops covering < 20% of surface

☐ r – Minor- solid rock between 1 and 2 m. or shattered rock between 0 5 and 1 0 m

▮D Disturbed Land

Fig. 6.   Land factor restrictions — Bedrock.

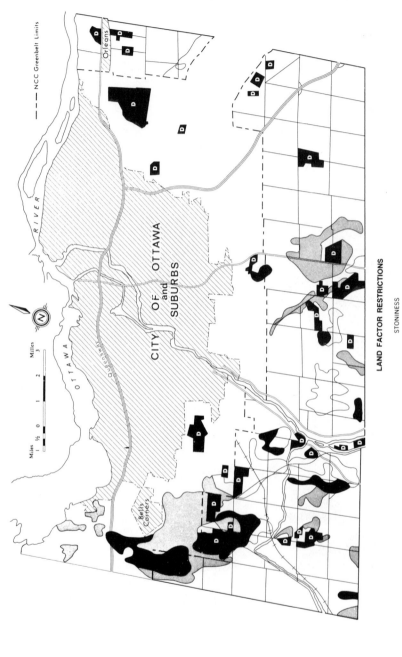

LAND FACTOR RESTRICTIONS

STONINESS

P' – Major – soils sufficiently stony to make use of machinery difficult. (3 to 15% on surface)

P – Moderate – stones cause a minor nuisance to operation of machinery. (0.1 to 3% on surface)

p – Minor – soils with few surface stones. (0.1% on surface)

D   Disturbed Land

Fig. 7.   Land factor restrictions — Stoniness.

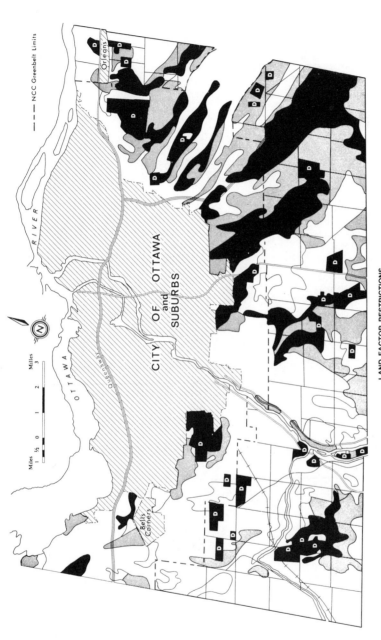

LAND FACTOR RESTRICTIONS

NATURAL FERTILITY

F' – Major - very low nutrient status and base exchange capacity due to low organic matter and/or clay content. Possible severe nutrient imbalance due to acidity or alkalinity (pH < 4.5 or > 7.6)

F – Moderate - low nutrient status due to low organic matter and/or clay content or moderate nutrient imbalance due to adverse acidity or alkalinity (pH 4.5 - 5.5 or 7.4 - 7.6)

f – Minor - minor nutrient imbalance due to low organic matter content and/or unsuitable reaction (pH) Affects only a few crops and may need moderate lime

D – Disturbed Land

Fig. 8. Land factor restrictions — Natural fertility.

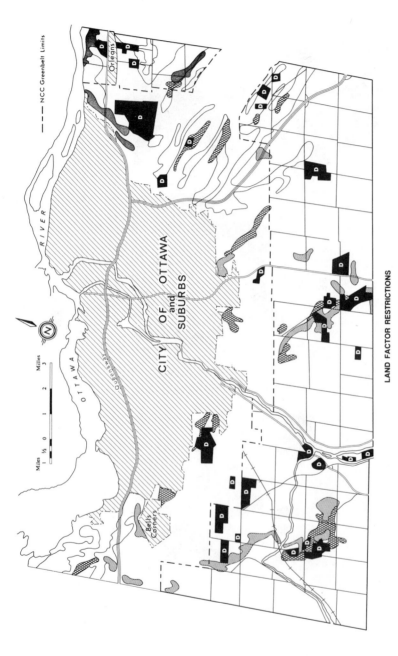

LAND FACTOR RESTRICTIONS

SOIL STRUCTURE

D' - Major* - Massiveness, poor structure and/or firm consistence, causing poor aeration and slow moisture distribution. Tillage is difficult and requires special management, and trafficability is poor when wet.

D - Moderate - massiveness, poor structure and/or firm consistence, causing poor aeration and root penetration through subsoil.

d - Minor - poor structure, causing minor air and water movement problems.

Disturbed Land

DROUGHTINESS

M' - Major - a condition generally found in well to excessively drained sands and gravels which require irrigation for normal crop growth under average weather conditions. Such soils may undergo wind erosion when non-irrigated and unprotected.

M - Moderate - generally found in well to excessively drained loamy sands, coarse sandy loams, and fine sandy loams or loams overlying sands or gravels. Without irrigation crop yields may be acceptable during average to wet years, but not in dry years.

m - Minor - well drained fine sandy loams or loams which, with proper soil moisture conservation practices, give acceptable yields under average climatic conditions.

° - This category does not exist in the area

Fig. 9. Land factor restrictions — Soil structure. Droughtiness.

Table 1. Area (ha) and proportions of land factor limitations

Land factor	Severity of limitation			Total area affected
	Major	Moderate	Minor	
Wetness	7910(18%)	14 520(33%)	2710(6%)	25 140(57%)
Variation in drainage	290(–)	3 100(7%)	5100(11%)	8 490(18%)
Inundation	140(–)	370(–)	950(2%)	1 460(2%)
Rockiness	2070(4%)	1 830(4%)	340(–)	4 240(8%)
Stoniness	1830(4%)	3 310(7%)	1630(3%)	6 770(14%)
Topography	3050(7%)	540(1%)	5330(12%)	8 920(12%)
Soil fertility	7350(17%)	8 380(19%)	3900(9%)	19 630(45%)
Droughtiness	1230(2%)	1 120(2%)	70(–)	2 420(4%)
Soil structure	–	410(–	3840(8%)	4 250(8%)

if they are located in marine clay, and sand over marine clay soils. Permanent structures and roads should not be built on such areas as the soil is subject to flow slides if situated on the undercutting side of the river (Lajoie 1974). Eroded scarps on bedrock, however, are generally stable and these provide an attractive touch to building sites.

The factors "rockiness" and "stoniness" are shown in Figs. 6 and 7. Rockiness is related to the amount of bedrock exposed at the surface, and the relative depth of materials overlying the bedrock. The worst rockiness condition, affecting 8% of the total region, is found mostly around Bells' Corners and along Highway 31.

Rockiness interferes strongly with many uses, but more so with some than with others. Although rocky areas are unsuitable for agricultural uses they are used successfully for forestry, conservation and some restricted recreation activities in the study area. Certain large-scale, urban-related projects such as high rise apartments, industrial parks and estate development are feasible, and the extra cost of developing such lands may be partly offset by the lower costs of acquisition. As well, these areas provide easily-accessible quarries for building materials in many cases.

The problem of stoniness differs with varying land-uses. Stones interfere least in forested lands and lands retained for conservation or watershed management. An abundance of large stones, while not an insurmountable problem for construction poses special design problems and may raise the cost of development.

The factors of soil "fertility," "tendency to drought" and soil "structure" are shown in Figures 8 and 9. Because these are primarily soil-related factors, their influence relates predominantly to biologically oriented uses. The most extensive of these are soil fertility limitations which affect about 45% of the area. Major fertility limitations are found in sand and gravel-derived soils. They have a restricted capability for agriculture, being suited more for forestry or conservation. With careful design for erosion control and septic tank siting, however, they can be used for residential housing.

Soils susceptible to drought are exclusively the deep sand or gravel-derived soils on well drained positions, primarily on ridge tops. These ridges are often used as sand and gravel pits, but in many cases they are suitable for residential and industrial buildings. However, they are highly susceptible to wind and water erosion and should be continually protected, particularly during construction.

Soils of inferior structure are restricted to the marine clays exposed in the former drainage channels of the Ottawa River. In this area, soil structure is not a major restriction to use except for agriculture.

Figure 10 illustrates the use of the land factor concept in extrapolating physical land

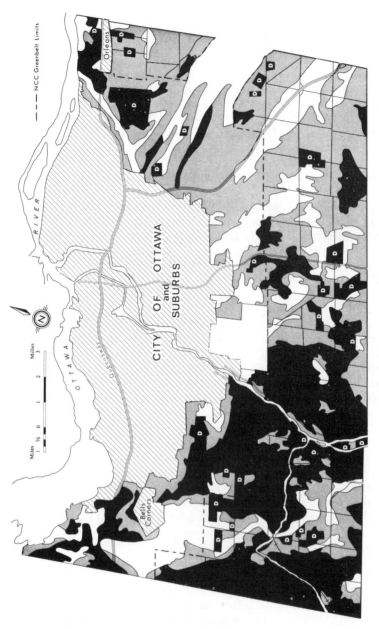

SOIL CAPABILITY FOR AGRICULTURE

Classes 1 & 2

Classes 3 & 4

Classes 5 6 7 and Organic

D   Disturbed Land

Fig. 10.   Land areas "suitable" for urban expansion.

data for other than agricultural uses. The factors major wetness (W'), moderate and major rockiness (R and R') and major topography (T'), along with areas of agricultural capability Class 1 and 2, organic soils and soils with peaty surface horizons (I), and areas with gravel potential were eliminated as being either hazardous, excessively difficult for construction or "socially desirable." The areas resulting after this selection procedure were classed as "suitable" for urban expansion.

This information indicates that approximately 6900 ha or 25% of the area south of the greenbelt is "suitable" for urbanization. With a population density of 35 persons per hectare this area could accommodate about 240 000 additional population. This more than meets the projected future requirements for the region (Regional Council 1974), and it could be accomplished without encroaching on quality agricultural lands or encountering unusual construction difficulties.

The prime areas with potential for urbanization are west of Barrhaven, south of Uplands Airport, in the Leitrim area, in parts of the Carlsbad Springs region and around Orleans. This analysis agrees somewhat with certain of the intentions of the Ottawa-Carleton Official Plan (Regional Council 1974) but it contrasts with others. The area of major conflict is the location of the south urban community which is sited primarily on quality agricultural lands (Figs. 2 and 11). Further, the analysis indicates that Barrhaven should expand westward, onto poorer soils, rather than eastward, and Orleans should expand to the south rather than to the north. Also further considerations could be given to the possibility of urban expansion in parts of the Carlsbad Springs and Leitrim areas.

DISCUSSION

The single factor maps discussed in this paper are examples of what could be called basic land factor limitations. Such factors are easily measured in the field and their effects on a land use are generally singular even though amelioration may be complex.

Not all basic factors necessary for land use planning can be generated from a physical land survey. Factors associated with the weather, those describing mineral potential and subsurface conditions at depths greater than 2 m, as well as those generated by human activities, must be collected at source. As a consequence, physical land data and the factors they show pertain especially to those land use activities associated most closely with the surface of the earth, primarily the biologically oriented uses of agriculture, forestry, landscaping, recreation and waste disposal, as well as certain of the non-biological uses such as subdivision design, servicing and road construction.

Land factors, as used and outlined in this paper, are based on the concept of limitations to use. They assist in identifying those uses incompatible with the character of the land or those conditions needing correction before a use is instituted. They do not indicate directly the uses for which the land is best suited. It is only through a process of careful elimination of certain uses from certain areas, or by designing to overcome limitations, that the latter aspect can be defined.

Knowledge of the land factors present in an area permits the evaluation of feasible land use alternatives and this assists in the definition of final or best use for an area. In many cases, however, it does not control the final or best use as this is as much affected by social, economic and political factors as by the character of the land. The proper role of physical land data in the planning process is to catalogue those factors relevant to various feasible uses, and to interpret the environmental effects of any of these uses in a given land area.

BRINKMAN, R. and SMYTH, A. J. 1973. Land evaluation for rural purposes. International Institute for Land Reclamation and Improvement, Box 46, Wageningen, The Netherlands. 116 pp.

Fig. 11. A portion of the Ottawa-Carleton official plan.

CANADA LAND INVENTORY. 1965. Soil capability classification for agriculture. Rep. No. 2, Department of Regional Economic Expansion, Ottawa, Ont. 16 pp.

DUMANSKI, J. 1976. Agricultural resources and patterns of land use in the Ottawa urban fringe. *In* Land use planning and resources in the Ottawa region; seminar paper, Ontario Inst. Agrol., Ottawa. Unpubl.

GIBSON, J. A. 1977. On the allocation of prime agricultural land. J. Soil Water Cons. **32**(6): 271–275.

GIERMAN, D. M. 1977. Rural to urban land conversion. Occasional Paper No. 16, Lands Directorate, Fisheries and Environment Canada, Hull, Que. 74 pp.

HILLS, G. A., RICHARDS, N. R. and MORWICK, F. F. 1944. Soil survey of Carleton county. Rep. No. 7, Ontario Soil Survey, Guelph, Ontario. 103 pp.

JURDANT, M., LACATE, D. S., ZOLTAI, S. C., RUNKA, G. G. and WELLS, R. 1975. Bio-physical land classification in Canada. *In* B.

Bernier and C. M. Winget, eds. Forest soils and forest land management. Les Presses de L'Université Laval, Québec, Qué. pp. 485–497.

LAJOIE, P. J. 1974. Les coulées d'argile des basses-terrasses de l'Outaouais, du Saint-Laurent et du Saguénay. Rev. Geogr. Montr. XXVIII: 419–428.

MARSHALL, I. B., DUMANSKI, J., HUFFMAN, E. C. and LAJOIE, P. G. 1979. Soils, capability and land use in the Ottawa urban fringe. Ontario Soil Survey Rep. 47. Agriculture Canada, Ottawa, Ont. (in press).

NOWLAND, J. L. and McKEAGUE, J. A. 1977. Canada's limited agricultural land resource. Pages 109–118 *in* R. R. Kruger and B. Mitchell, eds. Managing Canada's renewable resources. Methuen, Toronto, Ont.

REGIONAL COUNCIL. 1974. Official plan, Ottawa-Carleton planning area. Regional Municipality of Ottawa-Carleton, Ottawa, Ont. 143 pp.

SCHMUDE, K. O. 1977. A perspective on prime farmland. J. Soil Water Conserv. **32**(5): 240–242.

20: LAND CAPABILITY ASSESSMENT FOR A SMALLHOLDERS SETTLEMENT SCHEME IN JAMAICA

Wim Andriesse and Jules J. Scholten

International Soil Museum, Wageningen, The Netherlands

ABSTRACT

Andriesse, W. and Scholten, J.J., 1983. Land capability assessment for a smallholders settlement scheme in Jamaica. Geoderma, 29: 195—214.

In the framework of the land-reform programme in Jamaica, a detailed quantitative land capability assessment was carried out in order to determine viable land uses and related farm sizes for the development plan of a smallholders settlement. The assessed area (Burnt Ground) is located in western Jamaica. It consists of two landforms, both developed in limestone: an undulating erosion surface with deep, acid soils (Orthoxic Palehumults) surrounded by steep-sided hills with shallow, stony soils (predominantly Lithic Tropudalfs). The land capability assessment of the area is based on the principle of Land Utilization Types (LUT's) as subjects for classification. Three viable LUT's were determined and specified in line with government policy, socio-economic considerations and traditional land uses in the area. Farm inputs and outputs were quantified and a maximum productivity value (added value expressed in dollars per hectare) was established for each LUT. Next, the requirements of each LUT were matched against a number of diagnostic land characteristics which are related to the soils and topography. This approach has the practical value that, once the target farm-added value per year is established per LUT, the corresponding minimum viable farm size can be determined for land without limitations and for land with various degrees of limitations to that use. This is done by dividing the target farm-added value by the hectare productivity value. The approach also permits a direct quantitative comparison between productivities of different LUT's.

INTRODUCTION

Lands acquired by the government of Jamaica for its land reform programme are subdivided for long-term lease or sale to small farmers. In the preparation of development plans for these areas (settlement schemes), quantitative land capability assessment plays an important part, because it helps to determine relevant and promising land use alternatives and related minimum farm sizes.

The aim of this paper is to provide an example of practical interpretation of soil information, in relation to other physical and socio-economic data, for rural land use planning.

DESCRIPTION OF THE STUDY AREA

Location

The study area is the Burnt Ground settlement scheme located in the parish of Hanover in western Jamaica, approximately 25 km southwest of Montego Bay along the main road to Savanna-la-Mar (Figs. 1 and 2) at latitude 18°22'N and longitude 77°59'W. The total area measures 709 ha and is being developed by the government for settlement of small farmers, including the development of the necessary physical and social infrastructure.

Climate

Rainfall data are available for a recording station (Shettlewood) approximately 2.5 km east of Burnt Ground at an elevation of about 150 m above mean sea level (Table I). The elevation of Burnt Ground ranges from 170 to 340 m above mean sea level (MSL).

Evaporation (A pan) was measured at Smithfield station, approximately 14 km northwest of Burnt Ground at 270 m above MSL. Table II shows the mean monthly and annual evaporation and the calculated reference crop evapotranspiration (evapotranspiration = 0.75 X pan evaporation).

Van Zel (1979) has carried out an analysis of the rainfall (Shettlewood) and evapotranspiration (Smithfield) data in order to estimate irrigation needs in the Burnt Ground setting. This analysis (Fig. 3) shows that, even at 90% chance of occurrence, rainfall during the period from May to November is sufficient for rain-fed agriculture. The length of the rainy season permits rain-fed agriculture of two consecutive crops with a short to medium growing period. The December—April period is not as wet and does not allow successful cultivation of rain-fed annual crops. Grass (pastures) and deep-rooting crops (e.g. fruit trees) can be grown however, provided they are established in the wet season.

Mean daily minimum and maximum temperatures range from 20° to 28°C as recorded at Smithfield for the period 1970—1978.

Based upon the above data, the climate of Burnt Ground can be classified as Af according to the Köppen system of classification (Köppen, 1931).

The soil moisture regime of the area is classified as udic in terms of the USDA Soil Taxonomy (Soil Survey Staff, 1975) because rainfall exceeds evapotranspiration throughout the year (Tables I and II). The soil temperature regime is postulated to be isohyperthermic.

Physiography

The Burnt Ground area is underlain by the White Limestone Formation (Lower Miocene to Middle Eocene) which consists of hard, subhorizontally bedded limestone with inclusions of flint.

Two major landforms can be distinguished: i) an undulating to rolling

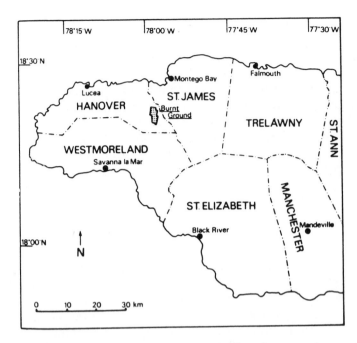

Fig. 1. The Burnt Ground area in western Jamaica.

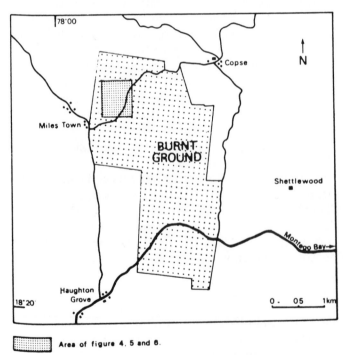

Fig. 2. The setting of the Burnt Ground settlement scheme and location of Figs. 4, 5 and 6.

TABLE I

Mean monthly and annual rainfall (mm) at Shettlewood (1931–1978)

Jan.	Feb.	Mar.	Apr.	May	June	July	Aug.	Sep.	Oct.	Nov.	Dec.	Year
86.4	86.4	96.5	190.5	354.4	276.9	246.4	299.7	302.3	320.3	147.3	86.4	2484.2

TABLE II

Mean monthly evaporation (mm) and calculated evapotranspiration (mm) at Smithfield (1970–1978)

	Jan.	Feb.	Mar.	Apr.	May	June	July	Aug.	Sep.	Oct.	Nov.	Dec.	Year
Evaporation	88.9	94.0	114.3	137.2	129.5	132.1	139.7	127.0	119.4	99.1	91.4	94.0	1366.6
Evapotranspiration	66.7	70.5	85.7	102.9	97.1	99.1	104.8	95.3	89.6	74.3	68.6	70.5	1025.1

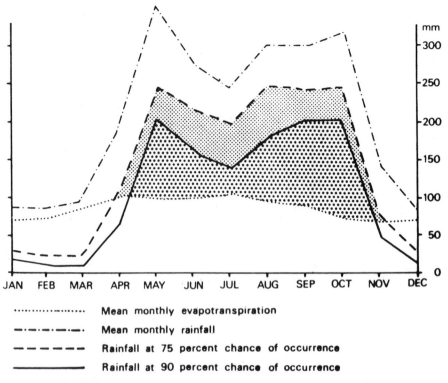

Fig. 3. Monthly rainfall and evapotranspiration pertaining to the Burnt Ground setting.

dissected limestone plateau (erosion surface); (ii) predominantly steep-sided limestone hills. The transition between the two landforms is abrupt. The dissected limestone plateau comprises nearly 80% of the total area. The range in elevation is between 170 and 260 m above MSL. The slopes are predominantly less than 15° (27%) with the majority being less than 7° (12%), see Table III. Subterranean dissolution of the limestone rock has resulted in sinkholes and depressions at the surface which usually are surrounded by steeper slopes. The sinkholes and depressions measure from a few meters to 100 m in diameter. Short and shallow gullies channel run-off into many of the sinkholes and depressions. Few gullies are longer than 500 m. Only the longest waterway in the area has a distinct flood plain, with a width up to 100 m in places. All surface drainage is intermittent.

The steep-sided limestone hills occupy slightly more than 20% of the area, mainly in the northern portion. They reach elevations of up to 340 m above MSL. Slopes are mainly steeper than 30° (58%) with the notable exception of small saddle areas that have slopes of less than 15° (27%). The hills occur as individual masses of elevated land (inselbergs) surrounded by the limestone plateau.

TABLE III

Distribution of slope classes in the Burnt Ground area

Slope class		Percent of area
(degree)	(percent)	
0– 7	0–12	47.1
7–15	12–27	31.5
15–20	27–36	2.6
20–25	36- 47	2.4
25–30	47–58	0.1
>30	>58	16.3
		100.0

Soils

In the area a total of 8 soil pits were described, sampled and analyzed and an additional 69 augerhole observations were made. From these observations and available analyses it appears that the dominant soil occurring on the dissected limestone plateau is deep, well-drained, strongly acid and well-structured. The surface layers (ochric epipedons) are dark brown, dark grayish brown or dark yellowish brown clays with moderate to strong blocky and crumb structure and with relatively high content of organic carbon (more than 1.5% and up to 11%). The high organic carbon levels may be related to the long history of pasture management in the area. Deeper layers (argillic horizons) are yellowish brown to strong brown heavy clays with moderate to strong blocky structure. Clay increase is perceptible (10–20%) and does not decrease by more than 20% from its maximum within 150 cm of the soil surface. Well-developed clay cutans were observed in the field and micromorphologically, in thin sections. Organic carbon content gradually decreases with depth but is still high (0.9% or more) in the upper part of the argillic horizon. The clays have low activity with CEC's (NH_4OAc, pH 7) less than 24 meq./100 g clay and effective CEC (sum of bases extractable with 1 N NH_4OAc plus aluminium extractable with 1 N KCl) less than 12 meq./100 g clay. Kaolinite is the largest component of the clay fraction, followed by 2:1 and 2:1:1 layer minerals (vermiculite– chlorite), quartz and goethite. Base saturation (by sum of cations) drops with depth and is less than 35% in the argillic horizon. Consequently, these soils are strongly to very strongly acid (pH H_2O 5.5–4.5). The classification at family level, according the USDA Soil Taxonomy (Soil Survey Staff, 1975) is: Orthoxic Palehumult, clayey, mixed, isohyperthermic (Scholten and Andriesse, 1982). In some depressions on the limestone plateau, gravel and stone contents of weathering flint may be more than 35% and such soils belong to the clayey-skeletal family of Orthoxic Palehumults. In depressions that are subject to severe flooding up to several months a year, soils are moderately well drained and genetically less developed. These soils were identified as Aquic Oxic Humitropepts, very fine, kaolinitic, isohyperthermic (Rural Physical Planning Unit, 1979).

The soils of the limestone hills can be divided into those of the predominantly steep side slopes and those on the gently sloping saddle areas. They all have slightly acid to neutral reactions (pH 6.0–7.5). On the steep slopes soils are mainly shallow (contact to the limestone within 50 cm from the surface), stony (more than 35% rock fragments in the solum) and rocky (more than 20% outcrops). These soils have well expressed (dark) yellowish brown argillic horizons with moderate to strong blocky structure and distinct clay cutans. Most soils have an ochric epipedon. They were classified as Lithic Tropudalfs, clayey-skeletal, mixed, isohyperthermic. Some soils have surface layers that meet the requirements for mollic epipedon: Lithic Argiudolls, clayey-skeletal, mixed, isohyperthermic (Rural Physical Planning Unit, 1979). The soils of the saddle areas are developed on colluvium from limestone and its weathering products. They are deep and well drained and have moderate to strong blocky structure. They have very dark grayish brown to dark yellowish brown clay surface layers (ochric epipedons) overlying yellowish brown heavy clays (argillic horizon): Typic Tropudalfs, very fine, mixed, isohyperthermic (Rural Physical Planning Unit, 1979).

Fig. 4 shows the distribution of most of these soils in a section of the Burnt Ground area.

Vegetation and land use

The Burnt Ground area is a traditional pasture area. Before 1980, when settlement of farmers in smallholdings commenced, most of the undulating to rolling land of the property (500 ha or about 70.5% of the total area) was under pasture. Under the management of a government agency, about 1240 head of cattle were kept in the area. Part of the pastures has been improved by means of planting Pangola (*Digitaria decumbens*), Guinea (*Panicum maximum*), Napier (*Pennisetum purpureum*) and Paragrass (*Brachiara mutica*). A network of stone walls, wire fences and gates subdivides the pastures into grazing enclosures. Drinking water for the cattle is available from several natural depressions and artificial ponds (total area of the ponds is 10 ha or 1.4% of the Burnt Ground area). Scattered over the pastures, individual mango (*Mangifera* spp.), citrus, star apple (*Chrysophyllum cainito*) and cotton trees (*Ceiba pentandra*) provide shade to the cattle. Most of the hilly and steep parts of the property (150 ha, or 21.2% of the area) is covered by forest and bush vegetation.

A citrus orchard of approximately 29 ha (4.1%) was established in 1953, on both sides of the main Montego Bay–Savanna la Mar road.

Small patches of land, covering a total of about 9 ha (1.3%), mainly occurring in the isolated interior valleys in the steep limestone hills, are being cultivated to yam (*Dioscorea* spp.), dasheen (*Colocasia esculenta*), banana

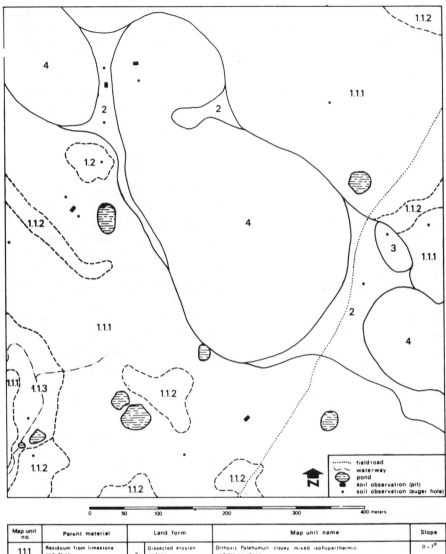

Map unit no.	Parent material		Land form	Map unit name	Slope
1.1.1	Residuum from limestone and flint	Limestone Plateau	Dissected erosion surface	Orthoxic Palehumult clayey mixed isohyperthermic undulating phase	0 - 7°
1.1.2				Orthoxic Palehumult clayey mixed isohyperthermic rolling phase	7 - 15°
1.1.3	Residuum and colluvium from limestone and flint		Flood plain of intermittent stream	Orthoxic Palehumult clayey mixed isohyperthermic nearly level severely flooded phase	0 - 2°
1.2			Depression in erosion surface	Orthoxic Palehumult clayey-skeletal mixed isohyperthermic nearly level slightly flooded phase	0 - 2°
2	Colluvium from limestone and flint	Limestone Hills	Saddle areas	Typic Tropudalf very fine mixed isohyperthermic sloping slightly gravelly phase	0 - 15°
3	Residuum from limestone and flint		Hillside slopes	Lithic Tropudalf very fine mixed isohyperthermic sloping phase	7 - 15°
4				Association of Lithic Tropudalf clayey-skeletal mixed isohyperthermic and Lithic Argiudoll clayey-skeletal mixed isohyperthermic steeply sloping phase	15 - 40° mainly over 30°

Fig. 4. Soils of a section of the Burnt Ground settlement scheme.

(*Musa* spp.), sugarcane (*Saccharum* spp.), coconut (*Cocos nucifera*), marihuana (*Cannabis sativa*), etc. by people living near the property. Also, newly settled farmers have started to prepare backyard gardens (approximately 0.14 ha each) in the area.

The remainder of the area (11 ha, or 1.5%) is occupied by permanent structures such as houses, cowsheds and cowpens, a concrete-surfaced water catchment with a storage tank and a few roads including part of the main road from Montego Bay to Savanna la Mar.

Land tenure

Historically, most of the region including Burnt Ground was farmed in large private holdings concentrating on beef cattle production. With the introduction of land reform, many of the large holdings were acquired by the government for subdivision among local landless small farmers in units of less than 5 ha in a system of leasehold or, since 1981, also as freehold. In some of the new schemes the farmers were settled in small villages but for the Burnt Ground area individual dispersed settlement has been selected for the establishment of dairy smallholdings. The settlements are equipped with the appropriate physical and social infrastructure, including farm roads, farm houses, water and electricity supplies, communal facilities, credit facilities, etc.

A number of privately owned large holdings of more than 50 ha continues to operate successfully in the region. They are either beef cattle or dairy farms.

LAND CAPABILITY ASSESSMENT

Objective

The main objective for the execution of a detailed quantitative land capability assessment of the Burnt Ground settlement scheme was to find a key to equal and fair subdivision of the cultivable land into individual farms capable of producing a viable target-income for farmer-settlers.

Method

The assessment was done in steps. First, relevant types of agricultural use or Land Utilization Types (LUT's) had to be defined for the area. The model of these LUT's is a simplified version of the concept of LUT's developed in the Land Evaluation approach (Beek and Bennema, 1971; Beek, 1974, 1978; FAO, 1976). The LUT's in the Burnt Ground example were characterized in terms of their produce (e.g., milk), their level of management (e.g., traditional family-operated smallholdings under rain-fed conditions) and related inputs (e.g., fertilizers).

The second step involved quantification of the inputs and outputs per LUT and determination of a maximum productivity per hectare which in the case of Burnt Ground was expressed by the added-value-factor share (added value is total value of output minus non-factor costs).

In the third step, the specific requirements of each LUT were matched with the physical land conditions occurring in the Burnt Ground scheme. These land conditions were inventoried in a detailed general-purpose soil survey involving slope analysis in the office plus field observations and laboratory analyses on samples from genetic horizons in eight soil pits. The results of the survey were presented in the form of a detailed soil map (see Fig. 4) with map units derived from taxonomic units at the family level of Soil Taxonomy (Soil

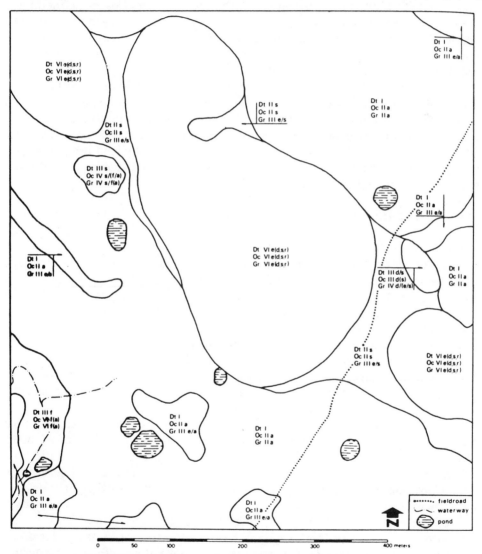

Fig. 5. Land capability of a section of the Burnt Ground settlement scheme (explanation of classification formula in text).

Survey Staff, 1975). Then, the soil map units were grouped into units of "land capability classes" and "subclasses" according to physical limitations ("diagnostic land characteristics") relevant to the various LUT's (Fig. 5). Land capability classes group tracts of land (e.g., soil map units) pertinent to quantified increasing degrees of limitation (e.g., 10% reduction in output for Class II land compared with Class I land). Land capability subclasses group tracts of land according to the various kinds of limitations (e.g., slope, soil acidity). It should be noted that, in the Burnt Ground example, land characteristics were selected rather than land qualities as the diagnostic physical limitations for matching with the LUT requirements. Although land qualities, as defined by Beek (1978), are better able to describe the relationship between environment and land use performance, single land characteristics were preferred because they can be derived directly from the soil map and their quantification is simpler than those of complex land qualities.

In the fourth and final step, minimum farm sizes were determined for the individual LUT's based on the productivity per hectare for each land capability class. The farm sizes were calculated so that they could generate the target farm income (or target farm-added value) which was established as a matter of government policy. This final step formed the basis for the land use planning and farm lay-out on the Burnt Ground settlement scheme (see Fig. 6 and the section on "Application of the Results").

Relevant land utilization types (LUT's)

Land utilization types relevant to the Burnt Ground settlement scheme have been selected and defined on the basis of the following factors: (a) government land use policy towards agricultural production in the region; (b) present land use and agricultural produce; (c) prevailing farm management level and technical knowledge in adjacent areas; (d) farm size and land tenure conditions; and (e) marketing aspects.

The first LUT selected deals with dairy farming. The presence of a dairy plant nearby Burnt Ground (10 km), a favourable milk price and the existing land use in the project area (mainly pastures) provide good prospects for dairy farming. Also an agricultural training centre in the vicinity (5 km) can provide training and technical support to selected farmer-settlers.

As the Jamaican government is implementing a resuscitation programme for citrus and citrus marketing prospects are good, citrus production was selected as a second LUT appropriate to the citrus orchard existing in the area (28 ha).

Further, backyard gardening of annual crops and vegetables is a relevant land utilization type inasmuch as most prospective farmer-settlers have experience in this kind of farming.

Produce is one of the attributes related to the determination of LUT's. Other attributes are the size of the farm, land tenure and farm management level. The land reform programme of the government aims at providing viable farm units to landless small farmers living in the vicinity of the project area. Thus,

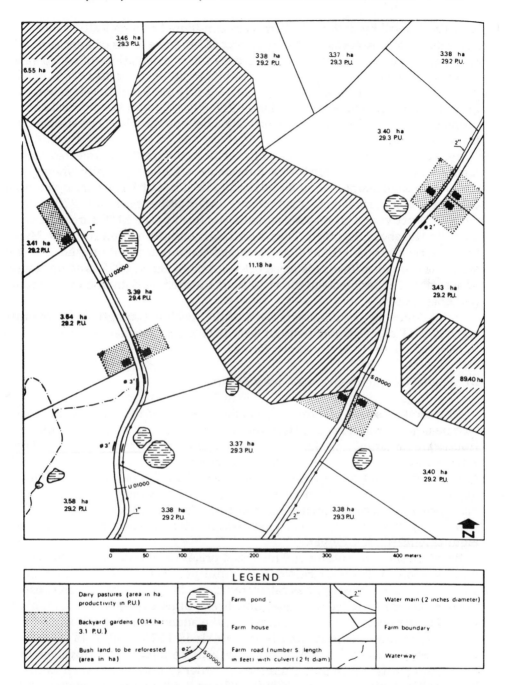

Fig. 6. Development plan of a section of the Burnt Ground settlement scheme showing the lay-out of farms, land for reforestation and infrastructure.

farm size is small by definition. Farms are considered economically viable if farm-added value exceeds J$ 3200 per year at the price levels of February 1977. This date was chosen as a standard reference for all calculations of added value in order to allow direct comparison of productivity of different LUT s. At February 1977, J$ 1.00 was equal to US$ 1.10. (First Rural Development Project, 1977.) Depending on the kind of land use, and on the physical condition of the land, this level of added value corresponds with farm sizes ranging from 2 to 6 ha.

Because of present skills of the prospective farmer-settlers, projected management levels in the LUT's are low to intermediate, including family labour, predominant use of simple farming tools and limited use of fertilizers, agricultural chemicals, etc. Farm labour requirements should not exceed 250- 270 mandays (md) per year. Output levels (yields) assumed in the LUT's are, consequent to the above, not high. They were based on information from the Ministry of Agriculture (Weir, 1974, and personal communication) on guidelines for agricultural credit officers (Jamaican Development Bank, 1977) and on results of agronomic experiments in the vicinity of the area on Orthoxic Palehumults (De Boer, 1981).

In the following, a summary is given of the specific assumptions for the three selected LUT's. The productivity of each LUT is also calculated. These calculations are made for fully developed farms.

Dt: Traditional family-operated dairy farming

Milk production on pastures is the main objective of this LUT. Additional income is generated however, from the sale of young stock and old cows. Houses are on farms, have farm road access, piped water and electricity. Basic assumptions underlying the calculation of productivity include: grazing density (one animal unit consisting of a cow plus calf per 0.8 ha), number of milkings daily (one only), milk production (1590 l per cow per year), pasture management (rotational grazing, bush cutting, fertilizing), use of additional cow feed (concentrates), animal sprays (disinfectants, detergents) and labour requirements (55 md/ha/yr).

Based on the assumptions and on actual prices of October 1978, the date on which this LUT was conceived, the output per hectare (revenue from milk, young stock and old cows) was calculated to be J$ 1375 per year. The cost of the non-factor inputs (concentrates, fertilizers, other expendables) amounted to J$ 340 per hectare per year. Therefore, the added value for this LUT, on land without physical limitations to this use, is J$ 1375—340 or J$ 1035 per hectare per year. Adjusted to the price levels of February 1977 this gives an added value of J$ 870/ha/yr. Therefore, in order to obtain the target farm-added value, a minimum size of 3200 ÷ 870 or 3.7 ha would be required for farms in this LUT. Total labour requirement would then be 204 man-days per year (md/yr).

Oc: *Family-operated citrus orchard farming*

In this land utilization type, ortaniques, sweet oranges and grapefruits are produced. Farm houses will be located in a little village at a distance of 700 m from the orchard. The houses are accessible by road and have piped water and electricity. Production assumptions include: tree density (267 trees per hectare), tree lifetime (40 years), replanting (on average 7 trees/ha/yr), yield (350 boxes/ha/yr), use of fertilizers and lime, pest control (fiddler beetle, slugs), and labour requirements (100 md/ha/yr).

According to price levels of March 1979, production under these assumptions would give an output value per hectare of J$ 2620 annually with non-factor costs of J$ 620 per ha/yr. Thus, the added value of produce is J$ 2000/ha/yr, or, if adjusted to price levels of February 1977, J$ 1600. A minimum farm size of 3200 ÷ 1600 or 2 ha of land without physical limitations would be needed to provide the target farm-added value. Total labour requirement on such a farm would be 200 man-days per year.

Gr: *Family-operated rainfed garden crop farming*

This land utilization type describes crop production in backyard gardens. The proximity of the backyard garden to the farm house and the small area of the garden allow for a relatively high management level in terms of labour input, fertilizer use and application of agricultural chemicals. Basic assumptions of this land utilization type are concerned with:
- choice of crops (yam, red beans, sweet pepper, tomato, pumpkin, cucumber, callaloo, all of which are commonly grown in the area. They represent a range of crops with different cultivation requirements and different economic risks. Yams, for example, are relatively easy to grow and have a stable market. Tomatoes on the other hand are vulnerable and they have an unstable market);
- crop yields (yams 14,000 kg/ha, red beans 550 kg/ha, sweet peppers 8500 kg/ha, tomatoes 6750 kg/ha, pumpkins 6750 kg/ha, cucumbers 5500 kg/ha, and callalooes 6750 kg/ha);
- individual crop area (yam will occupy 1/3 of the garden area, red beans and sweet pepper cover 1/6 of the area each, whereas cucumber, pumpkin, tomato and callaloo each make up 1/12 of the garden);
- cropping intensity (two crops of red beans and callalooes are grown per cropping season; all other crops are grown once per year only);
- use of fertilizers and chemicals (determined for each crop individually);
- application of lime;
- labour requirement (170 md/ha/yr; ploughing with small hired tractor).

At price levels of March 1979 production from this LUT would give an output value of J$ 3875/ha/yr, with non-factor cost totalling J$ 1100. Added value would then be J$ 2775/ha/yr. Adjusted to February 1977 price levels, this is equal to J$ 2220. A complete farm under this land utilization type would have a minimum size of 3200 ÷ 2230 or 1.4 ha of land without physical limitations to this use in order to generate the target farm-added value. This would require a labour input of 240 man-days annually.

Diagnostic land characteristics

Study of the soil survey data of the Burnt Ground area in relation to the requirements of the three selected LUT's resulted in the identification of a number of land characteristics with diagnostic significance to land capability due to their direct limiting influences on agricultural productivity. Most of these diagnostic land characteristics, referred to as limitations (and symbolized by lower case letters) in the land capability assessment, could be quantified by measurements in the office, field and laboratory. They are:

— Slope (limitation "e") affecting susceptibility to erosion. The subdivision in slope phases is derived from the Soil Conservation Service in Jamaica (Sheng and Stennett, 1975) and has practical significance in soil conservation treatments, e.g. for annual crops involving a large degree of soil disturbance, there is no need for permanent structures on slopes less than 7° (12%), mechanical construction of bench terraces is possible on slopes between 7° and 20° (12—36%), manual construction of bench terraces is possible on slopes between 20° and 25° (36—47%), whereas production of annual crops on slopes steeper than 25° (47%) is inadvisable.
— Effective soil depth or depth to hard bedrock impenetrable to roots (limitation "d") influencing rooting space and availability of moisture and nutrients. Effective soil depth co-determines the feasibility of conservation work, e.g. soil depth on a slope of 20° (36%) must be at least 67 cm to permit building of bench terraces of 2.5 m width (Sheng and Stennett, 1975).
— Stoniness (limitation "s") restricting availability of moisture and nutrients (by taking up effective soil volume) as well as soil workability. The adverse effects of stoniness can be diminished by stone picking and incorporation of stones into stonewalls and stone barriers.
— Rock outcrops (limitation "r") restricting effective soil surface and land management.
— Flooding (limitation "f") adversely affecting crop and pasture performance through physical damage and lack of oxygen.
— Soil acidity (limitation "a") adversely affecting soil fertility through one or more of the following: low effective CEC and related deficiency of bases through presence of clays with variable charges (kaolinite, goethite, haematite and gibbsite), aluminium and manganese toxicity and related phosphorus fixation.

Quantitative land capability assessment per LUT

In the assessment of land capability for the area of Burnt Ground the diagnostic land characteristics (limitations) were quantified relative to the three selected LUT's because some of the land characteristics have dissimilar effects on agricultural productivity in different LUT's (Table IV).

For each LUT six land capability classes (symbolized by Roman numerals I through VI) were distinguished according to the degree of the limitations and their effect on productivity. (A range of six classes was adopted following the practice of earlier soil survey interpretations in Jamaica which grouped land qualitatively into six capability classes for general agricultural use.) The effects of the various limitations on productivity in each LUT have been estimated on the basis of area-specific data (De Boer, 1981; Sheng and

TABLE IV

Land capability classes, productivity ratings and limitations for Dt: traditional family-operated dairy farming; Oc: family-operated citrus orchard farming; Gr: family-operated rain-fed garden crop farming

Land capab. class	Productivity (PU/ha)	Productivity (% of max.)	Slope (e) (degrees)	Effect. soil depth (d) (cm)[1]	Stoni-ness (s) (%)[2]	Rock outcrop (r) (%)[3]	Flood-ing classes[4] (f)	Soil acidity (a) (pH)[5]
Dt I	8.7	100	0—20	>50	0—15	0—5	0—4	4.5—8.0
Dt II	7.8	90	20—25	25—50	15—35	5—15	5	n.a.
Dt III	7.0	80	25—30	n.a.	35—50	15—25	6	n.a.
Dt IV	6.1	70	n.a.	n.a.	50—75	25—35	n.a.	4.0—4.5
Dt V	5.2	60	n.a.	n.a.	n.a.	35—45	n.a.	n.a.
Dt VI	—[6]	<50	>30	<25	>75	>45	7	<4.0
Oc I	16.0	100	0—20	>100	0—15	0—5	0—2	5.5—8.0
Oc II	14.4	90	20—25	50—100	15—35	5—15	3	5.0—5.5
Oc III	12.8	80	25—30	25—50	35—50	15—25	4	4.5—5.0
Oc IV	11.2	70	n.a.	n.a.	50—75	25—35	n.a.	4.0—4.5
Oc V	9.6	60	n.a.	n.a.	n.a.	35—45	n.a.	n.a.
Oc VI	—[6]	<50	>30	<25	>75	>45	5—7	<4.0
Gr I	22.2	100	0—7	>100	0—15	0—5	0—1	5.5—8.0
Gr II	20.0	90	7—15	50—100	15—35	5—15	2	5.0—5.5
Gr III	17.8	80	15—20	25—50	35—50	15—25	3	4.5—5.0
Gr IV	15.5	70	20—25	n.a.	n.a.	25—35	n.a.	4.0—4.5
Gr V	13.3	60	n.a.	n.a.	n.a.	n.a.	n.a.	n.a.
Gr VI	—[6]	<50	>25	<25	>50	>35	4—7	<4.0

n.a. = not applicable.
[1] Depth to hard rock impenetrable to roots.
[2] Stoniness expressed in weighted average of volume percent of coarse fraction in the upper 50 cm of the soil or to hard bedrock if shallower than 50 cm. The coarse fraction includes all particles with diameter larger than 2 mm.
[3] Rock outcrop expressed as percent of surface area.
[4] Flooding is defined as submergence at least 20 cm deep for a period more than one day. The following flooding classes were distinguished.
Class 0: no flooding.
Class 1: one or less floods of one to two days per two years.
Class 2: one or less floods of one to two days per year.
Class 3: one to two floods of one to two days per year.
Class 4: one or less floods of two to four days per year, or three to four floods of one to two days per year.
Class 5: one or less floods of four to ten days per year or ten to twenty cumulative days of flooding per year.
Class 6: one to two floods of four to ten days per year or twenty to thirty cumulative days of flooding per year.
Class 7: flooding conditions exceed those of class 6.
[5] Soil acidity expressed as weighted average of pH (H_2O) 1:1 air dried in the upper 50 cm of soil.
[6] No productivity unit is assigned to class VI.

Stennett, 1975; Weir, 1974) and general information (Soil Survey Staff, 1975; Sanchez, 1976).

Individual land capability classes were assigned "Productivity Units (PU)" which decrease proportionally from a maximum of 100% for Class I to less than 50% for Class VI. (Absolute values of PU were expressed in Jamaican dollars of added value per year, at price levels of February 1977: 1 PU is J$ 100).

Land capability class I: no limitation to the envisaged use, productivity 100—91% of the calculated maximum.

Land capability class II: slight limitation to the envisaged use, productivity 90—81% of the calculated maximum.

Land capability class III: moderate limitation(s) to the envisaged use, productivity 80—71% of the calculated maximum.

Land capability class IV: severe limitation(s) to the envisaged use, productivity 70—61% of the calculated maximum.

Land capability class V: very severe limitation(s) to the envisaged use, productivity 60—51% of the calculated maximum.

Land capability class VI: extreme limitation(s) which preclude(s) the economic use of such land under the envisaged use, productivity 50% or less of the calculated maximum.

Land capability classes were subdivided into subclasses according to kinds of limitations: e, d, s, r, f and a.

Land capability formulas were assigned to the units of the soil map to provide a land capability map (Fig. 5). The formulas are composed of the following elements in order of placement: (1) a symbol for the LUT consisting of a capital and a small letter, i.e. Dt, Oc, Gr; (2) a symbol for the land capability class, i.e. Roman numerals I through VI; (3) one or more lower case letter(s) symbolizing the limitation(s) in the land capability classes, i.e. e, d, s, r, f, a.

The following formula compositions were used:

(a) Land capability classes I have no limitations; formulas include only symbols for the LUT followed by Roman numeral I, i.e. Dt I, Oc I, Gr I.

(b) Land capability classes II have only one limitation, e.g. Dt IIs.

(c) Land capability classes III through VI may either have one limitation, e.g., Dt III f, or a combination of a major limitation and one or more minor limitation(s) which are shown in brackets, e.g., Oc VI f (a), or a combination of two or more equally intensive limitations, e.g. Gr III e/a. In the last example, "e" and "a" are both Class II limitations but their combination results in placement at Class III level.

APPLICATION OF THE RESULTS

In the preparation of the physical development plan for the Burnt Ground settlement scheme, the land capability assessment played an important part (Fig. 6). It showed that the larger part of the land on the steeply sloping limestone hills in the northern portion of the area, as well as scattered small tracts of land around large sinkholes, have limitations (slope, soil stoniness, rockiness) that preclude their commercial use for any of the three selected LUT's. Hence, it was proposed that these parts of the settlement scheme be in forest. The flood plain of the major waterway crossing the western section of the settle‑ment scheme has a severe flooding limitation rendering the flood plain unsuit‑ed for citrus and garden crops. The degree of the flooding limitation still allows use of the flood plain for pasture. Therefore, the development plan proposed that this area be divided among several dairy farms. Related farm houses and backyard gardens of these dairy farms were planned outside the flood plain on the undulating sections of the limestone plateau (Fig. 6).

In the subdivision of all remaining lands (the undulating and rolling lime‑stone plateau) that appeared to be suitable for commercial use under any of the three LUT's, the results of the land capability assessment assisted in the design of the two farm types proposed in the plan, each capable of producing the target farm-added value of J\$ 3200 (Febr. 1977). These two farm types are combinations of the LUT's dairy farming (Dt) plus garden cropping (Gr) and citrus farming (Oc) plus garden cropping (Gr), respectively. They are: (1) farm-type 1: traditional dairy smallholdings (3.4—4.0 ha) with garden crop farming (0.14 ha) as a minor component (Fig. 6); (2) farm-type 2: traditional citrus smallholdings (1.8—1.9 ha) with garden crop farming (0.14 ha) as a minor component.

This resulted in the delineation of 128 farms of type 1 and 14 farms of type 2.

CONCLUSIONS

The example of land use planning described in this article shows the central place that soil information takes in the execution of quantitative land capabili‑ty assessment for rural development planning.

The method of land capability assessment which was applied in Jamaica along lines related to the Land Evaluation approach (Beek and Bennema, 1971; FAO, 1976; Beek, 1978) matches the requirements of certain well-defined kinds of land use (land utilization types) with physical land attributes. The assessment provides a quantified basis for the delineation of farms, each capable of producing a target farm income, in detailed development planning.

The LUT's defined in Jamaica were patterned after the checklist prepared by Beek (1978, pp. 48—51) but were simplified. Also, for the characterization of physical land conditions, land characteristics were used instead of land qualities. Land characteristics, single attributes of land, can be measured direct‑ly (e.g. slope, soil depth, etc.), whereas land qualities are complex attributes of land, the expression of which is determined by a set of interacting single or compound land characteristics (e.g. moisture availability, erodibility, etc.). Moreover, the use of land characteristics has the practical advantage that the grouping of land capability classes and sub-classes according to diagnostic characteristics relevant to the various LUT's can be based directly on the soil map. The soil map units are described in terms of, and differentiate between, land characteristics. Another advantage of the use of land characteristics instead of land qualities is that the quantification of their relationships with the requirements of the LUT's and their effects on productivity is a somewhat easier process. Nevertheless, this matching process remains the weakest link in the land evaluation approach. In particular, this is a problem in the developing countries, where research data and farm records are often limited. Therefore, by necessity these relations have to be based largely on assumptions. In the making of these assumptions it is in the direct interest of the farmer-settlers that they do not overestimate productivity.

ACKNOWLEDGEMENTS

The authors wish to acknowledge their gratitude to the following agencies.

Directorate-General International Co-operation (DGIS) of the Ministry of Foreign Affairs of the Netherlands government for granting a three months study leave during which period this paper was prepared.

International Soil Museum, Wageningen, The Netherlands, for providing all facilities and support during the preparation of the paper.

The Ministry of Agriculture and the First Rural Development Project of the government of Jamaica for the opportunity to collect most of the background information for the paper during a three-years assignment in Jamaica.

REFERENCES

Beek, K.J., 1974. The concept of land utilization types. In: Approaches to Land Classification. FAO, Rome, Soils Bull., 22: 103—120.

Beek, K.J., 1978. Land Evaluation for Agricultural Development. Int. Inst. Land Reclam. Improvem., Wageningen, Publ., 23: 333 pp.

Beek, K.J. and Bennema, J., 1971. Land evaluation for agricultural land use planning. An ecological method. In: Approaches to Land Classification. FAO, Rome, Soils Bull., 22: 170—190.

De Boer, H.G., 1981. Final Report of the Agronomist, Cornwall Youth and Community Development Project, Montego Bay, 35 pp.

First Rural Development Project, 1977. Loan Agreement 1464 JM between the Government of Jamaica and the International Bank for Reconstruction and Development, Kingston, 47 pp.

F.A.O. (Food and Agriculture Organization of the United Nations), 1976. A framework for land evaluation. FAO, Rome, Soils Bull., 32: 72 pp.

Jamaican Development Bank, 1977. Handbook for Credit Officers, I. Crop Husbandry Guide. Kingston, 102 pp.

Köppen, W., 1931. Die Klimate der Erde. Grundriss der Klimakunde. Walter de Gruyter, Berlin-Leipzig, 2nd ed., 369 pp.

Rural Physical Planning Unit, 1979. Physical Development Plan Burnt Ground Settlement Scheme. Min. Agric., Montego Bay, 64 pp.

Sanchez, P.A., 1976. Properties and Management of Soils in the Tropics. Wiley, New York, NY, 618 pp.

Scholten, J.J. and Andriesse, W., 1982. Humic Acrisol (Orthoxic Palehumult). Int. Soil Museum, Wageningen, Soil Monolith Paper, 5: 64 pp.

Sheng, T.C. and Stennett, H.R., 1975. Lecture Notes Watershed Management and Soil Conservation Training Course. UNDP/FAO Project Forestry Devel. and Watershed Management in the Upland Regions of Jamaica, Proj. Working Doc., FAO/JAM 505, Kingston, 110 pp.

Soil Survey Staff, 1975. Soil Taxonomy, a Basic System of Soil Classification and Interpreting Soil Surveys. U.S. Dep. Agric. Handbook, 436, Washington, DC, 754 pp.

Van Zel, H.J., 1979. Analysis of rainfall and evaporation data for estimating irrigation needs, Cornwall Youth and Community Development Project, Hanover, Kingston, 24 pp.

Weir, C.C., 1974. Citrus growing in Jamaica. Agric. Inf. Serv., Min. Agric., Kingston, 53 pp.

INDEXES

AUTHOR CITATION INDEX

SUBJECT INDEX

About the Editor

DONALD A. DAVIDSON graduated with a B.Sc. degree in geography from the University of Aberdeen, Scotland. His graduate research took place at Sheffield University where he wrote a Ph.D. thesis on the effects of land conditions on agriculture. His research field is the evaluation of soil conditions relevant to land use. Most of his work has been in Britain, and he has made study visits to the Netherlands, Canada, the United States, and Thailand. Dr. Davidson has also been involved as a soil scientist on a number of archaeological projects in Greece and Scotland. His current research concerns the development of a computer-based land resource information system for application to land use planning. He is currently reader in the department of geography, University of Strathclyde, Glasgow; previously he held posts in the University of Sheffield, and St. David's University College, Wales. He has had short-term teaching appointments in Carleton University, Ottawa. Dr. Davidson is the author of *Science for Physical Geographers* (Arnold and Halstead, 1978), and *Soils and Land Use Planning* (Longman, 1980). He has coedited *Geoarchaeology: Earth Science and the Past* (Duckworth and Westview, 1976); *Timescales in Geomorphology*, (Wiley, 1980); *Principles and Applications of Soil Geography* (Longman, 1982); and the book series *Topics in Applied Geography* (Longman, 1979-1984).